Sport and Leisure Cultures

SPORT AND CULTURE SERIES
TOBY MILLER AND M. ANN HALL, EDITORS

Sport and Leisure Cultures

Alan Tomlinson

SPORT AND CULTURE SERIES, Volume 6

University of Minnesota Press
Minneapolis • London

Published by the University of Minnesota Press
111 Third Avenue South, Suite 290
Minneapolis, MN 55401-2520
http://www.upress.umn.edu

Library of Congress Cataloging-in-Publication Data

Tomlinson, Alan.
　　Sport and leisure cultures / Alan Tomlinson.
　　　　p. cm. — (Sport and culture series; v. 6)
　　Includes bibliographical references and index.
　　ISBN 0-8166-3382-7 (hc : alk. paper) — ISBN 0-8166-3383-5 (pb : alk. paper)
　　1. Sports—Sociological aspects. 2. Leisure—Sociological aspects. 3. Globalization.
　I. Title. II. Series.

　　GV706.5.T654 2005
　　306.48—dc22
　　　　　　　　　　　　　　　　　　2004026828

Printed in the United States of America on acid-free paper

The University of Minnesota is an equal-opportunity educator and employer.

12 11 10 09 08 07 06 05　　　　　　　10 9 8 7 6 5 4 3 2 1

Contents

PART III. LOCAL CULTURES

Acknowledgments

This book comprises studies of my main intellectual and academic preoccupations over recent years: sport and spectacle, sport cultures and power, consumption and leisure in everyday life. In conducting the research upon which the work is based, I have been consistently and generously supported by the University of Brighton and by colleagues in the Sport and Leisure Cultures research group in the Chelsea School Research Centre at the university. Many invitations also provided funding and research opportunities in numerous countries across Europe, North America, South America, the Caribbean, Asia, and Australia. Work in Colne, Lancashire, was funded by the British Academy. A trip to Buenos Aires was funded by the British Council. Travel to Japan was funded by the Japan Society for the Sociology of Sport, to Korea by the Korea/Japan 2002 World Cup symposium (the plane fare was handed to me on the Saturday morning of my trip, in the bar of my hotel lobby, in a white paper envelope). A wonderful opportunity to conclude the final full draft of the work, alongside delivering sessions to able and animated students and organizing my final phase as editor of the *International Review for the Sociology of Sport*, was provided by the Faculty of Social Sciences, the University of the West Indies (St. Augustine, Trinidad and Tobago), in October and November 2002. I am grateful too for funded invitations to speak in Boston, Iowa, Dublin, Lausanne, and numerous other venues in North America, Europe, and Australia.

The contents of this book are based on research studies conducted over the past decade or so. Books don't spring from nowhere or from one summer's inspiration. Well, at least mine don't. All of the chapters in this book have had earlier lives of one sort or another. They are all expanded, reworked, and updated in relation to previously published pieces or presentations. The responses of anonymous reviewers and professional networks and editors to those versions of my work are gratefully acknowledged. They have been absorbed into the studies in this book.

For chapter 3, I am grateful to personnel at and within FIFA for provision of materials and expression of views, to Rose Marie Breitenstein for access to her collection of Sir Stanley Rous's papers, to the (English) Football Association for access to their records and archives, to numerous individuals in world football who have agreed to speak to me, and to Professor John Sugden for editorial responses to earlier drafts of some of the material included in this chapter. Parts of this chapter draw on collaborative work with Professor Sugden, which was included in the books *Great Balls of Fire: How Big Money Is Hijacking World Football* and *Badfellas: FIFA Family at War*.

In relation to chapter 5 I would like to record my thanks to Dr. Wayne Wilson of the Amateur Athletic Foundation of Los Angeles for directing me to some key sources; and to Professor Andy Markovits, then of the University of California, Santa Cruz, and now at the University of Michigan, for generous and stimulating response to the book *Hosts and Champions*, a response that included hospitality and good conversation in the best spirit of international scholarship in both Southern California and Michigan.

The early 1980s fieldwork and newspaper research upon which material in chapter 8 and the case study of knur and spell in chapter 9 are based was funded by a personal research grant provided by the British Academy's Small Grants Research Fund in the Humanities. In 2000 fieldwork was supported by the Chelsea School, University of Brighton. I would also like to express my thanks to the knur and spell players of Colne, who welcomed my inquiring intrusions with a heartwarming openness. Thanks, too, for limitless support from personnel at Colne Library: in 1981 from Mr. P. Wightman, deputy district librarian, and Mildredge Ellis, librarian; in 2000 from Christine Bradley, reference and local studies librarian.

I am especially indebted to colleagues in my Brighton research group, particularly Dr. Ben Carrington, Professor Graham McFee, and Professor John Sugden. Ben Carrington has sought to keep me intellectually fresh, providing an invaluable tutorial service in contemporary cultural and sociological theory. Graham McFee consistently suggested that the studies were worth pursuing, and he has been particularly supportive of my work on Olympism and spectacle. John Sugden worked with me on some dimensions of my studies of football culture and football politics (and as coproducer or presenter of aspects of pieces and papers from which chapters 2, 3, 5, and 6 have been reworked). When an unreliable Brighton builder rendered me homeless, Ian McDonald provided refuge and wonderful vistas of Brighton and Hove seas and sunsets, in full view of which I planned the final work on this volume.

Professor Garry Whannel has been a constant source of intellectual support and friendship for over twenty years. He likes recalling when we first met, at a joint Centre for Contemporary Cultural Studies and Department of Physical Education (University of Birmingham) symposium on "Sporting Fictions." Evidently, I went up to him and said, "Hello, I hear you're lonely." It felt like that in those days working on sport. It's remarkable to this day how sport is still seen as a relatively minor part of the cultural studies boom. But it's not lonely any more. With support from the Leisure Studies Association, the British Society for Sports History, the British Sociological Association Sociology of Sport Study Group, the North American Society for the Sociology of Sport, the International Sociology of Sport Association, and the Sport and Media Section of the International Association for Media and Communications Research, we've had lots of people to talk to in more recent years. My thanks are therefore also due to people who have heard me talk at events organized by all of those organizations. All of your responses were valued.

Dr. David Rowe and his colleagues at the University of Newcastle, New South Wales, Australia, provided unfailing support and stimulation during my period as "their" research visitor from July to September 2000, during which the introduction and rationale for the volume were first drafted. David Rowe, as reviewer of the initial proposal to the University of Minnesota Press, made constructive and insightful suggestions concerning the structure and balance of the text. Professor Toby Miller, coeditor of the series in which this book appears, first asked me to think about whether there might be a book tucked away somewhere in this body of work, and he has been a constant source of support as well as a resourceful guide to some of Manhattan's most seductive eateries and bars (in the West Village at least). Toby and Professor Ann Hall provided astute and insightful editorial responses to an initial manuscript and have been stimulating, sharp, but always sensitive and supportive reviewers and series editors. Not least, they recognized my twin claim, my own source of the professionally schizophrenic: that is, my affiliation to my humanities roots throughout my own graduate-school journey toward the intellectual diaspora of the social sciences. Crudely materialist it may sound to some, but even ideologies have social bases: we must start with things in the world as we know, see, and seek to understand them. In commenting that this volume comprises both "good sociology (of the classical kind) and good social history," my editors have reaffirmed my long term belief that the best sociology needs a historical dimension, and the best social history needs a sociological awareness.

Jennifer Moore, acquisitions editor at the University of Minnesota Press when this volume was contracted, was patient and civil beyond reason as the submission date slipped back. Her successor, Carrie Mullen, has been keenly supportive of the project as it moved toward completion. It will be readers alone who will testify as to whether the wait was at all worthwhile.

In a long overdue double acknowledgment to my teachers, I would like to thank the recently retired Mr. David Clayton, who taught me history at Burnley Grammar School, and Professor Zevedei Barbu, who taught me the kind of sociology I believe in at the Graduate School of Social Sciences at the University of Sussex, from 1972 to 1975. When I went to the University of Kent (Canterbury) to study English and philosophy, where I then spent most of my time slipping toward social history and sociology alongside my English studies, my schoolteacher who had wanted me to aspire to historical studies at an ancient university (he was Merton, Oxford) said that the punting wouldn't be very good in Canterbury. Well, he was right, but punting never interested me anyway. I never turned my back on history, though, and when Mr. Clayton invited me, more than thirty years later, to address the Bolton Historical Society at the splendid site of Bolton School, Lancashire (England), on my research into global sports politics and football, I tingled after the applause when he said that it made him "proud to be able to say that I taught this man." The late Professor Zevedei Barbu ("Zev" to all who knew him) was the post–World War II diasporic intellectual par excellence. Interviews for the Economic and Social Research Council (or *Social* Science Research Council as it was then) studentship were personal affairs, one-to-one sessions in his office, eye-to-eye encounters across the haze of the clouds of his tobacco smoke. Did he take to you? Would this relationship work? Induction with Zev for his master's and research students was discussions of Chekhov plays in his elegant book-filled home on Montpelier Road, Brighton, ice cream, and good wines in the garden. He smoked like Humphrey Bogart ("don't Zevedei that joint, my friend"), talked like Claude Rains in *Casablanca*, and thought and wrote like an interdisciplinary dream. Zev had been culture minister in a brief utopian moment in postwar Romania's communist experiment. Fleeing for his safety, he joined R. D. Laing at Glasgow before heading back south to Sussex, forming an unforgettable partnership with Professor Tom Bottomore in heading up the graduate delivery of sociological studies. Just before he made his last, lonely journey to Brazil, he asked me what I was doing slipping toward the study of leisure and sport. It seemed a long way from *Daphnis and Chloe* and the Spanish picaresque. Yet another teacher wondering why I was wasting my time, taking the wrong turning. But it wasn't as far away as he thought. All that I did with Zev in sociological and cultural theory, the sociology and social history of art and literature (what was that about if it wasn't about identity and ideology?), and comparative studies (I had the pleasure of adapting and teaching his splendid undergraduate course on this) has stood me in good stead as I've worked on the place of sport and leisure cultures in the contemporary world. If Zev had lived a little longer, a little less adrift, I'm optimistic that he would have seen the point of the sort of work that's at the heart of this volume.

Closer to home, my daughters Alys Tomlinson and Rowan Tom-linson, with their respective photographic and literary perspicacity and insights, have continued to remind me of what really counts in life in a turbulent and uncertain yet—as several studies in this book demonstrate—curiously persistent and predictable world. Finally, Bernie Kirrane—and Jo and Sinead, the Kirranettes—appeared during the final phase of revision for this volume. I've never been so close to an MBA before. Until then, I never knew that time management could be so pleasurably and produc-tively counseled for.

Introduction

Analyzing Sport and Leisure Cultures

Locating Sport and Leisure Cultures

The German intellectual Walter Benjamin, while engaged with his study of German tragedy, reported boastfully that he had collected "over 600 quotations very systematically and clearly arranged" (1970, 47). He was aspiring, as Hannah Arendt put it, to "a sort of surrealistic montage," in which the assemblage of quotations constituted the major work itself, not just some secondary, illustrative appendage. Benjamin wrote that "quotations in my work are like robbers by the roadside who make an armed attack and relieve an idler of his convictions" (38). He aspired to produce a work made up of nothing but quotations, arranged in such a way that no further text would be necessary. The attractions of the Benjamin ideal are clear but also oppressive, showing up those haunting fears concerning the paucity of one's own thought. Mercifully, too, such a form of delivery would border on the arcane for any orthodox academic constituency. In this book, then, the numerous quotations are linked by conventional critical commentary, analysis, and discussion; and in this general introduction, quotations are kept to a minimum. An opening piece is too early a point to swamp or surrender the author cum idler's convictions.

The primary empirical focus of this book is sport and associated leisure forms and practices in their variously manifest local, national, and international contexts and in historical and comparative settings. The main institutional forms and settings of sport with which the analyses are concerned are professional, organized male ones (association football or soccer, for instance, features in several of the chapters), and the cultural contexts in which such sports have thrived, prospered, or declined. Several chapters, particularly those in part III concerned with local cultures and more general leisure practices, address questions about wider patterns of sport and leisure cultures and dynamics.

The study of sport has proved a fruitful empirical challenge for soci-ologists, social historians, and cultural analysts, informing major debates on structure and agency, globalization and Americanization, and identity and its sources and determinants. It has provided the most revealing of lenses through which to understand the impact of major social processes and changes, both upon the fabric of everyday life in the modern period and upon the genesis and character of related cultural forms such as the media. Taking culture—famously labeled by Raymond Williams (1983, 87) as "one of the two or three most complicated words in the English language"—as the meanings and values of and, crucially, within a particular society or his-torical period, it is beyond doubt that sport in the contemporary world is a rich cultural seam that can be mined in order to open up and expose the character of and dynamics within a wider culture or set of related cultures. Sport and leisure can also be illuminative of the nature of ideologies (dom-inant sets of interests) in a society.

In this sense, sport should be understood not as some quasi-autonomous institution, as some kind of self-sufficient social institution or subsystem related in various ways to parallel institutions within the society, but rather as a constitutive element of everyday life and popular culture, within particular social and historical settings. For example, take the (in)-famous example of college sports in the United States. What sense does it make to speak of the institution of college sport and to describe the estab-lished order represented in its gendered hierarchies and its financial infra-structure as if it is somehow a phenomenon apart? For surely any adequate understanding of the cultural form of college sport must be based on a recognition of how the core values of masculinity at the heart of that sport are bound up with the dynamics of profit, patronage, and civil pride, in par-ticular in small town/big college America.

Sport and leisure cultures must therefore be researched firsthand and in close-up for the meanings and values that they express, represent, confirm, or challenge and for their varying relationships with other (to paraphrase Bourdieu 1986) social fields. Such analysis can demonstrate the importance of cultures in times of seismic cultural change or—as is more widely and commonly the case—in times of cultural stability and continuity and, most importantly, in relation to more broadly impacting social forces and trends. Two such trends show how sport is resonant of the sounds and the signs of the times: first, the making and remaking of modern nations, with the concomitant expression or formulation of national identity; and second, the rise of consumer culture, lived locally but manifestly global, in both conspicuously public and more privatized and individualized forms.

While nations have expressed through sport some sense of a neces-sarily imagined collectivity (Sugden and Tomlinson 1994a), consumer cultures have increasingly flattered a sense of individuality within a globalizing world (Tomlinson 1990a; Philips and Tomlinson 1992). This is shown, respectively, in the buoyancy of international sport competitions and the individual consumer choice one makes as to what sports gear or footwear to purchase (in far from just a few cases, this purportedly individual choice expresses a collective celebration of the team). Your Adidas or Nike shoes or sweatshirt might speak not just for you but also for your locality or country or nation and, of course, the global cultural economy (Klein 2000).

There is no global production without a form of local appropriation at the point of consumption; there is no national identity without the participation of the individual and the cultural accretion of the local. Local, national, and global practices are increasingly interconnected, but they are not graspable by theory alone. In studying sport and leisure cultures, one must recognize the need to produce theorized case studies, to acknowledge theoretical legacies, and to generate afresh open-minded forms of theorizing. The importance of the theoretical is paramount. But the studies and analyses in this book are premised on a view that to theorize with an empirical focus, while avoiding empiricism, is the main task of the open-minded critical analyst.

Framing Theory, Theorizing, and Theorizing About

I claim in this book to be engaging with historical concerns as well as sociological issues, so contributing to a form of contemporary history of sport and leisure cultures. Some historians, for wholly understandable professional reasons sometimes motivated by a self-protective territorialism, are skeptical about such claims. The work of John Hargreaves (1986), for instance, has been subjected to strong criticism by social historian Richard Holt (for a summary of this, see Tomlinson 1999f). Holt's critique (1989) includes a serious point about language—ways of saying—and sociologists do, sometimes, masquerade the banal as the brilliant, rendering the obvious in obfuscatory fashion. But John Hargreaves is not guilty as charged on this one, and it is the theoretical strength and rigor of sociological work that seem to threaten historical scholars, in whose work the conceptual and the theoretical often play an important but not always explicitly acknowledged part. In both historical and sociological work, though, the task is to seek the appropriate balance of theorization and focused selective analysis of empirical cases.

This is not to say that theory should ride roughshod over or across the interpretive process. It is helpful to distinguish between three different types of theoretical endeavor: framing theory, theorizing, and theorizing about. A concern with theory—its impact on past analysis and the concepts that have framed or dominated a particular field of inquiry—is valuable. It provides a sense of where things have got to in a field. All academics can benefit from such a sense, a form of intellectual history of one's own field, a history of the ideas of one's predecessors. It is important to know how a field is moving on, and it is hard to see how this can be accomplished if a knowledge of what one is moving on from is lacking. Acquiring such knowledge is not always as easy as it seems, and it can be especially difficult in an academic discipline that is perpetually pre-paradigmatic, claimed by many theorists, though none can demonstrate an established dominance in the field. So a concern for the concepts and theories that have tussled for position and influence in a field is not a diversion or an irrelevance. It is an obligation for any serious academic. It is why territorial arguments are more than trivial and have historical and epistemological overtones.

A comprehensive review of diverse framing theories of relevance to the analysis of sport and leisure cultures would trace the impact of a range of approaches from functionalism to feminism(s), queer theory to cultural studies, market-led research to cultural studies, Marxism(s) to postcolonial theory (a list suggested by Toby Miller, in personal communication). It is emphatically not the task of this general introduction to review in any comprehensive fashion such a full range of framing theory(ies) in the sport and leisure studies field. For that, the mapping exercise of Jarvie and Maguire (1994) offers a valuable starting point. More modestly, the studies in this book recognize, as appropriate, relevant theoretical legacies that have framed particular debates and issues.

Then there is theorizing, forms of theoretical thinking that neither encourage nor entertain any serious engagement with the nature of empirical phenomena or with the actualities and realities of the practices of everyday life. By this, I mean forms of business-class sociology, the goldfish-bowl restricted vision of celebrity sociologists whose analytical antennae tune in to little beyond the airport lounge or their own side of the first-class curtain. There are, thankfully, few such theorizers working on the sociological analysis of sport and leisure cultures. Such theorizing is at best an apologetic kind of applied philosophy, as some, condemning the excesses of social theory as opposed to the rootedness of sociological theory, have implied (Mouzelis 1995, 9). Mouzelis warns against dissolving "the specific identity and logic of sociological theorising . . . into an adjunct of philosophy" or some other discipline. For Mouzelis the chief objective of sociological theory is to provide and assess conceptual tools and frameworks and construct new ones. These tools are, he elaborates, the means whereby the empirical investigation of the social world is facilitated by "asking theoretically interesting questions, providing conceptual means for comparative work," for instance.

Some excesses of the theory fallacy, burying Mouzelis's double objective under the rubble of ranting tendentiousness, can be seen in the thought-killing predictability of the pseudoanalyses of someone like Jean-Marie Brohm in his Althusserian attack on the role of sport in modern societies (Brohm 1978). Here theorizing purports to be about something (high-performance sport and international competitive sport), but the object of the theorizing is taken for granted, unexamined, and of apparent minimal interest to the theorist. *Sport: A Prison of Measured Time* is a brilliant polemic but offers little in the way of sociological theory. Brohm's analysis remains little more than unsubstantiated situationist politics, a footnote to the intellectual history of its period.

Theorizing about an object of investigation is, on the other hand, surely what theory is for. We use theory to grasp and debate general social processes, to make sense of the particular type of society, or some selected aspect of that society, or of a culture of or within that society. We do not then simply rush out to gather theory-supporting trophies; if we do, we should question our motives as social scientists. Theoretical understanding, rather, is reviewed in the light of data, findings, and evidence. It might be confirmed, but it might be disputed. Strong concrete analyses of empirical phenomena—institutions, cultural forms, lived practices—act back on theory. If we theorize about sport, the analysis of sport could in turn provoke a reformulation of theory and promote debates between different theoretical positions and stances. Eric Dunning appeals for an end to paradigm rivalry in the sociology of sport, which he believes can be destructive in its effects, and argues for a more constructive approach geared toward a "synthesis which . . . will help to counter these centrifugal pressures" (1999, 246). I am in total agreement with Dunning's general sentiment.

Informed overall by a concern with how cultures contribute to the cohering of societies, often through ideological processes representing particular sets of interests, the studies in this book are in an overarching sense stimulated by what one might broadly call the social history and sociology of consumption and a cultural-studies informed sociology, including forms of what has been termed cultural Marxism. But that is not to say that Max Weber's analyses are therefore irrelevant or that a Durkheimian notion of anomie is a redundant concept for the contemporary thinker. Dunning is right to call for a potentially synthesizing inclusiveness in the field, and one way to generate serious scholarly exchanges across the field and its paradigmatic rivalry—or, strictly speaking in a Kuhnian (Kuhn 1970) sense of paradigmatic science as a dominant consensual approach to the conventions of doing science, its pre-paradigmatic rivalry—is to examine closely the findings of our respective studies, to use them as appropriate in our own reconceptualizations and theory development, and to revisit with an open mind the dominant conceptualizations with which we launch our studies and analyses.

There are serious problems in the second version of theoretical endeavor, theorizing as it is done so often in the abstract. In reviewing any field of study, it is the first and third versions of doing theory that are invaluable, one for locating oneself in a developing field, the other for grounding any theoretical evaluation in studies of particular cases or practices. At the same time, no analytical mind arrives at the empirical case carrying no interpretive baggage. In all of the studies included in this book, that baggage is made explicit by stating my intellectual debts and by showing how the particular case is being theorized about.

It is theorizing *about* the empirical cases that furthers our understanding of global trends in sport and leisure, the relationship of those trends to expressions of national identity in sport, and the place in that wider context of local cultural forms and practices. Dislocated theorizing with some half-hidden, theory-led agenda will not further much understanding at all. Featherstone (1996) concluded his overview of localism, globalism, and cultural identity with a call for focused studies:

> It can be argued that the study of culture, our interest in doing
> justice to the description of particularities and differences,
> necessarily directs us toward an ideographic mode in which
> we are acutely aware of the danger of hypostatizations and
> overgeneralizations. (70)

In such an ideographic mode, based on an appropriate openness to empirical sources, a range of concepts should be available in the sociologist's interpretive toolbox, and the sociologist should be flexible as to what is included in that toolbox.

Auto-critiques have confirmed the contingency of the conceptual. In his foreword to the 1999 reissue of Gruneau's *Class, Sports, and Social Development*, Connell locates Gruneau's contribution in "the intellectual moment of the late 1970s and early 1980s" and "the project of a democratic social transformation, radical transformation on the large scale. He judged the contributions of conservatives, liberals, and radicals alike by that yardstick" (Connell 1999, vii). Colonialism, imperialism, gender, race, and the body were, Connell argues, underplayed in Gruneau's book. So what was the abiding, enduring quality of Gruneau's study? For Connell, it was that sporting activity is not fixed, that sport is historically produced by combinations of social forces, and that such processes have to be grasped historically and can be changed in history (ix). His corrective to the 1983 book's "little sense of imperialism as a system" is that sport needs to be seen "as part of a world structure of hegemony in social relations" (viii). In his afterword to the 1999 edition Gruneau calls for "better histories" and "more inclusive theories" (123, 124) in the continuing "study of sport as a field of constitutive social practices viewed in the context of the enabling and constraining features of social structures" (123). Connell's reminder that there are forms of global hegemony and Gruneau's plea for theoretically informed histories are in the spirit of this volume. This book contributes to the continuing recognition that sport and leisure forms and practices must be understood simultaneously as manifestations of culturally specific meanings and values, economically driven forces, and politically generated processes — in short, that culture and power must be understood in an integrated fashion, as the conceptualization of the potentially hegemonic place of sport in society has consistently sought to do.

SITUATING SPORT AND LEISURE CULTURES

The studies in this book are rooted in an interdisciplinary rationale that blends social history with sociology, cultural analysis with political science. They seek to demonstrate the importance of sport and leisure cultures in the generation and the articulation of contemporary social processes and cultural meanings. They are avowedly — though not exclusively — qualitative in approach. The historical studies combine original oral historical data with available documentary sources. Analyses of sport in particular social contexts — World Cup USA 1994, various Olympic Games sites, Switzerland, Japan, the United Arab Emirates, Ireland, and South Africa, for instance — are based on study visits and the ethnographic challenge laid down by MacAloon (1992) to those of us working in British cultural studies and a critical sociology of sport.

In the first part of the book my concern is with the supranational organization of sport in the case of football's world governing body, the symbolic ceremonial enveloping global sport events such as the Olympics, and questions of identity and determinism in contexts such as Northern Ireland, South Africa, and the football World Cup. The second part comprises studies of nationhood and national identity in the case of Switzerland, the global marketing of sport and the resistance of U.S. sports space to worldwide trends, and the politics of sport and leisure cultures in the case of Asian and Middle East societies. Local culture is the focus of the third part, which offers studies of patterns of leisure activity and consumption in contemporary urban space, the place of local sport in harmonizing class relations, and the persistence of a regionally distinctive working-class cultural form (knur and spell). Without sensitive and detailed analyses of such local cultures, it would be far too easy to accept unquestioningly the momentum of global trends and to give priority to the definitions and rhetorics of powerful institutions over the meanings of the everyday practices of people. The local, the global, and the national have always been in fascinating interplay, as theorists have consistently noted (Hall 1991; Featherstone 1996;

Miller et al. 1999). Any close study of the nuances of local cultural practices, the strategies of national identity making, and the projects of powerful supranational bodies makes this clear. This pivotal point is reasserted in the short theoretical introductions to each of the three parts of the book.

The studies in this book trace some specific features and distinctive diversities across the local, the national, and the global, but they also locate historical breaks in the primacy of one or another of these dimensions. They show, too, despite the sectional nomenclature within the volume, how false it would be to artificially prize apart these dimensions. They embody my interdisciplinary commitment to historical and sociological work, an open-minded commitment to critical methodologies (Tomlinson 1999b), and a central concern with power (Tomlinson 1998a). The chapters start with a focus on global sport cultures and the supranational and go on to argue for the recognition of the persisting power of (sometimes pernicious) local cultures in the increasingly globalized world. The specific examples of the national basis and context of sport and leisure cultures illustrate the continuing hold of a sphere between the local and the global. The final concentration on the local shows how human actors have been bound to local cultures and to principles of cultural bonding while showing awareness of the possibility of being drawn more and more toward forms of the supralocal, or how basic inequalities and differentials of power constrain choice in such matters, constraining some to the sphere of a mediated global culture, including widespread forms of banal broadcasting, in circumstances in which the cost of the local lived culture might well be out of reach. At all these levels the local negotiates the global, the global meets the local, and the national, in terms of provision and policy and regulatory aspects of production, mediates the two.

The analysis of such sport and leisure cultures has provided fruitful foci for the integrated interdisciplinary study of some central themes of contemporary social science. In all the studies, at all the levels addressed, identity is a recurrent theme, power a constant analytical concern, the social constraints inhibiting people's lives and possibilities and the conditions whereby power is gained and held (or hegemony established or not) a recurrent emphasis. A primary concern is with the ways in which sport and leisure cultures embody the power games (Sugden and Tomlinson 2002b) played out in the public cultures of the day. My primary case studies are of how such power games operate in men's sports, in a number of instances giving close scrutiny to the politics of (association) football, nationally and internationally. Adopting the international term for association football, this book calls the men's game with which several chapters are concerned simply "football"—not "soccer," which is the preferred term in the United States. But the book is about more than just the world of male sport. It addresses central social historical and sociocultural issues. If this book, and the project that underpins it, has any value, it is not least that it could encourage severely dislocated forms of theorizing back toward the world of human beings, social structures, and the complex processes of meaning making and power relations that make our societies and cultures what they are.

Walter Benjamin (1978) observed that "only the more feeble and distracted take an inimitable pleasure in conclusions" (64) and so correspondingly advised the writer not to "write the conclusion of a work in your familiar study. You would not find the necessary courage there" (81). Another strategy might be to dispense with any single concluding statement. Therefore any conclusion to this introduction remains an invitation to read on, to situate sport and leisure cultures within the focused analyses themselves, embodying as they do the theoretical and methodological priorities sketched out in this introduction. One should resist the temptation to extract ungrounded yet grandiose theoretical overviews, whether from the base of one's familiar study or elsewhere. Nevertheless, the attempt to make sense of the micropolitics of everyday life found in the sports world and leisure practices and to locate this within a broader understanding of culture and social process may make a modest contribution to the wider sociological project in which a recognition of the importance of sport and leisure—as consumption, consumerism, and spectacle—is becoming increasingly established.

PART I. GLOBAL THEMES

Global Themes

Extensive debate on the theory of globalization as it applies to sport, and on the genesis, emergence, and increasing significance of processes of globalization in and of sport need not be reproduced here. This has been accomplished by others, most notably Maguire (1999). Rather, some central features of the process are outlined and considered in terms of the intensifyingly global profile of mediated sport cultures. There is widespread agreement among commentators and theorists that in the final quarter of the twentieth century globalization had become one of the major forces or pressures that would affect all cultures and societies in a world order constantly being negotiated and in the process of remaking. Its relevance to the sports sphere has been widely debated (see, for instance, Harvey and Houle 1994; Maguire 1994; and Houlihan 1994a, in a dedicated issue of *Sociology of Sport Journal*). Miller et al. (2001) have also provided forceful argument and analysis concerning the effects of the new international sport-cultural order upon particular distinctive sport cultures within the wider globalization process. Here, I seek merely to present the central arguments in the broader theoretical debate to contextualize the chapters in the section, focusing on the level of the economic and its cultural concomitants, issues of modernity and self-identity, and the question of modernity and the globalization of media cultures.

Jacques (1989, 236–37) sees globalization as coterminous with internationalization and argues that on the economic level the capitalist crisis of the 1970s "accelerated the trend towards global markets," stimulating technologies "whose production and markets were highly internationalized." The outcome of this change was that an international economic order increased the interdependence of national economies. Jacques notes too that the "trend towards globalization" cannot be reduced to the economic alone: it also involves "the growth of an increasingly internationalized culture, with the spread of satellite television or the growth of English as an international language" (237). Jacques observes that the tunnel linking France to mainland Britain means that Paris can now be perceived as being as close to London as the Northern English city of Manchester and that "events in a far part of the globe can be brought live to your sitting room," which presages "a new sense of global intimacy and interdependence." At the same time, this process and the new sensibility that it engenders are locked in tension with a "tendency towards localization. There is a new search for identity and difference in the face of impersonal global forces, which is leading to the emergence of new national and ethnic demands." Here in the identification of simultaneous trends toward economic and cultural interdependence and political and cultural distinctiveness, Jacques could be describing some of the driving and defining features of modern international sports: high-profile international sport is premised on globalizing forms of interdependency and interconnectedness yet prospers on the cultivation of a separatist and distinctive cultural politics. The dynamic pointed to by Jacques has been noted with specific reference to sport by Maguire. Warning that the "conceptual snare" of the conflation of globalization with a homogenization thesis must be avoided, he points out the "unevenness" of globalizing processes but observes that despite such unevenness:

> It is more difficult to understand local or national experiences without reference to these global flows. The flow of leisure styles, customs and practices from one part of the world to another, "long-haul" tourism, and global events such as music festivals and the Olympic Games are examples of these processes at work.
> (Maguire 1994, 400)

Maguire traces five phases of the process of what he calls "global sportization," the last two of which cover the Cold War years of the twentieth century, and a process of "creolization of sport cultures," leading Maguire to the observation that we "need to develop criteria by which to judge the 'reach' and 'response' of global flows on local cultures" (Maguire 1999, 87). Giddens (1991), in his more general theoretical scope, had of course already recognized the increasing importance of the relationship between the local and the global in his reflections upon self-identity, self, and society in the late modern age. For him, the "dialectic of the local and the global is a basic emphasis of the arguments" (22) developed within those reflections. Globalization, Giddens implies, is nothing more or less than the growth and spread of the modern across the contemporary world, involving "an ongoing relation between distanciation and the chronic mutability of local circumstances and local engagements" (21–22). This is a gloomy view of modernity and the conditions of self-identity, in which spheres of locality are presented as uncontrollably fickle and those of the supralocal as remote and beyond one's control. Indeed, Giddens describes the "late modern world" as "apocalyptic . . . because it introduces risks which previous generations have not had to face" (4). Giddens identifies the dynamic at the heart of modernity between the existential angst of wondering who one is and the supraindividual forces that situate one precariously and catch one up perturbingly in "massive waves of global transformation" (184). Global sporting events can express the complexity of such a condition—making the study of such sport cultures more than a marginal social scientific task and potentially catapulting the analysis of sport to the heart of the sociological agenda. Such sporting events—in terms of their impact on the self-identity of individuals and the profile, pride, and identity of nations—are premised on an infrastructure of communications and a sophisticated global media system.

John B. Thompson recognizes the most general sense of the term "globalization" as referring to "the growing interconnectedness of different parts of the world, a process which gives rise to complex forms of interaction and interdependency" (J. B. Thompson 1995, 149). He notes, however, that in this general sense the term is often used interchangeably with terms such as "internationalization" and "transnationalization." For him, the term and the process need to be defined more clearly, as something beyond just the "expansion of activities beyond the boundaries of particular nation-states" (150). He specifies three conditions on which a more adequate conceptualization of globalization is based: first, an identifiably global arena in which activities take place; second, a global scale of organization, planning, and coordination of activities; and third, an established degree of reciprocity and interdependency of activities, with activities of a local kind around the world having the capacity to shape each other. "One can speak of globalization in this sense only when the growing interconnectedness of different regions and locales becomes systematic and reciprocal to some degree, and only when the scope of interconnectedness is effectively global" (150). Can one speak of international sport and the major events in the international sports calendar as truly globalized phenomena in these terms? The first two criteria are certainly met: sports competitions are staged in stadia and venues resonant with an internationalism that is central to the rationale of the event, and the television and media coverage of the biggest of those events internationalizes them from the beginning, while transnational organizations such as the International Olympic Committee (IOC) and the Fédération Internationale de Football Association (FIFA) provide a global scale of planning and organization. It is less obvious how the final criterion is met, but the combined effects of a layered form of administration and control (from the local to the regional to the national and the supranational), linked with the extensive media coverage of local-based sports and its immediate transition worldwide within the context of an expanding consumer culture, ensure a constant diffusion from the local or regional to the global and vice versa.

These theoretical issues and conceptual concerns run through the whole of this book but are particularly central to this first part. In part I, instances of sport's growth as a global force and some of the ways in which it accomplishes particular kinds of ideological work are analyzed, but I never lose sight of the ways in which sport continues to provide a means for the articulation of different kinds and levels of identity (the conceptual pedigree of which is overviewed within chapter 2). Indeed, the struggle to express new cultures in hybrid forms (Bhaba 1994) need not be wholly separated from the question of how cultures are often negotiated into being within the context of power relations. Pieterse (1995, 45) argued that we should view globalization as a process of "hybridization which gives rise to global mélange" and offered interesting classifications of static and fluid cultural relations: "a sociology conceived within the framework of nations/societies making place for a post-inter/national sociology of hybrid formations, times and spaces" (63). Social historians might call this the study of the balance between continuity and change in social and cultural life, in an increasingly international context. In studies of sport's place in the contemporary world order, it may not be necessary to seek a wholly new conceptual and analytical agenda, jettisoning concepts seen as compromised by some particular time and place.

Creolization, hybridity, whatever—to talk of globalization is not to deny locality or cultural identity and, in some circumstances, the capacity of human actors to build anew or at least reassemble the elements of their lived cultures. Hannerz, with reference to religious groups in Zaire, has observed that "to deal with globalization is to deal with diversity under increasing interconnectedness" (1999, 326). Appadurai, writing on ethnic violence, confirms that it is "not hard to see the general ways in which transnational forces impinge on local ethnic instabilities" (1999a, 321). To deal with globalization is also to deal with new sets of interest, including economic ones, and forms of governance (G. Thompson 1999). There is no single theory of globalization. Theoretical arguments over interesting theses, positions, and detailed cases are important, as counseled by McLennan (1998, 15). But such arguments must be informed by developed analyses of the kind that feature in this part of the book. Appadurai (1999b, 238) reminds us that "all forms of critique, including the most arcane and abstract, have the potential for changing the world." This catholic point needs to be constantly reasserted. And a potential for change is stronger if researchers are willing to speak to and read each other. Any critical analysis of sport can hardly fail to recognize how what Miller et al. (2001) call the "global sports complex" is a product of five processes—globalization, governmentalization, Americanization, televisualization, commodification—and is characterized as much by "commodification and alienation" as by "utopian internationalism" (4). The argument is in the detail, but the theoretical argument is impossible without the analytical detail. Sklair has argued that a new class, the transnational capitalist class, is emerging across the world, pursuing "people and resources all over the world in its insatiable desire for private profit and eternal accumulation . . . composed of corporate executives, globalizing bureaucrats and politicians, globalizing professionals, and consumerist elites" (2000, 4). Go to any of the Grand Slam tennis tournaments in Melbourne, New York, Paris, or London, and Sklair's theoretical claim is staring you in the face. Sport and other high-profile and internationalized forms of leisure consumption and practice are the lucrative sites of such a class's speculations and ambitions. Understanding the shift in the nature of sports governance is scarcely a dry backwater of public administration studies. It is a study of the making of globally significant changes, of international power and status, and of the transformation of worldwide capitalist markets.

What is of most interest for the critical analyst of contemporary sport culture(s) remains the knowing ways in which powerful interests within sport can exploit the identity-affirming capacity of a sport culture to suit their own priorities and needs. It is precisely in this way that sport can be simultaneously a conservative and traditional as well as a progressive and innovative force. That paradox is the central analytical theme in the critical understanding of global sport cultures and their associated leisure practices. Chapter 1 analyzes the recurrent rhetoric of Olympic ceremonies, showing how the universalistic idealism of such events blends with nationalist sentiment. In chapter 2 the place of male football cultures in an international and increasingly globalized sport culture is evaluated in terms of the politics of identity and social and cultural limitations on the influence of globalizing trends. Chapter 3 demonstrates the motives that have driven those who have been attracted to positions of power in the international development and administration of football, identifying a shift in the political economy on which international sport is based in a world of the media event and increasingly lucrative profits and outcomes for those recognizing the financial potential of sport.

1. Magnificent Trivia

Olympic Spectacle, Opening Ceremonies, and Some Paradoxes of Globalization

Juan Antonio Samaranch, president of the International Olympic Committee (IOC), presided over his final Olympic Games in Sydney, Australia, in September 2000. To the undisguised elation of Bob Carr (premier of New South Wales), John Howard (prime minister of Australia), and Michael Knight (minister for the Olympics), Samaranch declared, at the closing ceremony, that Sydney 2000 was "the best Olympic Games ever." "The accolade so wanted and so deserved," observed BBC television commentator Barry Davies. Samaranch poured praise in all directions, hailing the Games as "a glorious chapter in the history of Australia . . . fantastic success . . . the most dedicated and wonderful volunteers ever. . . . Thank you for these exceptional Games . . . indeed we did celebrate humanity." Samaranch claimed the Olympic Truce as a reality, citing the unity of the South Korea and North Korea teams in the parade of the athletes. "They could not have been better. You have presented to the world the best Olympic Games ever," Samaranch went on, and asked them to please accept an "expression of our satisfaction for a perfect organization." Barry Davies commented that "there are those who criticise him for the corruption of the ideal" but also "those who say that he reflects the realities of the modern world." No wonder Samaranch was smiling. He might have had a little linguistic difficulty with the word "Aboriginal" in the opening ceremony, his hesitant English rendering it as more like "operational," which is what he was no doubt mightily relieved to be after a terrible two years of IOC scandal (Jennings and Sambrook 2000; Lenskyj 2000). But now everything seemed nicely back in place.

Sydney had been promising a very big show indeed for the opening ceremony, the initial showpiece for the highest-profile event in a globally mediated world of international sport. The bigger the show, the better for the IOC boss. In an ambitious Australian spectacle, the IOC could begin to restore its tarnished reputation, Samaranch's own culpability in the corruption cases conveniently sidelined as the eyes of the world switched to the stadium and the spectacle. De Coubertin, founder of the modern Olympics, believed that "man is made up of" three parts: "body, mind and character. Character is not formed by the mind, it is formed above all by the body. That is what the ancients knew, and that is what we are relearning, painfully" (2000, 532). Whatever the dubiousness of this healthy body/ healthy mind rhetoric, it would be in Samaranch's interest to get the focus back on to the body. A glorious celebration of the qualities of youth and physicality would be ideal for this purpose, elided as those qualities still become with the idea of sound character. Samaranch, anticipating the predictable hyperbole and dramatic spectacle of Sydney's opening, might also have recalled de Coubertin's encomium to Olympism, uttered in the Sorbonne, Paris, in 1884, two years before the first Olympics of the modern era: "I raise my glass to the Olympic idea, which has crossed the mists of time like a ray from the all-powerful sun and is returning to shine on the gateway to the twentieth century with the gleam of joyful hope" (532). Sydney's millennial games provided the IOC with the perfect opportunity to play out its own version of the Olympic refrain. It is remarkable that such rhetoric has been sustained and legitimated across three centuries, and the symbolic and ceremonial elements in which such rhetoric is embedded have provided the concrete manifestation of this rhetoric. The following section reviews Sydney's contribution to this tradition.

G'DAY: WELCOME TO SYDNEY

Australian Ric Birch was director of ceremonies for the Sydney Olympics. He has an impressive pedigree, as director of production for David Wolper's spectaculars at the Los Angeles Olympics in 1984. Few who saw it will forget the Rocket Man who flew down into the Coliseum at the opening ceremony, the eighty-four grand pianos swiveling into view as Gershwin classics played, the dancing cowboys and cowgirls wagon-training it the wrong way across the North American continent. And, in the closing ceremony, a giant extraterrestrial thanking us for the hundred years in which we—the "family of man"—have managed to show such great achievements. This was selective U.S. history at its peak, cultural inventory and political bias rolled into one (Tomlinson 1989a).

Birch also had an executive producer role in Barcelona's ceremonies, but despite all his experience he wasn't saying much in the run-in to Sydney's opening. In fact, he was saying nothing at all. SOCOG's (Sydney Organizing Committee for the Olympic Games) media adviser Steve Cooke closed up on the ceremonies: "Ric's not speaking to anyone. We've had some trouble with the local media." But it's "tipped to be as Australian as possible," Cooke confided, with "athletes out on the field, creating fifteen thousand more seats." It would certainly include large numbers of children, young people, and volunteers, and there had been disputes about importing U.S. and Japanese boys and girls to play in the bands. Ten thousand professional, amateur, and volunteer supporters were lined up for the act at the opening, five thousand at the closing of the event.

All such ceremonies try to balance regional (city), national, and global interests. Sydney had a go at this with its unsuccessful mascots. Syd the platypus was the city's. Millie the echidna spoke for the millennium. Olly the kookaburra was named after the event itself. They were so unsuccessful that they were left offstage as the ceremonies played out the modern Olympic narratives of national rebirth and international and global cooperation, and Olivia Newton-John and Australian former Essex-man John Farnham sang songs of welcome to the world.

Birch's opening ceremony was widely hailed in Australia as a masterpiece of showbiz presentation, an uninhibitedly ambitious show of national and historical pride and cosmopolitan sincerity. What follows is a reminder of the primary themes and narrative, blended with my commentary, from close to ringside.

Sydney's welcome to the global audience in the world's most watched television event was like an advertisement for your local riding school. Or outdoor overcoat supplier. One hundred twenty riders draped in dry-as-bone Aussie bush coats romanticized the taming of the Australian outback. Riders aged fifteen to seventy-seven, astride their Australian stock horses, kept their cool in front of the 111,000 in the Olympic Stadium. The horse master didn't mince words: "We're breaking world records with this event and its scale will blow the world away." And sitting fifteen rows back, the emissions from the panting horses' nostrils wafting into the faces of those who paid $1,400 for their seats, it was certainly stirring, as the riders also sang the Australian national anthem. There weren't many more live animals to come after that—a couple of stray dogs and dingoes. But there were lots of imagined ones—imagined in a little girl's dream and realized like a play-school orgy of the fantastic.

Olympic ceremonies share the same preoccupations. The host nation wants to show that it can put on a global show but must also feature a quota of Olympic-style spirit—youth, universalism, peace, and the like. Such a recipe can draw and hold the audience, for we all become gleeful spectators again, watching vastly sophisticated technologies reduce complex histories to showbiz formulas. For Sydney 2000 the Sydney Symphony Orchestra worked overtime backing a lineup of Australian popular singers, as well as haunting soloists and choirs, in pop classic and middle-of-the-road numbers stressing dreams, heroism, and the power of the symbol of the flame. And political messages get slotted in there too. The governor-general of

Australia told the world that the Olympic Games are "a powerful tool for reconciliation." But it's the cultural spectacle that grabs you the most, that takes you back to the front row of the stalls or the big top.

The beginning of Sydney's cultural spectacle, after its welcome to the world, echoed the four-year-long Olympic arts festival, which had opened with the theme of Aboriginal dreaming, the life force and spiritual basis of the longest surviving of human civilizations. Deep Sea Dreaming placed center stage the Hero Girl, an innocent Shirley Temple look-alike or refugee from the cast of Peter Pan, who descended into the depths of a pool of fish, and so began a bizarre dream sequence journey guided by the great tribal dancer Djakapurra, the Songman. Hero Girl, suspended at great height, performed somersaults in the sky, chased by several glowing yellow creatures—they turned out to be young swimmers training, bellowed on by legendary Australian swimming coach Laurie Lawrence in video close-up. Hero Girl can't keep up, and the giant figure of the Songman waits to save her and guide her safely to salvation. Then followed Awakening, revolving around the uniting of diverse Aboriginal nations, and the appearance of Wandjina, the creation spirit, arching the stadium like a sunrise and igniting bushfires that prefaced the third theme, Fire, as a creative but not destructive force. Circus-time this, with an array of fire-eaters. This elemental emphasis persisted in the theme of Nature, the Australian landscape and its plants and animals emerging out of the chaos of fire—with just the one swift guest appearance from a kangaroo, which was then sidelined by the organizers as an undesirable national symbol after the scathing response to the bicycling kangaroos that had represented Australia in the handover phase of the closing ceremony of the previous summer Olympics in Atlanta. The threat of a dark force of modern culture was then represented with the Tin Symphony, which included Ned Kelly types in iron masks (several performing flying feats), dancing cog wheels, and merry fiddling music ushering in cheerful jigs. At the end of this segment, Hero Girl looked like she was about to be gobbled up by a mechanical dragon—or was it a horse? She survived, though, and after a few British sailors arrived on a contraption resembling a penny-farthing and the penal colony roots of western settlement were conveniently overlooked, the dream could continue.

Arrivals, the sixth theme, depicted the coming (all fit and dancing) of groups of immigrants from all over the world, hailing the New Australia of multiculturalism, celebrated ultimately (an Australian in-joke, I knew instantly from my time promenading the suburban streets of New South Wales) in a move from shantytown to suburbia, represented in the opening up of gyrating packing boxes transformed into jovial domestic gardeners, lawn mowers their dancing partners. The last segmental theme, thankfully, didn't live up to its name. In Eternity, the blue-collar egalitarianism of Australia was celebrated, workers building an enormous bridge on which one thousand tap dancers beat out an anthem of celebration, Songman and Hero Girl reconciling in the center of things.

Some experienced Australian commentators were nervous at the world's reaction. Would this be too Australian, too parochial? A concentration on the Aboriginal roots of the country, an encomium to the Australian countryside (the bush), and the making of the industrial culture, dominated. Multiculturalism, ethnicity, and reconciliation were central to the display, hailing the cultural diversity and cosmopolitanism of the New Australia. Artistic director and producer David Atkins states that the Sydney ceremony is important because it is about Australians themselves, and no other culture could have attempted what they did: "They couldn't have matched our mixture of youth, naivete and larrikinism." "Larrikinism" is the term in Australia for that streetwise, even connish, wit and cunning that helps you get on in life. It's an illuminating claim, showing how strong that "see what we can do" spirit is rooted in an Australian consciousness still afflicted by a deep sense of inferiority, undoubtedly fueled by the continent's geographical marginality.

After the host city/nation's narrative, fire and water were reconciled in a magician-like trick for the official ritual of the lighting of the Olympic flame. The last lap of the torch relay was inside a fountain. Far from extinguishing it, the fountain streamlined the flame, a still more dramatic effect when the cauldron burst into flames. It was runner and soon-to-be gold medalist Cathy Freeman who emerged to light the flame, rounding off the ceremony's depiction of the history of Australia as an Aboriginal meta-narrative.

This was the new Australia, reworking its history and its tensions, offering a vision in which Wendy learns to fly and all, however different, live happily ever after. Fairy tales do come true after all. Birch stated confidently that the Sydney spectacle would be "the greatest ever" opening ceremony. That is until next time, when the likes of Birch and his team, or some rival outfit, would be in Athens, telling the same story anew and making us all instant classicists and historians.

For all its claims to uniqueness and distinctiveness, the opening ceremony of Sydney 2000 followed not just official Olympic protocol but also inexorable Olympic rhetoric and hyperbole—universalism of youth, peace, and joy, with the added spice of reconciliation, sitting alongside an assertive national narrative of the making of a new nation, retold as a harmonious process of genesis from the earliest human spirit to the multicultural hedonism of a globalized world. If the template for this was forged anywhere, it was in Los Angeles in 1984. Before reviewing the predecessors of Sydney in this quarter century of transformation of the scale and impact of Olympic symbolism, it is useful to consider the material contexts of such events. This can help show how, in the 2000 Games, the Los Angeles legacy was intact.

MEDIA SPORTS EVENTS ON THE WORLD STAGE

It has become a truism within the sport and media industries that the Olympic Games and the football World Cup are the most widely watched—and therefore in a sense the biggest—television media events in the history of humankind. Statistics are presented that indicate the grip of these sporting events upon the popular consciousness of peoples throughout the contemporary world. The IOC produces its own publications on the place of the Olympic Games in the viewings and ratings hierarchy of the global television industry. In the preface to its report on this broadcast analysis, Samaranch claimed, following on from the 1992 Winter Olympics (in Albertville, France) and Summer Olympics (in Barcelona, Spain), that they "achieved the highest level of interest in Olympic history . . . best evidenced by the television coverage, as it is through television that the world experiences the Olympics" (IOC 1992, 3). The Winter Games were seen by a gross cumulative television audience of 8 billion viewers in 86 countries; the Summer Games by a cumulative audience of 16.6 billion in "a record 193 countries . . . Barcelona, as host city, provided 2,800 hours of live sports coverage. In several countries, ratings records were set" (3). This calculation represented 2.3 billion people, 85 percent of all people with televisions. The gross cumulative figure of 24.6 billion for 1992 was an increase of 44.7 percent on the cumulative figure of 17 billion for the 1988 Games (10.4 billion for Seoul, 6.6 billion for Calgary).

In its bullet-pointed summary titled "The Whole World Watches the Olympics" the report positions the Olympic Games right at the top of the global ratings, the Barcelona Games being "televised in more countries than any other event, including the World Cup Soccer Tournament, the Super Bowl, and the Formula 1 Grand Prix Series" (6). Surveys in the United States, Spain, and the United Kingdom are cited, indicating that in those countries nine of ten people "tuned in to watch" the Barcelona Games. It is such impact that prompts television companies to invest so much in television rights to the Games. North American giant NBC Sports won the rights, in 1994, to the 1996 Atlanta Summer Olympics, with a record bid of $456 million, confident that such outlay would be repaid by advertisers unable to resist the profiling guaranteed by the anticipated viewing figures for a North American–based Games that would be broadcast so comprehensively worldwide. Audience estimates for Olympic events, particularly the opening ceremony, have risen dramatically from 600 million for Mexico in 1968 to 900 million for Los Angeles in 1984, 3 billion for Seoul in 1988, up to the 3.5 billion claimed for Barcelona in 1992 (Moragas et al. 1995, 213). Although there are serious deficiencies in such estimates, it remains incontestable that the Olympics can "be labeled as a global television event of extraordinary proportions around the world" (221).

Television has enabled global sports events to be projected on increasingly grand and spectacular scales. The flickering black-and-white television images of the 1964 Rome Olympics were revelatory in their time. More sophisticated broadcasting techniques and the advent of color television have meant that those innovative images of 1964 now appear as quaint and inadequate records of sports events for the worldwide sporting audience. Fueled by Cold War rivalry throughout the 1970s and the 1980s, made-for-television Olympic ceremonies became a major source of audience figures, justifying the investments of the television industry and the main sponsors of the Olympics. The Los Angeles Olympic Games of 1984 can now be seen as a watershed in this regard, providing spectacular opening and closing ceremonies to assert the superiority of the Western, capitalist, free American way over the oppressive Eastern, communist, totalitarian Soviet way. The Soviet Union and many of its allies boycotted the 1984 Games in a direct response to the United States' boycott of the Moscow Olympics in 1980 (in response to the Soviet invasion of Afghanistan). In this context, the Los Angeles Games in 1984 were a statement of the strength of American ideals, ever stronger in the face of Soviet disruption. Allying Hollywood showbiz flair with U.S. political rhetoric and ideology, the ceremonies set a standard and an expectation for spectacle that succeeding host nations felt compelled to emulate or to surpass (Perelman 1985). In Seoul in 1988, Barcelona in 1992, Atlanta in 1996, and Sydney in 2000, the Summer Games opened to magnificent ceremonies celebratory of the different levels of the regional, the national, and the supranational—and simultaneously resonant of some central tensions within an increasingly globalized world of sports consumption.

Seoul's games were a statement of the political and economic accomplishments and aspirations of an aggressive and thrusting emergent political power as well as a statement, by contrast with North Korea, of the superiority of a capitalist model of development over a communist model. Barcelona's games were symbolic of the rehabilitation of Spain in the post-Franco period and of the status of the Catalan region and the city of Barcelona, vis-à-vis the central state and the metropolitan center, Madrid. Atlanta's staging of the games was pitched as a profiling of the American South and Southeast, a claim that it could be seen as a kind of capital of the South. Sydney staged the games as a celebration of a new multicultural, reconciled, and vibrant Australia and as a way of reminding international tourist and business markets of the worldly cosmopolitanism of the city and the country.

Each Olympic Games would repay detailed and intensive consideration as fully developed case studies of event management, civic boosterism, national pride and cultural identity, and media sport. For the purposes of this chapter I concentrate on the last two aspects, while recognizing the importance of the other aspects. The made-for-media ritual and ceremonial surrounding the opening of the events attracts, as we have seen, the largest global audience. A concentration on the features and qualities of these moments, as purveyed through television, points to some of the anomalies characterizing the intensifying globalization of sports events through the media. The analysis is based on textual readings of (British) television coverage of the 1984, 1988, 1992, 1996, and 2000 Summer Games discussed at the beginning of the chapter. In this sense the interpretations should be understood as specific to a British context. My own viewing and speaking position is not that of neutral and omniscient social scientist; it is based in the realities and specificities of the British media's presentation of Olympic spectacle—and some distinctively Anglocentric mediation by British television professionals, such as the commentator David Coleman. At the same time I provide readings—analyses and interpretations—that are anthropologically sensitive, and I locate any Anglocentric ethnocentrism at its source—within British television discourse itself. The analysis and interpretation are informed, too, by observations generated by my presence in Barcelona for a time during the 1992 Games and my presence at the Summer Games in Sydney in 2000. Contextual insights were also gained at developmental events in Calgary in 1987 and at Atlanta in 1994, during the processes of momentum-building prior to those cities' staging of the Winter Games of 1988 and the Summer Games of 1996 respectively.

Symbolizing the Global and the Local: The Recurrent Motifs of Olympic Ceremonies

Considering selected aspects of globalization and their relevance to international sports and those sports' worldwide influence, as outlined in the introduction to part I, it is clear that sports can be usefully described as globalized phenomena, but there is more still to be said. Sports do not simply demonstrate the nature of globalization. They are generative of it: they are globalizing as well as globalized, and they embody dramatically the tensions of the global and local dualism, offering as they do forms of subglobal identity and affiliation within the globalized discourses of international sporting contacts and exchanges. These tensions are ingrained in the ceremonies and spectacles of events such as the Olympic Games, in which allegedly universal values such as the "Olympic ideal" are reworked in different times and places, necessarily arrogated, as particular histories and cultures are brought to bear in the restating of the ideal. By the conceptual term *arrogation* I mean the process whereby values are inevitably reshaped, while being claimed as preserved. As globalizing processes and regional and cultural traditions meet, the local has the capacity to absorb the global in an *arrogating* process of remolding. The following analytical cases seek to show these processes at work. Los Angeles 1984 is in many respects the prototype of the contemporary televisual Olympic spectacle. Although the scale of the opening ceremony at the Moscow Olympics in 1980 was, according to accounts of those present at the event, magnificent, the event was not widely broadcast in the Anglo-American world. In media terms then, Los Angeles 1984 set the pace for its successors in its unadulterated celebration of American culture and values (Tomlinson 1989a, and 1999a, 217–31). In my full account of Los Angeles 1984 I argued that the spectacle was what Adair (1986, 76–80) has called "Spielbergian" or "para-Spielbergian," mixing visions of a simple, untainted, and yet retrievable past with the impact of new and sometimes alien forces in an optimistic blend for the future, exemplified in the closing ceremony by the giant spaceman who hailed the games as an example of "the family of man involved in the limitless possibilities of human achievement. For almost 100 years you have celebrated the best that humanity has to offer. You call it the Olympic Games, and for that and the cities that have kept the Olympic ideal alive, I salute you" (Tomlinson 1999a, 224). For Adair, the Spielberg film *ET: The Extra-Terrestrial,* which "was predicated on a universe of infinite spiritual consciousness" and "groping towards a literal theology of space," is a form of Christian science fiction. The opening ceremony of the 1984 Los Angeles Olympics and the persisting themes in its closing ceremony addressed the world in an accessible language of popular entertainment, offering their own version of the miraculous route to future salvation. In Los Angeles, the language of the ceremony drew upon

> a reservoir of meanings, deep wells of cultural prejudice and national solipsism . . . for all its apparent harmlessness and innocence . . . one of the most fascinating "necessary arrogations" of the "Olympic ideal." (Tomlinson 1999a, 228)

Analyses of ceremony and spectacle at the Summer Olympics in Seoul, Barcelona, and Atlanta demonstrate the continuing prevalence of the themes dramatically depicted in Los Angeles and climaxing in the spectacle of Sydney.

Seoul 1988: Ascendant Worlds and the Korean Miracle

After much controversy in the lead-up to the 1988 Summer Olympic Games, South Korea's capital offered a spectacle combining the spiritual with the physical, the contemporary cultural with the historical-anthropological. In the BBC studio in London, the background music was the Vangelis soundtrack to the film *Chariots of Fire,* the widely reproduced audio anthem of a past and pure Olympic—and very British—ideal (Tomlinson 1988b). An occidental fan had opened up to reveal images of the Korean flag, the event's logo, and the Olympic rings, an elegant screen-consuming flame, and then a sequence of images of Korean dancers and Olympic athletes. Noting that prices of £1,000 per stadium ticket were being demanded on the black market, London's anchorman then welcomed viewers to "what promises to be one of the most spectacular opening ceremonies of all time. . . . It's become traditional that the host nation" welcomes the world to the games "in the most lavish style possible." This was a cue to display some clips of the choreography in Moscow in 1980, backed by the image of the Russian bear, and of Los Angeles in 1984 — the immortalized eighty-four grand pianos, the Rocket Man, and the choreographed letters of "welcome." "Pageantry, spectacle, and showbiz" were promised for the forthcoming ceremony, in which ninety-five hundred athletes would eventually parade, representing 160 of 167 eligible nations. When the baton in this commentary relay was passed to David Coleman in Seoul, the theme of "pageant and spectacle" was reaffirmed but celebrated as a miracle: a "rebirth of the Olympic Games . . . that must be thought of as an Olympic miracle," for "today in the most unlikely country . . . NOCs [National Olympic Committees] are more united than ever." With so few eligible nations choosing not to attend the games, Coleman could claim that this was "truly the most international sports gathering in history." That theme of internationalism was immediately conflated with a rhetoric of global unity. For "the chosen theme [of the ceremony] is peace, harmony, and progress," which, Coleman commented, had already been achieved in Olympic terms by the record turnout of nations. Before a moment of the ceremony had passed, the central motif was put in place by Coleman: the notion of the Olympics as reconciliation, as a progressive force for peace.

The ceremony began, unprecedentedly, with a procession outside the main stadium, on Seoul's main river, focused on the progress of the Korean Giant Drum to the stadium. A flotilla of 160 (the number of competing nations) boats and 160 windsurfers and waterskiers moved toward the stadium, each individual carrying a flag of a competing nation. Twenty-four (the number of the Olympiad, the period or cycle of the Games) boats led an armada, followed by five boats representing the world's oceans and six boats representing the world's continents, in style, shape, and impact "forming a fascinating mixture of old and new," as Coleman put it. In the Olympic Stadium this aquatic procession was being watched on huge screens, while Coleman prepared Western viewers for the forthcoming spectacle. The imagination of those of us in the West might well, he remarked, be stretched by what was to come, "but in Korea it is not just fanciful but it's also meaningful." Marching into the stadium as background to Coleman's attempt at anthropological sensitivity were 1,200 traditional Korean drummers, beating out a welcome presaging the arrival of the Giant Drum and enacting a ritual of origins.

The ceremony revolved around a theatrical reenactment of the beginning of time, of the first morning, of the greeting of the first sunrise, the percussion symbolizing the human heartbeat. The drummers performed, too, an ancient ritual allegedly going back thousands of years: the purifying of the land, which, we were told by Coleman, "on this historic day has special Olympic significance . . . symbolizing making sacred the site of the 24th Olympiad." The vision was completed when, after three thunderous booming strikes of the Giant Drum, the World Tree, posited as the link between Heaven and Earth, exploded skyward in a celebration of the world's first sunrise, fireworks and balloons cracking and floating Heavenward.

This representation of the birth of the world was followed by the entry into the stadium of white-robed dancers: "In celebration of the first dawn Greek goddesses and Korean angels pour into the arena," Coleman observed, symbolizing the unions of Heaven and Earth and of East and West, "the dance expressing the serenity of a world at peace." A moment, he reflectively added, for the troubled Olympic family to treasure. Here, in the assertion of connectedness and unity between ancient Greek mythology and contemporary Korean ritual, and between geopolitical blocs in the modern world order, the flexibility of Olympic-related values is shown. Specifically rooted in a particular genesis and history, they are nevertheless intertwined with a transhistorical celebration of the common values of humanity. Above the action down on the ground in the arena, a large screen flickered the motto in ultramodern neon: "The Light of Genesis."

The birth and genesis sequence was followed by a choreographed performance by fifteen hundred acrobatic young people, dancing in and out of the formation of the year of the event, "88," the universal greeting "welcome" and its South Korean equivalent, as the Olympic fanfare played by eighty-eight trumpeters accompanied the arrival of the country's president. From the Korean word for "welcome," the dancers broke formation and regrouped into the shape of the five Olympic rings, to metamorphose yet again into the form of the Olympic emblem, suddenly resplendent in the colors of white, yellow, red, and blue. Thus was concluded the main opening show as the event moved toward the more official and formal opening rituals: the march into the stadium of the teams, the formal opening declarations, the raising of the Olympic flag, the arrival of the Olympic torch, and the lighting of the sacred flame. Around a rhetoric of reconciliation, but immersed in a Cold War subtext, the Seoul ceremony accomplished a simultaneous celebration of the local and the global, of its own culture and the grander narratives of human history, bathed in the glow of a quasi-religious and spiritually universalist emphasis. What would be offered in Barcelona four years later? As the media look constantly for personal bests and world records from the athletes during the Games, expectations are also high with regard to the spectacle and the ceremony. After all, that is what the global audience initially and in its greatest numbers consumes.

Barcelona 1992: Classical and Conflictual Cultures in Cooperation

In July 1992 viewers of the BBC's coverage of Barcelona's opening ceremony were greeted with the claim that "history will be made" in yet another "new chapter in the Olympic story." The BBC introduced an alphabet of the story: at C, the English runner Sebastian (now Lord) Coe was featured while the soundtrack of *Chariots of Fire* played; at E, the notion of the eternal nature of athletic achievement was invoked; at L, the legends of Jesse Owens, the great black athlete at the 1936 Berlin Olympics, and Carl Lewis, his equivalent in the 1980s. The TV host for the ceremony, David Coleman, told how he always has a feeling of triumph, joy, and elation at such a moment, "with half the world's population" watching. It was a tense assignment, too, for Coleman, not just with over 170 nations present (and a number of the "new" ones among them symbolizing the post–Cold War resurgence of ethnic nationalism), but also with the arrangements for the ceremony having been the focus of much negotiation and struggle between the Catalan organizers and the Spanish state before an eventual compromise was reached between the Catalan regional claims and those of the national government (Jennings 1996; John Hargreaves 1996). An opening sequence of birds, flowers, and gymnasts was followed by a focus on the Olympic logo, with the colors of red, yellow, and blue intended as a representation of life, sun, and sea. The flags of Catalonia the region, Spain the nation, and Barcelona the city were displayed as the king and queen of the country waved and smiled their way through the Catalonian national anthem and then paid solemn attention to the national anthem of Spain.

Seven jets then sculpted the five Olympic Rings in the sky above the stadium, as a Carama folk dance was performed below, again mimicking the Olympic rings. Attention then switched to the vocal acrobatics of José Carreras and Montserrat Caballé, and the dancers reformed from the five rings into a heart shape: "the message from the Olympic stadium . . . the people of Catalonia open their hearts" to the people of the world, as Coleman stated, noting too how the simultaneous release of doves acted as a message of peace and harmony. The Catalan opening was then followed by a Spanish welcome, with Aragon drummers and a brass band "brought together from many parts of Spain." Replicas of the works of Picasso and Goya, manifested in animated cardboard form, then stumbled across the arena as Placido Domingo serenaded a troupe of dancers, vocally flirting with one of the dancers who was on horseback. After dancing a solo to the accompaniment of a traditional Spanish guitarist, the dancer remounted and departed the stadium on horseback. More singing was followed by the ceremony's set piece, a novel interpretation of Greek and Mediterranean history and culture. Hercules at the ancient Olympics was evoked, as Mediterranean sailors also discovered Barcelona as a haven. Coleman contextualized, in a script that could have been preserved from Seoul 1988: "The story begins at sunrise," with "the sun's journey through the Universe." The giant Hercules undergoes a test by passing through the source of life, the sun, making possible—in some way or other—the making of the Mediterranean Sea. Dancers had formed a representation of this forming and then foaming sea, and the ceremony then moved toward a narrative of the birth of Barcelona, with sea monsters tamed as the culture of the city was established. Back in the London studio, the anchorman Des Lynam was tactfully noncommittal—"it was certainly different"—and English football superstar turned media pundit, Gary Lineker, was cued to recall how, when he scored four goals for England against Spain in an international encounter, he was cheered on by Catalan fans (at the time he was a player for Barcelona) for his demolition of the Spanish side (headlines in the Barcelona press roared out "Catalan player beats Spain"). This was a heady mix indeed, of classicist and contemporary mythmaking.

After the march of the athletes and the opening declarations, the cultural festival continued. Highlights included the Greek soprano Agnes Baltza, for instance, "singing for the immortal spirit of antiquity," in Coleman's words. John Hargreaves observes:

> Agnes Baltza was to be seen on rear centre stage in silhouette, a stark priestess-like figure dressed entirely in black, shrouded in stage mist, and making her delivery with exaggerated dramatic gestures, to all intents and purposes a phantom in full cry. The festive atmosphere was having to give way at that moment to what, clearly, was being signalled as sacred ritual. (2000, 116)

The raising of the Olympic flag, the rendition of the Olympic anthem, and the presentation of flags of lost Olympic Games (Berlin, 1916; Tokyo, 1940 and 1944) followed and then came the presentation of art-based tributes to previous host cities. For an Olympics at which Nelson Mandela marched in celebration of South Africa's rehabilitation, former Soviet satellites paraded as independent nations, the 107 athletes from Kuwait and Iraq participated (after the Gulf War of 1990–91) only nine nations apart (although Iraq was greeted by widespread negative whistling), a united German team paraded, and individuals competed in the name of Serbia and Macedonia, the harmonizing symbolism of the Olympics was an irresistible emphasis. Maragal, on behalf of the IOC, declared that this city—where the people's Olympics of

fifty years ago had been aborted by the Fascist uprising and the civil war—
"is today *your* city," and he referred to the negotiations between the United
Nations and the new states in the former Yugoslavia in attempts to effect
an Olympic truce. Thanking the sixty thousand volunteers who were making
the staging of the Games possible, he talked of the beginning of a lasting
peace that young people deserve. He was followed by Barcelona-born IOC
president Samaranch himself, a former Franco appointee (Simson and Jennings 1992) who, rewriting personal and national history, claimed that "the
dream of my generation has come true. On behalf of the Olympic Movement, thanks." He praised the persisting ideals of de Coubertin with the
best of the world's youth again gathered together at a point when "the
greatest festival of our contemporary society is about to begin." Barcelona's
ceremony bears comparison with Seoul's in at least two ways: the collapse
of history into a contemporary mythical narrative and the symbolic sup-
pression of difference, with international sporting encounters acting as a
form of supranational global cultural politics.

Atlanta 1996: Rekindling the Flame

Atlanta's problem was that it did not want to appear as simply another part
of the United States (Tomlinson 1999h). Los Angeles had set the pace in
1984, and ten years later the area had also hosted, in the Rose Bowl, Pasadena,
the final of the football World Cup. Things were beginning to look like a
U.S. monopoly. And of course Coca-Cola, the longest-running sponsor of
the Olympics and football, had its headquarters in downtown Atlanta. Atlanta
didn't want to be subsumed under a homogenizing U.S. identity, but how
could it be both American and global and follow on credibly from 1992,
when Barcelona's historical and mythical sense of its own history and identity
had provided such a tough act to follow?

At the "Olympic Experience" exhibition in the city, a buildup to the
games, a letter from the boss of the local organizers, Billy Payne, articulated
the pitch to the few browsers (a crowd hugely outnumbered by the queues
clamoring for entry into Coca-Cola's own theme museum a little way down
the road) curious enough to see what lay behind the images of the mascot
Izzy and the torch and flame logo. We were rewarded for our efforts with a
call to dream with Izzy, "our fun-filled Olympic character, of what might be
in 1996, when the Olympic Games come to the American South for the first
time ever." The letter from Billy Payne and associated literature were at
pains to mark out anything special about Atlanta's success and forthcoming
challenge. Payne drew upon the platitudes of official Olympic history:

> Our mission is to conduct the Centennial Olympic Games with
> sensitivity, integrity, fiscal responsibility and commitment to the

needs of athletes . . . to share with the world the spirit of America, the experience of the American South and the vision of Atlanta . . . and to leave a positive physical and spiritual legacy and an indelible mark upon Olympic history by staging the most memorable Games ever . . . I hope you will sense the anticipation we feel and return in 1996 for the "Celebration of the Century"—the 100th anniversary of the modern Olympic Games.

"For the first time in Olympic history," visitors were told, "the Games are awarded to a US city east of the Mississippi River and the Olympic Movement will touch the American South for the first time ever."

The two prominent Olympic symbols, the flame and the torch, dominated the opening ceremony that was to culminate in Muhammad Ali's ascent to light the flame. Hometown boy Billy Payne had never traveled beyond the shores of the Americas. Perfect for him in an era of globalization, he could show Atlanta to the world by bringing to Atlanta one of the world's biggest cultural events. The opening of the Atlanta games had something of the continuation of a dream about it, in its mixture of fantasy and light entertainment, absurd storytelling and clichéd mythmaking.

The most representative images of the city of Atlanta must be the Coca-Cola bottle, the archetypally ugly urban landscape and skylines, and the inspiring image of the civil rights martyr Martin Luther King Jr., whose dream was more sincere, more necessary, and more noble than anything that went on in Billy Payne's head. At least the organizers showed some good taste in leaving Coca-Cola out of the ceremonial reckoning—the IOC still prides itself on keeping advertising boards out of the Olympic arena, seeking to purvey a pure, pristine message of untainted, uncommercialized sporting contest. The proceedings began with five Olympic spirits—each one a color of the five Olympic rings, red, black, green, yellow, blue—bursting out of the perimeter walls of the Olympic stadium. The colors represented the five continents, and the stadium surface was draped in these colors as golden singer-dancers looking like robotic sunflowers writhed their way through their itinerary. The television commentator noted that "young tribes of the various continents flood the arena," which was as good a description as any of the amorphous blob of colorful and chaotic dancers, drummers, and gymnasts that gradually assumed a recognizable shape as fliers descended from the stadium rim, in respective Olympic colors, and five ragged rings and a wobbly "100" (the latter, in recognition of the centennial birthday of the games, made up of children in white garb) materialized uncertainly in the heart of the stadium.

At this point John Williams—long-time collaborator and score-scribe of Steven Spielberg the moviemaker—brought some cadence if not credence to the proceedings and conducted the centennial Olympic theme, "Some of the Heroes," while the figure "100" reshaped into a dove of peace. The participants left the stadium like a drug-crazed exodus of refugees. The stage was now set—with flags of the Atlantic paramilitary and U.S. army bands—for Billy Payne's biggest moment. President Bill Clinton walked into the arena and up to IOC President Samaranch and Payne himself. Twilight was falling as Clinton was trumpeted in to the U.S. national anthem, and six fighter pilots executed a flyby. An Atlanta Welcome Wave gave all present a slice of the action. Atlantan culture was now center stage. Mixed-race gospel singing, frenetic aerobic dance (former actress and fitness guru Jane Fonda was a local celebrity), and cheerleaders were illuminated by the headlights of pickup trucks that had rumbled into the stadium.

The pace slowed as locally born Gladys Knight sang the anthem of the state, "Georgia on My Mind," and a sequence revolving around summertime was offered as a "tribute to the beauty of the South, its volatility of climate, its history, spirit and culture." Things were certainly heating up: Billy Payne joked about how he lied about the climate to the IOC a year or two before, saying that it would be "75 [degrees], not 92, for the Opening Ceremony." An elaborate dance drama then symbolized the birth of the South, issuing from the new day generated by the meeting of the moon and the sun. For this serious generative moment the musical accompaniment was a haunting aria. The set changed dramatically, with the arrival of a huge scaffolding trimmed at its bottom edge by what seemed to be rolls of barbed wire. This was real hometown stuff, though, and turned out to be a representation of a giant catfish pulling Old Man River and one of his riverboats (no slave ships here). Stilted Southern gents patrolled the river edges as "When the Saints Go Marching In" played, to be interrupted by a staged violent storm of thunder and lightning. To the recitation of the words of William Faulkner on the American South's qualities as "something that did not exist before," the Southern spirit appeared to reclaim the landscape from the storm. The "landscape bursts with new life," said the television commentator, and a hallelujah refrain celebrated the restoration. A little more audience participation with flashlights after a countdown, and then the gospel singers really let go, and dancers with headgear sprouting several flagpoles offered a spectacular accompaniment.

The theme moved back toward the broad Olympic theme, as the building of a Greek temple was reenacted, the Greek poet Pindar was quoted on the greatness of the Olympic Games, and the set was transformed into a cast of silhouettes of archers, discus throwers, jumpers, wrestlers, and dancers, resonant of the Greek statues of the athlete and of Leni Riefenstahl's cinematic depiction of those representations. This was a truly striking set and heralded tributes to the achievement of de Coubertin the founder. It was he who rekindled the flame of the Olympic idea, we were informed. The fabric flames came to life at this point, as the first and succeeding Games were represented by runners with flags of the host cities. As the Atlanta runner sprinted to the front of the procession, and approached the representation of the stadium at Olympus, the pillars collapsed backward, a triumphalist anthem blared out, young black women carried the Atlanta flag up the steps, and the interminable march of the nations began. After that fashion parade of participants, Muhammad Ali emerged to light the flame, in a moving moment that some, including myself, have argued diminished his world-historical significance and recast him as a bit actor in an all-American showbiz spectacle (Tomlinson 2000b).

The Symbolic Impact of Media Sports Spectacle in the Globalized World

John B. Thompson (1990) has argued forcefully for the adoption in media analysis of a depth hermeneutic approach that recognizes the three critical stages in the sociocultural production and the interpretive consumption of media meanings (Tomlinson 1999a, 76–78). Within his framework, analytical work can be conducted upon the sociohistorical or sociological conditions of production of the cultural phenomenon. A discursive analysis can subject the phenomenon to rigorous and multifaceted textual critique and analysis, and the potentially drawn-out and frequently complex process of understanding of the phenomenon can be studied as a form of interpretation of interpretations. Not all stages of this analytical framework are equally accessible to the critical analyst: how could the third phase be comprehensively undertaken when Olympic ceremonies are relayed to every technologically equipped nation in the world? In many respects it is the first and second stages that are most conducive to the research of the contemporary historian, cultural critic, or critical sociologist. Evidence of the production values underlying the ceremonies is documented by the key social actors themselves in official accounts, for instance, such as the official records and documentation of the Los Angeles Olympics Organizing Committee (Perelman 1985; LAOOC 1984). These provide revealing background detail on the production and the staging of the Games, from its accreditation system and architecture through to disputes over the logo and the color schemes adopted for the ceremony, making the production values explicit in an everyday and accessible account of the staging process and thus providing extensive data and sources for analyzing the formative ideological values underlying the production process. Textual analyses are also accessible, in particular of the recordings of the televisual version of the events, which, along with the media guides distributed to the press, offer a more reliable source than any other for the content and form of the events themselves. It is, therefore, the first two aspects of Thompson's model that can most usefully be developed in the kind of analysis presented in this chapter and that would repay more research.

Contemporary debates about the Olympic movement and the status of Olympic ideals will be sterile if they remain uninformed by any developed sense of history, of the formative moment of "this great symbol" of the Olympics (MacAloon 1981), and of the material basis of ideologies in past as well as present times. Despite the early Olympic message calling for peace and cooperation between the youth of the world, the local celebration of the Games as expressed in ceremonies leads inevitably to forms of nationalism and nationalist self-aggrandizement, recurrent sets of ideologically complex contradictions (Tomlinson 1984b). The Games are not usually "officially" begun until after the opening extravaganza, "cultural entertainment" as the British Olympic Association describes it (British Olympic Association 1996). This is then followed by the Olympic movement's own quasi-traditional rituals, such as torches, flag changes and flag troopings, anthems, team parades, opening declarations, the taking of oaths: "the lighting of the Olympic flame . . . a symbolic release of pigeons" (IOC 1995, 100). In this the nationalistic displays and assertions of cultural distinctiveness come to prioritize the local over the allegedly universal and the global, in ways that are hardly new. Leni Riefenstahl, in her film of the 1936 Berlin Olympics *(Olympia),* presented to the world a "technologically innovative and brilliant encomium to the aesthetics of the body" (Tomlinson 1999a, 230), which appealed to idealist universal values but was also, despite her denials, political propaganda for a particular nationalist ideology (Sontag 1983; McFee and Tomlinson 1995, 1999).

In all the cases considered in this chapter, the paradoxes of globalization are marked. Symbolic spectacle positions the nation as a player on the global stage, but national pride and local history are the real stuff of affiliation and "belongingness." The ceremonial inflection of the pseudo-global localizes — tradition and history are reappropriated into a local, arrogated version of the ideal. Compromises and negotiations abound as strands of Olympic internationalism, nationalism and pan-nationalism, and global consumer culture are woven together in made-for-television contemporary pageant and spectacle. As John Hargreaves (2000, 113) noted of the Barcelona case, four forces pulled the games in potentially different directions: "Olympic internationalism, Europeanisation, Americanisation and the question of global culture." Hargreaves might have added that acting centrifugally against these global forces there is always the nationalist formulation of the local.

In such a process of incontrovertibly intensifying globalization, the spectacles of succession and inauguration have become central to the media's expectations and expressive of some widespread and recurrent paradoxes in the globalization process. The study of Olympic spectacle offers a revealing basis for the comprehension of the complexities characteristic of the cultural expression of the persisting crises of modernity and globalization as well as an understanding of some aspects of media sport's contribution to both the expression and attempted resolution of those crises. Olympic ceremonies are magnificent trivia yet are seriously revealing of the dynamics of globalization and national identity as encapsulated in the mediated sports mega-event.

More prosaically, why do such ceremonies matter? Obviously, they matter because so many people are said to watch them and that makes them inherently interesting, even important. But they matter more because of how universalizing rhetorics of world sport—usually stressing peace, harmony, past-present continuity, rebirth, and hope for youth—are woven into the textures of the ceremonies (Tomlinson 1999h). And in some cases these rhetorics are little more than fronts for ruthless and ambitious companies, or operate as apologetic justifications for dubious political regimes, or veil the real motives of corrupt land dealers and asset strippers complicit with or close to those running the events. At the very least the ceremonies usually confirm stereotypes—the sentimental American, the wacky and eccentric French—rather than create intercultural and cross-societal understanding. When we know the corporate motives and political ambitions that drive both local organizing committees and world governing bodies of sport, it would be intellectually irresponsible to accept merely at face value the public rhetoric, symbolism, and ritual of such events. Pierre Bourdieu has argued that "the forces of great global ceremonies like the World Cup . . . can be combated either by caricature (which can ridicule or discredit) or utopia (which can propose alternatives to what exists)" (Bourdieu 1999, 21). This need not be an either/or. A critical cultural analysis can seek both to question by ridicule and to aspire to reform. Critical readings of global sports ceremonies can expose by ridicule and so prompt debate around and potential reform of the public face of some of the most prominent sports events and powerful sports organizations in the modern world. Transnational organizations are embodied, peopled, as Sklair (2000) is at pains to remind us. They and their spokespersons can be challenged, critiqued, the organizations questioned and potentially changed. A critical reading of Olympic ceremonies is therefore more than mere textual criticism. It is analytical work revealing of some of the ideological uses to which globalizing rhetoric can be put in the world of media sport.

2. Sport, Politics, and Identities
Comparative Sport Cultures

Football Cultures and Identity

In May 1997 500 million people from 202 countries were reported to have watched the television coverage of the final match of the Union Européenne de Football Association's (UEFA's) Champions' League. The Italian side, Juventus, which was a hot favorite to hold on to its title and to crown a season of achievement in which it had retained its Italian Serie A league title, had comprehensively defeated the French side, Paris St. Germain, in the European Super Cup and won what was effectively seen as the world club title by defeating River Plate of Argentina. Juventus's opponent, Borussia Dortmund of Germany, was widely considered to have little chance against a side described by the Ajax defender Frank de Boer as "a team from another planet." The legendary Dutch player Johann Cruyff, who swept his Ajax club side to three successive championships from 1971 to 1973, was quoted as saying of Juventus that "they can't fail." The Italian side's record in the progress to the final had been imperious, including brilliant victories combining tactical acumen, team discipline, and creative individual style. For almost the first half hour of the final Juventus swarmed all over an outclassed-looking Dortmund side, the latter's aging squad appearing to be outrun, outthought, and outexpressed. Then the German side overturned all the pundits' prematch projections, scoring twice in a few minutes with its first two attempts on goal, both emanating from corner kicks and clinically executed by the veteran Riedle, the first with his left foot, the second with his head. The German hero had told his teammates that he had dreamed that he would score twice, once with his left foot, once with a header. After the first strike, he recalled when the game was over, he told himself just to keep on dreaming. An impudently brilliant goal by the prima donna Juventus substitute, Del Piero, threatened to open up the game in the second half of play, but a stunningly executed lobbed goal by the German substitute Ricken clinched the game for the Germans. Ricken had been on the pitch for just 15 seconds, and the shot was his first touch of the ball. Juventus's French star Zidane had struck the post of the Dortmund goal just before halftime, and Vieri had drilled the ball into the German net soon after, only to have the strike disallowed for a handballing infringement. It is one of the great dramatic qualities of football that territorial domination does not translate directly into scores or points, that superior creativity counts for nothing unless translated into goals. The players and the managers know this. As Juventus coach Lippi said after the game, "We're not unbeatable, we have never said we were."[1] In football, as Bromberger has argued, can be found "the worth and allegorical depth of a great piece of theatre . . . a profoundly significant game is being played out on the field which intensifies and enacts the fundamental values of life" (1994, 281). Bromberger speaks against any interpretation of a football match as a "seductive fiction" or a "pernicious mirage," for it has the capacity to "mobilise and display loyalties"; he recognizes that, at a variety of levels, football is expressive of deep and complex meanings:

> Football in its current organisational format—from local and regional leagues to a world championship—provides a forum for the expression of affirmed collective identities and local or regional antagonisms. (283)

Thus, on the night of the Dortmund–Juventus game, fans in the stadium could unite around the colors, costumes, chants, and insignia of their respective teams. And the media pundits and commentators could set up a classic clash of national character: phlegmatic, disciplined Northern European German forces marshaled against the flawed genius of the Southern European Latin artists. Of course this was in one sense absurd: four of the Dortmund side—three Germans and a Portuguese—were former Juventus players, and the side also included a Scot and a Swiss; and the Juventus team included two Frenchmen, two players from the Balkans, and a Uruguayan. But this was not enough to hold back the English television commentary team, and as the game progressed, the "mental strength" of the German team and the wastefulness of the Latin side emerged as the prevailing interpretive themes. In domestic lounges, public bars, and sports clubs worldwide, the same interpretations of the collective symbolism of the game would have been read into the evening. For, "like a caricatural drama," football "lays bare the major symbolic axes of our societies. Its deep structure (the laws of the genre rather than the rules of the game) represents the uncertain fate of man in the world of today" (Bromberger 1994, 284). Within that deep structure, Bromberger also reminds us, "uncertainty and chance" can play a great part. Juventus personnel would testify to this.

Lest the Dortmund–Juventus encounter be dismissed as a one-off, the 1999 Champions League final between Bayern Munich of Germany and Manchester United of England embodied equally dramatic qualities. In Barcelona, Spain, in May, the English side played a lackluster match and trailed to a single goal for the duration of normal time. By the end of the ninety minutes of normal playing time, after striking the bar and the post during the second half of the game, the Germans looked to be brilliantly effective tactical winners. Then, in the last two minutes Manchester's two substitutes scored one goal each, and every superlative in the commentator's rhetoric was poured out to the global audience on the drama of the contest and on the devastated response of the stunned German players. Sport, then, and football in particular, can embody the polarities of hope and despair, generating simultaneously a certainty of commitment among both players and fans and an uncertainty of outcome and emotions. With this expressive capacity, football has become a significant source for the expression of identities—at local, regional, and national levels and in personal, social, and cultural forms. I watched the Manchester–Bayern match in a downtown bar in Iowa City, Iowa, along with a Liverpudlian colleague, a couple of Irish expatriates, and a black African student from the local university. We could have all claimed to support whichever team we wanted, in such a diasporic gathering. But if we were not so privileged as to be able to be there at all, we may not have had such identity-affirming options.

In this chapter, I cite comparative contexts of sport cultures and politics, with particular reference to football, in order to address some of these central themes in contemporary social and cultural theory. Sport, and particularly football—the world's most popular game—are critical sites of and sources for the expression of forms of collective belonging, affiliation, and identity. Yet sport itself has a surprisingly low profile in some of the wider debates around these themes—paradoxically, its high profile within prominent public sites of contemporary cultural life and the private spaces of media consumption is not matched by its prominence in academic analysis and theorization of the popular. When looking at selected examples of local, regional, national, and global football cultures, I will be concerned primarily with the lived dimensions of those cultures, while recognizing that the semiotics of everyday life rest upon a constant reworking or absorption of the textual within the lived. Before the sports fan—or indeed any traveler—arrives in a new city or country, interpretations, anticipations, and expectations are well established, from media-based rather than first-hand sources. Lived cultures are themselves in great part mediated by and negotiated through textual sources and discourses, though never—and especially so in the cases that I have chosen to consider in this chapter—necessarily or exclusively determined by them. They must also be observed, as appropriate participated in, and documented. It is observed lived football cultures, and the politics of the popular inscribed within them, with which I am primarily concerned in this chapter.[2] Observation and interpretation of the complex and changing nature of football cultures in an increasingly interrelated and interconnected world can contribute to an understanding of the politics of the popular and the relation of popular cultural forms to issues of cultural, collective, and social identity.

Football cultures in the modern period have been sources of cultural creativity in a variety of ways. The reformed football codes of the nineteenth-century public schools in Britain created an enormously influential model of team games, which was used as a basis for moral reform and the training of a male elite. Athleticism and the amateurist code became major expressions of elite male identity in the dominant culture of a transforming society (Mangan 1981). In new industrial communities in later nineteenth-century England and Scotland, the professional code provided vital sources for the expression of local identity—it is in the heartlands of the industrial communities of central Scotland, the English Midlands, and the Northwest of England that the roots of the professional game were most fully established (Holt 1989; Tomlinson 1991). Social and oral historians—as well as novelists and other storytellers—have testified to the impact and significance of the game at informal and amateur levels as well as in the professional mode (Davies 1992). Hill and Williams, in their volume on sport and identity in the north of England, note that "it is clear that in different social settings individuals could subscribe to conflicting identities, yet without feeling any sense of paradox or contradiction" (1996, 10). Hill has recognized that sports events—his example is the English Cup Final and the ritual of the singing of the solemn Victorian hymn "Abide with Me" at that Wembley event—can "flag" nationhood, acting as an element of Michael Billig's "banal nationalism," the making and expressing of a sense of community in everyday settings. To study such sources and articulations of identity, Hill argues for the application of "some of the approaches and insights that have been developed on the borderland where history, literature, sociology and anthropology converge" (1999, 2). Historians of national identity, he argues:

> might acknowledge rather more than has been their custom the
> role played by the Cup Final, and indeed other sporting practices
> and institutions, in helping to fashion a sense of being. . . . They
> will need to turn to newer methodologies to probe their sources,
> to take, even ever so slightly, a "linguistic turn." (18)

Football historians have demonstrated the spread of the game across the world and the appropriation of the game of colonial and commercial elites by the indigenous populations of third-world and underdeveloped countries (Mason 1980, 1986; Murray 1994; Giulianotti 1999). With the expansion of the international dimensions of the game, football has become a major source for the expression of national identity. As the European Championships of 1996 showed, this has been as true in a world of post–Cold War revivalist nationalism as it was in the post–Second World War period of the dissolution of empires. Through football, East European states in the 1990s expressed aspirations and tensions comparable with those of African and Asian nations, which expressed their autonomy and world significance through football from the 1960s onward (Sugden and Tomlinson 1996b, 1997, and 1998c, chapters 6, 7, and 8). Some boundaries of affiliation have become more blurred than before in an age in which Paris St. Germain versus Manchester United can be watched by someone in Santa Cruz or Sydney, wearing the replica shirt and cheering on players from all over the world. But—as attendance at major events such as the World Cup, the Olympic football tournaments, Euro 1996 and 2000, or the final matches of the African Cup of Nations illustrates—the dominance of globalized media industries has not eroded the capacity of football to express complex layers of identity. Queuing for entry into the Pasadena Rose Bowl for the final of the World Cup in 1994, a colleague and I were teased mercilessly by a Londoner in a black-and-white football shirt—a Brentford fan, intertextually cross-referential in his joking: "of all the gates, in all the world . . . I end up next to a fucking Scouser." Trekking back from the Brisbane Cricket Ground through the resplendent riverside gardens of the city, after watching South Africa's energetic young side defeat Brazil in the 2000 Olympics, I was trailing behind a fan wearing a Blackburn Rovers shirt, the colors of one of the English clubs that my grandfather played for before the Great War. Choosing whom to chant with in Santa Monica on the eve of the 1994 World Cup final between Brazil and Italy, we chose the Italians, expressing a sense of Europeanness against, perhaps, a more focused footballing judgment.

Such complexities, and sometimes choices, of identity and affiliation are deep-rooted in football culture, when rivalries at the local or regional level can so easily be superseded at the national and international level. Fans and players alike can unite at the more all-embracing level, in an authentic yet transient expression of a higher collectivity. In a section on cultural history, Chaney notes how the "interesting cultural form of sport" offers a "commentary on the fictions of collective life": spectacles express invented traditions, particular norms of conduct are interpreted and transmitted in sport settings, and sport can provide "a tangible focus for popular experience and the sense of community" (1994, 55). Sociological and historical work on football cultures—from local leagues to the World Cup—bears out these general points. Yet in some contexts, of course, meanings are more restricted than in others—this is Chaney's second point—interpretations are imposed, conducts constrained. Football cultures operate within and often upon the politics of everyday life. The more overarching collective expression might veil over intensely complex tensions, or a particular set of historical, political, and cultural circumstances might make any flexibility impossible. It is such complexities that are portrayed in this chapter, as a way of reflecting on central themes in the analysis of the popular and its contribution to expressions of identity. As a way of understanding the varied interrelationships of sport, identities, and politics, I consider three cases of football cultures: football in Northern Ireland, the professional game in post-apartheid South Africa, and the global pinnacle of the professional game, the World (Football) Cup. Prior to those cases, I review the intellectual historical pedigree of the concept of identity.

IDENTITY

It is always interesting to consider the pedigree of any prominent concept. As historians of ideas would be quick to point out, concepts embody the preoccupations and concerns of their times. Alienation, for instance, captured the sociological imagination of the mid-twentieth century for at least two reasons: first, it referred to a concrete material reality within the work experience of modern industrial societies, that sense of being cut off from the products of one's labor in the increasingly complex division of labor; and second, it embraced aspects of a modern consciousness in which the contemporary self was said to be cut off from some sort of inner core of being. Both these elements could be traced back, in Marx's thought, to his early and more philosophico-Hegelian phase (Mandel and Novack 1970). This second element shared certain concerns with the Durkheimian sense of anomie (normlessness), which referred to a crisis of values in modern society, in which the norms and values according to which contemporary life is lived are increasingly vague, uncertain, and crisis-ridden. In talking of the ethical and moral inadequacies of professional organizations, Durkheim refers to the "state of anomie" as a condition in which the "entire sphere of collective life is for the most part removed from the moderating action of any rules" (1984, xxxii); he observes that in such an absence of moral presence or authority, anarchy follows. It seems remarkable that powerful concepts of such pedigree have become so little mentioned in late twentieth-century thought, precisely at the time during which the currency of the concept of identity has achieved great prominence. But in an intellectual climate under some influence from postmodern strands of thought, these concepts appear to refer too unproblematically to some essentialist core of unalienated normality.[3] For some, this renders such concepts out of touch with a complex contemporary world in which old certainties have collapsed, difference is normative, and cultural identity is constantly in the making. Theoretically, this is an attractively open-ended scenario in which any sphere of cultural expression can be seen to have its own internal coherence; any cultural identity is there for the taking. Transient populations adopt new citizenship identities; ethnic cultures reassert their ancient territorial rights; sexual identities are renegotiated in courtrooms and operating rooms; men marry men and women marry women. In this sort of cultural climate a limitless set of possibilities exists for the expression of identity. Within such a framework, as Cole Porter might have ruefully put it, "anything goes." Clothes, sports, food choices, shopping preferences, media interests become signifiers of a floating self, identifiers of identity. Self is still constituted by some identifiable notion of non-self, of the Other, but it is, so to speak, constantly "up for grabs." We can be anybody we choose, just so long as we have the basis for the making of informed choices.

The biggest flaw in placing at the center of the interpretive stage such a conceptualization and elevating it to the status of a general theoretical framework is the lack of detailed and sustained research into the everyday realities of creating, acting out, and reproducing cultural identities and of any adequate recognition of the social and structural contexts of and constraints upon identity formation. Theoretically, Larrain is surely right in his observation that any formation of cultural identities "presupposes the notion of the 'other'; the definition of the cultural self always involves a distinction from the values, characteristics and ways of life of others" (1994, 142)—in fact, this was the fundamental insight of classical interpretive approaches of a microsociological kind. In the perspective of symbolic interactionism, for instance, in George Herbert Mead's or Charles Cooley's terms, there is no self without the interacting other. Cooley's "looking-glass self" identifies three elements: "the imagination of our appearance to the other person; the imagination of his judgment of our appearance; and some sort of self-feeling" (1969, 217). Mead, in *Mind, Self and Society* as cited by Coser, posited categories of the "I" and the "me" which both are inherently related to social experience, but are distinct in the following way:

> The "I" is the response of the organism to the attitudes of the
> others; the "me" is the organized set of attitudes of others which
> one assumes. The attitudes of the others constitute the organized
> "me," and then one reacts toward that as an "I." (Coser 1971, 338)

From such perspectives there simply is no meaningful self without the other: the individual self is an assemblage of responses to social contexts and situations. Such a premise is illustrated brilliantly, of course, in the interactionist sociology of Erving Goffman, whose work is so firmly rooted in chosen institutional and anthropological settings (1959, 1968). Yet the minutely articulated ways in which the play of appearances and the dynamics and distinctions of the "I" and the "me" are expressed, reaffirmed, and at times challenged and resisted rarely feature in the broader theoretical syntheses that have made the notion of identity such a prominent and pervasive one. Let us consider an example from a major theorist in the sociological field—Anthony Giddens, for whom the notion of identity features centrally in *Modernity and Self-identity* (1991).

In his concern with identity, Giddens offers no reductionist rejection of the structural realities of modern societies to the experiential realities of the interpersonal relations of social actors. On the contrary, his concern with self is justified as a type of holistic theorization of a complex world of interrelated structurizing macroforces and lived microrealities. In "high modernity," he believes, "for the first time in human history, 'self' and 'society' are interrelated in a global milieu" (32). High levels of "time-space distanciation" contribute to this and to "the relation between self-identity and modern institutions." In such circumstances, "the self becomes a reflexive project." What does this mean for sociological analysis and for an understanding of the cultural forms through which certain kinds of meaning are conveyed and transmitted and categories of identity expressed? I will consider this question in the light of Giddens's discussion of "the body."

For Giddens, through his analysis of Janette Rainwater's *Self-therapy*—a how-to manual for self-realization—the contemporary body can be seen as itself (as Giddens himself puts it, consistent with his understanding of Rainwater), "part of an action system rather than a merely passive object." Body awareness is a means of

> constructing a differentiated self, not as one of the dissolution of the ego. Experiencing the body is a way of cohering the self as an integrated whole, whereby the individual says "this is where I live." (Giddens 1991, 77–78)

Although Giddens recognizes that there are questions that can be asked about the ideological context of Rainwater's conceptions, he argues that "they signal something real about self and self-identity in the contemporary world—the world of late modernity." Here Giddens starts from a text and textual discourse and moves toward the contexts about which that text is claimed to speak. Analysis of what may be an arbitrarily chosen instance proceeds to theorization of the wider sociocultural condition. Giddens prioritizes self-identity over social identity, the analysis of the individual body over consideration of contexts in which bodies might express cultural identity or collective identity. Reading Giddens, it is as if to talk of collective identities is to talk of some past romantic age. He recognizes, in a discussion of dress and social identity, that group pressures and factors such as socioeconomic resources and advertising have influences upon dress and can "promote standardisation rather than individual difference" (99). But appearance still, for Giddens, "becomes a central element of the reflexive project of the self" (100).

There is an enormous body of contemporary writing on the concept of identity—social, cultural, personal. For Stuart Hall, identity has become a central concept: he points to "two different ways of thinking about 'cultural identity'" (1990, 223). The first way of thinking sees cultural identity as a single, shared culture, reflecting "common cultural experiences and shared cultural codes," providing "stable, unchanging and continuous frames of reference and meaning." Hall's second way of thinking, or position, acknowledges the "deep and significant difference" that contributes to "what we really are":

> Cultural identity, in this second sense, is a matter of "becoming" as well as "being." It belongs to the future as much as to the past. It is not something which already exists, transcending place, time, history and culture. Cultural identities come from somewhere, have histories. But, like everything which is historical, they undergo constant transformation. Far from being eternally fixed in some essentialised past, which is waiting to be found, and which, when found, will secure our sense of ourselves into eternity, identities are the names we give to the different ways we are positioned by, and position ourselves within, the narratives of the past. (225)

Narratives of the past are social products too, and any talk of the "reflexive self" and of the "constant transformation" of identities must never be at the expense of an awareness that self and identities are in part determined and constrained by society and social structure. To talk about identities in any sociologically adequate way, it is useful to draw upon Durkheim's analytical categories of mechanical and organic solidarity (1984). For Durkheim, mechanical solidarity was the cement that bound the individual to the collective social order, so that ascribed aspects of life determined actions, in relatively unreflective ways. In a situation of increased differentiation, an organic form of solidarity could establish a sense of unity and connectedness that could accommodate more individual difference. In Coser's words, "Mechanical solidarity was founded upon likeness, organic solidarity arose because of complementarity between actors engaged in different pursuits" (1984, xvi).[4] As the scope for the development and negotiation of identities around an increasing range of such "pursuits" expands, sport has become an important site for the expression of unity within difference, an organic solidarity, at a level of national identity.[5] Multiple identities become possible in a differentiated society but can also be expressed as one in appropriate collective settings: the Manchester United, Arsenal, Burnley, and Everton fans suspend regional identities and rivalries when supporting the English national side. Sporting events — in terms of their impact on the self-identity of individuals and the profile, pride, and identity of nations — capture and articulate such contradictory forces, premised too upon an infrastructure of communications and a sophisticated global media system.

In spheres of popular culture embracing the collective, subcultural, and individual dimensions, identities are not always there just for the taking or the making. Many collectively experienced and consumed popular cultural forms are far from a matter of individual choice. Their meanings and impacts can be bound up with the political dynamics within and between societies. The "reflexive project of the self" or the "constant transformation" of cultural identity is not an easy or even available option to the individual born into the sectarian culture of Northern Ireland or the black majority of a South African township, and it may be that very option or prospect that the cosmopolitan World Cup fan is striving to reject. In the following section I look at some particular settings in which football cultures have found their expression, arguing that collective and cultural identities as expressed in football can be seen as elements in a less reflexive project of the self, in which is sought a meaningful cultural identity and collective affiliation, and in which fewer choices of identity are available than some orthodoxies would recognize.

COMPARATIVE FOOTBALL CULTURES:
ISSUES OF CULTURAL AND POLITICAL IDENTITY
Northern Ireland 1995: Peeping through the Peace Process
Scenes from a 1995 Summer

In the summer of 1995, from a distance and through the mist and the drizzle, Belfast looked like any other Northern European seaport. It is only when you get down to the streets that the city's pronounced sectarian geography is revealed. Even in the political optimism of talk of the peace process, the urban iconography of sectarianism dominated the public culture of the streets. Curbstones painted red, white, and blue marked the fixed territoriality of space. Orange Halls and commemorative archways in Protestant North Belfast flew the Union Jack, the flag of St. George, and the orange lodge flag, testifying to the significance of flags and emblems in the expression of identity. In this community your religious affiliation and your political persona, and any involvement in public or popular culture, were not for negotiation. Bunting across the Shankill Road professed an assertive politics of identity. Woven in with the flag of the Union and the red, white, and blue decorations were political statements about the status of loyalist "prisoners of war." Loyalist paramilitary murals were prominent in the shadow of the Shankill Leisure Centre. One featured deceased *city councillor George Seawright, famous for the speech in Belfast City Hall council chambers in which he proclaimed that "all Catholics should be incinerated along with their priests." He was also famous for climbing onto the roofs of leisure centers in nationalist areas and waving his (legally held) pistol to keep the mob at bay as he hauled down the Irish tricolor. Ironically, his head was blown off by the Provisional Irish Republican Army while waiting in his car in the parking lot of the Shankill Leisure Centre, fifty feet from this mural.*

In another part of town, more painted curbstones mark the boundaries of sectarian territories. Green, white, and gold curbstones off the Falls Road mark the territory of Catholic nationalism and Republicanism. The Gaelic game of football is played at Casement Park, home ground to County Antrim Gaelic Athletic Association. Gaelic spelling—Páirc Mhic Aismaint—makes a culturally specific statement, as do the Gaelic game's distinctive goalposts at the end of a playing area surrounded by barbed wire. An empty sports ground can be a desolate, apparently soulless place, innocent or meaningless. But cultural spaces have narrative histories and cultural identities too. Casement Park is named after Sir Roger Casement, hanged by the British for treason for negotiating with the Germans to supply arms to the Irish Republican Army around the time of the Great War. In more recent years, two army corporals were dragged from their car and beaten before being shot, "executed," inside Casement Park. The ground was occupied by the British forces for a while in the 1970s—given the symbolic and ceremonial significance of the site, this incensed local nationalists. Next door is Andersonstown Leisure Centre, symbolically claimed by the Irish flag. Fifty yards up the street from the Leisure Centre is the headquarters of Sinn Fein.

Less than a mile from Sinn Fein headquarters is loyalist South Belfast— known locally as the "village" and replete with the insignia and the iconography of its inhabitants' identity—a warren of streets and terraces looking like so many inner-industrial communities at a time of celebration or festival, until the cultural and political specificities of the red, white, and blue, and orange alter the everyday landscape of the gable end, the ice cream salesman's patch, and the sport and leisure facilities. Inside these sectarian stockades this atmosphere of the "village" is a felt and lived reality. It is also an appropriate metaphor for the cultivation of forms of mechanical solidarity: such forms of solidarity constrain and inhibit the possibility of breaking free and selecting alternative identities. In the center of the village is Windsor Park, home to Linfield Football Club and also the "national" stadium. Named after the House of Windsor (the British Royal Family), it is replete with loyalist symbolism, reinforcement of a separate and persisting identity. It is a hostile environment for Catholics, despite their sporting preferences and passions, for they are seen as having pledged their football alliances to the Republic of Ireland.

(Sugden and Tomlinson 1998a, 179–80)

Windsor Park was named in honor of the rulers of the day, in tribute to a made-over imperialist regime. It carries with it the pedigree of the British monarchy. The second son of Edward VII, George V, was also a first cousin of Czar Nicholas II of Russia and of the Emperor William II of Germany, as well as monarchs in Spain, Romania, and Greece. He was born into a royal house entitled Saxe-Coburg-Gotha, popularly the house of Hanover or Brunswick. In June 1917 George V announced that any princes of his family who were British subjects but bore German titles should relinquish them in favor of British names. A month later it was announced that King George had abandoned all his personal and his family's German titles and that henceforth the royal house of Great Britain and Ireland would be known as the house of Windsor. The national stadium in what emerged as Northern Ireland was therefore a monument to European imperialism and the British monarchy.

Casement Park remains, by any historical consciousness, a poignant echo of opposition to the house, dynasty, and legacy of Windsor, to many beyond Ireland itself. Sir Roger Casement did not just espouse the case of what he called the "white Indians of Ireland" but had a more extensive record of progressive interventionism. He was born in County Antrim, to a Catholic mother and a Protestant father. He served as British consul in Boura, the Belgian Congo, and exposed the crimes against the native peoples during the brutal exploitation of that country's natural resources. He reported this to the foreign secretary Lord Lansdowne, and though Casement was commended and decorated (with the CMG), the Belgian King Leopold intervened to ensure that nothing was done about the revealed injustices. Transferred to South America, Casement exposed the merciless annihilation of the tribes of Peru, Colombia, and Brazil conducted by the Amazon Company, based in London. The British establishment responded "by knighting Casement, in express recognition of his services to the oppressed peoples of the earth":

> The injustice which had been borne by the Irish for centuries
> increasingly filled his consciousness. He could not rid his thoughts
> of the fact that almost half the population of Ireland had been
> murdered by Cromwell's soldiers, that thousands of men and
> women were later sent as white slaves to the West Indies, that in
> recent times more than a million Irish had died of starvation, and
> that the majority of the young generation were still forced to emi-
> grate from their native land. (Sebald 1999, 129)

Driven to action by the defeat of the Liberal government's Home Rule program in 1914, he returned his decorations to London, refused a pension, and traveled in 1915 to Berlin, seeking arms supplies for the Irish nationalist cause and urging Irish prisoners of war to form an Irish brigade. The mission was unsuccessful and, returned by German submarine, he walked ashore at Tralee, on Ireland's west coast, a doomed fifty-one-year-old who was immediately arrested. His message that "no German help was available" could not stop the momentum that culminated in the 1916 Easter Rising. The outcome of his trial for treason was inevitable, and he was hanged in Pentonville Prison, London, in 1916. Casement Park is therefore named as testimony not just to an Irish hero but to a prophetic champion of the oppressed peoples of the world, ignored, sidelined, and then killed off by the British state. Casement was condemned and hanged by the system whose ruling family would within months change its name to Windsor. There could hardly be any more evocative and reciprocally provocative and excluding naming of the two most prominent stadiums in Northern Ireland.

Close observation of the place and meaning of sport in Northern Ireland challenges any crude view of the homogenizing effects of globalization. In the province, "soccer fandom is frequently constructed around masculinity and place-centered narratives of devotion and belonging" (Bairner and Shirlow 1998, 163), with the sports stadium providing "an important symbolic space in terms of a wider cultural resistance or representation" (165). Cultural hostility and the refusal of "pan-cultural contact" produce "cultures of besiegement" distinguishing the "we" from the "they": "In the localised nature of politics of territorial control and resistance . . . imperatives of communal difference, segregation and exclusion have predominated over the politics of shared interests, integration, assimilation and consensus" (167). Unionist activity surrounds football at its highest levels in Northern Ireland, and alongside this, Bairner and Shirlow show, Protestants are alienated from nationalist sporting spaces. Irish League football games are hotbeds of Protestant/loyalist feeling, and national football games at Windsor Park have consistently expressed strong anti-Catholic sentiment (170–71). "Space and its social meaning" remain profoundly determining, sport/football making "the imagined community of Ulster as a Protestant place . . . more real for young loyalists as they express their affiliation at Windsor Park or the Oval" (173).

What do we learn from these reports and observations on sporting sites and cultures in Northern Ireland? And from reflections on the symbolic impact of sport spaces and sites?

- Affiliations in sport and football are far from malleable and flexible—they are marked by culturally and politically specific and entrenched meanings.
- Football in its public form is a site for symbolic reaffirmation of cultural affiliation and identity.
- Football spaces, with their legacy of cultural and political meanings, can inhibit or block potential forms of cultural transformation.
- Cultural identity in and through sport is not a matter of personal

choice; cultural identity is fixed and constrained by the weight of history and supraindividual influences.

To summarize the case:

> It is difficult to ignore the proximity of sport to politics when during a Gaelic football match a heavily armed helicopter hovers deafeningly just above the heads of the players before disappearing into the confines of a corrugated-iron fortress built by the British army on an adjoining field, an area of land which was, before the "Troubles," part of the playing area—or when a number of expensive new municipal sport and leisure facilities are constructed, at taxpayers' expense, alongside military and police stockades in the most troubled areas of Belfast. (Sugden and Bairner 1992, 155)

The British government has had a statutory duty to provide public sport and leisure in Northern Ireland and an overriding responsibility for maintenance of public order and, ultimately, union with the United Kingdom. However, the ownership of the facilities that it provided in the furtherance of these goals is contested. As one civil servant put it: "A lot of community centres and some of the leisure centres throughout the Province are being virtually run by paramilitaries, and the decent citizen is just not welcome" (160). Thus, in these ways, sport and leisure, often hailed as matters for individual choice, are, in such a context, the suppliers of prescribed and nonnegotiable cultural identities.

The moves, in the second half of the 1990s, toward a negotiated peace in Northern Ireland, culminating in the 1999 Belfast or Good Friday agreement, offered a hopeful vision of change and intercultural tolerance, but the outcome of the political process would remain dependent on the extent to which cultural identities could be at least diluted and modified if not wholly remade. Bairner (1999, 128) has confirmed that a deep-rooted masculinity is critical to the politics of identity and, therefore, that gender must be recognized as a key reference point alongside nationality and ethnicity in any consideration of the potential for and the constraints upon change in any peace process. "Heavy drinking, sexism and profanity" (Bairner 2000a, 182) characterize football cultures in Northern Ireland, parallel to patterns of male working-class culture in other parts of the United Kingdom, but with the vicious edge of sectarian goading, as in the Unionist/Protestant taunt to supporters of predominantly nationalist/Catholic teams: "'We're up to our necks in Fenian blood, surrender or you'll die.' This song celebrates the deaths of Catholics" (184). There may be spaces of alternative cultural expression opening up during the peace process—such as the Belfast Giants ice hockey team, playing to packed houses in 2000–2001, and emblematic of a suprasectarian, cosmopolitan aspiration among some of the population (Bairner 2003)—but even so "the politics of identity will persist" in the cultural and social divisions of the society (Bairner 2001b). Sport and the affiliations expressed in sport can "intensify these divisions. Sport contributes significantly to the construction and reproduction of certain identities and, by implication, to the maintenance of the gulf that exists between particular social groups. In this respect, the north of Ireland has been no different from a multitude of other deeply divided societies" (Bairner 2000b, 67). The Sports Council for Northern Ireland appointed a community relations officer in 1996. She recognizes the importance of sport in the "telling" dynamics of interaction in the society. When meeting people you "tell" them who you are by revealing your name, saying what school you attended and what sport you play or follow. All of these cases of "telling" are statements of identity. In Northern Ireland, "even the most obvious things in life become political—*everything* in Northern Ireland becomes political" (Muldoon 2001)—the siting of a hospital, the coaching of a sport, the chanting for a team. The surveys undertaken for the Council showed the unchanging patterns of sports, and as the community relations officer, Maura Muldoon, observed, the deep-rootedness of the sources of sectarian identity in the Northern Ireland case, peace or no peace, issues a huge challenge to the policy process to "go beyond cosmetic" responses, initiatives, and solutions. Any realistic appraisal of prospects for change in the policy arena must recognize that it needs a time frame of human generations rather than cycles of governmental administrations to effect significant forms of cultural transformation.

South Africa 1996: Scenes from Soccer City

At the First National Bank (FNB) Stadium (more popularly known as Soccer City) on the edge of Soweto, Johannesburg, on Saturday, February 3, 1996, Nelson Mandela donned a replica shirt of the South Africa national football side and presented the African Nations Cup to the team captain in front of an ecstatic home crowd and, as ever, the lenses, cameras, and eyes of the world media. South Africa had defeated Tunisia to win the trophy, and it seemed that sport was tailored by some spiritual or supernatural force for the president and his Rainbow Nation. Before its victory against Ghana the previous week, Mandela had exhorted the team with a pledge of faith: "My children, I'm leaving the country and its people in your hands" (Block 1996, S12).

In winning the Rugby World Cup in 1995, humiliating England in cricketing matches in 1995–96, winning the continent's football championship, and producing the country's first black African Olympic gold medalist (marathon runner Josia Thugwane) at the Atlanta Olympics in August 1996, South Africa has presented, through sport, an image of cross-cultural unity and harmony resonant of the political rhetoric around claims concerning its transformation into the Rainbow Nation. The scenes in the FNB were unforgettable ones of collective celebration. Mandela—seen by many as "the cheerleader as sport unites all South Africans" (van Niekerk 1996, 19)— led the celebrations, hailing the rapturous crowd from the pitch, escorted out there and protected by an elaborate choreography of heavily armed militia. Beneath the surface of such an integrated expression of collective affiliation, the tensions of a society reared in conflict—with different elements in the society endemically mistrusting of the other elements—were still there: in the stadium, heavily armed white paramilitary police patrolled the concrete moat between the crowd and the pitch.

This was hardly surprising, given the ways in which sport itself had so often been used to bolster the apartheid regime. As Jarvie noted, sport in apartheid South Africa might have been claimed, in the international arena, as multiracial. But "internally sport for the majority of Africans is controlled through a number of economic and political factors which militate against the free playing of multi-racial sport" (1985, 80). This was so entrenched that while much can be claimed for the symbolic role of sport in the anti-apartheid struggle, close analysis shows that sport's influence was less than has been widely assumed. Its value lay in its profile as a "symbol of the anti-apartheid movement," the sport campaign representing "a stepping-stone to other more effective arenas and sanctions" (Keech and Houlihan 1999, 118, 119). Sports diplomacy on the international stage was important in the mobilization of worldwide opposition to apartheid. But such diplomatic achievements did little to change the divided sport cultures of the apartheid system. These were deeply institutionalized. The National Party's sports policy in the early 1960s was based on four principles:

> Each social group would form a separate controlling association
> in each sport, white associations would control the code, send
> representatives to the world federation, and assist the development
> of black associations, racially mixed teams would not represent
> South Africa, and sports officials would not invite racially mixed
> teams from abroad to play in the Republic. (Booth 1998, 61)

Football nevertheless had the power, with its extensive base in black culture, to bind the different ethnic elements of the society together in unprecedented, symbolic ways. Football was more than merely marginal and in important ways expressed that "black people's agency in shaping the world in which they lived and played . . . gave meanings to ordinary people's lives in the apartheid era" (Alegi 2000, 16). Yet in January 1996, as South Africa progressed to the victory rostrum at the African Cup of Nations, the tournament seemed to be turning into a celebration of a single new nation. Elaborate costumes and face painting captured the carnival atmosphere of the occasion. Black and white, men and women, stood together on the terraces, where there was a genuine mingling of difference, a multicultural fandom, uniting around favorites like white star Mark Fish, soon to play in the top two divisions of the English professional leagues. This was a genuine expression of cultural commonality and national unity. The witty puns of Soweto's tabloid, the *Sowetan*, were transformed into banners of support for the South Africa side, "Bafana, Bafana" (boys, boys), throughout the tournament. "Pharoahs, go home to mummy," mocked one directed at the Egyptian side. Inside the stadium, just before the final, the South African cricket team—all white, but for one Asian—paraded on the pitch, fueling the collective spirit.

But the cultural harmony of the moment did not erode a cultural politics for which large-scale sport has always provided an opportunity. A figure of revilement for the crowd was the Nigerian dictator Abacha, responsible for the hanging of Ken Saro-Wiwa, the dissident poet, and in alliance with the Shell Company in environment-threatening industrial developments in Nigeria. "Shell and Abacha must go to hell," proclaimed one banner under a picture of Abacha, with a picture of Saro-Wiwa on the other side (Sugden and Tomlinson 1999a, eighth plate after p. 96). Meanwhile, overhead, and in full view of Nelson Mandela, a light aircraft circled Soccer City, trailing a banner with the slogan "Go Well Go Shell." Sponsored in their celebrations by such a representative of global domination, the South African fans were unlikely to sustain the collective euphoria and symbolic solidarity of the moment into a troubled future.

These images of and moments in South Africa's remarkable sporting renaissance are reminders that, in particular sets of circumstances:

- Football can create a cultural identity over and above deeply rooted cleavages and difference.
- Collective identity can be expressed in highly distinctive ways by forms of sport and popular culture.
- Within collective expressions of identity there are complex intralayers of meaning.
- Expressions of cultural and collective identity in sport are dramatic but often transient, reflecting the frailty of cultural and political alliances.

In South African sport, as expressed by the country's most expert football journalist, white South African Mark Gleeson, football remains the "Mafia sport . . . the sport of thugs," at least in the administrative sphere, with a succession of corruption scandals that have robbed the game of finances and facilities.[6] And no national victory can change such a profile overnight. Indeed, deeply rooted organizational forms and practices could hardly be reformed on the spot. Keech (2000) has shown the scale of complexity and interorganizational rivalry that characterized the organization of sport during the apartheid period, including among the sports bodies seeking to speak for the black majority. But there was widespread optimism at sport's potential within the post-apartheid nation. After the collapse of the formal apartheid system, great efforts were made to galvanize the positive side of sports around a perceived "need to entrench" the country's "new democratic ethos in sport as part of the transformation process for the upliftment of the quality of life of all South Africans" (DSR 1995, 3–4). Sport could be mobilized as "a unifier, healer of wounds, creator of work opportunities, booster of the national image, promoter of national health, consolidator of international ties, restorer of the culture of learning and teaching, redeemer of the so-called marginalized youth, etc." (4). It is not at all easy to see what more could be "etcetera-ed" in this roll call of sport's virtues and functions.

Despite such a virtuous agenda, the complex of organizational structures and interests could not be unraveled overnight, and in the "new" South Africa the vested interests of the past could not be veiled for very long. In the Transvaal, top members of the "old Afrikaner establishment" could not account, in late 1996, for "R7 million that was earmarked for black rugby development" (Black and Nauright 1998, 146). By mid-1997, half a decade since rugby's post-apartheid unity, "neither Transvaal nor Orange Free State had fielded a single black player" (147). Beneath the worldwide profile of the continental football victory of 1996, long-established divisions were likely to reassert themselves in the world of sport, across the country and in the regions. As Tommy Ballantine, veteran white sports journalist, in Durban, put it to me: "Can you ever see a Zulu playing Rugby?"[7] For rugby was still the sport par excellence of the Afrikaan male elite. Comparably, football in South Africa remained an essentially black working-class sport, with its own history of off-field maladministration and financial scandals as well as a history of considerable achievement on the playing side. One high-profile tournament and success would hardly miraculously transform its historical, social, political, and cultural base.[8] Indeed, the rainbow metaphor was soon to lose its gloss, as the residues of apartheid recurrently resurfaced within South African sport cultures. As Guelke and Sugden (1998, 93) put it: "The political legacy of both rugby and soccer and the significance of these sports in the working-up of separate cultural identities present major obstacles for those who would harness them in the service of community relations." In early 1997, the coach of the Springbok rugby team, André Markgraaff, was dismissed after making racist remarks, calling black South African sports and rugby administrator Mululeki George a "fucking kaffir," a "massively derogatory term used by some whites to describe blacks . . . during the segregation and apartheid eras" (Black and Nauright 1998, 147). And soon after the historic football victory in the Africa Cup of Nations, white footballer Sean Dundee accepted German citizenship, claiming that he had been discriminated against, as a white, within South Africa's football culture. Jennifer Hargreaves has noted that "women in sport in the new 'Rainbow Republic' are finding ways to celebrate *unity out of diversity*" (2000, 45). The enduringly divided sport cultures of male South African sport remain a long way removed from any such celebratory culture of sport. In the case of cricket, it has been recognized that some degree of post-apartheid transformation has "loosened race identity," but only marginally: "cricket has failed to create an imagined South African community," indeed has continued to reproduce class privileges and the status quo; "the elite-centred nature of transformation . . . is validating the established capitalist status quo by providing opportunities for select Blacks (Vahed 2001, 319 and 333).

World Cup USA 1994 and France 1998: Football, Commodity, and Spectacle
As any student of media reception and the process of consumption would confirm, cultural products are open to a variety of interpretations. The World Cup final, for instance, is both a global spectacle and a local cultural event. This multifaceted nature of the single football match was captured in a television documentary coordinated by Andreas Rogenhagen (1995), drawing on footage shot by directors from forty countries during the broadcasting of the 1994 Brazil versus Italy final.[9] Production lines were stopped in a Tehran car factory, workers moving to a space where a screening had been set up. In Cameroon, Mongo Faya's harem was feasting, dancing, and celebrating with him throughout the event. In Argentina, fans chanted their support for the Italian side, allies in their arch rivalry with Brazil. The vodka and orange was out for the game for the remote couple in Lapland. The street party in jubilant Rio moved into the ecstasy and the hysteria of triumph when Italian Roberto Baggio failed to score in the penalty shoot-out half a continent away in Pasadena, California, while the despondent Italian fans in Turin were speechless and drained. Monks in their monastery in Prague, myriad groups of people from Belorussia to Costa Rica, gathered around televisions, from giant public screenings in Beijing to smaller-scale viewings of black-and-white portable sets. Choosing to let the global culture of football speak for itself, director Rogenhagen offered no commentary, no subtitles, just name labels for countries and cities and for the players who featured most tellingly in the dramatic finale of the shoot-out. The global reach of sport and television was vividly captured and conveyed in this documentary. Differences of age, status, gender, ethnicity, and culture

seemed, however fleetingly, superseded by a shared passion for and response to the event and its outcome.

Cultural phenomena such as the Olympics and the football World Cup have the capacity to engage audiences across the world, whatever the various modes of reception and cultures of consuming expressed in the process and the act of viewing. Such sports events have undeniably claimed a hugely prominent place in the world media's calendar. As high-profile media events, they generate histories and traditions, as in the Argentine-England cycle of football encounters (Alabarces et al. 2001). Because competitive events such as these are staged regularly and in planned sequence without overlapping, they can provide a source for continual review and anticipation, a context in which histories can be developed, soap operatic narratives fostered, and the intensifying symbiosis of top-level performance sport and television reaffirmed. As live events, they provide opportunity for the expression of cultural and national identity as well as a cosmopolitan consumerism that is a prerequisite for participation. As it has grown in scale, the World Cup has offered the opportunity—to those privileged and resourced enough to be able to get there—for the simultaneous expression of their local identity and their cosmopolitan self.

The USA World Cup was successful as spectacle and investment (see chapter 5). To the watching billions around the world, the blue-shirted (Azzurra) fans of Italy and the yellow-shirted followers of Brazil would have blended into anonymous homogeneous hordes. But at the entrance turnstiles and on the bleachers, it was clear that this was far from the case and that spectators' motivations and identities were varied and complex. My ticket had been acquired from the Irish Football Association, and two pugnacious and pinkish Irish Protestants were in the same row. For them, the appeal and qualities of the game were of little interest. Regularly, throughout the event, they unfurled their own flag, a red cross on a white background, and brandished it proudly and defiantly: for them, if they had been football fans, there would have been a problem, for both the finalists were from predominantly Catholic countries. For these two "fans," the game was an opportunity to make propaganda in a nation known for its Republican sympathies on the Irish question. The more carnivalesque and celebratory dimension of the event can be seen in the female fan who flaunted her green top with the screaming slogan "Brazil yes, Havelange no"; the Brazil side was "her" team: though she was Colombian, not Brazilian, her affiliation was straightforward enough on the basis of continent, history, and tradition. For some Brazilian fans themselves, the final was an opportunity to engage in a politics of protest, to demonstrate against the effects of the FIFA president Havelange's influence upon domestic football in his home country.[10] A form of reductive individualism could retell the World Cup final event as a series of unique individual narratives, minidramas of choice and life chances. That this would be at all possible is indicative of the organic solidarity that is characteristic of the international sports event. For the moment of the event at least, a unity-in-difference is accomplished: all those at the Pasadena Rose Bowl had at least one thing in common. They were there, sharing in the staging of a major event of globalized consumer culture (Wagg 1995), their presence supporting some of the world's largest companies, "exploiting the world's most popular game for what in advertising parlance is known as 'global mileage'" (Sinha 1994, 1996).

Four years later, when winning the football World Cup on its home territory at the Stade de France in a northern suburb of Paris, the French football side showed the persisting power of sport to speak for a society and its culture (Markovits 1998). A shift away from a sense of French identity as style, toward a sense of identity as competitive success, showed how for "a few weeks at least sport became a metaphor for society, particularly regarding questions of ethnic and cultural integration, but also for issues of tension between modernization and tradition. . . . The World Cup afforded the opportunity to ask whether France can, or must, maintain distinctively 'French' values, which may appear to be out-of-step with contemporary processes of modernization and globalization" (Dauncey and Hare 2000, 344). The despondent Brazilians, sambaing languidly in the bars of Montmartre as millions of (mainly French) revelers squeezed onto the Champs Elysées, would recognize this tension, as embodied in the tournament and its outcome. And whether winner or loser, the very presence at or around the event confirms the impact of the pinnacle of the world game as a celebration of global consumerism (Sugden and Tomlinson 1999a, 55–71).

Concluding Comment

I have taken three examples in which football has expressed, respectively, constraining forms of inherited cultural-political identity, emergent and spectacular (yet frail) forms of collective and politically progressive identity, and cosmopolitan forms of consumerism within a globalized political economy. They show how cultural identity and particular forms of social solidarity can be given expressive form in sport, in some cases (involving sufficient complementarity of interests in collective contexts) counterbalancing the alienating and anomic dimensions of contemporary life. In examples such as the three considered, identities are theoretically open to negotiation and renewal, and might provide the possibilities of effective contestation, but they remain practically constrained by the contexts of their initial production and the flexibility or rigidity of the social setting.[11]

Football cultures contribute in myriad ways to forms of personal, cultural, social, and national identity, but never regardless of the social structure and relations of the society. Identity is contingent on the ascribed dimensions of a society in which mechanical solidarity prevails in the Northern Irish case; it is a modified mechanical solidarity that is expressed in football in the South African post-apartheid context; on the world level, the World Cup mobilizes a much more fluid set of identities, on the basis of a football culture whose collective expression represents the quintessentially organic solidarity of a supranational world order and globalized consumer economy and culture.

Global sporting events can express the paradox of a condition in which individual angst, the dilemma of identity, can blend with collective empathy and sometimes constraint. As I have previously put it:

> The exhilaration of following events of worldwide interest, of involving oneself in matters of cosmopolitan modernity, sits alongside a recurrent sense of unease concerning who one really is. Rooting for the nation, in the context of a global discourse of competitive sport, is both an expression and a resolution of this paradox. (Sugden and Tomlinson 1994b, 10–11)

As a cultural phenomenon in which fate plays such an important part, football retains a capacity to confound expectations. One could hardly imagine that Juventus could fail against Dortmund, Patrick Urbini of *L'Équipe* commented to the Italian side's French star, Didier Deschamps, before the 1997 European Champions League final. Deschamps was more fatalistic:

> DESCHAMPS: That's what a lot of people are thinking, yes. But we, we know that we'll be facing an experienced and high-quality opponent, capable of being very good in the final. In a match such as this, there's no margin of security. Thus, one can lose.
>
> URBINI: With Dortmund, where are the dangers?
>
> DESCHAMPS: In all ways, with the Germans, the matches are always battles. It is in their mentality . . . they never let go.[12]

Football is a game of fate, but protagonists in the varying theaters of the game cannot reinvent themselves totally, and historical traditions persist: Deschamps was to be proved right about the major strength of the German team, whatever the cosmopolitan roots of its players. The fates meet history in the realm of sport and international sporting exchange and cannot escape the politics of a particular time and place. If cultural identity is a zone of possibility in Hall's optimistic conceptualization, sport space in Northern Ireland, in its zonal reaffirmation of exclusion, all but erodes such possibilities. Football cultures have histories and are framed by the realities of politics, the politics of the popular, and political economy. The football fan might switch replica jerseys as some fluctuating meanings of time and space are negotiated and may sway not just with the crowd but with the heady challenges of a symbolic interactionist angst. But such switches of affiliation and identity are not equally available or open, and in societies in which a sporting cultural identity is an element of that society's mechanical solidarity, the collective chant of the terrace culture can veil—as the popular speaks for the political—an agonized inner scream of the suppressed self.

3. FIFA and the Men's World Cup
The Expansion of the Global Football Family

Dr. João Havelange was president of La Fédération Internationale de Football Association (FIFA), world football's governing body, from 1974 to 1998, a critical phase of transformation in the political economy and cultural profile of world sport. At FIFA House in Zurich, even in his absence the Brazilian was talked of in hushed tones—always as "the president"—when talked about at all. When the phone rang in FIFA House and it was Havelange on the line, the arched backs of the FIFA apparatchiks straightened and stiffened. The man was in South America: the FIFA secretariat was in mid-Europe. But when he was on the line, it was like a royal visit. "Oui, Monsieur le Président" was the reported general response to any such calls. No discussion, just the affirmative and the reaffirming. FIFA House was like a court of the old ancien régime, with Havelange wielding individualistic, autocratic, and charismatic power. How did FIFA fall into the hands of this ruthless Brazilian and then his protégé and successor as president Joseph "Sepp" Blatter? How did such men sustain their power base in this phase of growth of globalized sport? These are the main questions posed in this chapter. In answering them, it is essential to examine the network of alliances that sustained the power base of such men for more than a quarter of a century, combining the interests of world football and global sport more closely than ever with commercial partners and with business and professional interests (Sugden and Tomlinson 1998c, 1999a). Tracing the growth of FIFA is a form of mapping seismic shifts in an increasingly global consumer economy and the wider geopolitical landscape. Following a brief historical overview of the birth and growth of the organization, personal profiles of FIFA's presidents are presented and their impacts evaluated and located in the wider history and politics of the game. The political and economic base of the long-term domination of the politics of the sport by Havelange and Blatter is then explicated.

FIFA's FOUNDING FATHERS

FIFA was founded by seven European footballing nations in 1904. Almost a century later, FIFA could boast 204 member nations. From its roots in a Eurocentric initiative, world football has come to represent a global passion, capable of mobilizing national sentiment and pride in unprecedentedly dramatic and, more recently, sophisticatedly mediated forms. The founding members of FIFA were Belgium, Denmark, France, the Netherlands, Spain, Sweden, and Switzerland. The football associations of Great Britain were initially haughty and hostile (Tomlinson 1999c, 99), English hauteur helping Frenchman Robert Guérin become the first president of FIFA (Wahl 1986, 12). The volatile relationship among the English Football Association (FA), the other UK countries, and FIFA has been related in detail (Tomlinson 1986, 1994, 1999c; Moorhouse 1995; Sugden and Tomlinson 1998c). The FA joined in 1905, stayed until 1920, joined again from 1924 to 1928 (leaving over disputes concerning payments to amateurs) and then rejoined in 1946. Yet FIFA's eight presidents have included three Englishmen, who between them presided over the organization for thirty years, a third of its existence. The presidents wer:e

Robert Guérin	France	1904–1906
Daniel Woolfall	England	1906–1918
Jules Rimet	France	1921–1954
Rodolfe Seeldrayers	Belgium	1954–1955
Arthur Drewry	England	1956–1961
Stanley Rous	England	1961–1974
João Havelange	Brazil	1974–1998
Joseph Blatter	Switzerland	1998–

For the first seventy years of its life, FIFA was controlled by Northern European administrators. The first English president, Daniel (D. B.) Woolfall, had a clear mandate from the English to "regulate football on the Continent as a pure sport" (Tomlinson 1986, 87). Woolfall was a civil servant from the northern English town of Blackburn and had been a contributor to Blackburn Rovers's domination of the English FA Cup competition in the 1880s. He led FIFA through a period of steady growth up until the end of World War I, but disputes over sporting relations between "former enemy nations" led to ostracisms, resignations, the temporary dissolution of FIFA, and the setting up (by Denmark, Finland, Norway, Sweden, and Italy) of a new Federation of National Football Associations. FIFA emerged from this challenge at the turn of the decade, with Jules Rimet, the French lawyer, taking the position of provisional head of FIFA in 1920 before becoming official president in 1921, a post he was to hold for thirty-three years, during which time his name was given to the World Cup trophy. During Rimet's presidency, the number of member associations grew from twenty to eighty-five, and five World Cup tournaments and finals took place.

FOOTBALL PATRICIANS: THE PIONEERS

The dramatic growth was consolidated during the presidencies of the Belgian Rodolfe Seeldrayers and the Englishmen Arthur Drewry and Sir Stanley Rous. The men who ran FIFA have symbolized their eras, but they have impacted, rather than merely reflected, their societies and their times in important ways. The character of the protagonists in the FIFA saga warrants attention, not from any "great man" theory of history but from the recognition that "men make their own history, but they do not make it just as they please; they do not make it under circumstances chosen by themselves, but under circumstances directly encountered, given and transmitted from the past" (Marx 1979, 103). Rimet, Rous, Havelange, Blatter, and the social and political relationships in which they have been embedded are indicative of the distinctive globalizing forces that drove the world game throughout the twentieth century.

Daniel Woolfall's years at the helm were obviously blighted by the Great War. Arthur Drewry was close to Stanley Rous, who, though at the time general secretary at the English FA, was the effective power behind the presidential position. Seeldrayers was a veteran football diplomat who held the post for a mere two years. Belgian Seeldrayers was, like Rimet, a lawyer, but also a classic all-round sportsman of the old school tradition. He was founder member of a prominent football club, a hockey international, and national champion in the 110-meter hurdles, and he had been president of both the Belgian Olympic Committee and the Belgian Football Association; throughout his life he espoused the virtues of British athleticism (Guldemont and Deps 1995, 19). He was a figure very much in the Rimet mold. Drewry was a faithful football administrator, president of the English Football League from 1949 to 1954, a fish-processing businessman from Grimsby in Lincolnshire (Inglis 1988; Tomlinson 1999c, 155). Drewry had been chairman of the FA's International Selection Committee since 1944 before becoming president of the Football League. In November 1945 he was with Rous in Switzerland, negotiating the four British football associations' reentry into FIFA, and was appointed vice president of FIFA by Rimet. After service in the Middle East during World War I, Drewry had returned to Grimsby and married the daughter of Grimsby Town Football Club's chairman, beginning to work too in his father-in-law's fishing business. He became chairman of the Grimsby club and was increasingly involved in the administration of the English game and its international dimensions, through both the league and the FA. He left the league to become chairman of the FA in 1955, to Rous's general secretary, just before succeeding Seel-drayers as FIFA president. Drewry was by now in his mid-60s and died, after a year-long illness, in March 1961.

FIFA's first two presidents established the foundations for the French and English domination of FIFA for its first seventy years. Guérin was an engineer and newspaper editor who did all he could to bring the English and the British in to FIFA at the beginning (Tomlinson 1999c, 100), but with little success in the face of English arrogance and obduracy. But once FIFA was formed, the FA considered it wise to become involved, and began operating behind the scenes. A special FA committee invited Continental nations to a conference on the eve of the 1905 England-Scotland match in London. The outcome of this meeting was that the British associations accepted FIFA's general objectives and expressed willingness to cooperate. The French president Guérin's early optimism at bridge building proved short-lived, and he resigned after his efforts to organize a first international competition came to nothing. The English were by now ready to step in and offer leadership (101). So the British, and particularly the English, joined in when it was clear that they would be at the helm. It was now time for the dependable Englishman to take over, and Daniel Woolfall, championing footballing excellence but rooted in amateur values, got himself elected as FIFA president. Under his leadership, FIFA's membership expanded from seven to twenty-four by the eve of World War I. This included some non-European members—South Africa in 1909/10, Argentina and Chile in 1912, the United States in 1913.

FOOTBALL PATRICIANS: RIMET, ROUS, AND FOOTBALL'S EDUCATIONAL MISSION

It was after the Great War that FIFA became more truly international, with Rimet as president.[1] Rimet was a self-made professional and religious do-gooder who dominated the growth of international football. Like so many senior sports administrators Rimet was trained in law. As an older man, the bearded, bowler-hatted, and thoroughly bourgeois Rimet was an established figure among Parisian polite society. But he came from humble origins. Rimet was born in 1873 into a modest family in rural France and from an early age helped his father in the family's grocer's shop. He was a conscientious and able schoolboy. From the age of eleven, he was raised in Paris where his father had moved in search of work. He lived in the heart of the city, learning to survive and play football on the street and to work ambitiously at school and at church. The young Rimet worked his way toward a full legal qualification and was active in encouraging football among the poorer children of the city. He was a philanthropist for whom sport was a means of building good character.

Rimet was Christian and patriotic. His love of God and nation came together in his passion for football. He believed in the universality of the church and saw in football the chance to create a worldwide "football family" welded to Christian principles. Like his countryman, founder of the modern Olympics Baron Pierre de Coubertin, Rimet believed that sport could be a force for national and international good. Sport and football could bring people and nations together in a healthy competitiveness, he thought. Sport could be a powerful means of both physical and moral progress, providing healthy pleasure and fun and promoting friendship between races. His philosophy of sport was more egalitarian than de Coubertin's, and he promoted full-time professionalism as a form of meritocracy. In World War II his principles marginalized him in Vichy France, when he resigned from his position in charge of French football, opposed to the nationalization of the game implemented by the Vichy regime. Generally, though, Rimet embodied the imperial project of politico-cultural colonization through cultural forms and practices such as sport (Mangan 1985) and the paradoxes and contradictions of any such modernizing project and establishment, just as was the case in the formative phase of the Olympic idea (Tomlinson 1984b). Most critically, Rimet preached in FIFA's mission the benefits of a global reach for the world footballing family, but denied the opportunity to huge parts of that family to mature. In effect, Rimet stunted the growth of his beloved family.

Rimet resisted the development of continental confederations and the empowerment of football confederations in Africa and in Asia, finding it difficult to loosen Europe's imperious hold on the sport. He did not believe that the administration of world football should be based on geographical or regional groupings. His consistent goal was to preserve FIFA as a family unit, and he argued that "decentralisation will destroy FIFA, only direct membership will retain FIFA as one family." He was traditional and conservative, but clever. As Rous recalled, elderly and inert committee members were useful to Rimet, who saw such "dead" committee men as preventing unnecessary change. The Rimet philosophy was reaffirmed in his opening address to the FIFA Congress in Rio in 1950, in which he listed four "finest human qualities" that football should impart. These were discipline, guided toward the achievement of a common goal; loyalty to the spirit of the game; moderation in competition and sporting rivalry; and solidarity in clubs and games. He proposed that such idealistic qualities be transferred from the game to everyday life. With one heart and one will, he preached, the world football family showed a "perfect unity that holds us together, the spiritual community to which we all adhere..." (Rous 1978, 131). The speech endorses Rimet's vision:

> World unity of football, the essential goal of FIFA, has been an accomplished fact: unity both moral and material.... These

results are not a matter of chance; they are the pursuit of voluntary
action resolutely pursued, the consequence of the magnificent
enthusiasm displayed by an elite of directing minds in all the
national Associations, of the work, often obscure but always
persistent, of the devoted moving spirits of large and small clubs,
of the referees who put up with abuse because they have faith,
and finally of the patient plodding of all, apostles and disciples,
towards a common ideal that fully deserves to be held aloft.

This is the language of the messianic visionary, linked to a sense of volun-
tarism as a form of vocation. But initially Rimet found it difficult to embrace
the whole world within his vision. At the first World Cup in Uruguay in
1930, only four of the fifteen competing teams were from Europe. Rimet
had worked hard to establish the World Cup, and in many ways Uruguay
was the obvious choice. Uruguay had shattered the world football establishment by winning the Olympic football championship in 1924 and 1928.
These were the most dramatic achievements of the emerging football super-
powers of South America. Football was also well established in Brazil and
Argentina, where the game had been growing for half a century. It thrived
initially in the ranks of nomadic British diplomats, planters, and engineers
who took their football togs and the Football Association rule book wherever they went. The colonials' love of the game soon spread among the local,
poorer classes. But however much it spread, Rimet saw no case for the
devolution and decentralization of the game's administration.

The sport took hold most strongly around the River Plate, and games
between Argentina and Uruguay were played regularly from the turn of the
century. The South American confederation—CONMEBOL—records its
founding date as 1916, long before any other continental confederation. In
its early days FIFA was so Eurocentric that no need was seen among the
European establishment for any separate European organization (the European football confederation, Union Européenne de Football Association
[UEFA], was founded in 1954). Rimet's concept of the world football family was deeply rooted in an entrenched colonialism. His successors would
need to be aware of the dynamics of a postcolonial world if the football
family was to hold together in the second half of the century. It was a bourgeois Englishman who inherited this challenge.

Sir Stanley Rous, although not assuming the FIFA presidency until
1961, was an influential force in the world game after World War II. He was
secretary of the English Football Association from 1934 to 1961, and even
though England was not a member of FIFA, he retained relations with the
world body (Beck 1999). Taking over at FIFA in his midsixties, he grasped
this new challenge with typical energy and commitment. Walter Winterbottom, England's first manager, says that "in our own country he took us

out of being an insular Association Football League and got us back into world football and this was tremendous." Winterbottom also praised Rous's exceptional charm and diplomatic skills.[2] Charm and skills: the lauded characteristics and qualities of the patrician colonizer.

A son of the middle classes (his two elder sisters were schoolteachers), his father had planned for him to go to Emmanuel College, Cambridge. But his father died, and after service in Africa during World War I, Rous studied at St. Luke's College, Exeter, and then taught at Watford Grammar School. He was not born into the establishment, but through football he became an establishment figure. For him, teaching and football were acts of public service. Rous played football at college and then in the army during the Great War, and he went on to become a referee of international repute. This is where he made his first impact on world football. His rewriting of the rules of the game was immensely influential. In administration, he went on to modernize the English game, establishing a more efficient bureaucratic base, introducing teaching schemes for all levels of the game—coaching, playing, refereeing. But this mission was about more than just football. Britain was in crisis after World War II, losing an empire and looking for a role. Educating football players as coaches, practitioners as educators, was one way of restoring British prominence in what Rous saw as a radically altered postcolonial world.

The FA had left FIFA in 1928, and Rous believed that it should be reintegrated into the world football family. In a paper which he presented to the Football Association, first drafted in May 1943, he claimed that the activities of the FA's War Emergency Committee had boosted football's international profile by fostering relations with government departments and by establishing links with influential people through cooperation with the armed forces. "The unparalleled opportunities which the war years have given the Association of being of service to countries other than our own," he wrote, "has laid an excellent foundation for post-war international development."[3]

Rous, recognizing that Britain's formal political empire was about to shrink dramatically, saw in football a chance to retain some influence over world culture. From the old world of the English middle class but negotiating the volatile world of postcolonialism, Rous's life and philosophy were a bundle of contradictions. Rous could be both innovative and traditional, adventurous yet crabbily cautious, modern yet steeped in traditional values. These contradictions and controversies over China, South Africa, and Chile/Russia, in particular, were to be cleverly exploited by Havelange (Sugden and Tomlinson 1998c, 1997a). With World Cup finals looking increasingly lucrative and emerging third world nations wanting more representation in the world game, Rous was to appear more and more old-worldly. Even within

Europe, he was viewed as too English as his home country strolled to its home-based World Cup victory in 1966. An English FIFA president, Drewry, had been in place when Rous secured the 1966 World Cup finals, and one Swiss commentator saw this and the culminating triumph in the tournament as far too cozy and collusive. In a fascinating document called "Thoughts on the 1966 World Championship," within FIFA's technical study of the event, the coach to the Swiss national team, Dr. A. Foni, argued that top Latin American and European teams were favored in their respective continents, meeting the weakest teams in opening games and having more rest than their distant cousins. In Chile, for instance, European teams had only forty-eight hours of rest between games, the Latin Americans recovering and preparing for a day more. Foni had some genuine complaints:

> Four years later the story was repeated in England, naturally with the necessary changes being made and, let me add, with a subtlety that worked still more . . . in favour of the host country.
>
> I mean simply that England won its victory with the last two games, but also that the premises for this victory were created well in advance: selection of a definite ground, longer breaks between games, decisions by referees that were slightly but very clearly favourable. It is very likely that English football, no doubt one of the best in the world, did not need these little "nudges," but it is a fact that they were given, they were not refused.[4]

To raise the "moral and the athletic level of the World Cup," Foni proposed a more representative participation. The 1996 finals had offered just one place for a team from Africa and Asia, promoting a boycott by those confederations and a wild-card entry from North Korea. "The Jules Rimet Cup will have attained its aim only when the five continents are effectively represented—football probably being the most universal of all sports," prophesied Foni. Rous's response, in immaculate longhand, was "disappointed—unfair, shows himself partisan, attacks referees officials organisers, is *bitter* . . . inaccurate, uninformed." But there was an objectivity to Foni's analysis—after all, England played all its games at London's Wembley Stadium—and a widespread concern throughout FIFA that Rous was unwilling to recognize. The resentments of the football world would simmer throughout the ensuing years.

So when he stood for reelection as FIFA president, claiming that he wanted "just a couple of years to push through some important schemes," Rous either had a confidence that was misplaced or had miscalculated the institutional politics of FIFA. Ten years later Rous put his defeat down to the limitless ambitions of his rival: "I know what activity was being practised by my successor, the appeals that he'd made to countries" (Tomlinson 1999c,

113). Rous, parvenu member of the cricketing fraternity of Lords/MCC (the Marylebone Cricket Club), of Wimbledon's All England Club (tennis), and of Hurlingham (polo), made "appeals . . . to countries" sound like a nasty disease. Rous's recollections have some truth in them, for Havelange did run a ruthless, aggressive, and corrupt campaign, based on disappearing monies from the accounts of the Brazilian sport federation of which he was president (Yallop 1999; Sugden and Tomlinson 1999a). But football administrators in the third world believed that Rous viewed them and their problems through the eyes of the British imperialist. Rous was no modernist. He ran the world game with the concerned air of the reforming patrician schoolmaster. When his pupils got out of hand he hardly knew what had hit him or what had undermined his authority. In the years leading up to the 1974 election Rous could have sought to challenge and change the perceptions of him as out of touch and out of time, but he chose not to do so. Rimet and Rous represented more than a knee-jerk cultural imperialism. In their well-intentioned paternalism, their own version of a kind of multicultural understanding and tolerance, they effectively legitimated an ethnocentric ideology, contributing to a form of what Žižek (1997) has called deeply entrenched racism within their own cultural assumptions and dominant worldview.

Football Entrepreneurs:
FIFA's Corporate Transformation

If football people the world over had been charmed by Rous's old-world diplomacy, they were awed by Brazilian Dr. João Havelange's new world presence. Havelange carried himself with the aura of the despot, and he had a physical presence and power that he was never slow to use in his presidential role. "Havelange had such an aura about him," comments vice president David Will, "people were actually physically scared of him, were frightened of him, in a one-to-one situation. He's devastating. His control of himself is amazing."

Havelange recalls with relish and self-congratulation how he made his way in the world.[5] Son of a Belgian industrialist and arms trader, Jean-Marie Faustin Godefroid Havelange was born on May 8, 1916, in Rio de Janeiro. He went to his father's arms company as a youngster and learned the rudiments of business administration. His father died when he was eighteen, and he went to work and studied part-time: "I wasn't earning very much, but I was learning something for life." He worked for an iron and steel company that had a Belgian connection before serving as a lawyer for a couple of years and then going on to become managing director of his own transport company. Early in life he decided that he could not work for anyone else. After working as an employee for six years, he went to the company boss and told him that he was resigning and never wanted to work for another boss in his life: "I have never had another boss in my life, except maybe my wife," he boasted. He branched out on his own, building a business empire in the transport and financial industries of a modernizing Brazil. In 1997 Havelange boasted that 20 million people a year were transported by his company, which he'd been with for fifty-seven years (fifty-three as chairman). He had also been the director of the biggest insurance company in Brazil: "When I became president of FIFA," he said, "I had to take a step down in that company."

Young Havelange was an athlete of some distinction. He had played junior football with Fluminense, the amateur sporting club for Brazil's elite. To belong to this club, it was necessary to belong to a family of means — which meant being white. When a famous mixed-race player, Carlos Alberto, sought to pass himself off as white by powdering his face in the locker rooms, they called it the "face-powder club." Professionalism would later bring more opportunities for nonwhites and also herald the end for mediocre upper-class footballers like Havelange. Not good enough to play alongside the talented professionals, he redirected his energies to swimming. From the mid-1930s to the early 1950s Havelange competed at the top, elite levels of his two chosen performance sports, representing Brazil in the Olympics in Berlin in 1936 in swimming and in Helsinki in 1952 on the water polo team. He said that "water polo served to discharge my aggressiveness and all my occasional ill humour" — it is a common boast of his that he swims every morning of his life.

Havelange's memories of the Hitler Olympics are extraordinary. "The first thing I remember is that the organisation of the transport was perfect, and the equipment and the facilities for 25,000 people were very well arranged." He remembers the convivial hospitality provided by the Nazis and the seven visits some athlete guests made to hear the seven hundred musicians playing in the Berlin Philharmonic. "From the start it was a pleasure to be in Berlin," Havelange recalled, and like many others he received the travel and privileges that Hitler's and Goebbels's friends in the Olympic movement laid on. Trains could be booked for 75 percent discount, and the twenty-year-old Havelange saw twenty-five different cities. The young Havelange appears to have greatly enjoyed his sojourn in Hitler's Germany.

Returned from 1930s Germany, Havelange spent the years of his own peak sports performances building up business and social contacts in Brazil's capital, São Paulo. Brazil declared war against Germany and Italy on August 22, 1942. Brazil had a quiet war. It joined the defense of the South Atlantic against Axis submarines and also sent an expeditionary force to Italy in 1944, which conducted itself courageously in several bloody engagements. Back home, the young entrepreneur sensed some real business openings in the transport industry. The state had taken over public transport, and this would be reprivatized after the war. Brazil had nuzzled up to the United States during the war, giving it use of naval and air bases. In exchange, the two countries signed a number of agreements for economic development and for the production of Brazilian raw materials. With the state in temporary control of the economy and a black market thriving, it was a busy and productive war for a young businessman on the make. The city government requisitioned the transport system, creating a municipal company. This was not to Havelange's liking, nor in line with his individualist market philosophy, but he was not slow to spot a business opportunity around the corner. In his own words, the postwar years were for him ones of opportunity for fighting government interference in the market. "Since I did not want to be a public servant, I and some friends founded the Viação Cometa in 1947." Highway construction was at the top of Brazil's postwar agenda of modernization. It did not take Havelange long to see the crucial, expanding public transport market. In the last year of the twentieth century, it was still the vehicles of Viação Cometa that dominated the urban hinterlands of São Paulo and Rio and transported the lost and the dispossessed around Havelange's huge home country, as so brilliantly shown in Walter Salles's 1998 movie *Central Station*.

By the mid-1950s Havelange had established a power base in national business networks. His time with the steelmaking company Belgo-Mineira helped him learn how to oil the wheels of bureaucracy. Senior partners realized that if they wanted to speed their imported buses through customs, Havelange was their man. Havelange was a minority shareholder but was chosen as director-president of Viação Cometa. Contacts in the sports world were big-business contacts too. During his São Paulo years, Havelange had swum and played water polo at the Espéria rowing club, cultivating and consolidating friendships with some of the country's leading industrialists. From his midtwenties onward, he was displaying the qualities of the wheeler-dealer that would serve him well for the following half century. No other world sports figure had combined sports and business networking and interests so closely, so early in the century of modern and global sport (see too Simson and Jennings 1992, 39–40).

In Havelange's view, just being a Brazilian made him the man for FIFA's top job. "It was an advantage for me when I became president of FIFA," he says, "that since a small child I have lived together with all the different races and understood their mentalities. It is nothing new for me to be in FIFA's multi-racial environment. . . . In São Paulo and Rio there are streets with Arabs living on one side and Jews on the other side and they live in the same street in perfect harmony." Havelange points out that Brazil is the eighth industrial power in the world, that São Paulo is a city just like industrial Germany. Yet Northern Brazil is less developed, a little like Africa. He can claim therefore that Brazil is both a midpoint and micro-cosm of the world: a leader of the nonaligned nations with first, second, and third world features. With this self-image Havelange cleverly positioned himself as representative of the advanced world, as much as of the third world but with an empathy for the whole world.

Trading on his achievements in the swimming pool and associated networks and contacts, in the late 1950s Havelange brought his business and administrative skills into Brazilian sport. His base in the Brazilian Sports Federation (the CBD) gave him authority over all the country's major sports as well as football. "I brought with me the entrepreneurial skills, the busi-ness skills from my own company to the federation," he says. "There were just [sports] coaches, but I brought in specialist doctors, administrators for the federation to give it a wider basis. This is what made the difference and why we won the World Cup in 1958, 1962 and 1970." Havelange recognized the potential football had to promote Brazil's international image and his own global profile in both sport and business. He used his experience of restructuring football in Brazil, with an expanded national and regional league and cup setup underpinned by commercial intervention, as a model for the expansion of the world game when he seized FIFA's reins of power from Englishman Sir Stanley Rous in 1974 (Sugden et al. 1998, 11–31, esp. 15–19). Once at the FIFA helm, Havelange set about taking control of world football from its established North European, Anglo-Saxon stronghold. To do this he would have to fulfil the commitments he had made to the devel-oping world—especially Africa and Asia—during his election campaign. There were eight of these: the increase in the number of World Cup final teams, from sixteen to twenty-four; the creation of a junior, under-twenty World Championship; the construction of a new FIFA headquarters; the provision of materials to needy national associations; help in stadium devel-opment and improvement; more courses for professionals; medical and tech-nical help; and the introduction of an intercontinental club championship. Rous was no match for this manifesto, and Havelange won the presidency on the second ballot.

When Havelange took over at FIFA, operating from its picturesque headquarters in Zurich, it was a modest operation with few personnel and negligible finances—less than a hundred members and operating a single tournament, a sixteen-nation World Cup finals. After a quarter of a century, when Havelange stepped down in Paris in 1998, on the eve of the first-ever thirty-two-nation senior competition, according to his own estimates, FIFA had more than $4 billion on its way into its coffers, and as a global industry he reckoned football to be worth in the region of $250 billion annually, way in excess of General Motors' $170 billion. This huge expansion, including the addition of a series of world championships for youth and women, was achieved in partnership with transnational media partners and global business interests, including the giants Coca-Cola, Adidas, and McDonald's. Toward the end of his twenty-four years in power, Havelange listed the eleven competitions that FIFA now staged and summarized his achievements:

> For all of these 11 competitions, FIFA bears the cost of travelling, board, accommodation and local transport.
>
> Allow me to inform you that the principle for the evolution of industry lies in improvement and this also applies to football. Since I have been President of FIFA, which is now 22 years, we have organised courses for technical matters, refereeing courses, sports medicine courses as well as administration courses in every continent on a permanent basis, for the benefit of approximately 40,000 people. This is the reason for the global expansion of the game, which you mentioned in your letter.
>
> Apart from that, the FIFA administration service may be considered perfect. The economic and financial situation due to the development which has taken place has been envied. Under the economic aspect, I would mention the buildings which have been constructed and acquired in favour of the continuity of football development. On the financial side we are, together with our sponsors, attaining such conditions which will permit us to reach all our aims. (letter to author, dated Zurich, October 29, 1996)

Not much false modesty here! A mere six weeks or so later, Havelange was to announce that he would not stand again, fueling endless speculation on his succession and giving Sepp Blatter plenty of time in which to plot his strategy. Havelange bowed out from the presidency with a sense of mission accomplished.

Havelange, with the help of his close ally and confidant, the late Horst Dassler of Adidas, had been the first to recognize the full commercial potential of sport in the global market and to open the game to the influences of new media and new markets (Tomlinson 2004). Aided by his faithful general secretary Blatter, who had been with him at FIFA since 1975, initially as technical director, he could talk and deliver on bigger commercial deals than world sport had yet seen. Former FIFA media director, Guido Tognoni, welcomed back into the FIFA fold in Blatter's organizational purge after his 2002 reelection victory but sacked after the publication of *Badfellas: FIFA Family at War* (Sugden and Tomlinson 2003) in which I cited his 1996 observations to me on the nature of FIFA and the character of Blatter the president, said that on a clear and sunny day "Havelange could make you believe that the sky was red when it was really blue." People wonder at Havelange's almost supernatural powers of strength and concentration. "Havelange was a master of managing meetings," Tognoni recalled, "he was also a master of giving people the feeling that they are important without giving power away. He was just a master of power." There is a physically competitive side to Havelange's use of power. "He was always the toughest guy and even when he was tired he didn't want to stop the meetings," said Tognoni. "He was always fully informed about everything, whereas the members, they were not professionals, they had to eat what was served." Havelange "had the power to do everything that he wanted." And he certainly knew what he, and others, wanted. Havelange's football family included business and media magnates who stood to profit dramatically from football's commercial growth. Long-term ally Guillermo Cañedo, a media baron from Mexico, would soon be installed as chair of FIFA's media committee, brokering global deals in television sport's most expansionist phase.

Havelange has not refused personal honors and benefits. The FIFA president had not marked out France as a favorite in his early pronouncements on the race to host the 1998 World Cup finals. In late 1988—within five months of receiving his Nobel Peace Prize nomination from the Swiss Football Association—he praised Switzerland for its good transport network, telecommunications systems, hotel provision, and stable currency. Havelange told the Swiss what they wanted to hear, that it was "able to organise an outstanding World Cup as in 1954, but brought up to date." The stadiums would require extensions and renovation, but "given the financial strength of the country," Havelange could see no problem there. But it was France that gained the finals, and Havelange himself a Légion d'Honneur from the French state along the way to the decision.

Havelange manipulated the loyalties of small nations brilliantly, perhaps most blatantly in the case of Palestine, which was accepted as a full FIFA member at the June 1998 congress. It was a defining moment when the Palestine delegate carried its flag around the Equinox stadium, welcomed along with a few other nations as the newest members of the FIFA family. There were few doubts as to where its vote would go in the election for the FIFA presidency won later in the day by Havelange's faithful servant Blatter. Havelange claims that FIFA is truly democratic, with each member country having one vote. But the secret ballot, one-member-one-vote system gives him absolute control. Vanuatu has the same voting rights in a FIFA congress election as does Germany, the Faeroe Islands the same voting weight as Brazil. For years this has worried more powerful football nations, as voting outcomes and decisions can be assured from the accumulated commitment of tiny constituencies. Majorities necessary to change the rules, procedures, or statutes of FIFA are exceedingly difficult to mobilize or muster. Havelange and Blatter cultivated key loyalties in Africa, Asia, the Americas, and the Caribbean in a hugely effective fashion that guaranteed

Havelange five uncontested reelections and Blatter two sweeping victories against challengers from Europe and Africa respectively.

Among Havelange's claims is that FIFA is noncommercial as well as democratic. Under Swiss law it has noncommercial, almost charitable status—despite its $4 billion in the coffers, as claimed by Havelange in September 1997—and escapes the usual company reporting requirements. A FIFA document in 1984 claimed that Havelange was a "football magnate who combined the qualities of far-sightedness and openness, an entrepreneur in body and soul" who "in no time transformed an administration-oriented institution into a dynamic enterprise brimming with new ideas and the will to see them through, so that now the administration is managed in the form of a modern firm."[6] Guido Tognoni, though, said that "people say that he was leading FIFA like an industry—but he was leading FIFA like a private enterprise, like a proprietor." "As if he owned it?" I asked. "Yes, exactly," said Tognoni.

As late as the end of the 1990s, deals on the scale of the television rights for the World Cup finals of 2006 were completed without reference to FIFA's executive committee, deals that would lead to the collapse of FIFA's long-term commercial partner ISL (International Sport and Leisure), the brainchild of Horst Dassler and widely recognized as FIFA's "black box" of unaccounted-for monies. FIFA executive committee member David Will wearily observed: "It's depressing. I think we just have to keep chipping away at this. The first task is to have the committees properly chosen, and not to have committees packed with pay-offs. We don't know how the [2006 television] deal was made. We know the money and we know everything else." Will added: "Per Omdal and I have seen the contracts, but we asked that the contracts be laid before the Executive Committee for final approval, and instead we were told at the Executive Committee that the contracts were signed that day" (personal interview, June 1998).

So Havelange's self-proclaimed "perfection" has come at a price, with FIFA operating essentially as a cartel for the biggest event in world football, the World Cup, and the expansion of the global game based on networks of insider deals, noncompetitive contracts, and electoral manipulations. Even as he planned for his retirement in 1998, Havelange worked ceaselessly behind the scenes to ensure that the regime that he had installed at FIFA House would continue through the election of his hand-picked protégé, Joseph "Sepp" Blatter. Henchman Blatter would be the Brazilian's ideal successor, if he could make the leap from general secretary to president and exhibit the gravitas to go with the position. Throughout his decades of power wielding in world football, Havelange has believed that he has done no wrong. Responding to criticism of his visit to Nigeria as dissident Ken Saro-Wiwa was about to be executed, he uttered a stunningly revealing personal philosophy: "I don't want to make any comparisons with the Pope, but he is also criticised from time to time, and his reply is silence. I too am sometimes criticised, so explanations about such matters are superfluous."

Sepp Blatter emerged victorious in the battle for the FIFA presidency in June 1998.[7] He had persuaded enough African and European countries to vote for him, to add to his extensive base of votes safely delivered from Asia, the Gulf states of the Middle East, the Americas, the Caribbean, and the South Pacific, to fracture the Europe-Africa alliance on which UEFA president Lennart Johansson's candidacy depended. Blatter's run-in to the election was masterfully organized, with the support of a Swiss commercial partner and a private jet provided by Qatar. Blatter prospered on the back of his long-standing working partnership with Havelange and all the infrastructure of FIFA that had aided his bid long before he formally declared himself just a few months before the vote. The circumstances in which so many nations supported Blatter are shrouded in controversy (Yallop 1999; Sugden and Tomlinson 1999a), but his campaigning strategy was so effective that he came out of the first ballot with 111 votes to Johansson's 80. The devastated Swede soon realized that there was little point in proceeding to a second ballot.

Havelange, with heavy irony allied to consummate diplomatic skill, praised the European president as "sportsman, gentleman, leader and friend," whose "qualities and values" would help the football family enter the next century. Blatter hailed his defeated rival as "a great personality, fair and realistic" and pledged "to unite football" and establish "continuity in the good sense." "I am a servant of football," beamed Blatter. "I shall play, live and breathe football," he said. "I am deeply, deeply touched, deeply, and offer a message of friendship, openness, understanding, a message of solidarity."

Blatter had learned well under Havelange's tutelage, and he understood football politics in Africa. While Johansson busied himself working on the hierarchy of the African confederation, Blatter, often accompanied by Havelange, had visited Africa in a private jet, meeting with the representatives of some of the continent's remotest and poorest countries, making personal contact with the men in the national associations who would be marking the ballot cards in Paris in June. It was a strategy that had worked for Havelange in 1974 and it worked again for Blatter in 1998. Blatter was steeped in the world of international sports politics. He had business and administration experience as an organizer of the 1972 and 1976 Olympic Games. He had headed public relations for a Swiss tourist board in the 1960s and been general secretary of the Swiss ice hockey federation. As director of sports timing and public relations at Longines SA, he was noticed by Adidas boss Horst Dassler. Dassler alerted Havelange to Blatter's qualities, and Havelange brought him in to FIFA, where he worked on the implementation of Havelange's program and the funding needed from early commercial partners such as Coca-Cola and Adidas itself. Blatter rose quickly through FIFA's hierarchy, becoming general secretary in 1981, even marrying the former general secretary's daughter on his way into her father's job.

At the launch of his presidential campaign Blatter claimed that football stands for basic education, shapes character and combative spirit, and fosters respect and discipline. It can make a valuable contribution to health, he added. And it is theater, entertainment, art. "But, first and foremost," he told his audience, "it is an endless source of passion and excitement. It stirs the emotions and can move its enthusiasts to tears of joy or frustration like no other game and it is for everybody." Let football keep its human touch, its spirited play, and its constant challenge, pleaded Blatter, "but above all its universality." The key word here is "universality," a veiled reference to the European base of Johansson's campaign. Blatter was nominated by several national associations, initially by Jamaica and the United States. Others included countries from the Gulf and South America.

At the Equinox congress hall on June 8, 1998, freelance heavies and government agents patrolled the razor-wired fences. A few hours later the FIFA family anointed Blatter as its new president. With a public fanfare, England had jumped ship from Europe at the last minute. In the congress hall Alec McGivan, England 2006 campaign manager, looked smug. Graham Kelly, chief executive of the English FA, looked as mournful as ever, as if he was yearning for a wet day back at Football League headquarters in Lytham St. Anne's, when life must have been so much simpler. Perhaps he was uncomfortable in his seat, maybe he just saw his future six months on, when he would be forced into resignation over the financial gift he'd pledged to the Welsh FA in seeking to get its backing for Blatter, as England curried favor with him in its bid campaign for the 2006 World Cup.[8]

In his last presidential address Havelange said that he took his leave with indelible memories of "Sepp Blatter at my side for twenty-three years. I leave, with a clear conscience, the governing body of the world's, the planet's most popular sport." With his protégé in charge, Havelange would be close to the action for the foreseeable future. In the Equinox hall the postmortem on the result soon got under way. Questions were still swirling. Mihir Bose of the *Daily Telegraph* asked Blatter, "Was your campaign corrupt? Is FIFA not clean?" Blatter's face tightened, his smile subsided. "The accounts were cleared in congress," he snarled, "no questions were asked then." Show me my accusers, demanded Blatter. "It might become uncomfortable for anyone whose name you mention." The day after Blatter's victory, Kenya's *Daily Nation* reported how grateful the Kenyan football federation was to former president Havelange for promising to pay team travel costs to an obscure regional tournament in Rwanda. Chairman of the federation, Peter Kenneth, said in Paris, "It has been a gruelling battle but in the final analysis we are proud to have been associated with the winning candidate." "You've got the FIFA you want, you want this FIFA of corruption, that's what you've got. Get on with it," said one executive committee member to another. The cocky and acidic response said it all. "Sure it's all about money. Your side didn't spend enough money." The disillusioned Johansson, still in charge at UEFA, raised in the context of Swedish principles of democracy, transparency, and solidarity, confirmed: "I have had enough. I would never again go for the FIFA presidency. I will never engage myself in such dirty business," though he recognized that "we must be prepared to fight against corruption and bribery and dishonest people" (Bairner and Darby 2001).

Once in power new president Blatter moved swiftly to neutralize his opponents and enemies. In his first Exco (executive committee) meeting he dropped a controversial proposal to create a special bureau—an inner circle empowered to take decisions outside of the executive committee "to cope with FIFA's increasing volume of work." Johansson and his supporters would never have stood for this. Cleverly, Blatter withdrew his proposal at the last minute, proposing instead to double the number of full Exco meetings. Members would have to jet to world capitals twice as often now for the continuing (FIFA's motto) "good of the game." In his second meeting Blatter reshuffled the FIFA committees, giving his supporters key positions but also making sure that potential opponents were kept inside the FIFA family. David Will was rewarded for his open commitment to Johansson by being removed from the chairs of the prestigious referees and legal committees and was handed the grand-sounding but lower-profile national associations' committee. Blatter also proposed that for the first time Exco members should be paid in addition to already generous expenses. He suggested $50,000 a year. There were no objections from committee members.

Blatter provided FIFA with continuity, and though within his first year he showed a lack of the presidential gravitas of his Brazilian mentor, he consolidated the hold on power of the Havelange/Blatter dynasty. His suggestions that the World Cup be held every two years and his vigorous promotion of a World Club championship would be controversial issues. But his profile was high. He accepted the invitation to become the International Olympic Committee's 108th member, in the wake of its expulsion of exposed corrupt members and its ethical drive to clean up its act following bribery and voting scandals. He at times lacked authority over the FIFA congress. In Los Angeles, in June 1999, the Asian delegation walked out in protest at not getting an extra place in the 2002 finals to be cohosted by South Korea and Japan. In July 2000, his favored candidate for the staging of the 2006 World Cup, South Africa, lost his executive committee's vote to Germany, a triumph for a Johansson-backed Euro-Asian alliance.

But when it came to the reelection contest of June 2002, in a climate of unprecedented negative publicity as his own general secretary made allegations of corruption and incompetence, in the wake especially of the ISL collapse, Blatter easily defeated his challenger, the president of the African confederation, Issa Hayatou from Cameroon.

Hayatou never got close, mustering a mere 56 votes against Blatter's 139, a comfortable first-round winning majority of 83 for the embattled incumbent. Nine FIFA members, for reasons of suspension and the like, could not vote. The 195 that did vote not only reelected Blatter but granted him a more than doubled winning majority. Blatter had offered "tailor-made solutions" to development problems of small nations in the run-in to his initial victory in Paris in 1998. He knew his constituency intimately and played a trump card halfway through his beleaguered first term, doling out US$80 million to small nations for pilot projects that would be completed in 2001, early 2003, and soon after. What did Issa Hayatou have to offer against this, to the minnow nations of his own continent, to tiny countries in Asia and Oceania? Only 17,000 people live in the Cook Islands. Five hundred forty thousand dollars is a lot of development money for the footballers among that population. Blatter's scheme, the Goal project, was a masterstroke among those he'd played over his seventeen years as general secretary and his first few years as president. While the world press was interrogating FIFA's integrity, Blatter was visiting small countries, turning the turf on schemes for national academies and football pitches. What did it matter to these countries how FIFA managed its finances, as long as these kinds of subsidy were flowing in from Zurich? Samoa was benefiting to the tune of more than US$900,000 for the J. S. Blatter Football Fields Complex in Toleafoa. Blatter couldn't get there for the inauguration in July 2001, but arrangements were made for his executive committee colleague Mohamad Bin Hammam of Qatar, chairman of the Goal Bureau, to attend. Bin Hammam and Qatar had aided Blatter's election in 1998 by providing private jets for Blatter's whistle-stop visits to potential supporters. The same team was on the campaign trail again in the year up to the 2002 election, with the Goal project headlining the manifesto. The skeletons would clearly stay locked safely in many national associations' out-of-the-way cupboards. And borrowing from the future revenues for the 2006 World Cup—"securitization," as the accountants put it—and bringing marketing business in-house (including all the key ISL people with long-term insider knowledge), Blatter's FIFA was also overcoming the financial disasters of 2001.

So as Brazil and a revitalized Ronaldo took the 2002 World Cup back home to please football romantics across the world, as South Korea celebrated its third place in the tournament, and as the emperor of Japan watched the final in a country that for the previous month at least had taken the sport to its heart, FIFA controversies seemed a long way away. If the tournament was such a memorable fairytale for the hosts and the giant-killers from Turkey and Senegal, if the passion and flair of the Brazilian champions overcame a regimented, disciplined, but dull German challenge in the final, then what does it matter how FIFA conducts its business, one might ask? And media commentators and sports fans commonly do ask this. Several answers are offered in the concluding section of the chapter.

FAMILY FORTUNES

The global football family has not lacked its problems and tensions. The legendary Brazilian player Pelé, the biggest star of the United States' football initiatives in the 1970s, was not present at the Las Vegas World Cup finals draw in December 1993. Embroiled in a row with Havelange's son-in-law Ricardo Teixeira (president of Brazil's Football Federation), Pelé held his own press conference in Las Vegas. "Already facing a law suit for defamation, he was not prepared to be specific, but said: 'I cannot accept corruption, and football has a big problem with that in Brazil. . . .' For speaking out, he had been given no part in the draw" (Lovejoy 1993a, 32). Clearly, the structure of Brazilian football and Havelange's "means of gaining unassailable power" (Tomlinson 1986, 97) in the game had left some legacy of resentment. After almost two decades in power at FIFA, though, Havelange clearly felt little dependence on a former player, of whatever stature.

Despite instances and allegations of corruption in the higher economic levels of the game, the profile of the game has continued to grow. Part of football's global appeal has been that it does not demand expensive or extensive equipment. It has gained footholds not just in the stadia of the modern world but also on the cobbled streets of condensed working-class communities in Britain, on the beaches of Brazil, and the plains of the African continent. It guaranteed mass sport at its cheapest and most cheerful and the possibility of gaining international profiles in top-level performance, so contributing to the political agenda of a nation through the expression — and sometimes manipulation — of national sentiment. By any criterion of global representation, football became the world's greatest game, and FIFA — one of the earliest organizations operating as what Sklair has called a "transnational practice," more recently operating on combined "economic" and "cultural-ideological" levels (Sklair 1991, 6) — has created, in the World Cup, the world's greatest showcase for its most popular game.

The construction, expression, and maintenance of forms of national identity is a complex process, and identities can be fragile, the reactions to the expression of them unpredictable (Arbena 1993, 153). Global forces marginalize more culturally distinctive sports: Guttmann concludes an erudite review of sports' diffusion with the comment that "the international dominance of Western sports continues and resistance to this form of cultural imperialism remains weak" (1993, 134). But in the case of football a different process is at work—not merely the either/or of the domination of the imperialist or the resistance of the oppressed. Rather, in the FIFA story and the way in which nations have expressed the imaginings of their own community and national identities, the story has been one of appropriation. The form of football has been taken and remolded into the style and the culture of the recipient; football has been appropriated and remade in these ways, to the extent that the traditional centers of power in the world game have lost their "natural" dominance. There is an element of continuity in the vision of the FIFA presidents, in that they understood this global reach of the game and its simultaneous capacity to speak for distinctive national and regional cultures and interests. Yet the center of control of the modern game has continued to represent the vested interests of multinational capital and football entrepreneurs' associated benefits.

Havelange's success represents a superb irony in the FIFA story. The challenge of the developing world to the advanced world was led by a glamorous figure resonant of the modern and consolidated economically by money from the capitalist centers of mid-Europe and North America. The third world had been aroused and in footballing terms was on the ascendancy, but in power terms, the alliances within FIFA combined the political and cultural interests of emergent nations with the market aspirations of multinational and transnational economic interests still based firmly in the first world of capitalism. It is a further irony—yet at the same time a truism of a globalizing world based on the driving forces of a capitalist political economy and the search for new worldwide consumer markets— that the increased representation of third world nations at the World Cups of 1994, 1998, and 2002 was celebrated in the heart of the first world capitalist system (despite the Asian symbolism of the last of these events). But this was hardly an accident. FIFA's deal with Coca-Cola was hammered out in the mid-1970s at the company's headquarters in Atlanta, Georgia. That deal can be seen as a pivotal moment in the history of modern football, and from the moment that deal was struck it became likely—regardless of the state of the game within its own sport culture—that the United States would host the biggest football event in the world. With the World Cup in the United States in 1994, the centenary Summer Olympic Games in Atlanta in 1996, the women's World Cup in the United States in 1999, and the Winter Olympics in Salt Lake City in 2002, modern sport's and football's impact and appeal beyond their Western roots can be seen to be premised on the patronage of the transnational political economy. The exclusive sponsors for the 2002 finals were Adidas, Avaya, Budweiser, Coca-Cola, Fuji Xerox, Fuji Film, Gillette, Hyundai, JVC, KT-Korea/NTT-Japan, Mastercard, McDonald's,

Philips, Toshiba, and Yahoo (fifteen official general sponsors, more than ever before, paying a total of US$527 million for the privilege, ranging from between $18 million to a little over $36 million each). The host nations bore the brunt of the staging costs—between them, around US$7.5 billion on infrastructure (Szymanski 2002, 11)—and 35 billion viewers are said to have tuned in (over five times the population of the world). Despite FIFA's internal financial crises, it is unlikely that the sponsors will withdraw from this level of global market penetration. The political capital that could accumulate from hosting the event might evaporate quickly after the event (Dauncey and Hare 1999), but countries will still compete vigorously to stage the finals.

The story of FIFA's expanded football family is one of alliances between emerging cultural and political interests in the developing world and entrenched economic interests in the developed capitalist world. Yet throughout the turbulent family rows and breakups in this story, football has continued to provide gripping drama and sporting spectacle. FIFA, for all its contradictions and flaws, has made much of this possible in its later developmental phases in ways and initiatives that would not have been undertaken or embraced by the traditional old guard of the Eurocentric founding fathers. The atmosphere up at FIFA House in the modern bunker might be less charming than the quaint villa that housed Sir Stanley Rous's FIFA coterie, but a bunker in the Gnomes of Zurich's neighborhood is a fitting resting place for the dealmakers of world football and the vast riches that have accumulated on the back of FIFA's initiatives.

In the earlier days of FIFA, figures such as Rimet and Rous led world football almost as volunteers, as idealist missionaries, with backgrounds in education and public service. Their successors have far different backgrounds, in business, economics, and marketing. While a politics of football has driven FIFA dynamics throughout its history, the motives of the men who made FIFA have differed as the power base switched from France and England to Brazil and nonaligned Switzerland. While FIFA men of the last quarter of the twentieth century could promote and puff their organization's work "for the good of the game" in glitzy surroundings created by modern communications technology, they would be gleefully rubbing their hands knowing that FIFA was now one of the most high-profile and lucrative businesses in the global consumer and cultural industry. That is why it is vital to subject to analysis and scrutiny the practices and conventions of such organizations that have come to dominate the political economy of global sport. There are at least three good reasons for undertaking such work.

First, the level of hypocrisy underlying the gap between FIFA's claims and practices should surely be challenged. Anyone appealing to ideals of international friendship and cooperation, to the causes of youth and the developing world, must be called to account and be seen to be aboveboard in its fundamental claims. Second, the money generated on behalf of the global peoples' game, doled out to the 204 FIFA members, needs monitoring. Regular handouts of a million dollars could change a lot of lives in small nations, if it were guaranteed that those monies don't go directly into the private bank accounts of individuals or the unmonitored accounts of self-serving associations. And third, bodies such as FIFA cannot be immune from consideration in any global debate about the nature of corporate governance. FIFA may be based in the land of neutrality, international tolerance, hush-hush bank accounts, and Nazi gold, but as businesses such as Enron, Worldcom, and Xerox are exposed for their dubious accounting practices, bodies such as FIFA can no longer be allowed to hide behind a rhetoric of global goodwill and bogus organizational democracy.

The challenge to FIFA president Blatter subsided after his June 2002 reelection, just as it did in Paris in 1998 in the weeks following his initial election victory. Those Europeans, Africans, and Asians who led the challenge knew what a good beating was when it came their way, and they had little choice but to be realistic about the nature and scale of the Blatter re-election victory. But the issues would not go away. Numerous football associations were for Blatter not just because of past favors and the spiderwebs of patronage and dependency. They were also adamant that no African—for this, read black man and the myriad alternatives to that term floated in some nations of Europe, particularly the newer nations in the east of the continent—could be contemplated as FIFA president. "For the good of the game," FIFA's slogan, the organization must begin to vet its membership, cleanse its organizational and financial practices and procedures, weed out prejudices and racism, open itself to scrutiny, and set a model of above-board, ethical, and transparent corporate governance for those organizations seeking and claiming to speak for a globalized world.

PART II. NATIONAL STUDIES

National Studies

There is an enormous literature on national identity and nationalism, some of which has been reviewed in the context of sport (Allison 2000). More particularly, with reference to the politics of world football, emergent national identities in the postcolonial world have been expressed through the vehicle of sports organizations and sports events (Sugden et al. 1998). Hargreaves has studied in illuminating depth the contribution of an event such as the Olympics to the resolution of issues of regional and national identity, specifically in the case of the 1992 Barcelona Olympic Games and its relation to both Catalan political interests and those of the national Spanish state (John Hargreaves 2000). Allison emphasizes sport's capacity to give collective expression to deep-rooted values: "A national dimension . . . starts with the immense added meaning that a sense of shared national identity gives to watching a team and (sometimes) an individual perform" (2000, 345). Countering one case with another, case after case, he exposes the fragility of the posturings of archtheorists yet is still drawn to conclude that "sport sometimes channels, sometimes releases, sometimes even creates complex and powerful nationalist sentiments" (354). National identity can be powerfully felt, as sport provides a vehicle for the articulation and often public demonstration of a national identity and nationalist sentiments. It can also be garnered for political purposes, sport providing a means for the expression of national pride on an international stage.

Bairner (2001a) has shown in his comparative study of the national contexts of sport cultures and systems how the reach of globalization is, unsurprisingly, limited by the capacity of sport to speak for the national sentiments of a population or to be mobilized in the interests of national identity formation fueled by politicians. In studies of the national sport cultures of Scotland, Ireland, Canada, the United States, and Sweden, Bairner shows convincingly that "the process described by the term *globalization* has" far from "successfully eradicated either completely or in part the central role of nationality in the contemporary world" (6). Rowe writes that Bairner

> notes at the commencement of his book *Sport, Nationalism, and Globalization* that while many tentative propositions can be presented concerning sport, identities, and social practices: "One theory, however, that is put forward with a greater degree of confidence suggests that, as a result of the process known as globalization, the relationship between sport and *national* identity is self-evidently unravelling to reveal an increasingly global sporting culture." (Rowe 2003, 283)

Rowe has taken some of Bairner's points as a starting point and argued that "the project of globalisation will have to look elsewhere for an ideal socio-cultural institution that is not likely to trigger, with considerable intensity, the kind of cultural nationalism evidenced by sport. There is certainly no immediate prospect of the uncoupling of the sport-nation nexus . . . such a re-conceptualisation of sport would simultaneously erode (if not destroy) a key component of the affective power that is translatable into economic capital." (292)

Bairner notes the wide acceptance of "the linkage of sport and nationalism" (2001a, 163) but points also to "a lack of precision" concerning what particular types of nationalism are linked to sport and what ways those types interact with sport. He comments too on the considerable variation in how national issues are expressed in one formation rather than another. But in many cases it can be seen clearly that "sport has greatly assisted national endeavours to resist or, at the very least, to domesticate globalizing impulses" (164). Nationalists used sport, Bairner, reminds us, with regularity and consistency, throughout the twentieth century, "whatever their situation and respective aspirations," and though the selected case studies may look initially like evidence for the influence of an homogenizing global process, the analyses make it clear that "cultural convergence is still some way off" (177). The studies in this section further support the theoretical positions of Bairner and Rowe and the analytical inductions of Allison. One of the chapters, on emergent societies and sport cultures in the Middle East and Asia, is a reminder of how sport nationalism can be inculcated from above, the product of societies in which there is no substantial separation of civil society and the state. Some would argue that postcolonial theory can open the doors to an understanding of some of these remarkable cultural experiments. But it should never be forgotten that national sport cultures are almost always cultural-political formations, the understanding of which requires the insights of the anthropologist alongside the analytical agenda of the sociologist and the political scientist. In the case of some postcolonial societies it is vital that the subtleties of power and culture are not lost in the imposition of any all-embracing theoretical framework.

Postcolonial theory has offered a trenchant critique of established analytical categories, warning quite rightly against the perpetuation of Western-based and dominant ethnocentric readings of dominated cultures (see, for instance, Hall 1991). But as Rojek has rightly observed (2000, 110), the speculative theorizations of the postcolonial and the hybrid in Stuart Hall's later work have yet to be applied in any substantive fashion in leisure studies, though some applications have been developed in relation to feminist theory (Aitchison 2000). I am not competent to review the fors and againsts of the postcolonial debate, and the chapters in this part do not stand or fall on the basis of their contribution to that debate. But I do offer analysis and comment on societies whose histories have been dramatically shaped by transitions from colonized pasts, whether this be the United States, the United Arab Emirates, or (South) Korea, and it seems to me that there is a perfectly adequate conceptual toolbox in Western social science for undertaking such analyses. Yet in widespread deliberations within the postcolonial debate, there is a momentum and even a consensus that particular emphases within that debate constitute a paradigm shift, an epistemological break, rendering invalid much of that which preceded it. One particular point is of most importance here for my own conceptual and analytical agenda. It relates to the claim within postcolonial theory that the "tyranny of the present" must be refused (Childs and Williams 1997, 23). Spivak is feted as the high priestess of this kind of self-denial. In fact, following her thinking on the "politics of interpretations" reveals her approach to be a very much traditional theoretical exercise. Identity as a "working notion" is recognized as critical to the act of interpretation. "Ideology in action is what a group takes to be natural and self-evident, that of which a group, as a group, must deny any historical sedimentation" (Spivak 1987, 118). This could also be Gramsci talking of "common sense." But Spivak's postcolonial theory does not allow her to sound too certain, as in a truism of the postcolonial she implies that all knowledge is compromised: "It is impossible, of course, to mark off a group as an entity without sharing complicity with its ideological definition. A persistent critique of ideology is thus forever incomplete" (118). Good for business, but hardly for project completion! Spivak undermines completely the prospect of a cultural analysis that is anything but tainted by the language and conceptual baggage of the analyst or the subject or group that is the focus of the analyst. If Spivak is right, I am unable to speak a language of relatively objective social scientific analysis. But we can analyze ideologies in their construction and their effects and, in terms of the focus of the studies in this section of the book, their manifestations in sport cultures. As I researched the sport histories and cultures of different countries featured in this part I did not know with any programmatic certainty what I would find. But I am confident that what I have found has been adequately interpreted with appropriate concepts and that the postcolonial realities of sport cultures in some of these national settings are conducive to illuminating sociocultural analysis without the gnashings and intellectual self-flagellations of Spivak's variant of the post-colonial agenda.

It is not a mystery how forms of culture have been used in post-colonial moments to promote and bolster forms of national identity and to inform the expression of national identities. What the critical social historian or social scientist needs is an open-mindedness to the meaning of the data and the materials. Sport cultures have been widely cultivated by and claimed for national political interests. In this they have been used to accomplish much ideological work, very often serving the interests of powerful groups, but also providing a means whereby dominated groups can contest and explicitly resist the imposition of cultural meaning. The studies in this section confirm the persisting influence of national cultures in the making of the sport and leisure sphere in federal democracies such as Switzerland (chapter 4) and the United States (chapter 5), in state-centralized capitalist societies in the Asian tiger economy, and in despotic theocracies of the (Middle Eastern) Gulf region (chapter 6). They are studies of the ways in which national cultures interact with international or global trends, and it is the study of the national and the persistence of the national (as in the case of the study of the impact of football's event in the United States in 1994 on the wider dominant sport culture of the United States) that can inform usefully any sweeping claims concerning the influence and the reach of global trends.

4. Sport, Cultural Diversity, and National Identity

The Swiss Case

Yes, truly, Switzerland has been organized as a training ground.
Everything is there, smilingly accessible, and nothing is in the way.
— PIERRE DE COUBERTIN, 1920

Situated in the heart of Europe, Switzerland is famous for its long-established neutrality in regional and global conflicts, its economic and fiscal independence and strength, its exceptionally striking natural environment, and its institutionalized multiculturalism. As one drives from the German center of Zurich in the north of the country to the French-influenced Geneva in the south, passing through a consistently beautiful landscape of lakes and peaks, one travels from strasse to rue and from German-language place names and motorway signs to their French counterparts. In this high-profile linguistic and accompanying cultural variety and difference, the Swiss federation is experienced as a society-of-difference, though not necessarily of division. This chapter explores some of these dimensions as they manifest themselves in sport and leisure cultures, and as they have been produced by the specificities and nuances of Swiss political and cultural history.

Stereotypes of Switzerland abound, emphasizing the natural beauty of the country's rolling green valleys, the rising snow-capped peaks, and the vast yet unthreatening lakes,[1] as well as the administrative and technical efficiency of its service, business, and commercial organizations. Pierre de Coubertin, founder of the modern Olympics, chose Lausanne, Switzerland, as the headquarters for his International Olympic Committee (IOC). Writing in 1920, he identified the "future mission of Switzerland in terms of sport" as "popularisation, simplification, facilitation, democratisation, fortification" (1986, 603). He idealized the neutrality of the country, calling it "the only true democracy existing in Europe at the present time" (602), and also its sporting culture and populace. Lakes, mountains, bucolic traditions—"Swiss shepherds passed on untiringly from one to another the secrets of freestyle wrestling" (601)—hikers and climbers: all offered de Coubertin a vision of civilization preferable to the militaristic aggrandizement practiced by the great European powers. It was to Switzerland that de Coubertin turned as the alternative to "the armies of France, Italy, Germany . . . signing up bold volunteers ready to urge war under foreign flags for glory and profit" (601).

He recognized, writing in 1919, that the new world order involved the powerful new player of the United States, giving "warning of the vast wave of Americanism which is crossing the ocean and is about to break on Europe. The phenomenon is expected; it is in the natural order of things. But it is not only language, lavatories, railways and banks which are going to be Americanized; it is going to happen to the universities too, for let us not forget that the universities of the United States played the leading part in the preparation and the launching of the war—as in its conduct" (de Coubertin, 2000, 172). The "formula" of the U.S. universities would come to dominate the world, de Coubertin predicted, and integral to this formula was the allocation of "a very considerable part to sporting culture." De Coubertin urged a new, antimilitaristic form of internationalism through sport, but realistically recognized the potentially military functions and benefits of a developed sport culture.

De Coubertin's paean to Swiss virtues included therefore their military preparedness with arms and horses as well as their commitment to winter sports. "Harmless play," "serious sport," "competitive athleticism" (2000, 600)—all were blended for the French aristocrat in the Swiss sport culture. The "desire" and "instinct" of the Swiss citizen provided de Coubertin with a template for the IOC's "summary of aspirations for the near future . . . 'All sports for all'" (1986, 602). In the wake of the carnage and mayhem of World War I, therefore, de Coubertin saw Switzerland as an emblem of hope for a better future, and as the perfect location where he could "democratise and simplify the machinery of the sporting life" (603). De Coubertin's deification of Swiss polity and culture both typified and reinforced strong stereotypes of the society and its values.

The Swiss themselves are fiercely defensive of their political, cultural, economic, and environmental legacies, resenting the parochialism of the far from untypical visitors from the United States who glance at the wrong bit of the European map and express surprise that they're not on the road to Stockholm. Swiss sensibility is bound up with a form of self-image that asserts a distinctive and common geographical, historical, and political legacy, alongside the recognition of the cultural and linguistic traditions of the German, French, Italian, and Romand constituencies within the country. To be mistaken for Swedes, or anyone else for that matter, is both a joke and an insult, for the Swiss claim that their multicultural society based on negotiation, compromise, and reciprocal respect for difference should be acknowledged more widely. Indeed, the Swiss polity and the multilinguistic character of the society must be understood before any particular cultural form within that society can be properly assessed.

SWISS MADE: HISTORY, POLITICS, AND CULTURE

The Swiss Federation has experienced several formative moments in its political constitutional history, a history that, for several reasons (Rappard 1936, viii–ix), has been of continuing interest to American political scientists. First, Switzerland offers a fascinating long-term history of a relatively stable republic, which was established long before the heroic phase of the republican tradition in the nineteenth century. Second, over five centuries it developed from a loose confederacy of sovereign states into a federal union, and its 1848 constitution was modeled on (with its bicameral form of central and regional structures) the U.S. precedent of 1787. The Swiss model therefore inspired and was in turn inspired by the U.S. model. Democratic institutions such as the referendum also originated in Switzerland. Third, the composite nature of its demography can be linked to the country's policy of neutrality and isolationism with respect to international conflicts, in that the diverse cultural, ethnic, and linguistic character of the populace rendered the taking of sides no simple matter. The long-established interest of political scientists in the Swiss polity has consistently recognized the distinctive but complex interplay of politics and culture in a society in which the political imperative has been to provide an all-embracing political ethos that simultaneously respects and preserves the cultural diversity of a multicultural and multilinguistic population. Speaking in Zurich in September 1946, the British politician Winston Churchill could claim that there was a moral to be learned from the Swiss success in "achieving unity based on tolerance" (cited in Thürer 1970, 175) and overcoming differences of race, language, and customs. Churchill proclaimed further that in Switzerland politics was a civic task, not a matter of power, and that the Swiss benefit from "an ingrained faith in mutual help and solidarity."

This historical, political, and cultural pedigree has created the base for and expectation of a culturally diverse pluralism, and international interest in this accomplishment has been aroused after global crises and conflicts such as the two great world wars of the twentieth century. A former president of the Swiss national council could therefore write, just after World War I, that Switzerland had as many democracies as it had cantons and demicantons and that—as "the oldest of all" examples of "the political system of the future . . . a federative organization" and along with the United States "the completest" type of this form of political organization—the Swiss Confederation could pride itself on its long tradition of freedom and democracy (Bonjour 1920, 30). The war had provided a threat to the moral unity of the country, with German-French rivalries becoming manifest within its own populace to the extent that in October 1914 the Swiss Federal Council considered it necessary to reaffirm the core values of the confederation "to reassert 'the ideal of our country' as a cultural community and as a political idea above the diversity of race and language. 'First and above all are we Swiss, then only Latins and Germans'" (cited in Kohn 1978, 128).

The defining moments of this national ideal were in the thirteenth, sixteenth, eighteenth, and nineteenth centuries. Effectively, up until the time of the French revolution, Switzerland comprised a miniature league of nations, with no national citizenship, representative government, or federal structure. For five centuries the "country" was based on agreements between separate sovereign states or cantons with differing political characters—at the time of the invasion by French armies in 1798 these numbered thirteen and included democratic communities, urban aristocracies, and oligarchies. Covenants between these bodies and treaties with contiguous communities perpetuated core principles of mutual defense against external aggression and peaceful negotiation of internal disputes. These principles had been first documented in a historically recorded treaty in 1291 among men of the Alpine valleys around Lucerne. What bound together this diverse set of interests—despite some tensions such as a civil war throughout the 1430s and 1440s before Zurich renounced its pact with Austria and rejoined the confederation in 1450 (Thürer 1970)—was "pressure from without and the cohesive vitality of certain traditions" (Rappard 1936, 16; Codding 1961, 21). These traditions included the Landsgemeinde, political assemblies of the medieval communities. Neutrality as a principle dates substantially from 1515, when defeat in battle at the hands of Francis I convinced the Swiss that alliances to preserve the status quo, rather than imperialistic expansion, would best guarantee the future of the states and territories and the stability of the different religious groups within the alliances (Codding 1961, 152–53).

But the French invasion of its territories shattered this centuries-old federal bond. Throughout the Napoleonic period, the invention of the French lawyers—the one and indivisible Helvetic Republic—was reshaped and disputed in its strong centralism by those close to Swiss traditions. At the Congress of Vienna Swiss majority opinion triumphed, and representative liberal democracies were established in the place of the aristocracies and oligarchies. A short civil war in which seven minority cantons were routed in 1847 was followed by the adoption of the 1848 constitution by means of a constitutional referendum. The revised constitution of April 1874 confirmed the four main objectives of the confederation as national centralization, extended democracy, reinforced anticlericalism, and state intervention in social and economic spheres (25). This was mostly in line with the principles built into the earlier constitution, with the addition of the recognition of the interventionist role of the state. A Catholic, French-speaking minority, however, was clearly less powerful within the newly defined Swiss nation than were the Protestant liberal elements. Forms of continuity guaranteed by this constitution could even be noted in the urban topography of the country, with the "dispersed nature of political power which is so typical of Switzerland" working against the formation of any new towns from the middle of the eighteenth century onward (Phaidon 1985, 27).

The mainstream of Swiss political life was impregnated with more social democratic and even socialist principles and influence during and after a general strike in 1918. Alongside the stability produced by the unaltered nature of its international frontiers ever since 1815, this has ensured a continuity and neutrality and a championing of peace and freedom, the secret of which one commentator has claimed to be maintenance of "a fair balance between all the component elements of its society" (Thürer 1970, 176). Just a few months prior to the end of World War I, the confederation's president, Felix-Louis Calonder, appealed to his country to remain faithful to the national motto of—in the words of the German Swiss poet and patriot Gottfried Keller—"friendship in freedom." Extracts from Calonder's speech warrant extensive citation, embodying as they do the central values of a long-lasting Swiss polity. For him, Switzerland's history is one of

> consolidation of the principle of law and peace in internal relationships [through foreign policy].
> [Switzerland] embraces this rich diversity [and has a] profound unity as one people on the basis of mutual respect. . . . Complete confidence can only be conceived in an atmosphere of full freedom and sincere amity.
> [Swiss history is one of the] developments of international relations in miniature . . . [its state a] precursor of the future League of Nations.
> [Switzerland's international mission is] to be the harbinger of concord between all peoples by proving to the world, through its own example, that populations differing in race and language may unite to form a happy commonwealth on the basis of mutual confidence, freedom and equality of rights. (Bonjour 1920, 206–7)

As most of Europe was plunging toward the tragedy of World War II, the Swiss coined the term "ideological national defense" for the justification of their own joint principles of liberty and nationalism and their continuing neutrality. In response to the threat of a totalitarian collectivism prioritizing nation, race, or class over the individual, the Federal Council issued a message to the nation on the "meaning and mission of Switzerland," defending "the dignity of the individual" within the context of federalism and democracy. The author, Philip Etter (cited in Kohn 1978, 129), stressed the importance of the historical longevity and geographical centrality of the country:

> For the very reason that we reject the concept of race or descent as the basis of a state and as the factor determining political frontiers, we gain the liberty and strength to remain conscious of our cultural ties with the three great civilizations. The Swiss national idea is not based upon race or biological factors, it rests on a spiritual decision.
>
> The respect for the right and liberty of human personality is so deeply anchored in the Swiss idea, that we can regard it as its basic concept and can claim its defence as an essential task of the nation. . . . We recognize the individual human personality as the strongest creative force in the life of the spirit, and the state has accordingly limited its own sphere of power.

Such appeals, obviously more widespread in times of threat and international conflict, have nevertheless been typical of the ideals and the rhetoric by which a Swiss politics and culture has been explained and justified throughout its modern history. Some historical realities might appear to refute these claims. Doctrinal deviation in Geneva could not save Spanish anti-Trinity scholar Michael Servetus from being burned at the stake in Geneva during the Reformation, occasioning the "charge that Geneva represented a narrow intolerance worse than the papacy" (Johnston and Scribner 1993, 152). During World War II, trade relations with the Nazis were not halted until 1944–45, and Stalin called the Swiss "swine," as Swiss neutrality was squeezed when any access beyond the country became dependent on some degree of cooperation with the Axis powers (Robertson 1987, 29–30).

Hinde Fekete, a Belgian survivor of Auschwitz, recalls how "my family was expelled by the supposedly neutral Swiss and later died at the concentration camp. It took fifty years to unmask Switzerland. And I say it's important the world knows that Switzerland was not neutral. Germany was depositing the gold in their banks, and the Swiss were depositing Jews in their gas chambers" (Carpozi 1999, xx). Spain, Portugal, Italy, Sweden, Norway, and Turkey are also implicated by Carpozi in the acceptance of stolen gold bullion from the Nazis between 1939 and 1945, but "Switzerland . . . figured most prominently in ravaging Jewish resources . . . as the greatest plunderer of Nazi gold . . . the principal banker and financial broker for the Germans" (x). At the end of the war, Switzerland made a deal with the United States, Britain, and France, known as the Washington Accord, agreeing to pay $58.4 million of gold, in exchange for which the three Allied nations "would drop their post-war claim for the return of all gold received by

Switzerland from Germany during the war (namely some $400 million)"
(Sayer and Botting 1998, 341). Swiss banks were also still holding the so-
called dormant bank accounts of Holocaust victims.

This traumatic—but also lucrative—period for Swiss neutrality has
proved a recurrently embarrassing issue for the country, with its "wartime
role as bankers to the Nazis" (Jury 1997, 8) coming under increasing scrutiny,
culminating in a conference on the issue of the laundering of Nazi gold
in London in December 1997. Much of the Nazi gold that poured into
Switzerland during the war had been stolen from Jewish victims of Hitler's
death camps, and the Swiss were warned by the Allies that much of this was
illegally acquired, the spoils of plunder: "But Switzerland thought, and continues to think, that it had to trade with the Nazis as well as the Allies
because it was a neutral country" (8). This Swiss defense, of course, conveniently ignores the fact that as the war progressed there were no Allies
accessible with whom to trade. Surprised by the international furor over
the morality of its stance, Switzerland has suspended its bank secrecy laws
to help Holocaust victims, released large sums, and established two funds:
the Swiss Fund for Needy Victims of the Holocaust ($215 million) and the
Swiss Foundation for Solidarity ($5.5 billion). The first fund made its first
payments in December 1997 to Latvian survivors of the Holocaust. Its honorary chairman was Elie Wiesel, Nobel Peace Prize winner, Auschwitz survivor, and the man who adapted the word Holocaust (meaning a whole
burnt offering or sacrifice) to refer to the Nazi atrocity and genocide (Gow
1997). This was a sensitive diplomatic gesture by the Swiss to the international and Jewish constituencies. The second fund was aimed at making
annual awards to victims of catastrophe and poverty. At the same time as
recognizing a degree of responsibility in this area, the Swiss have remained
indignant at what they see as an unfair singling out of their relations with
the Nazis. Countries in Latin America and in Europe (Portugal, Sweden,
and Spain) are known to have also laundered Nazi assets and gold. But the
Swiss case lends itself to suspicion, its principle of neutrality looking like
self-serving amorality in the case of the country's relationship with Nazi
Germany. Other such issues have haunted the Swiss, its World War II labor
camps for Jews included (Watson-Smyth 1998, 3).

The problem for the country is that the ideal of tolerance and respect
for the other—if applied to the Nazis, for instance—can amount to a laissez-
faire and nonjudgmental amorality. Zurich has been home to exiles such as
Lenin and writers such as the Ulysses-drafting Joyce, but has also provided
the perfect basis for laundering $111 billion worth of Citibank bonds—Mafia
spoils from a New Jersey warehouse raid in the later 1980s (Honigsbaum
1997, 3). The dispersal of this loot, implicating not just the Italian Mafia but
also Swiss lawyers, Russian gangsters, mysterious Croatian militia, and even

the Vatican, has been traced to the base of Zurich antique dealer Pietro Zach, long under investigation by the Swiss police and the FBI but still able to enjoy boasting of his "fairy-tale pink castle in St Moritz . . . love of fast cars, beautiful women and fine champagne" (4), and, presumably, finding enough takers for what has been on offer from his global stings. It is the respect for privacy, banking secrecy, and claimed neutrality that can allow a figure like Zach—as well as rock stars such as David Bowie and Tina Turner—to prosper and flourish in Switzerland.

Moreover, the constant celebration of these core values can sound self-righteous, even smug. A literary historian can thus claim that Swiss literature, while representing the "different linguistic regions of the country," also shuns any taint of "immoralism." The Swiss "sense of civic-mindedness" produces a "guarantee of morality," even though limiting artistic freedom and lacking imagination (Calgari 1963, 5). Nevertheless, in many of the most prominent spheres of everyday life, comparative autonomy has been important. No ministry of education at the federal level has interfered with the educational policies of the different cantons, so that a national Concordat on School Coordination in 1970 offered no threat to the separate cantons' authority and depended on consultation with all citizens, resulting in an "extremely diversified" but harmoniously developed overall picture of educational policy throughout the confederation (Egger and Blanc 1974, 46, 47). The story of Jura separatism also sustains the view that policy developments and political conflicts be settled peacefully. The rugged topography of the Jura region had kept it almost exclusively French speaking for centuries, but from 1815 to 1978 Jura was part of the canton of Berne, known as Bernese Jura. In the 1978 referendum 41.5 percent of electors voted, and of these 82.3 percent favored the formation of the new canton. South Jura—59,000 people in fifty communes—voted for the status quo. Ancestry rather than religious affiliation was found to be the main influence on those choosing to vote for separatism (Jenkins 1986). It is striking that, unlike in the cases of Basque separatism or Irish republicanism, violence against human life played no part in the separatists' campaigning. Symbolic violence against objects was employed, but rarely in circumstances endangering human life.[2]

Local identity is clearly strongly felt in Switzerland, linguistic and cultural differences having quite as many excluding consequences as integrating effects. But the arguments made for the positive benefits of the Swiss system are that they benefit all subsections of the population, producing stable institutional structures. One analyst points to the strong family structure and low divorce rates—lower only in Western Europe's other most linguistically divided nation, Belgium, in 1979, and to the Swiss dedication to "goals of self-sufficiency and social responsibility"—in a society that concentrates its resources at the level of the community and has "little serious disorganization" (Segalman 1986, 190–91). Segalman also argues (196) that Switzerland can be seen as a model for the expression of Etzioni's communitarian values.[3] Interestingly, newcomers to the Swiss dream of citizenship and tolerance might tell another story. Community-based welfare organizations or churches have been traditionally unresponsive to immigrants, encouraging them to turn for help to official homeland organizations. But it appears that one immigrant response has been wholly within the spirit of Swiss values, that is, immigrants have "cultivated a regional identity (that is, as Fricelians, Sicilians, Andalusians and the like) that imposed less of a choice between Swiss and homeland identity" (Ireland 1994, 251). Such a choice, stressing locality and language, is entirely consistent with the idea, the polity, and diverse cultures of the Swiss model. In a sense, what has been called "tyrannical institutional arrangements," offering little support, drive the immigrants into a semblance of self-sufficiency, even though still barred from a full or equal sense of citizenship. This creates a desired form of assimilation, but based on exclusion, and neutralizes any threatening aspect of the newcomer (270).

The most specialized analysis on the nature and effects of Swiss multilingualism is contained in Macrae's (1983) work. He recognizes that the costs of varied languages, political tensions around these, and the need for conflict resolution can be high, "ranging from chronic alienation and intergroup hostility to serious political conflict, mass violence, secession or partition, and even civil or international war" (ix). The Swiss case is special, he notes, for the tradition of mediation established so early in its history, so that conflicts were usually resolved short of open hostilities (47). Nevertheless, economic inequalities can sometimes fuel minority sensitivities, and Macrae notes that the French Swiss—once prominent through the financial weight of Geneva—have come to feel a sense of "increasing comparative disadvantage" alongside the industrial strength of the German Swiss. These differences and inequalities remain despite the nature of Swiss development in the second half of the twentieth century, "the multiple, cross-cutting cleavage structure of the postwar period" (117) (clearly bolstered by the strength of the different language traditions), and the protection of the languages within the constitution. Three general rules protect and preserve this. First, based directly on article 116 of the revised constitution of 1874, an absolute equality of all Switzerland's languages is recognized.[4] Second, cantons are sovereign on language-related matters. And third and relatedly, cantons or linguistic areas can defend their own language against any external threat, the citizen having "to adjust to the linguistic milieu of the canton" (122). The two consequences of these rules, points out Macrae, are that the federal authorities must deal with the canton in the official language(s) of the canton, and the individual must deal with the canton in the canton's own language or bear the costs of translation. These consequences guarantee that the federal administration is defined in some of its major functions by the region and that entrants or newcomers to cantons or areas must communicate in the manner of the canton. This potentially subordinates the center and homogenizes the local. In such circumstances, a progressive democratic system can serve the most conservative of interests. Consequently, Macrae can observe that the socialist and catholic gymnastic and sports federations, the "two smaller, ideologically oriented, gymnastic and sports federations have maintained or even improved their relative position since the interwar period" (116). Again, the delineation of difference at the regional or local level can be claimed as the basis of common political affiliation at the central overarching political level.

One of the potential sources for the expression of this crucial unity-in-difference that is fundamental to the Swiss polity, society, and culture is the terrain of sport, both domestic and international. Sport within the country might be bound up with separate cultural legacies and traditions, while the international arena provides a forum for the expression of the nation itself, the political entity. Also, how might the Swiss principles of neutrality and negotiation have contributed to particular aspects of the international sporting scene? The country has a long experience of participation in international organizations, and even if the country has chosen at times not to join certain organizations, such as the United Nations and the European Union, the old League of Nations' buildings in Geneva were nevertheless made available for the United Nations.[5] As a basis for the exploration of these questions, the profile of Swiss sport internationally is reviewed, prior to consideration of broader sport and leisure patterns within the country. This provides a foundation for an informed and adequate understanding of the place and role of sport within the society.

SWISS SPORT: ITS INTERNATIONAL PROFILE

What, then, is Switzerland known for in international sport? A consideration of its achievements in the arenas of the world's two highest-profile sporting events—the Olympic Games and the football World Cup—provides an answer to this question. First, the Summer and Winter Olympics (see Wallechinsky 1993, 1996, for medal details). With its ideal location at the heart of the European Alps, Switzerland has produced champions regularly in the Winter Olympics, in particular from 1936 onward, once Alpine skiing was accepted in the program of the Winter Olympics, so undermining Nordic domination of the discipline. Particularly notable performances were in the games of St. Moritz (1948, ten medals, third position), Cortina d'Ampezzo (1956, six medals, fourth position), Sapporo (1976, ten medals, third position), and Calgary (1988, fifteen medals, third position). Such achievement and performance at elite level has been achieved in specialist individual sports or small-team sports: two-man and four-man bobsled and the subdisciplines of Alpine skiing, in later years more by men than by women. Medals in the Summer Olympics have been harder to come by, particularly since the competitive world of the Olympics became more specialized and professionalized. In the second modern Olympics in Paris in 1900, Switzerland was fourth in the medals table, with eight medals, and sixth place was secured in 1906 (Athens, fifteen medals), 1924 (Paris, twenty-five medals), and 1928 (Amsterdam, fifteen medals). A ninth position was attained at the 1948 relaunch of the Games after World War II (London, twenty medals), but since then—apart from a blip in 1984, when four gold and four bronze medals were won at the Soviet/Communist–boycotted Los Angeles Olympics—the spasmodic Swiss achievements have been based more on random individual triumphs than on systematic strategies. For instance, the Barcelona gold for men's tennis was won by Marc Rossett, ranked only forty-fourth in the world, in a five-hour match against Spain's third-ranked player, Catalan Jordi Arresse from Barcelona. Top seeds had tumbled early, beaten by the "brutal heat, the slow clay surface, and the patriotic emotions of their unheralded opponents" (Wallechinsky 1996, 692). Rossett seized his chance, annihilating South African ninth-seeded Wayne Ferreira in straight sets, and confirming his giant-killing intent with a 6–4, 6–2, 6–1 demolition of first-seeded Jim Courier of the United States. Rossett sprang from nowhere and won as an outsider.

Swiss achievements in both the Summer and the Winter Games were based on a combination of influences. Its excellence in specialist sports that thrived in the country's alpine environment (winter sports and cycling) was bolstered by inherent forms of commercialized professionalism. This generated a sort of topographic determinism so that, as journalist Martin Putter has noted, until the 1980s and 1990s "it was unthinkable that successful skiers would come from outside the Alpine regions (i.e the lowlands and the 'Jura')."[6] Competence in amateur sports in the earlier phases of Olympic history produced creditable performances and sometimes fairly high rankings, especially when highly competitive nations such as Soviet Union–influenced Eastern European countries did not yet compete or when those such as Germany were excluded from the Olympics after their defeats in world wars. Otherwise, forms of support could be targeted toward dedicated individuals, home-born or imported, the latter case exemplified in the late 1990s tennis prodigy, Czechoslovakia-born Martina Hingis (her first name a tribute by Hingis's tennis-mad parents to the Czech-American tennis champion Martina Navratilova). There is little evidence of coherent sports development programs aimed at the production of future champions and, though champions have been respected, they are far from idolized or transformed into national heroes. In the first decade of the twenty-first century young tennis player Roger Federer was poised to challenge the world's top players, but without the pressure that a Tim Henman faced regularly from his expectant British public; Federer became Wimbledon 2003 men's singles champion.

Football in Switzerland has a long history.[7] The country was one of the founder members of the world governing body, FIFA, in 1904, and the Swiss Football Association, founded in 1895, is one of the oldest associations in mainland Europe. Internationally, Swiss sides have not been in the top grade, although in 1924 its silver-medal winning side held the champion Uruguay to 3–0 in the Olympic final in Paris; and, in predominantly European fields, in 1934 and 1938 World Cups in France and Italy respectively, the national sides progressed as far as the quarterfinals; as hosts, too, in 1954, the Swiss reached that stage again, going down 7–5 to Austria. Outstanding performances seem to have been followed by anticlimactic dips in performance, as in the United States in 1994 when, after beating the highly fancied Romanian side 4–1, the Swiss lost 3–0 to Spain in the second stage.

Early British influence on football in Switzerland is evident from the names of its pioneer clubs—Grasshoppers of Zurich and Young Boys of Berne, for instance. But it has been argued, by Lanfranchi (1998), that the origins of the game in Switzerland were not just a local affair, and that in the process of the diffusion of football throughout Europe "the Swiss played a role which was essential and which is too often neglected." German Swiss, Britons, Austrians, and Italians mixed in early Swiss football clubs in Geneva, and Swiss involvement in international commerce influenced football development in other European countries such as Spain and France. Swiss technical colleges of the 1880s welcomed students from abroad to study engineering, technology, and international banking. Football was in many cases part of their wider cultural education and was one asset with which they returned home on completion of their training. The founders (in 1900) of the French Mediterranean club, Olympique de Sete, first encountered football during their technical training in Geneva, as did Henry Monnier, a young banker who in 1901 established the Nimes football club. The most renowned of such "Swiss footballer technicians" was Vittorio Pozzo. Initiated into football during his period of study at technical institutes in Winterthur and Zurich, where in 1908 he obtained a diploma in languages and commercial techniques, Pozzo went on, thirty years later, to guide Italy to its two World Cup triumphs of the interwar period. Lanfranchi lists a number of reasons for this Swiss influence. First, Switzerland favored English middle-class sports in the athleticist character-building model, rather than popular and paramilitary gymnastics, more so than was the case in any other European country, and Swiss private schools adopted English sports, as well as climbing and rambling, as early as the 1860s. The Swiss Alpine

Club was formed in 1863, a mere six years after the English original, and football was offered and played in La Chatelaine School in Geneva as early as 1869. Boarding schools established their own sports fields.

Beyond Switzerland itself, the Internazionale club derived its name from the large number of Swiss players on its team. Bari, also in Italy, was founded in 1908 by a Swiss flour and cereal merchant, Gustav Kuhn, along with German, French, Swiss, Spanish, and Italian friends. In Naples, Swiss and English international businessmen formed the city's first football teams. In Marseille, the Stade Helvetique (Swiss), three-times national champions between 1909 and 1913, was created at the same time as a Swiss commercial circle. These Swiss internationalists, argues Lanfranchi, expressed in their commitment to football a strongly felt Anglophilia, the "perfect expression of their conception of modernity." The rational use of spare time that the games of the British elite represented was consonant with the central tenets, in Zurich liberalism, of the interconnectedness of money and spirit. The Swiss promoted and facilitated the game widely and in varied roles: "In 1912, even, a match between Barcelona FC and the English team Auckland Wanderers was refereed by a Swiss pastor" (Lanfranchi 1998). The sporting sphere could here be seen as part of a wider religious mission and suited central Protestant values especially. In Switzerland itself sports associations were promoted more in the Protestant community. Lanfranchi describes a sporting culture of a cosmopolitan kind, taking as its inspiration the British team games and the amateur ethos associated with them. This was not to last. A distancing from the British fair-play model was apparent in the years after World War I, and in 1920, for the first time, the Swiss Football Association was obliged to take up positions: "If the German-Swiss clubs supported a match with the German national side, the Romand-Swiss clubs were unflinchingly opposed." Away from Switzerland, Swiss merchants and businessmen had used football as a uniting force for the international business elite. Back home in Switzerland, football became a focus for an everyday politics of cultural identity. It has been claimed by commentators and fans that the Swiss national side, or the country's top sides when engaging in European competition, underachieve because of language-cultural schisms in the locker room. Such views were expressed to account for the Swiss national side's decline in form and deteriorating results at the end of its qualifying match schedule for the 2004 European championship in Portugal, though by then an efficient and well-organized Swiss quad had already qualified comfortably for the finals.

The origins of organized sport within Switzerland were characterized by an early prominence of the German gymnastics movement and a later adoption of the English model of games and sport. English upper-class hedonists exported their games ethic to the slopes of the Swiss Alps. Arnold

Lunn, sports enthusiast and travel entrepreneur for the English elite, founded the Public Schools Alpine Sports Club in 1902, organized downhill race events, and established an enclave for privileged socialites and amateurs at Murren in 1912. He organized the British Ski Championship in 1921, the first-ever downhill national championship, a full nine years before the Swiss started their own (Holt 1992). Such figures in the heyday of derring-do athleticism found many sympathetic and empathetic responses among the embryonic Swiss sporting elite. Not all observers shared Lunn's enthusiasm for opening up the Alps. The German sociologist Simmel, writing in 1895, saw the access granted by new transport systems generative of "an average sensibility." He cited Murren as one such place where "higher and finer values" would be depressed, "without elevating those at the base to the same degree" (Simmel 1991, 95). Simmel would have approved of Lunn's and his compatriots' social and cultural exclusivity but not of their rah-rah cheerfulness and life-threatening risk-taking on the slopes. The nationalistic militarism of the Swiss model of the German gymnastics movement would overlap more fully with this Anglo-British games ethic, though early tensions between them displayed the schisms that could arise in the sphere of popular culture and sport.

If Switzerland has not been hugely prominent in the international sporting scene, it has drawn on its traditions of neutrality and international diplomacy in welcoming to its lakeland shores international sports organizations such as the IOC (in Lausanne), FIFA (in Zurich), and UEFA, formerly in Berne and now in Nyon, on the edge of Lake Geneva and a short commute from Geneva itself. All these organizations originated in Paris, but were soon drawn—the idealist rhetoric of de Coubertin and his like notwithstanding—to the advantages offered by the Swiss to international, nongovernmental organizations functioning as offshore companies with wide international or global remits. It was the Gnomes of Zurich and their encouragement of sport's new commercial barons who were confirming the suitability of Switzerland as a site for such international organizations, a site conducive to those organizations for reasons far removed from the sport culture of the nation itself.[8]

Sport and Leisure Cultures in Modern Switzerland

Regardless of its relatively limited international impact in sport, Switzerland has been described as "one of the most fully organized countries with respect to sport" (Stamm and Lamprecht 1996b, 1). It has approximately one sports club for every 250 members of the population and around 100 national and international sports organizations; about a quarter to a third of the Swiss population is estimated to be actively involved in a sports club. Tennis, squash, hiking, jogging, and skiing may have taken place in other less formal organizational settings, but the most influential strand in the development of Swiss sport has remained the club-based organization.

As in the case of Germany (Merkel 1999, 144–46), the gymnastic activity of Turnen was prominent in the nineteenth century, the first clubs being founded in Germany in 1819 and in Zurich in 1820. These clubs were formed by fugitives from Germany, where the egalitarian, democratic, and progressive values of the Turnbewegung had led to the movement being banned in 1819. Three points favored their growth. First, liberal strands in the Swiss polity saw the clubs as models of desirable democratic organization. Second, the Swiss movement saw itself as integrated to the social order, promoting military skills and citizenship. Third, the movement linked with a folk games revival. The Swiss Rifle Association, founded in 1824, also emphasized military skills and Swiss independence. In 1874, sport policy was formally located in the federal military department, where it stayed until 1983, when responsibility for sport was shifted to the department of the interior. Only seven other sport associations were established before the end of the nineteenth century, the Alpine Club being the first of these, and cycling, rowing, soccer, and tennis becoming well established. All these were for middle- and upper-class men, many of whom would also have received compulsory gymnastics at school since this was inaugurated in the revised federal constitution of 1874. Women were for a long time excluded. The women's gymnastic association was not founded until 1920, and though some women participated in gymnastics, cycling, and hiking, it was not until 1972 that the provision of physical education for girls was formally included in the constitution.

Whatever the vicissitudes in popularity or profile of a particular sport, and the more individual and commercial settings in which sport is played, the sports clubs have retained an important place in the wider sport culture. Stamm and Lamprecht account for this well, in terms of the framing features of Swiss culture and polity:

> The large number of different sports clubs and sport-related clubs is indicative of a well-known feature of Swiss culture — namely Switzerland's high density of any kind of clubs. With some irony it is sometimes said that wherever three or more people meet regularly in Switzerland, they establish a club. As a consequence there exists a wide variety of clubs encompassing such diverse activities as music, pet care, stamp collecting, sports or political activities. Against this background it is not surprising that most Swiss are members in at least one or two clubs.
>
> Clubs in Switzerland are much more than regular gatherings of people with common interests, however. The term club refers to a specific legal construction that acts as a juridical person and is able to enter contracts etc. in its own right. The Swiss civil code specifies several prerequisites for clubs to attain

their legal status. Each club needs written statutes that spell out
its goals, means and organizational structure. By law clubs are
democratic non-profit organizations whose highest authority is
the meeting of all members which votes on important club matters,
fixes membership dues, considers new members and elects the
president and other executive charges which act as official
representatives of the club. (Stamm and Lamprecht 1996a, 9)

Clubs also rely extensively on volunteer labor, which is an economic imperative but also has roots in the values of sport and leisure as special spheres in which involvement and action are based in solidarity and enjoyment.

Beyond these broad and common institutional features of the sports club, the historical legacy of the gymnastic and rifle clubs was political, ideological, and integrative, with competition relatively marginal; new clubs based on an English model prioritized competition and modernity. Although it has been claimed that the politically conservative gymnastic and rifle clubs — *Vereine* — prevailed in the German-speaking regions, and the modern clubs — *Klubs* — were stronger in French and Italian parts of the country, the regional distribution of the 28,000 clubs of both types matches the distribution of the population: "three quarters of the clubs [are] in the German speaking part, about a fifth in the French speaking part and the remainder in the Italian speaking part. Thus there is no clear preference of the German speaking population for organized sport" (Stamm and Lamprecht 1996a, 10; see, too, Schlagenhauf and Schiffer 1976). Nevertheless, sports clubs of whatever sort would certainly be identified by separate language traditions. Traditional clubs are only slightly stronger in the German-speaking regions then, but traditional and folk sports vary in the different language regions. German Swiss play tug-of-war, the folk game *Hornussen,* and handball and wrestle, whereas *pétanque, boules,* and *boccia* are restricted to the other two main language communities. French Swiss are comparatively more involved in basketball, waterskiing, weight lifting, and boxing; Italian speakers in basketball, soccer, and ice hockey. The largest clubs have remained the rifle and gymnastic associations (Bose et al. 1994). One hour's shooting a year is prescribed for men under forty able to do military service and is organized by local rifle clubs in which eligible males had to be compulsory members up until 1996, thus obviously inflating their membership figures. But it is the gymnastics movement—with almost a third of a million active members — that has remained the strongest organized sport in Switzerland: "Apart from its long tradition and deep roots in Swiss popular culture, the success of the gymnastic movement in terms of membership figures certainly also relates to its ability to integrate people beyond the sphere of 'pure' sports into a more encompassing social club" (Stamm and Lamprecht 1996b, 12).

Beyond the formal framework of the club, activities such as hiking, cycling, swimming, and skiing are the most popular. Participation rates, expressed as the percentage of the population regularly participating in the activity in 1994 (Stamm and Lamprecht 1996b, 13) are highest in the outdoor sports—hiking, 31 percent; swimming or water gymnastics, 29 percent; cycling or mountain biking, 29 percent; and downhill skiing, 28 percent. Rates are nowhere near as high for any other activity, with only three others engaging more than 10 percent of the population—fitness training or body building, 14 percent; jogging, 16 percent; and gymnastics or jazz dance, 18 percent. Tennis (10 percent) and soccer (9 percent) have the next highest participation rates. Seven percent participate in cross-country skiing or tours and do fitness trails. Six percent play basketball or streetball and table tennis. Badminton and volleyball or beach volleyball attract rates of 5 percent. Though analyses of the Swiss situation might suggest "a high degree of freedom in the choice of general leisure activities" (Stamm and Lamprecht 1995, 235), evidence also indicates that "leisure remains closely linked to the overarching social order . . . embedded in different spheres of life."

The size of club memberships varies widely, with golf clubs and alpine clubs having large mean memberships of around eight hundred and five hundred respectively; tennis and field hockey clubs, around two hundred; shooting, soccer, ice skating, swimming, and skiing, one hundred or so; and snow biking, cycling, weight lifting, boxing, motor sports, and bobsled clubs, an active average membership of under ten people. The only sport associations in which female members form the majority are ice and roller skating, volleyball, dancing, and two gymnastic associations. Women comprise a third or more of the membership in another nine sports, including sport for disabled people, snowboarding, the academic sport association, another gymnastic association, golf, badminton, horse riding, and squash. Male preserves are shooting, ice hockey, football, and cycling (Stamm and Lamprecht 1996b, 14; and Lamprecht and Stamm 1996). Organized club-based sports are less conducive to women's participation than are informally generated forms of involvement. So even though frequency of involvement may to some extent have been leveling out between men and women, types of activity and involvement have continued to reflect gendered differences: "A closer examination of the *patterns* [my emphasis] of sport involvement shows that the traditional field of competitive, physically demanding, and club-organized sport remains the preserve of younger men" (Lamprecht and Stamm 1996, 284).

Although an expanding infrastructure for Swiss sport can be identified (Bulletin of Sports Information 1991), Switzerland has no official sports policy, and there is no federal-level department with responsibility for sport: "Formal independence from political intervention is not only an important feature of organized sport in Switzerland but also applies to other segments of sports." A federal agency—the Federal Sports Commission—coordinates physical education and youth sport policies, and the educational and communications center at Macolin acts as a federal sports school and an executive body to the federal agency.[9] It is at the regional level, within the cantons, that sport departments dispense budgets to support a coordinating function and at which proceeds from the national sports lottery are allocated and distributed. The most important providers are the towns and villages that provide for primary school sport and can rent out facilities, at generously low prices, to independent sports clubs. Across the sports sphere, the Swiss respect for intrasocietal independence is translated into a pluralist scenario of self-organization and respect for difference—but one which for obvious reasons might favor tradition and existing inequalities as well as cultural difference and diverse cultural practices and identities.

Some newer and more fashionable sports have challenged traditional practices and structures, and Stamm and Lamprecht (1996b) note that the gymnastics clubs have failed to adapt, leaving activities such as aerobics out of their programs and looking staid and out of touch alongside commercial fitness centers that are open all hours and boast high-tech facilities and scientific fitness programs.

Lamprecht and Stamm conclude that traditional norms continue to affect forms of age and gender-based participation in sports; that where women and older people are participating more, it is in areas that organized forms of male-dominated sports do not consider to be "'serious' sports"; and that if broadening forms of participation in sport can be seen as contributing to a process of democratization of sport, persisting forms of differentiation in sports lead in an "opposite direction" (Lamprecht and Stamm 1996, 284–85). "Expansion" and apparent "inclusion" therefore lie alongside a process of "differentiation and pluralisation," generating outcomes that shore up traditional divisions and inequalities in Swiss society and culture (Lamprecht and Stamm 1995).

Everyday Leisure and Consumption in Switzerland

The variations in types and structure of clubs and sports involvement may not be as wide as often supposed, but at the turn of the last decade of the twentieth century a large-scale national survey could still identify variations in cultural practice on the basis of geographical and linguistic influence.[10] Sporting items in newspapers and on television rank as almost as important in the weekly free-time schedule of the population as radio music programs, movies on television, and light entertainment television programs. Sports clubs and gymnastics clubs were the types of clubs with the most members, "more or less 10 percent of the population." Almost half of the people interviewed considered that such societies were important social elements in their place of residence, citing especially gymnastic and sports clubs, associations for the protection of nature, orchestras, or singing clubs/choirs. One in three of respondents saw pedestrian walkways, cycle routes, and sporting facilities as important in their localities. The general participation figures indicate that for physical exercise offering a break from daily routine—such as walking outings, sport, even do-it-yourself—there is minimal variation among the different groups of the population.

Nevertheless, detailed figures do indicate some variations that draw on cultural tradition. German speakers engaged in more do-it-yourself, use of musical instruments, reading of political journals, and intensive watching of television game shows and soap operas than French-speaking respondents. German speakers went out drinking less and took more walks, picnics, and excursions, though taking part in only half as many organized programs. Big local events such as festivals or sports meetings were attended in greater numbers by French and Italian speakers than Germans. The same was true of village, neighborhood, and society fetes, though German speakers were more likely to be found in orchestras and carnival events.

What is interesting in such variations is the cultural or linguistic and religion-influenced legacy, of a kind of German Protestant worthiness in everyday life, and a more hedonistic and communal public culture among the French- and Italian-speaking, predominantly Catholic, communities. It is likely therefore that though broad participation figures might suggest few or only small differences in participation, the mode of participation and the meaning of the activity may, in many cases, reflect the separate linguistic and cultural tradition.

Sport and the Social Order in Switzerland

The task in this chapter has been to explicate the nature of the Swiss polity and culture and of accepted and respected divisions within the society and to consider sport's place in the Swiss scheme of things. While there are histories of pedagogic, traditional, and international sports organizations and initiatives in Switzerland, these have usually had little to say about the wider values of Swiss society and culture.[11] It has been emphasized in this chapter that any consideration of sport apart from a fuller appreciation of Swiss values and prevailing ideologies would be a futile task, for clear historical and cultural reasons. Where does sport lie in the linguistically divided society of Switzerland?

While sport might appear to be of relatively minor significance in the constitution of Swiss national, regional, and cultural identity, it is more important than first meets the eye. The history of its oldest organized ideological sports clubs, blended with some appropriation of a folkloric essence, imbues Swiss cultural history with a longevity and a national robustnness

that bolsters its centuries-old tradition of political autonomy, cultural separatism, and international neutrality. Maguire has observed acutely how
"ultra-modern Switzerland" or at least "sections of Swiss society" have used
traditional forms of wrestling and cross-country running (carrying weapons)
"to reaffirm a specific tradition, habitus and identity" (1999, 88). Despite
swings toward "the global sports formation," as Maguire terms it, traditional sports persist in their cultural significance. In Swiss society, types of
clubs may be more evenly distributed across the separate language communities than some theorists of division care to admit, but mode of participation and the meaning of sports as a cultural practice continue to express the
distinct values of the different constituencies. The deep-rootedness of the
regional and local cultures is also such that symbolic and fanatical expressions of national identity seem deeply un-Swiss. Swiss national identity
itself is, no more and no less, the multiculturalism of the regions and the
politics of consensus. It seems entirely fitting that most national Swiss sports
champions are rewarded for their individual labors on the tennis court, the
ski slope, or the bike saddle or in small teams of enthusiastic experts such
as the bobsled champions. Switzerland is a managed diversity too in its
community and recreational sports. That such difference can be controlled
and administered harmoniously is explained by the constantly reaffirmed
principle of social closure, as explicated by Weber. For the language and
area-based subpopulations of Switzerland are defined and respected status
groups, language being "the common characteristic shared by many people" (Weber 1978, 48). Although Weber could observe, with irony, that his
concept could be applied to a "pure" form of modern "democratic" society,
in "some of the smaller Swiss cities," where "only families belonging to
broadly similar taxation groups dance with each other" (49), it is his notion
of social closure that more generally illuminates the Swiss situation. Parkin
(1974, 3) expands:

> Weber means the process by which social collectivities seek
> to maximize rewards by restricting access to rewards and
> opportunities to a limited circle of eligibles. This entails the
> singling out of certain identifiable social or physical attributes as
> the justificatory basis of exclusion. Weber suggests that virtually
> any group attribute—race, language, social origin, descent—may
> be seized upon provided it can be used for "the monopolization of
> specific, usually economic opportunities."

This is critical. For inherent to this dynamic of closure and exclusion is the
potential for exploitation and, certainly, a lust for tradition. In Switzerland,
it is this dynamic with all its potential outcomes that is central to the pluralist political constitution. Difference is not merely tolerated but encouraged.

Homogeneity at the national level is, concomitantly, unwanted and discouraged. Culturally varied and modern individualist bourgeois sports and physical activities as well as traditionally conservative *Turnen*-based gymnastic clubs and English team games all fit into the Swiss pluralist jigsaw. It will never, of course, be as plain sailing on the inside as it might seem from the perspective of history and an analytical exterior. Pick up a paper in Switzerland and the traveler will soon see that. The *Geneva Post* reported in May 1996 on a proposal to introduce bilingualism in primary education in the canton of Geneva and raised the question of whether such a second language should be English (the language of global communication) or German. This was front page news:

> The motion comes at a time when the linguistic division of Switzerland is today more than ever straining relations between the Swiss Romande and the German-speaking part of the country. That division has been aggravated by Zurich's economic weight and its ties with Germany, while international Geneva is said to be more of a dollar rather than Deutschemark-oriented area. (*Geneva Post* [English language], no. 10, May 23–29, 1996, 1)

No doubt the tradition-steeped German-speaking gymnastic clubs will seem quaint and amusing to more cosmopolitan consumers. But such tensions stand as continuing testimony to the harmony of the wider entity. In the case of sports clubs of any kind, a respect for their differences, for their forms of closure and exclusion, can be both separatist and uniting. That is the paradox at the heart of the Swiss trick. It might not cheer you up if you are a French-speaking Swiss on the eve of a national referendum, knowing that if the German-speaking Swiss all turn out and unite on an issue then you might as well stay at home. But in the Swiss case, the contribution of sport is not to generate and promote social division; rather, it is to celebrate cultural diversity. At local, regional, and national levels sport is one of the cultural forms that expresses and symbolizes an authentically felt social harmony and unity in difference. Difference and diversity do not, in this sense, constitute division.

The IOC has, in the shams and hypocrisies of later leaders, distorted the early Olympic ideals of de Coubertin, and its apologists extorted the Olympics for personal aggrandizement and corporate profit (Jennings 1996; Tomlinson, 2000b; Jennings and Sambrook, 2000). While claiming to speak for the interests of the youth of the world and the peaceful interaction of nations and peoples, the long-term IOC president Juan Antonio Samaranch, veteran of Spanish and Catalan politics in the Franco era, could still massage his biography as late as November 1999 by listing the qualities and achievements of Franco in modernizing Spanish society, keeping it out of the two great wars of the century and easing the transition to a democracy and a monarchy (BBC World Service 1999). But whatever the likes of Samaranch have done, in his case blending his own brand of Swiss ideals with his fascist pedigree, de Coubertin was right to see Swiss neutrality and stability as preferable to the barbarism produced by jingoistic nationalism. It was prescient of the French zealot to see in sport a distinctive potential, if not inherent capacity, to harmonize cultural dissonance. Juan Antonio Samaranch and his successors, using sport for their own ends in the Swiss context, would do well to reconsider their own positions in the light of such ideals. In doing so, they might contribute to the more positive side of the Swiss legacy in politics and culture and so enhance both the tarnished image of international sport and the sullied reputation of the Swiss polity.

5. Stateside Football
The Men's World Cup USA 1994 and Its Legacy

The 1994 World Cup produced a turnover of $4 billion with 32
billion television viewers. I mean no disrespect to other sports by
saying that even the Olympic Games cannot compare. The World
Cup was a fabulous success.
—JOSEPH "SEPP" BLATTER (1994), FIFA general secretary

In June and July 1994 the major event in television sports across the world
was the football World Cup, the world championship of football, as the
host nation of that year preferred to call it. Yet in the United States itself
there was much skepticism about this event, for the United States had
never embraced football as a major competitive, spectator-based, and high-
performance sport. Alongside baseball, American football, and basketball
(the big three)—and the claimant to entry into a big four, ice hockey—football, the world's most popular sport, has looked unquestionably minor league.
And yet at the World Cup finals of 1994 ticket sales exceeded those of any
previous World Cup, the games were widely recognized as splendidly enter-
taining, and television recording and reproduction techniques guaranteed
high-quality coverage of and feedback on almost any aspect of the game, its
players, and the tournament. How was this possible? And what has been
the impact of the successful staging of the tournament on sport culture in
the United States? And on football itself?

The answers to these questions have far-reaching implications for
an understanding and theorization of contemporary sport, bearing as they
do on the issue of globalization. Debate in sociology and associated social
sciences and within the sociology of sport itself has highlighted the importance of globalization as a central contemporary social process. Robertson
has argued that a historical, comparative, and interdisciplinary social science
framework can be developed if social theory is "refocused and expanded so
as to make concern with 'the world' a central hermeneutic, and in such a
way as to constrain empirical and comparative-historical research in the

same direction" (R. Robertson 1990, 19); for Robertson, the concept "should be applied to a particular series of developments concerning the *concrete structuration of the world as a whole*" (20), and with "the question of the actual form of recent and contemporary moves in the direction of global interdependence and global consciousness" (22). With these concerns and questions in mind, Robertson offers "in unavoidably skeletal terms" a fivefold classification of "the temporal-historical path to the present circumstance of a very high degree of *global density and complexity* . . ." (26). Early "germinal" and "incipient" phases are followed by a third phase that Robertson labels the "take-off phase," covering the last quarter of the nineteenth and the first quarter of the twentieth centuries. In this phase, instances of international communication and international relations escalate, and global competitions are developed—"e.g. Olympics, Nobel Prizes" (27). The governing body of world football is also established at this time (Tomlinson 1986, 1994), and the first World Cup (expressing many tensions between the established elites of the Western European world and the emergent football-playing powers of the Americas) is staged in 1930 in Uruguay, as described earlier in chapter 3. Such tensions embody the core characteristics of Robertson's fourth phase, which he calls a "struggle for hegemony," running from the 1920s through the mid-1960s. The final phase in his model is one of "uncertainty," with intensifying forms of global consciousness achieved in a "consolidation of global media system[s]," alongside an increase for many societies in "problems of multiculturality and polyethnicity." It is interesting that Robertson specifies the Olympic Games as evidence of early forms of globalization. Clearly, the features and dynamics of supranational sporting organizations and events revealed some of the core characteristics of globalization processes. Houlihan observes that "while the World Cup has been free of overt politics by comparison to the Olympic Games it has not been able to avoid the intrusion of politics completely" (1994b, 27). Indeed, the World Cup and the worldwide development of football by FIFA and those social actors and human agents within and associated with FIFA can be seen as a revealing source for the study of globally resonating cultural politics. Some trends within globalization embody the aspirations and ambitions of particular individuals; some forms of concrete structuration can be identified as the projects of networks and alliances of powerful individuals. A comprehensive grasp of trends in the globalization process must recognize this. Analysis of the context and nature of such processes and cultural phenomena can provide a rich dividend not just for a specialist sociology of sport but also for social theory more generally.

Harvey, Rail, and Thibault have listed Americanization, mundialization, and modernization as terms that are sometimes conflated with globalization and note, too, that such "conceptual clutter has led to theoretical confusion" (1996, 1). On the basis of their readings of social theorists such as Robertson, Anthony Giddens, and others, they propose that "the most important point about globalization is the fact that it is characterized by tendencies and processes that take place beyond the reality of nation-states" (1996, 2) and that the extent of the globalization of the world is "still open to debate" (3). An analysis of the impact of the premier tournament of the world's most popular game upon the sport culture of the United States can contribute to an understanding of some prominent "tendencies and processes" of globalization and of the extent of their impact on global and national sport cultures.

Globally framed historical scholarship has also noted the importance and distinctiveness of sport, in its complex relationship to political domination and cultural standardization. In his survey of "The Arts, 1914–1945" Hobsbawm asserts that in "the field of popular culture the world was American or it was provincial," but with one exception: "The unique exception was sport" (Hobsbawm 1995, 198). He recognizes football as a "genuinely international" sport: "The sport the world made its own was association football, the child of Britain's global economic presence. . . . This simple and elegant game, unhampered by complex rules and equipment, and which could be practised on any more or less flat open space of the required size, made its way through the world entirely on its merits" (198). But not in the United States. A study of the impact of the World Cup when it did give elite football its highest-ever profile within the United States will illuminate the extent and nature of sport's contribution to tendencies and processes of globalization.

More specifically, it is clear that some sports organizations operating on the supranational level constitute forms of transnational practice that have little if any accountability, except to themselves—certainly the International Olympic Committee is such a body, as most trenchantly shown by Simson and Jennings (1992). FIFA, the world governing body of football, is another such body, and its decision to place the 1994 World Cup in the United States was its decision alone. Evaluating the outcome of this decision contributes to what Sklair has summarized as the "transnational relations" approach: "an injunction to researchers to pay more attention to non-governmental entities" (Sklair 1991, 3) and to Sklair's own particular project, "a conception of the global system based on *transnational practices*" (6). From the basis of a blend of social history, critical sociology, and cultural analysis, and in the light of theoretical concerns with the nature of transnational practices in sport and their contribution to globalization processes, this chapter evaluates the genesis, impact, and legacy of one of the world's highest-profile sports events. In this context, the Markovits (1990), Sugden (1994), and Sugden and Tomlinson (1994b) theses on the marginality of football in the sports space of the United States are reviewed in the light of the profile and impact of World Cup USA 1994.

METHODS

In constructing the case study of USA 1994, I have adopted a multimethod approach, the analysis drawing on a range of sources. These include secondary sources such as established survey databases, media representations of sport and football, archival sources on the political economy of world sport, insider and cultural commentaries on the nature of the event, and forms of participant observation for one week at the beginning of the finals and a second week at the culmination of the event. Time was spent going to games, talking to fans of many nationalities, and gathering sources and materials as the finals tournament unfolded. One week was spent on the East Coast of the United States, immediately prior to and after the opening of the World Cup finals. This included time among immigrant Irish and American Irish fans in Rhode Island; with sports academics and football cognoscenti in New Haven, Connecticut; and with immigrant Irish fans in Manhattan. In particular, in Manhattan, football games were viewed in two typical Irish American sports bars across the first full weekend of the finals tournament. Throughout the tournament, responses to the event were reviewed in both the general print media and specialist magazines and the television coverage of games monitored in both the United States and the United Kingdom. Over the last days of the tournament, participant observation was conducted in Los Angeles, Pasadena, and Santa Monica; both the World Cup final and the playoff game for third place were attended.

Further materials were gathered, after the event, from specialist sources and archives in the Paul Ziegler Resource Center at the Amateur Athletic Foundation of Los Angeles, pertaining to the economics of the event, networks of sports entrepreneurs in California, the media impact of USA 1994, and the nature of sponsorship of football in the United States. The range of methods used in this analysis is not justified on the basis of any model of triangulation, as multimethod approaches have been by methodologists such as Smith (1975, 271–92). Rather, the multimethods approach employed here embodies a commitment to a critical investigative sociology (Douglas 1976; Sugden 1997; Sugden and Tomlinson 1995b, 1999c) informed by an openness to the pertinence of sociologically relevant, if at times sociologically unorthodox, sources (Tomlinson 1984a). Such an approach can be controversial, as Hammersley and Atkinson, in an annotated bibliographic comment on Douglas, note (1983, 240), adjudicating Douglas to be cavalier in his "treatment of philosophical issues" (240). But in work on the past where the sensitivities of the present are no threat, the use of such a range of methods is commonplace; in critical social history, the scholar must utilize and interpret what is available and accessible. The analysis presented in this chapter constitutes a form of critical social history of the present, in which no faith is placed in the superiority of one method or another or in the foolproofness of pseudoautonomous methods whose internal validity is presumed to guarantee the reliability of some shared finding. Critical sociological work at times depends on following leads, rather than implementing ready-made methods or techniques, and on making connections between fragments of information, the relevance of which will not always be clear at the outset of the investigation. For the following analysis, a range of conventional and nonconventional sources is drawn on within this investigative and critical framework.

Prior to the analysis itself, the main arguments concerning football and U.S. sport culture are reviewed, with particular emphasis on the concept of sports space.

FOOTBALL IN U.S. SPORTS SPACE

Classic sources on the history and sociology of American sports have paid little heed to the story of football in the United States, though enthusiasts for the game have sought to remedy this. Foulds and Harris (1979) retrieve some of this ignored if not hidden history and report that the American League of Professional Football Clubs opened its season on October 6, 1894. An early blend of professional and amateur players in Boston were from the textile communities of the region, players emerging from "large, immigrant football-educated populations" (13). Only six years after the formation of the professional Football League in England, teams such as the Boston Beaneaters, the Brooklyn Superbas, the Washington Senators, and the New York Giants were competing (under the name "football") in football matches. Despite optimistic reception in some quarters of the press, matches staged on weekday afternoons failed to capture a large following. As Foulds and Harris put it, "the failure of the promoters to realize that the basic support in the initial stages of the league rested with the large football addicted foreign-born blue collar working population of the Eastern industrial states was unfortunate" (13). Despite evidence of subcultural popularity—among Jewish communities and teams in the New York area, for instance, in the 1920s (Murray 1994, 262)—attempts to introduce high-profile professional football remained short-lived, if initially successful, or merely marginal (265–72). As Markovits and Sugden have demonstrated, the historical, social, and cultural odds were stacked against football becoming a mainstream professional sport in the United States.

For Markovits, a European-raised intellectual, sports fan, and football aficionado, the lack of American response to football World Cups (particularly when the finals took place in a contiguous neighboring country) has been intriguing. He noted that when the 1986 World Cup finals were hosted by Mexico in 1986, "this event failed to capture the imagination of the American public," and he described the American interest in "the world's most important media event" as "strikingly minute in comparison to that exhibited in virtually every country in the world" (Markovits 1988, 125). His explanation for the failure of football to gain a hold in U.S. sport culture revolves around a notion of sports space and the argument that in the formative period of U.S. nation-building three vigorously characteristic American sports took shape—baseball, American football, and basketball. This had the consequence that "America's bourgeois hegemony and legacy of the 'first new nation' . . . contributed substantially to the continued absence of the world's most popular team sport as a major presence in American popular culture" (125). The sports space, Markovits eloquently and convincingly argues, was occupied early in the United States, so that a fully matured form of association football, or football as developed formatively in Britain and its imperial and trading networks, had little chance of gaining any serious foothold in the United States' sports territory. Football was crowded out from below by baseball, with its mythlike resonance of rural community, and from above by American football, with its initially college-based rationalistic personification of the new industrial order. Indoors, basketball also took a hold on the sports consciousness of the expanding nation—very much, though Markovits does not touch upon this—in waiting for its development in its professional form by black Americans (Novak 1976; George 1992).

Where football took some hold, Markovits reminds us, before World War I, it "remained closely associated with immigrants, a stigma which proved fatal to football's potential of becoming a popular team sport in the 'new world'" (1988, 135); even on its reintroduction as a university or college sport in the latter half of this century, "football has remained largely the domain of foreigners and recent immigrants, both as players and spectators" (136).

Sugden and Tomlinson, referring to other spheres beyond just sport, have commented that "as a nation," the United States "has often appeared reluctant to import cultural forms which might highlight its own cultural and ethnic diffuseness" (1994b, 9), and this theme dominated Sugden's discussion of the United States and football. Taking Markovits's brilliant initial insights further and citing Oriard's work on images of sports in American culture, Sugden (1994) developed more fully the notion that the quest for distinctive forms of homegrown sport represented a thrusting new nation's yearning for self-identity—not least by evolving nativist cultural forms. Indeed, one might go further still from this perspective and note that the United States' big three are evidence of a unique society's quest for an appropriately unique sport and popular culture. With "the working class and middle class 'sport space' of the American public already crowded . . . there was little or no room for another outdoor team ball game, particularly one, like football, which could be readily associated with anti-American traditions" (235). Sugden emphasizes the notion of American nativism, which is manifest in the celebration of one's own identity and, simultaneously, the denigration of what one can only call the Cultural Other, shown in "an intense distaste for and suspicion of foreign subcultures and alien traditions" (235). He also argues that when football did take a hold in American high schools in the 1970s and the 1980s, alongside its "elevated status as an intercollegiate sport," it did so on a middle-class base and on the basis of "a youth caucus which was not so obviously dependent on immigrant and ethnic involvement" (243). Football, ironically (given its status across the world as a proletarian and working-class rooted sport in its professional spectator form), now offered the indigenous American middle class a positive and essentially reconstituted amateurist alternative to the excesses of violent professional sports and, especially, American football.

Compounding this antimasculinist, non-American status of football in the perception of the American public, the U.S. women's team became world champions in 1991, beating Norway 5–2 in China. Norway avenged this defeat with a 1–0 semifinal victory in the 1995 Women's World Cup in Sweden and went on to become champions, defeating Germany in the final. The U.S. team secured third place with a 2–0 win over China and went on to win the inaugural women's football event in the 1996 Atlanta Olympics, defeating China 2–1 in the final. In 1999 the United States again defeated China—this time in a penalty shootout after a 0–0 reciprocal shutout—to win the Women's World Cup in the United States. Norway kept this three-way battle for world supremacy going, winning gold in the Sydney 2000 Olympics. Nothing in the later 1990s occurred to challenge Sugden's conclusion that "no matter . . . how well the World Cup is organized, and regardless of how many tickets are sold, so long as football in America continues to be viewed as a game for foreigners, rich white kids and women, its chances of becoming established as a mainstream professional sport there are minimal" (Sugden 1994, 250). These chances were heightened, it might be argued, by the profile of the U.S. men's team in competing in the final stages of three World Cups in succession and its success in reaching the last eight at the 2002 World Cup in Japan and Korea, including its defeat of Mexico. An increasing consciousness of and pride in the U.S. team by the public has been labeled "football's tripartite Gestalt" (Markovits and Hellerman 2003), based on an expanded middle-ground awareness of football among the general sporting public along with the grassroots commitment of recreational players and the commitment of football's "coterie of enthusiasts." It would take more cycles of World Cup participation and success to establish the rootedness of this gestalt.

These analyses do not suggest that space is simply full, like some popular restaurant with a waiting list for reservations. The concept of sports space should be understood as referring to that which is culturally constructed, not merely physically determined. There is no reason why any particular society should have two rather than three, or three rather than four or five dominant sports—and of course this is particularly true of advanced societies with large populations such as the United States. But sports space refers to the cultural meanings of a sport and to the capacity of a society to value a particular kind of sport and render it meaningful and of social significance. There are socially determined and culturally specific conditions in which cultural forms such as sport are established and developed in particular societies and times. In Cuba, for instance, the postrevolutionary sport culture could harness well-established sports such as boxing and baseball to the explicit values of the revolutionary society (Sugden, Tomlinson, and McCartan 1993). Other societies keen to excel at Olympic level have also demonstrated how the available sports space can be reallocated. These include not just the communist societies of Cuba, the former Soviet Union, the former East Germany, and China, for instance, but also Spain and the hugely successful Australian host nation in Sydney 2000, among liberal-democratic capitalist societies. Sports space should therefore be seen not in any oversimplified spatiophysical terms but in the context of culture and power relations in particular societies. Criticisms have been made of the concept of sports space and of its explanatory limitations. Waddington and Roderick criticize both Markovits and the football historian Tony Mason for what they call "an implicit—and therefore unexamined—assumption that in each society there is a limited amount of 'space' for sports, and that once this 'space' has been 'filled' by one sport, there is no room for other sports" (1996, 45). But space is not "filled" simply on a first-come, first-served basis. It is disputed and contested by social groups and actors with particular sets of interests. Positions within any society's sports space can thus be denied by dominant groups and alliances of interests. This sense of sports space as contested cultural territory as well as a sphere of established institutional interests is fundamental to the conceptualization of football in the United States.

Other analysts (Williams and Giulianotti 1994) also adopted the predictive mode in analysis of the forthcoming finals and argued that a "predilection for the present" so characteristic of North American forms of popular cultural consumption would hardly guarantee "a stable or lasting future" for professional football. For them, "American" participation would be a "'fad': a pleasurable leisure experience while it lasts, and perhaps profitable for sponsors and manufacturers, but unlikely to be replicated through a settled and successful national American league to replace the failures of the past" (14). Such social scientific analyses and commentaries were complemented by observations from inside the game. The English First Division football player Garry Nelson, striker for the South London side Charlton Athletic, was vacationing in Orlando with his family when the finals began. His diary for Wednesday, June 15, 1994, two days before the opening game, contains an entry in which he notes that whoever wins the World Cup, it will not be the United States. Therefore, he goes on, "football is going to resist all the commercial efforts to catapult it into the big bucks stateside. It will remain the passion of the ethnic minorities and the 'safe' game that middle-class Wasp kids are allowed to play before they're considered mature and tough enough to play American football" (Nelson 1995, 13).

In the light of these analyses and predictions, some themes and discourses around the buildup to World Cup USA 1994 are considered, and then the event itself and its legacy are subjected to informed retrospective evaluation.

THE BUILDUP: SOME THEMES AND DISCOURSES

In 1988 FIFA awarded the 1994 World Cup finals to the United States. The United States Soccer Federation's (USSF) bid "received more votes than Brazil and Morocco put together" (Palmer 1994, 1), supported as it was by an infrastructure of stadiums, hotels, transport networks, and projected sponsors.

The choice of the United States as host for the World Cup finals was greeted with a combination of disbelief, hoots of derision, and skepticism among journalists, commentators, and professionals, both within and beyond the United States. The draw for the tournament was held in December 1993, and even at that stage, just months before the event itself, print media columnists could seek to mobilize nationalist sentiment against the most popular sport in the world on the basis that it was very strange indeed to give so much credence to a sport that was based on the skillful manipulation of a round ball by the foot. Tom Weir commented that spectators in the United States are thrilled most of all by action from the waist up:

> All arms and hands, things that happen from the waist up. . . . The World Cup draw is Sunday and admit it, you don't care. And no matter how much this event gets crammed down your throat . . . you still won't care. But don't feel guilty about it. There's a good reason why you don't care about soccer, even if it is the national passion in Cameroon, Uruguay and Madagascar. It's because you are an American, and hating soccer is more American than mom's apple pie, driving a pickup or spending Saturday afternoon channel-surfing with the remote control. (Weir 1993, 3C)

Such rhetoric is of course fueled by the columnist's eye for controversy, and there are many other places beyond the United States where pickup driving and channel surfing are well established and extremely popular. But the implication is that (however globalized they have become) these are quintessentially American activities, and football is not. The subtext to Weir's tirade is a separatist and nativist one.

If U.S. journalists were dismissive of football on the basis of an ethnocentric celebration of their own culture, other writers were uncritically celebratory of football and dismissive of U.S. culture and mores. One British journalist, for instance, stressed the more absurdist side of the draw in a puritanical piece on Las Vegas and U.S. culture:

> Filthy lucre it is that bought one of sport's great events for a
> nation of philistines who continue to treat it with yawning
> indifference. . . . the American organizing committee called a
> media conference for 12 noon, and arrived 65 minutes late. What
> followed was truly Pythonesque, with Roy Post, of the US Mint,
> treating the world's football writers to a lengthy dissertation on
> his commemorative coin programme. (Lovejoy 1993a, 24)

Monty Python's Flying Circus (the classic surrealist British comedy series) and further references to Mickey Mouse and Disney—these were the cultural references and metaphors with which Lovejoy made sense of the draw. Though the metaphor of the circus is multifaceted, evoking notions of festival, fun, entertainment, and daring as well as clowns and ridiculousness, British journalistic responses to the draw touched more on the clownishness and the absurdity—as well as a perceived tackiness—of the event. Other British sports journalists (Lacey 1993; Wilson 1991; Gardner 1994) were skeptical about or dismissive of the stages of the buildup and the media events such as the draw (though nothing could be less slick, sophisticated, or engaging than the televised draw for the English FA Cup, even in its revised prime-time format as launched in autumn 1995).

The draw itself was broadcast in the United Kingdom on the obscure Eurosport cable channel, in a mid-evening slot up against the competitive schedules of the terrestrial network channels. It opened with a series of welcomes from apparently high-profile television, film, and sports celebrities, including the movie stars Jessica Lange and Jeff Bridges, and several sports stars. "Hello world, welcome to the USA" was the repeated line as these celebrities performed, for the most part, limited tricks with a football ball. President Bill Clinton then appeared to state that the country was "proud and excited" to host the World Cup and that "World Cup fever" had gripped the whole nation right through to the White House. He relayed some participation statistics showing that football was the fastest growing youth sport in the United States. Three thousand guests at the Las Vegas draw were then offered snippets on the world profile of the game, with movie celebrity Faye Dunaway cohosting the program. Dr. João Havelange, president of FIFA, was welcomed for what the host acknowledged as "one of the most complicated draws" ever to have been conducted, linked as it was to a seeding system and the demographics of ethnic and immigrant communities across the venue cities and regions. The holders of the World Cup trophy passed the cup to Havelange, and he passed this on to Alan Rothenberg, lynchpin of the organization World Cup USA 1994. Rothenberg stated that it was with "pride and humility" that he accepted the trophy for the period of the finals, which would, he was convinced, "establish a legacy for USA football to flourish at every level of play," including at the level of a new professional league—the proposed Major League Soccer—which would soon rank with any other in the world, and for which Rothenberg himself was responsible. Soon after awarding the finals to the United States in 1988, Palmer (1994) reports, FIFA had been active in campaigning against the USSF's incumbent elected president, Werner Fricker, and was directly implicated in the election of Rothenberg as his successor. Palmer reports Rothenberg on this: "The World Cup was dead in the water when I came in. . . . There was even talk about taking it away from America" (Palmer 1994, 2). The draw, and the lineup at the draw, were testimony to Rothenberg's revivalist impact.

Roberto Baggio of Italy was presented with not just the Player of the Year award but also with the Adidas Energizer trophy, and then a few welcomes were shown from some of the host cities: a Mickey Mouse mascot introduced the viewer to the attractions of Orlando, Florida; and nightlife, cars, and people were highlighted as the special qualities of Detroit, for instance. Nike, Delta, and Opel graphics then led into a sustained Nike advertisement—"You can't live without . . . Just do it"—which conflated football, sex, and youth style, before the event returned to welcome the top FIFA careerist Joseph "Sepp" Blatter, four years later to take over the mantle of FIFA president. The razzmatazz of the buildup anticlimaxed in singer Diana Ross's penalty kick at the opening ceremony in Chicago on July 17. She struck the ball with a jerky mechanical swing of the leg. The ball rolled painfully and apologetically wide and simultaneously the goal itself collapsed. Coincidentally, the Italian star Baggio was to shoot the deciding penalty of the final over the bar in Pasadena just a few weeks later.

Nevertheless, early concerns at the staging of the event in the United States were assuaged by the time of the later stages of the buildup. The goals would stay the same size; the matches would still be played in two forty-five-minute halves rather than in quarters; all the matches would be played on grass. Indeed, skepticism among some was tempered by an eager anticipation of the effect of some brave innovations by FIFA: a subtle amendment to the offside law that would favor attacking play; the stricter interpretation of foul and violent play that would inhibit the more physically intimidating side of the game, especially among defenders, and so promote creativity; a strict line on how to deal with injured players; and the award of three points to teams for first-round wins. These innovations matched the image of football in the United States that sponsors were keen to promote—a free-flowing, creative game with few of the trappings of overt aggression and violence characteristic of other top-level professional team sports.

THE EVENT

A barrage of quantifiable facts can be marshaled in support of a case for the success of the event. Media viewing figures, both for the United States and the rest of the world; ticket sales and capacity crowds; merchandise turnover; computer innovation—all these features of USA 1994 cannot be ignored, but they are not the primary focus or concern of this chapter. Such data alone cannot evoke the cultural impact of the event. Though before, during, and in the immediate wake of the event these indicators seemed to set the stage well for the legacy anticipated and predicted by Rothenberg, the actual nature and impact of the event cannot be captured by such quantifiable indicators. In this section, therefore, I emphasize much more the cultural dimensions of the event, based on observations on the East Coast for the opening days of the tournament and on the West Coast for the final stages, and on an interpretive and empathetic immersion in the event itself within U.S. and UK sport culture.

One Night in New York

On the eve of the Ireland–Italy game we arrived in New York City, meeting up with Irish American football fans in Manhattan. P.J.'s Irish bar on the first night of the tournament revealed the cognitive complexities of contemporary forms of global sports affiliation.

To enter P.J.'s on any night is to step into a twilight world between the United States and Ireland. To enter the bar the night before the Republic of Ireland's opening World Cup game against Italy in Giants Stadium was more like stepping out of New York and into Dublin. The place was decorated as it would be on the eve of St. Patrick's Day. It was packed with Irish Americans, Canadian Irish, and other diaspora Irish from as far afield as Japan and Australia and countless fans who had made the trip from Northern Ireland or the Republic of Ireland. Many were gathered around a large screen at the far end of the bar watching reruns of and postmortems on Spain's surrender of a 2–0 lead in its opening game with South Korea. Others were hanging around the counter, quaffing beer and competing with the hard rock blaring from the juke box with their own mixture of Irish laments and football songs.

On a smaller television set, some were watching the fifth game in the NBA basketball finals between the New York Knicks and the Houston Rockets, live from Madison Square Garden. There was plenty to watch here. But suddenly a groan issued from P.J.'s as live coverage of both the soccer tournament and the basketball game was suspended to bring live coverage of an even bigger, unfolding sports drama: former all-American football star and media personality O.J. Simpson's flight from the system of justice. On the screen appeared a white sport utility vehicle being pursued along a Los Angeles highway by a phalanx of black and white patrol cars and a swarm of police and media helicopters. The start of what would be one of the longest-running sport-related stories in the United States was upstaging basketball and the World Cup. That week, the New York Yankees also beat the Baltimore Orioles in Yankee Stadium and Tabasco Cat was hot, winning the Belmont Stakes at Belmont Park. In American football, the New York Giants and the New York Jets were to begin preseason training the following week.

(based on Sugden and Tomlinson 1994c)

As Markovits asserted, on the basis of his historical and social scientific analysis, there are few openings in the fiercely contested American sports space. This truth was subjectively experienced by every occupant of P.J.'s Irish American bar on the night of the first day of USA 1994 (Sugden and Tomlinson 1994c; see, too, for corroborating accounts, Wilson 1994; and Usborne 1994). Scottish novelist Don Watson, elsewhere in New York, was at that moment in "a place called 188 Houston, which is usually a music bar but has been taken over tonight by Knicks fever. . . . The Knicks will win this game, to put them 2–1 up in the series and in sight of the NBA Championship, but this will be dwarfed on TV by the news that breaks as we watch in the bar, dumbfounded. . . . O.J. Simpson has been found, and that now famous scene of him driving up LA Highway 405 in the white Bronco is being broadcast live on one of the six television screens in the bar. . . . Obligingly, Channel 4, which is broadcasting the Knicks game, puts an insert of the O.J. chase on the picture" (Watson 1994, 72). The matches of the opening day of the World Cup football tournament were low profile in comparison. In the sports bars across the United States, where visiting fans and football fans among ethnic minority populations gathered, cultural misunderstandings and disputes were manifest on this inaugural night of the football World Cup. This reaffirmed the reciprocal ethnocentrism that can characterize culture clashes in sport, as portrayed in, for instance, Rayner's idiosyncratic account of the noncommunication between American and British males on the theme of "football" (Rayner 1992, 44–45). The reported observations, corroborated by other writers, analysts, and commentators, show such interpretive conflicts over the meaning of football to be widespread in the dynamics of U.S./non-U.S. sports publics. Nevertheless, where football's cosmopolitan roots were manifest, a truly international event was under way. Earlier the same evening Don Watson had been celebrating the South Koreans' comeback in the game against Spain: "In a bar in New York City a Honduran and a Scot slap palms in celebration of a goal scored in Dallas by a South Korean" (Watson 1994, 72).

One Day in LA

The carnival atmosphere in Southern California on the weekend of the World Cup final reaffirmed football as the worldwide people's game, with cosmopolitan parties on the streets of Santa Monica and Pasadena and a global festival at the Rose Bowl, Pasadena, for the final between Italy and Brazil. The event was a resounding success (television executives no doubt sweated at the lack of goals in a goalless draw, but revived for the dramatic climax of the penalty shoot-out). The final was a quintessential celebration of sport's contribution to global consumer culture, with flags of competing nations matched by banners of sponsoring multinationals. The prematch spectacle included cheerleaders, massed bands, rock-and-roll singers and jazz musicians, clowns, flybys by the U.S. Air Force, and an invasion of the Rose Bowl playing area by hundreds of children drawn from the United States' ethnically diverse population. And, for the first time in World Cup history, the team of the host nation did a lap of honor at the tournament final, with the youngsters. The great Brazilian soccer player Pelé also skipped in, with singer Whitney Houston. The establishment of the world sports organizations—Samaranch of the International Olympic Committee, the late Nebiolo of the International Amateur Athletic Federation, and Havelange of FIFA—sat in the best seats in the house, along with Alan Rothenberg.

In a spectacular postmatch finale, fireworks displays recolored the Californian skyline, and vintage biplanes meandered through the colors. For this concluding scenario, Darryl Hall boomed out the soundtrack, with a gutsy rendition of Glory Land, *the World Cup 1994 anthem.*

Three and a half million tickets had been sold for the fifty-two matches of the finals, a FIFA record, and much to the delight of the sponsors and the TV moguls, several billion viewers had tuned into the games all around the world. The fans were happy; FIFA and the organizers and their contractors could be congratulated on a challenging job well done; the official sponsors had had undoubted value for money— good news for Canon, Coca-Cola, Energizer, Fuji Film, General Motors, Gillette, JVC, Master Card, McDonald's, Philips, and Snickers; the media were content, some even apologetic and eating humble rather than mom's apple pie. Grahame L. Jones, for instance, recognized not just the creditable performance of the U.S. team in getting beyond the first round of the tournament, but also the "drama and pathos and emotion and passion and patriotism" in a "World Cup filled with spectacular games and stirring upsets" (Jones 1994, 28); and there would be a huge windfall for noble causes such as UNICEF.

(based on Sugden and Tomlinson 1995a)

The World Cup final was a truly spectacular and memorable climax (with music, dancing, fireworks, celebrities) to a buoyant tournament. There may have been a lack of goals in the final throes of the tournament, but Roberto Baggio's imitation of Diana Ross finished the action in unforgettably theatrical style. Would, though, the legacy promised by the U.S. organizers be grasped? Would the people's game, the global game, thrive when the circus left town? In responding to this question, glib prophecy and thin history must both be avoided. The deep-rootedness of the long-term trends that have affected the context and profile of football in U.S. sport culture would be unlikely to be overturned overnight.

THE LEGACY

The World Cup had a bigger media impact in the United States than many pessimists had anticipated, hailed as "the surprise sports story of the year" with television ratings "20%–30% higher than many expected" (Media Sports Business 1994, 10). Live games on the ESPN cable channel attracted viewing figures equal to the rating for prime-time Wednesday Major League Baseball games: "The July 17 championship final, Brazil vs. Italy, drew an unprecedented 9.5/24 (8.95 mil.) on ABC plus another 1.62 mil. on Univision, the Spanish network available on cable and off-air TV" (10). Press coverage also exceeded expectation.

In the light of this profile of the event, substantial impact was widely assumed. Claims have been made that the 1994 World Cup generated a high level of interest and recruitment to the grass roots of the game. The U.S. Youth Soccer Association reported that in the follow-up to the World Cup its membership increased by 9 percent to 2.1 million; the American Youth Soccer Organization's membership was claimed to have increased by 14 percent to half a million (*Sports Industry News* 1995). And certainly young people were the primary marketing target—"The US Soccer Federation claims 16m registered players—more than any other Fifa member—of whom most are children" (Berlin 1994). But the professional game continued to face difficulties in "attracting investors, finding adequate stadiums and local franchise control" (*Sports Industry News* 1995).

The professional game was fragmented, with the five-year-old American Professional Soccer League (APSL) continuing to plan its own expansion from seven to twelve teams at the same time as the proposed full-time Major League Soccer (MLS) initiative was stalling. Yet the highest average gate in the APSL was 5,300 (for the Los Angeles Salsa in the 10,000-capacity California State Fullerton Stadium), followed by averages of 4,200 and 4,873 for teams from another country, the Montreal Impact and the Vancouver 86ers respectively (Media Sports Business 1994, 11). The situation a year after USA 1994 did not augur well for the future of professional football in the United States, as Paul Gardner's overview (1995) also indicated. The new professional league (MLS) pledged to FIFA when the finals were given to the United States had still not started up, and its starting date had been put back from the postponed date of April 1995 to a further postponed date of April 1996. Ten teams were planned, but only eight sites had been found by April 1995. Gardner describes a divided, fictionalized part-time football culture in the United States, with four existing leagues (two of these indoor) currently in existence, and none of them willing to give up any share of the football market. The U.S. public is used to paying to see the best and to hailing its indigenous sports as "world-class." An English professional football star with many years of experience of the game in the United States, Rodney Marsh, pinpointed this, three years before the event, as a problem for the future of the game after the World Cup: "1995 will be the kill or cure year. . . . Assuming the World Cup is a success in football terms . . . assuming the football captures the American imagination, the pro clubs here will have to show a big improvement or go under. Once people have seen the best there is no way they'll go back to watch second-rate stuff" (P. Wilson 1991, 39). The ever-acerbic football journalist Brian Glanville reiterated this point after the finals: "Having watched the World Cup, Americans were never going to settle for junk football" (1995, 72).

Where football did thrive in the immediate wake of the USA 1994 adventure was where it had thrived before—in the schools, among particular ethnic communities, and among some women. This is where the sponsorship had already been targeted. The banana retailer Chiquita Brands International sponsored the Chiquita Cup, Fair Play, Clinics, and Soccer Challenges, essentially grassroots programs for youth football. Chiquita was also an Olympic football and U.S. football sponsor. But its World Cup marketing drive confirmed football's specific market: "According to Chiquita the company will be focusing on its football sponsorship through World Cup 1994. . . . Chiquita Brands target 3 demographic groups: children ages 15–16; women ages 25–34; and adults 55+ . . . looks for quality events with a 'healthy image' and family image" (Team Marketing Report 1994, 48).

But thriving Mexican leagues playing their matches in Southern California, Hispanic crowds flocking into a Los Angeles stadium for an El Salvador versus Denmark match (Kuper 1994, 157), healthy and athletic women (even if world champions and soon-to-be gold medalists at the inaugural Olympic women's football tournament in Atlanta in 1996), and senior citizens and children—whatever commitment to football these groups represented would be unlikely to guarantee any inroads by football into the core sports space of the United States. In this respect the business community was focused and realistic concerning where football's potential in the U.S. market really lay—belying the rhetoric of Rothenberg and the like.

Staging the event well was a matter of civic pride for many and massive personal profit for a few. There are direct comparisons with the Olympic Games here. In Los Angeles in 1984 armies of volunteers were recruited to help stage the Summer Olympics at the peak of global Cold War politics. Controversies raged over whether these volunteers could be provided with working lunches; the Los Angeles Organizing Committee reported a surplus of $225 million. At the World Cup finals ten years later, this same productive—and certainly from some perspectives exploitative—dynamic provided the base for the spectacular staging of a global event of staggering profitability. Tony Mason has summarized the impact of the World Cup (1995, 152). Crowds averaged 68,604, and the aggregate spectator figure was 3,567,415. The 94,194 spectators at the final in the Rose Bowl paid $43.5 million for their tickets, an average price of nearly $462 per ticket. Three million dollars' worth of World Cup merchandise was sold at airport and hotel gift stores operated in the United States by the British company WH Smith. And Univision, the Spanish-language television network, generated twice as much advertising revenue as during the previous World Cup, Italia 1990.

This outcome was not merely accidental or a stroke of serendipity for the organizers. Scott Parks Le Tellier was featured in the British press in 1993 as not just "the managing director and chief operating officer" of USA 1994, but also as a missionary (well based with a Mormon background), visionary, and evangelist—for football (Lawson 1993, 25). He became keen on football while watching the World Cup in Germany in 1974, Lawson reports. Along with a "surviving hunger of commerce for new outlets," it was the Le Tellier–style "new breed of evangelists" who helped secure the football World Cup for the United States. Lawson presents Le Tellier as a force outside of that "hunger for commerce." In fact, on closer scrutiny, Le Tellier and other key players in USA 1994 were catalysts for that hungry commerce, not merely complements to it.

Le Tellier, speaking to journalist Ken Reich in the post-Olympics euphoria in early 1985, spoke less idealistically about his involvement in and motivation for the football cause in North America. He had spent his honeymoon in Spain in 1982 "at the World Cup championships learning how to run a major football tournament so we could do it two years later." He had actually moved to Los Angeles to seek to get involved in the 1984 Games, having been in Montreal in 1976, and as an ambitious young attorney met sports entrepreneurs on the appropriate sports and professional circuits. In discussion with Reich he noted the pressures of multicommitments in the case of Alan Rothenberg, co-commissioner for football in the 1984 Olympic Games: "Alan was the original commissioner, but he was so tied up doing other things and was never there, they figured that the job wasn't going to get done." Le Tellier relates how he had joined the Olympic Organizing

Committee in July 1981, after having become the tennis partner of Mike O'Hara, head of the sports department in the Organizing Committee. By the end of the following year he was concentrating on three sports (football, baseball, and equestrian events) and later worked in the finance department. After the successful Games bonuses were paid to employees, in three categories of $2,500, $1,500, and $700, Reich asked Le Tellier "Do you think the bonuses paid the employees were adequate?" Le Tellier replied "No, and I'm sure I'm not alone in feeling that way. . . . It is unfathomable to me that with that kind of surplus that you wouldn't want to leave a little bit better taste in some of the people that had been around for that period of time, and what led them to think, I wasn't in the discussion, obviously, at that stage, I don't know who was" (Reich Collection 1985 [interview March 22, 1985]). No doubt Peter Ueberroth, the man behind the organization of the Games, was.

A decade later, and working with Alan Rothenberg in a team that seems to have survived the bitterness and tensions of the Olympic exertions, Le Tellier reaped a richer harvest. Three months after the final game of USA 1994, the Los Angeles Times reported that "Alan Rothenberg will receive $7 million in compensation for serving as the World Cup Organizing Committee's chairman and chief executive officer" (Cart 1994, C1), out of the event's preliminary projection of a $60 million surplus. The $7 million comprised a $3 million bonus and a $4 million "deferred-compensation package for 'back-pay due,'" calculated at $800,000 a year, running from August of 1990 through next year" (C1). Prominent in defense of this decision was board member Peter V. Ueberroth. Cart also cites one board member who was not so supportive and stated to her that "I'm against paying a guy for a volunteer job." Le Tellier, chief operating officer of the World Cup Organizing Committee, was voted a $500,000 bonus.

For the 50 hours a week reported for 1991 (for roles of secretary, managing director, and chief operating officer), Le Tellier's documented annual "compensation" was $174,000, with a further $148,697 reported for "other allowances" (U.S. Internal Revenue Service 1991/92, part V). Le Tellier's address in this return is a Virginia one. For his 0.5 hours per week as honorary chairman and director, Henry Kissinger claimed nothing. For his 20 hours per week as chairman, chief executive officer, and president, Alan I. Rothenberg is documented as receiving no compensation and just $2,500 in "other allowances." In the following year, Le Tellier, still working 50 hours a week, received $186,000 "compensation" and $414,291 for "other allowances"—"Mr. Le Tellier's other allowances include the accelerated payment to him of certain vested post–1994 World Cup salary continuation benefits and of expenses and allowances associated with his relocation from Virginia to California" (U.S. Internal Revenue Service 1992/93, part V). In this same return Alan I. Rothenberg was documented as receiving no "compensation," as in the previous year, and $30,000 in "other allowances." But the IRS was also informed that "the Board of Directors has authorized the payment of salaried compensation to Mr. Rothenberg. Mr. Rothenberg has elected to defer the compensation pending a determination that a sufficient surplus exists from World Cup USA 1994, Inc. operations to satisfy all other obligations" (ibid.). Perhaps the World Cup Organizing Committee's board members did not all recognize the full implications of this authorization, made as it was at a time when Rothenberg, as Cart reports, declined a salary offer of $350,000 per annum (Cart 1994, C1).

Rothenberg had taken over responsibility for the World Cup organizing committee soon after election as USSF president and assumed a central position in the tangled networks of the United States' football developments. Palmer comments: "What bothers some people is that MLS, which is headed by Rothenberg, received £500,000 from World Cup USA, whose chairman is Rothenberg, to pay for its business plan which it submitted to the USSF, of which Rothenberg is president. . . . No-one was very surprised when MLS beat two other bids to set up the national league and then was given $3.5 million by World Cup USA for start-up costs" (1994, 2). No one seemed very surprised either when Rothenberg's claims about the legacy of the World Cup event looked to have little foundation.

This detail of the financial transactions at the heart of the USA World Cup administration is not an indulgent excursus, a mere empirical aside. It is fundamental to understanding the basis on which the USA World Cup was staged. Like the 1984 Olympics before it, the event was staged to celebrate the ways in which the United States could meet a challenge and put on an efficient and spectacular global show. But it was also a gold rush for a thrusting and entrepreneurial professional elite, whose commitment to football development has been questioned. A former English professional football player, Graham Ramsay, has said of Rothenberg that "All the reasons for him being involved are financial. He's not there for the sport. The World Cup is like a big circus going through town" (Palmer 1994, 2). British football journalist Brian Glanville questions Rothenberg's as well as Havelange's credentials: "Havelange . . . has this much in common with the Czar of American Soccer, Alan (£7 million or more) Rothenberg: neither has any real feeling for the game" (1995, 72).

As has been noted, "The World Cup provided a terrific sampling opportunity among American viewers" (Hudson and Boewadt 1995, 266). And some cash will certainly have flowed to the grass roots of the game: "The estimated economic impact of the circus on the USA was a cool $4 billion, with a direct profit of over $20 million to the US organizers" (Fynn and Guest 1994, 381). But the real legacy of the USA World Cup, once the circus left town, has been the model of mean, lean, and immensely profitable event management that the organizers of sports mega-events have long sought to emulate. You don't have to like sport to do that. It might help to make a success of the event if you do, but the driving force behind USA 1994 was a combination of local pride, global posturing, and personal ambition.

This initial evaluation of the nature and impact of USA 1994 shows that the Markovits thesis on the fullness of the sports space in the United States is not undermined by the success of the event. For the event was, in many ways, whatever its profile in the summer of 1994, marginal to that space. Even when the established sports space of the United States was disrupted and rendered theoretically vulnerable by strikes in major sports in the immediate wake of the World Cup in the autumn/winter of 1994/95, this could not be seized as an opportunity to establish professional football, for the public and the sponsors remained skeptical about the place of football within the canon of U.S. sport cultures.

Conclusions: 2010 Here We Come!

To combine historical, sociological, political, economic, and cultural analysis has been the interdisciplinary challenge of this chapter, drawing on an eclectic range of methods and sources, from market research surveys to my own and others' participant observation and investigative journalism. The analysis has been evolved in the tradition of the cultural sciences, as a pan-European might put it, and a tradition of critical social science and "investigative sociology" (Hargreaves and Tomlinson 1992; Tomlinson 1984a). On this basis I can provide answers to the three questions posed in the introductory section of the chapter. First, the successful staging of the 1994 World Cup finals was possible because the set of interlocking alliances and interests in world sport was conducive to its location in the United States and because the United States' sports administrators and entrepreneurs could draw productively on an expertise and pedigree in high-profile event management. Second, the impact of this successful staging on U.S. sport culture was minimal, due to the unavailability of appropriate forms of sports space within that society. Third, the impact of the tournament on football itself was negligible, though some of the playing reforms conducive to the marketing of the game in the United States have been implemented worldwide by FIFA, thus favoring attacking play and protecting the most creative skills. USA 1994 also confirmed that a country that successfully hosts a global sports event need not be one of the top competitors in that sport. This has certainly encouraged bids from emergent football nations, such as Japan and South Korea (fierce competitors for the right to host the 2002 World Cup finals before accepting FIFA's co-hosting compromise) and South Africa (beaten to the 2006 prize by Germany), which can argue that they have the economic, transport, and communication infrastructure in place for hosting an event of this scale. These answers have clarified the nature of the success of the USA World Cup as event and spectacle and the coterminous and persistent problems for professional football in gaining any significant foothold in the territory of dominant U.S. sports.

The analysis offered here is presented as a modest case study that can be used to inform some central debates in contemporary social theory and to base a critically informed sociology of sport—including themes concerning cultural affiliation and identity, the nature of national identity as expressed in a particular society's sport culture, and the process of the intensifying globalization of some aspects of popular culture. Maguire has warned against monocausal thinking on some of these issues and argued persuasively for the adoption of "multicausal analyses" through which "we can study the unintended basis of intended social actions that characterize . . . global commingling" (1994, 421). Houlihan, too, observes that classifications and typologies are useful in specifying different patterns and "varieties" of globalized relationships and presents a taxonomic model of "reach" and "response" as a means of developing "a more useful conceptualization of globalization" (1994a, 370–71). World football culture has "reached" only partially and unevenly into the sport cultures and space of the United States, met by responses across the last century ranging across the three included in Houlihan's model: the conflictual, participative, and passive. In USA 1994 the passive response gave way to some extent to an expanded participative response, but with scarce indication of any long-lasting transformation in the cultural position and social profile of the sport.

Analysis of contemporary forms of worldwide sports events shows the variety and complexity of forms of the reach/response dynamic characteristic of sports as they become more significant worldwide phenomena. Analysis of such cases can also benefit from awareness of Maguire's cautionary remarks concerning the dangers of monocausal thinking. But—and despite Maguire's comment that a form of thinking as represented in this analysis "remains locked in a 1970s conceptual time warp" (1994, 399)—this analysis of the impact of World Cup 1994 is also a reminder that central to some major trends in the globalization of world sport is a political economy that merges the interests of transnational bodies such as FIFA, multinational corporations, and national and regional elites. These interests merge to produce economically profitable outcomes that are entirely intended and, as the analysis demonstrates, identifiable. In this light the analysis is offered as an example of the study of an actual form of a globalizing tendency, to paraphrase Robertson, and of, again in Robertson's words, the concrete structuration of one of the world's premier sports events. The analysis is also testimony to the relevance of the economic and the culture-ideology dimensions of transnational practices (Sklair 1991, 6) for an understanding of globalizing sports. The false promises of some of the prophets and makers of USA 1994 can only really be explained as examples of the ideological—the masking of real interests and values geared toward a set of particular interests—exploitation of the situation. The embryonic football culture of the United States (Giulianotti 1999, 36–37) was never likely to make dramatically swift and significant inroads into the established sports space of that culture. Statistical trends and interpretive work throughout the 1990s have reaffirmed that USA 1994 was made possible and accomplished by a powerful set of interests, but at no expense to an ironically vulnerable U.S. sports establishment.

This is not to say that football has simply faded away in the post-1994 period in the United States. The national team qualified for the World Cup finals in France in 1998, but finished with the poorest record of all of the participating teams. Even so, a mere year after that low point, the MLS's public relations man Dan Courtemanch could talk a good game for the future of the sport in the United States. MLS has its offices just over from New York's Grand Central station in midtown Manhattan. I interviewed Courtemanch there in November 1999, in the plush but business-like boardroom of the MLS headquarters. He agreed that the 1994 World Cup finals were the critical showcase without which the MLS would never have got off the ground:

> At the end of World Cup 1994 we finally had American players
> who had done well at the top level at the World Cup. We had
> some recognizable names. In addition, the fans were familiar with
> some of the international stars, whether it be Carlos Valdarama
> from Colombia or Jorge Campos or Roberto Donadoni, and these
> were players that eventually ended up playing in Major League
> Soccer.

Some U.S. players also played in the English Premier League, the Italian Serie A, and the German Bundesliga, further raising the profile of the U.S. national side. A younger generation has more recently provided "a new breed of stars," in Courtemanch's words, establishing a platform for Courtemanch's optimistic, even bullish, projection: "and kinda that new breed of stars, you know. The United States' goal is to win the World Cup in 2010. You know, it's a very ambitious goal." This might seem a lofty ambition, but the new world, in the form of U.S. football entrepreneur Alan Rothenberg, was now firmly entrenched in FIFA's corridors of power. If they wouldn't triumph on the pitch, the United States was getting into a good position to prosper in the wider global politics of the game.

Football's representatives in the United States could easily talk up the prospects of the sport, but even after the successful World Cup 2002 venture, the MLS chairman Don Garber was honest enough to tell the BBC sports commentator Alan Green that in the United States "a deep cultural passion doesn't exist . . . yet" (BBC World Service 2002). Garber saw the challenge as to make the game economically viable, and so to invest in getting it "deeply ingrained into the community . . . into the culture." This involved embracing the ethnic demographics of football's fan base and drafting in, for instance, a Korean star of the 2002 World Cup to play for an MLS team in a locality with a prominent Korean expatriate and immigrant population, getting a Guatemalan to play in LA, bringing in Luis Fernandez, the Mexican star. For Garber, the football aficionado is more sophisticated than the MLS had initially recognized, and this kind of targeting of the audience can be of double value, boosting the team and the spectator base. By the 2006 World Cup, Garber projected, the MLS would have more teams; the U.S. national side would have done even better in the North and Central Americas confederation's (CONCACAF) Gold Cup; there would be more football-specific facilities for the top level: "There'll be progress every day, month, year, further along by 2006." But realistically, for the big objectives, it's 2020 he'd be aiming for: "We've not yet come close to developing" our capacity.

By 2002 there were signs of considerable progress in that development. Rothenberg, talking in the elegant and opulent lobby of Hotel Le Bristol at the heart of Paris during World Cup 1998, reprised his savior role:

> I saved the World Cup. FIFA was gravely concerned that the preparations were not going the way that it wanted them to and was seriously thinking about taking the World Cup away from the US. That's when they contacted me and asked me whether I'd be interested in getting involved. I said yes, and was told I should become president of the United States Soccer Federation. I had to admit I wasn't even a member of that organisation. I got elected president of the federation and shortly thereafter took over organisation of the World Cup. (Sugden and Tomlinson 1999a, 76)

Rothenberg rode to FIFA's rescue and wooed the North American sports industry. In August 1993 he was addressing the annual convention of the National Sports Goods Association, firing salvo after salvo of market statistics for the following year's event (Schlossberg 1996, 152). USA 1994 would have 32 billion television viewers across the world, twice the figure for the previous year's widely hailed Barcelona Olympics. One and a half million visitors would spend freely across the nation for almost a month. The 900,000 ticket packages were already sold out in two offerings, guaranteeing 3.5 million spectators at live games. FIFA's man Rothenberg—by 2000 leading technical inspection teams to Germany, South Africa, and England in the selection process for the hosts of the 2006 World Cup—saw the business potential of football even if it reached only modestly into U.S. sports space. Hardly a football man, Rothenberg has been described by one senior committee member of FIFA as a "quintessential American entrepreneur, a hard-nosed LA lawyer . . . not a football man" (Sugden and Tomlinson 1998c, 111). His arrival on the U.S. football scene catapulted the cozy voluntarist world of the U.S. football federation into a ruthless corporate machine, a big business operation. One former employee of Rothenberg's, suing unsuccessfully for breach of contract, told the *Los Angeles Times* in 1994 that "the man has the morals of a bandit" (Sugden and Tomlinson 1999a, 84). Rothenberg himself does little to discourage or contest such evaluations, recalling that "joining the US football federation was like joining the PTA. Some of these people had to realise there is a big difference between lining the field for a youth league game and running a potentially billion-dollar business. . . . I don't beat people up because I enjoy beating up people . . . but if I have to leave some strewn bodies in order to win, within the rules, that's the way you have to do it" (Sugden and Tomlinson 1999a, 84).

Rothenberg epitomized the brash worldview of the sports entrepreneur, and millions—over 18 million by the late 1990s—continued to play the game and ensured that the market base of the game was consolidated. Football remained, though, primarily an activity for "young, relatively affluent middle-class children" (Markovits 1998, 28), a sport of "normalized cultural values and ideals prized by suburban middle-class mores" (Andrews et al. 1997, 280). The lack of a fan culture for football in the United States is demonstrated most evocatively when the national team takes the field for a home game against a side that can call upon the other big fan constituency, the Hispanic ethnic following. Eric Wynola, of the U.S. national team, has observed that "American fans could learn a lot from the way that Haitians act, with their enthusiasm about the game" (Metcalf 2000, 26). The U.S. team had coasted to a comfortable 3–0 win over Haiti in the Gold Cup in February 2000. But most of the fifty thousand in the crowd in Miami's Orange Bowl were cheering on the Haitians. Defender Agoos added: "It's nothing new, us being the visiting team on our home soil. We played Iran in Los Angeles (last month) and it might as well have been Tehran." You could be an active football player but far from a fan, the big three or four still your main source of fan identity and affiliation (Markovits and Hellerman 2001).

Rothenberg remained the perfect embodiment of the corporatization of the game as a commodity form. "There is nothing that illustrates globalization better than football," commented British social historian Eric Hobsbawm (1999, 122) in his reflections on "Homo Globatus." But, he also observed, sport bestows "an extra authority in the definition of social

hierarchy" (135), and it is in this hierarchy of stardom that U.S. football players find themselves persistingly peripheralized. I asked Dan Courtemanch,
who beyond his market research-speak is an enthusiast for the game, "What's
Alan Rothenberg's relationship to Major League Soccer?" He looked like
I'd bitten his hand and responded in a high-pitched contralto, "He's an
investor." While football remains a huge global marketplace, people like
Rothenberg will continue to represent U.S. know-how and entrepreneurial
flair in the power and business circles of the world game.

There is no doubt that football has made identifiable inroads into
the consciousness of significant numbers of the U.S. population. Markovits
and Hellerman argue, in light of the U.S. team's strong showing at World
Cup 2002 in Japan and Korea, for the recognition of an "Olympianization"
of the game within U.S. sport culture and space. What they call a "formerly
bifurcated Gestalt of football in America"—comprising almost 20 million
recreational players with scarcely any "cultural connection to football" alongside small numbers of informed devotees following the game on all levels—
has, they argue, gone some way to becoming "tripartite." The game flour-
ishes at the grass roots, aficionados still follow the sport at all levels, but
there has emerged "a quadrennially recurring World Cup consciousness"
(Markovits and Hellerman 2003, 1545). Yet the domestic professional league
continues to struggle. In September 2003 the women's professional league,
the United Soccer Association, closed amid mounting debts and lack of sponsorship on the eve of the women's World Cup in the United States itself and
the U.S. team's valiant but unsuccessful defense of its title. The conclusion
is inescapable: any rising consciousness of either the men's or the women's
game is most focused on top international competition, where national pride
and prestige are at stake.

The United States will pursue its ambition to win the men's World
Cup in 2010 and, regardless of the claims of other parts of the world, may
even seek to stage the tournament again in that year. Simultaneously, the
social and cultural specificity of the roots of the game in the United States
itself—its exceptionalism, as so perceptively studied by Markovits and noted
by Hobsbawm—reaffirm the merely minor threat that football has offered
to the established interests in the U.S. sport culture and market.

6. Eastern Promise?

*Football in the Societies and Cultures of the
Middle and Far East*

The game of football was in numerous cases taken to colonized and newly expanding countries and associated markets by "some Englishmen and Scotsmen abroad" (Mason 1986). Thus, in the South Asian subcontinent, the oldest established football association was the Calcutta-based Indian Football Association (1893) (the All India Football Federation was not established until 1937). In Southeast Asia football made some institutionalized impact early, Singapore's football association dating from 1892. Little detail is known of this body's history, but the Football Association of Singapore (FAS) is certain that "the game was dominated by the British companies and the British forces that were stationed in Singapore during the colonial days" and that "Inter-Business Houses football matches started in the early part of the twentieth century," in which "there were many expatriate players, mostly from England." Occupying forces and international business were the seminal influences on what was then known as the SAFA (Singapore Amateur Football Association). Indeed, this legacy lives on, at least in the sphere of tradition and cultural heritage, in the context of Singapore's modern professional league, the S-League, modeled explicitly on Japan's J-League. The top and bottom clubs in the Pioneer Series B program of fourteen matches during Singapore's inaugural professional season in 1996 were, respectively, Singapore Armed Forces Football Club and Police Football Club.[1]

Much had happened in Asian football in the intervening century to indicate that although tradition might live on in matters of nomenclature and labels, the meanings, motivations, and aspirations underlying the game at the end of the twentieth century were a world apart from those that stimulated the pioneers of the game on the continent. This chapter examines this transformation and identifies the major influences on the growth, spread, and impact of football on the world's largest continent. The scale of this transformation and growth was captured by the comments on Asian football by the general secretary of the Asian Football Confederation (AFC) in December 1996:

> Football is a serious business. We need to reorientate our thinking to treat Asian soccer as a product which needs to be researched, produced and marketed on a planned and sustained basis through every available means throughout the continent.[2]

Football in Asia has acquired—in this seriously developed, produced, and marketed form—a wider global profile, in line with some ambitious objectives. For the general secretary, Peter Velappan, increasing success in FIFA tournaments at the world-class level—particularly in younger age-group categories—has demonstrated genuine development and authentic potential. This has been so much the case that Velappan could claim that "by 2005, Asia will be the equal to Brazil in terms of standards."[3] Much of this notable pace of development has required the promotion and management of change—organizational and cultural as well as sporting—in and among the forty-four (as of 1996) member associations of the confederation. This chapter is concerned with the underlying dynamics and principles that have made, for some Asian countries, such an optimistic projection possible.

ASIA ON THE WORLD FOOTBALL STAGE

The Asian presence in world football at its highest levels was most dramatically announced by North Korea's successes in the World Cup in England in 1966, most notably its defeat of Italy (Tomlinson 1994, 24–25). But that was prompted above all by the sporting imperatives of a Communist regime (other social formations were developing their football cultures and systems much more unevenly) and by that country's opportunistic response in going to England when the mass of Asian and African nations withdrew from the qualifying rounds, in objection to the confederation's lack of an automatic slot in the finals. Nevertheless, the succeeding thirty years saw some outstanding successes in football development. In November 1996, according to the FIFA/Coca-Cola Asian rankings, the more prominent Asian national sides were as listed in Table 1 (for this purpose, only those Asian nations featuring in FIFA's top one hundred world ranking are listed).[4] It is striking that (apart from Thailand and Iran) the top ten are dominated either by Arab Gulf states in the Middle East (Saudi Arabia, Qatar, United Arab Emirates, Kuwait, and Oman) or by established or aspirant superpower societies and economies of the Far East (China, Japan, and Korea). Thailand's ranking was based in part on its prominence within the Southeast Asia region—the ASEAN (Association of Southeast Asian Nations) grouping—having triumphed in the inaugural Tiger Cup. Its bubble, though, was burst at the Asian Cup in the United Arab Emirates, where it suffered confidence-shattering defeats at the hands of Saudi Arabia (0–6), Iran (1–3), and Iraq (1–4). Iran was emerging as a regional power in the wake of problems persisting six years after the end of the Iran-Iraq war. But the dominant regions, performing frequently and consistently enough to make a mark in world rankings, were the oil-rich societies of the Gulf and the thrusting capitalist and emerging tiger economies of the Far East. Performance on the World Cup stage has also reflected such patterns.

Asian national sides did not immediately follow up the 1966 success of the Korean Democratic People's Republic. As the AFC general secretary reflected: "Asia did not take the cue that Asian teams had the potential and the capability to take on the best in the world. Asia continued to slumber" (Velappan 1996). To put this point less poetically, but in a more explanatory way—no other Asian side was as yet supported by a centrist infrastructure, in this case along para-Soviet lines, nor were any yet undergirded by a supportive infrastructure from within a capitalist economy or a corporatist alliance of social, political, and economic interests. It is the societal type, and the deployment of resources within the society, that has promoted football enough to heighten levels of aspiration and raise levels of performance—along with an increased presence within FIFA and confederational organization, administration, and politics.[5] Many Asian countries were to experience, in periods of postcolonial independence and adaptation, the same type of developmental problems as did newly independent African nations. Sport could hardly be immune from this. Unless newly formed nations could provide

TABLE 1. FIFA/Coca-Cola Asian rankings, November 1996

Asian ranking	Country	World ranking	Change Oct.–Nov. 1996
1	Japan	22	−2
2	Saudi Arabia	40	0
3	South Korea	46	−1
4	Thailand	57	−3
5	Qatar	64	−2
6	United Arab Emirates	69	+4
7	Iran	77	−6
8	China	78	−12
9	Kuwait	79	+7
10	Oman	88	0
11	Malaysia	92	0
12	Singapore	94	−1
13	Lebanon	99	−2
14	Myanmar	100	−2

SOURCE: *Asian Football Confederation News* 3, no. 1/97 (January 1997): 6.

substantial resources and scrupulous and efficient administration, there was little chance of them reaching world-class performance levels. The record of Asian teams in World Cups after 1966 testifies to this basic but critical point. The Republic of Korea had the worst record of the sixteen finalists in Switzerland in 1954; after the honorable showing of the Democratic Republic of Korea in getting to the last eight in 1966, when Asian sides got into the final tournaments they performed consistently poorly until they hosted the tournament in Japan and Korea in 2002 (Table 2).

On the levels of performance among the established, developed elite of world footballing nations, Asian sides have been the minnows in the global sea. Prior to 2002, two performances in particular were hailed as break-throughs: the Saudi performance throughout USA 1994, in which the team beat Belgium and Morocco and shook a complacent Germany with a late rally in a quarterfinal knockout game; and a non–World Cup performance, Japan's defeat of Brazil (1–0) at the Atlanta Olympics in July 1996 (Brazil nevertheless advanced in the tournament, losing the final to Nigeria). Opinion is divided as to the realism of these claims. Otto Pfister, experienced German coach to African and Asian national sides including the famous "Black Stars" Ghana team of the early 1990s, remains unconvinced: "Asia is far behind.... Look, I take 10 football games, 9 times I lost, and won in one game. This game is in a big competition? It is not typical, it is not typical."[6]

TABLE 2. Finishing position of Asian sides in World Cup Finals

World Cup	Year	Asian side	Finishing position
West Germany	1974	Korea Republic	16/16
Argentina	1978	Iran	14/16
Spain	1982	Kuwait	21/24
Mexico	1986	Korea Republic	20/24
Mexico	1986	Iraq	23/24
Italy	1990	Korea Republic	22/24
Italy	1990	United Arab Emirates	24/24
USA	1994	Korea Republic	20/24
USA	1994	Saudi Arabia	12 (or 8)/24
France	1998	Saudi Arabia	28/32
France	1998	Korea Republic	30/32
France	1998	Japan	31/32
France	1998	Iran	20/32
Japan/Korea	2002	Korea Republic	4/32
Japan/Korea	2002	Japan	10 (or 11)/32
Japan/Korea	2002	China	31/32
Japan/Korea	2002	Saudi Arabia	31/32

Source: Compiled from AFC 1994, p. 48, and from complementary personal sources.

The resounding fact for Asian football remains—whatever the level achieved, anticipated, or predicted—that its leading performers have *systematically* produced the continent's elite squads, in some cases in astoundingly short-term phases of development. China's vast resources, for instance, could be harnessed behind sport, so enabling its footballers to set up a training camp in the Brazilian jungle, in the belief that there was something to be learned from proximity to and immersion in the football culture that had produced the most successful international side in the history of the World Cup (Bernstein 1995). So far, the men's game has not achieved the levels of international competitiveness attained by the Chinese women's side, though it has established itself as the third-ranking nation in the continental federation. In other nations in Asia, a coalescence of cultural, political, and economic forces, orchestrated from the center, could provide the necessary infrastructure for the development of top-level sport.

A GULF APART: THE CASE OF THE UNITED ARAB EMIRATES AND OTHER GULF STATES

The United Arab Emirates (UAE)—as World Cup qualifier in Italy in 1990 (finishing with the poorest record of all the participants in the finals) and as hosts of and finalists in the Eleventh Asian Cup in December 1996—provides one of the less well-known stories of successful football development. It is considered here, along with observations on arguably the most successful Gulf state, Saudi Arabia, as a revealing case of the conditions and nature of football development in the Arab Gulf states.[7]

The seven separate emirates united as a nation only in 1971, and the UAE Football Association affiliated to FIFA the following year. Within nineteen years the national side was playing in the World Cup finals and was a regular serious contender for honors in continental Asia and subregional Asian tournaments such as the Gulf Cup. For a nation with such a small population—in 1995 a mere 2,377,453, 66.5 percent of which was male—and with a heritage of sports much more resonant of the nativist sports of the Arab ruling class and the imported sports of the former ruling classes of the British Empire, this was a remarkable achievement. How and why was this achieved?[8] Football was developed consciously in the United Arab Emirates for political purposes in order to express parallel status with other Gulf states and, if success was achieved, to raise the profile of the United Arab Emirates across the world. This was done by deploying the power and resources of an enlightened despotic corporatist state and applying them in the sphere of public culture. Football was developed not just as a potential career for young athletes, but as a form of service to the nation and a contribution to its further development.

Football was introduced into the United Arab Emirates by British merchant sailors playing the game in their free time in port and soldiers based in the various statelets. Emirate nationals also encountered the game, filtered through British colonials, in India. The first school-based football side is said to date from the late 1920s, and neighborhood-based youth sides developed in the 1940s. This provided a basis for some growth and expansion of the game, but the critical date for the development of UAE soccer was two weeks to the day after the formation of the United Arab Emirates, when the UAE Football Association was established within the new Youth and Sports Ministry. The UAE president, Sheikh Zayed bin Sultan Al Nahyan, saw youth as having a major role in the development of the new nation, and from the very beginnings of the new country "sport became an official movement countrywide," and the major task of the football association was to build a national side capable of competing effectively in international tournaments. A creditable result (third place in the 1972 Gulf Cup just three months into the nation's history) in its first international competition convinced the authorities that football could promote effectively some major social and cultural objectives. An informal league established in 1973 developed into the full UAE League in 1974, when the President's Cup was also established. Attaining a competitive international standard of football was the priority, in pursuit of which limitless resources were directed. World-class coaches were recruited, including in the late 1970s England's Don Revie, known notoriously as Don "Readies" for his mercenary drive and greed. He received £5,000 a month tax-free during his two years as national team manager before managing the top club side Al Nasr.

By the mid-1980s local league structures were established as feeders or recruitment sources for the main UAE League. Modeling itself on successful European and Western football nations, the football association introduced new competitions and promoted continuity for the national squad from junior and youth through to the full side. This development was funded almost exclusively by the state.

The UAE president, Sheikh Zayed, was from the Al Nahyan family, the sheikhs of Abu Dhabi for more than 250 years. When oil was struck in the mid-1960s, he emerged as the chosen new ruler of the emirate, and on the formation of the new federation, "of which he was a key architect," he became president of the United Arab Emirates. In both the official history of the new nation and its modern public iconography, Zayed is celebrated as an active, outdoor sportsman: the horseman, the falconer, the horticulturist, the wildlife environmentalist, the camel owner, the dancer. In his own book on falconry (dated 1977), he described a hunting party of falconers as a cross between a male-bonding ritual, a therapeutic escape, and a political walkabout among ordinary folk. Unschooled in a land with no educational establishments when he was a boy during the 1930s, Zayed established himself nevertheless as the prominent leader who would make, in the words of his minister of information and culture, "a truly meteoric rise from hard pressed tribal leader to Head of State." Zayed has been successfully re-elected (obviously unopposed) at five-year periods. His family has filled the official positions of state, and he has been the mouthpiece for the collective voice of the nation for a quarter of a century. In his own expression of the enlightened despotism of his rule, in negotiation with separate emirates as the federation took shape: "I am not imposing unity on anyone. That is tyranny. All of us have our opinions and these opinions can change. Sometimes we put all opinions together and then extract from them a single common point of view. This is our democracy." The sheikh has traditionally led the people of his tribe on the basis of consultation and consensus. This Zayed recurrently claimed to have done in the United Arab Emirates's transition toward modernization, drawing on a deep awareness of a Bedouin tradition of mediation. His moderate, anti-extremist Islam beliefs have stressed the compatibility of heritage and progress.

In the context of such a one-ruler, dynastic, theocratic state, sport came to play a major part, with ruling family appointees placed in key positions in the body responsible for sporting policy, the Ministry of Youth and Sports. General fitness and exercise have been promoted, reputedly for the population as a whole. But international events (snooker, tennis, power-boat racing, golf) were attracted, and particular sports targeted for development, to bring the new nation, its modernization and its riches, to the attention of a wider world. The UAE Football Association was chaired in 1996 by Sheikh Abdulla bin Zayed Al Nahyan, undersecretary of the Ministry of Information and Culture. This was a high profile indeed for football administration during the finals of the Asian Cup. But to the visitor arriving in Abu Dhabi during the tournament, it soon became clear that the event was merely part of a national celebration of a more important moment, the twenty-fifth anniversary of Sheikh Zayed's accession. The extraordinary illuminated trimmings on Abu Dhabi's office blocks and high-rises and the bright lightbulbs along all the length of the airport road into Abu Dhabi city were not in the name of Asian football.[9] They celebrated the supremacy of the president. Very little publicity on the Asian Cup adorned the streets and thoroughfares of the city. Some young children in the city center might be playing football in an alleyway, inquiring of foreign journalists, "Will we win, will we win?" but as the United Arab Emirates progressed to the final the football remained very low profile within the public culture of the city. It could only be concluded that to a large extent the football culture was a manufactured one, lacking—despite full stadia for UAE games, the crowds made up in part of bused-in schoolchildren and security and military forces—a deep-rooted historical and cultural vintage and passion. For it is clear what the motivation has been for the promotion of football in the United Arab Emirates, as expressed in the "welcome" from the president of the football association, in his further role as chairman of the Higher Organizing Committee, at the draw for the Asian Cup finals:

> We are delighted and proud to welcome our brothers and friends. . . .
> The willingness of the brotherly and friendly federations of the
> countries which have qualified for the finals shows their keenness
> to contribute to the success of the Championship and also reflects
> the level of friendship and cooperation between the UAE and
> them.[10]

Here the stress is on diplomatic harmony and cooperation, couched in a language of fraternity and common interests. Nor is the opportunity passed over for a more flag-waving celebration of the United Arab Emirates itself and its own elite institutions. The draw for the tournament had been held at Dubai's Chamber of Commerce and Industry, and the sheikh's praise of that institution blended the themes of youth, progress, and economics:

> The Chamber is one of our most distinguished economic
> institutions with great capabilities and which cooperates with
> our national institutions to serve the march of youth and sports.[11]

Prominent sportsmen invited to the draw were thanked for helping to hoist the country's flag. Patriotism, diplomacy, veneration of national institutions, moral approval for the blend of sports and youth—these were the values characteristic of the United Arab Emirates's model of international sporting relations. The development of football in the United Arab Emirates was inextricably bound up with these values.

Technically, the UAE League players in 1996 were neither full-time nor professional. But in actuality, it was a version of classic Soviet models of central promotion and sponsorship of sports and athletes in the service of the state.[12] The minister of youth and sports was in charge of all the sports associations in the country, and stadia and clubs of the top division were sustained by government funds, each club receiving a regular revenue allocation. The United Arab Emirates permitted no foreign players to play in its league, nor any UAE player to leave the country. Officials claimed that players from Gulf countries like the United Arab Emirates did not want to play abroad, well remunerated and provided as they have been in their own countries. In the successful UAE squad in the late 1980s—coached by Brazilian Zagalo—to Italia 1990 players were stimulated by the prospect of promised bonuses that would make them millionaires. A Mercedes, a notable status symbol, would be a routine gift to a player for a victory. Ray Seqiqui of *Gulf News* recalled, to Yorkshire Television researchers, one star goal-keeper who had three Mercedes. Status mobility could be high; physical or geographical mobility was not an option. A player simply would not be permitted to play elsewhere. Playing for one of the United Arab Emirates' top clubs guaranteed a job for life, with related work available after a playing career and generous testimonials also providing for the future. All presidents of clubs were sheikhs, and provision for players was comprehensive. The government provided a free home for all locals and nationals:[13] "Very nice houses, free electricity and free water . . . quality and security in the UAE is very very good, top of the world," as my informant Abbas Mohammad Hassan stated. Technically, UAE players are part-time, hold down jobs, and play as amateurs. In fact, they are generously sponsored, close to full-time athletes. In 1996 there was some debate about the prospect of developing a squad of full-time professionals in the United Arab Emirates, along the lines of Saudi Arabia's setup. It was recognized that coaches can find it difficult coaching some players who for a part of the day might be working at something other than football. There was no doubt that such issues would be raised and decided on at the highest level of government policy, the football association president being at the heart of the state apparatus.

Football has benefited in the United Arab Emirates from the patronage of the corporatist state.[14] In corporatism, the functions of the state, the economy, and the society are coterminous. The direction and nature of policy are dictated by a sense of clear objectives, the achievement of which is seen to justify any choice of means. With the support of the highest echelon of the state itself, Sheikh Zayed, and in line with his support for improving the welfare of the people and the worldwide image of the nation, football was developed in the United Arab Emirates as a means of profiling the qualities of the new nation and presenting an image of progress and excellence to the wider world. That the football association of the country can be given to a twenty-one-year-old as a birthday present was further testimony to the integrated nature of the political-cultural project. FIFA affiliation and FIFA and AFC approval of the state-of-the-art facilities in which events could be held became hallmarks of modernity for a state and a society in which the legacy of Arab culture remained central—camel racing and eagle breeding and flying were prominent in the sport sections of UAE official literature for 1996. Sports that were legacies of the colonial imperialist days—rugby, golf, and tennis—continued to sustain a higher regular public profile than did football, even though the latter could claim to be the country's most popular spectator sport. It is the internationalism of football that has placed it at the center of UAE policy; the United Arab Emirates has offered the world sports calendar some of its richest events—the Dubai golf classic, tennis open, and snooker tournaments, for instance.

And the UAE's public relations policy has been imaginative. On his return from successful medical treatment in the United States, Sheikh Zayed was presented with the biggest birthday cake in the world, and such gimmicks could lay claim to mention in the *Guinness Book of Records*. The Asian Cup itself was in many respects no more than just another sideshow to the state machine's construction of a picture of the veneration and worship of the sheikh. Football, though, could deliver the international audience. In the continental and world terms of AFC and FIFA respectively, football could provide the opportunity to profile both the nation and its own sporting culture. Any means to such an end could be justified, on the basis solely of the corporatist project. Football was widely recognized in the region as a source of nation-building. In another case, that of the Republic of Yemen, which borders Saudi Arabia and Oman, "sports were one of the few visible expressions of the people's desires for one nation" (Stevenson and Alaug 1999, 204), and "sport induces peoples' participation in a national system" (Stevenson and Alaug 1997, 262). For two decades the Yemen Arab Republic (North Yemen) and the People's Democratic Republic of Yemen (South Yemen) had anticipated a unification that was achieved in May 1990. Throughout this period the two nations had kept playing football matches against each other, and this achieved, Stevenson and Alaug claims (1999, 184), the incorporation of autonomous regions alongside the molding of a new national identity and the promotion of nationalism.

The Saudi Arabian case offers many parallels to that of the United Arab Emirates. Football was legalized in the kingdom of Saudi Arabia in 1959. Before then, the royal family had doubly disapproved of football, morally because it allowed Saudi youths to expose naked thighs and politically because soccer clubs were seen as a cover for dissident and potentially subversive political activity (Wagg 1995, 170). Rather than seek to simply destroy the game, Prince Feisal saw it, along with other sports, as a popular cultural form that could be incorporated into the central apparatus of the state. The wealthy Gulf states are monarchies, ruled by royal decree. In Saudi Arabia, all aspects of society are dominated by the royal family, with its several thousand princes occupying pivotal positions of power. Once deciding that a project could be developed, the country has routinely committed almost limitless funds to its realization. English football journalist Paddy Barclay told Yorshire Television researchers, in 1988, how "money has been thrown at the game there. The stadium is palatial although the pitch is dreadful. It is a mix of the modern with the traditional." This mix was too much for assistant football coach Englishman Colin Murphy, who worked under successful coach Bob Houghton. His verdict on Saudi youth—"fucking millions, breed like fucking rabbits," with large-scale trials or newcomers' sessions "like a fucking zoo"—couched in appallingly racist language the xenophobic views of this particular kind of Englishman abroad. Saudi Arabia's male youth provided football with a mass following, with training sessions for club reserve sides (the second string squad) attracting five hundred people or more and crowds of ten thousand watching reserve team matches. Murphy had little to say about whether this was a voluntarist enthusiasm among the spectators or perhaps another smaller-scale case of the manipulation of public culture and the construction of the spectacle.

Saudi Arabia had, without doubt, established a strong infrastructural base for the development of the game, setting up small leagues for all age groups at district levels. The top league was set up in 1978/79, and with training sessions run for all levels and two hundred officials centered on the national football federation, Saudi Arabia produced impressive national results within the Middle Eastern and wider Asian region. Bob Houghton spoke of the plush facilities made available for the national side. The national team would be picked at the start of each season and taken from their clubs for the duration of that season. A training camp made available to the side was in a cool area used by the royal family as one of its retreats from the heat of the climate. The effective boss of Saudi soccer in Houghton's time was Abdul Fatah Nazer, brother of the Saudi oil minister. Fatah was a football fanatic with a doctorate from Manchester University and a collection of British television's *Match of the Day* videos going back over a couple of decades. Football was run by insiders at the highest level of the nation's elite. When the English Football Association mounted its bid to stage the 2006 World Cup, the British government's network of ambassadors and high commissioners soon reported that the two FIFA executive committee votes from Saudi Arabia and Qatar could not be pledged by independent-thinking individuals: "It became clear early on that the final decisions on World Cup 2006 would be taken not by the FIFA members but by their governments and ruling royal families" (DCMS 2000, 28). Setting football fixtures would be more than a simple job for sports administrators. In 1997 the England 2006 bidding team—including retired senior diplomat Frank Wheeler—became embroiled in tense negotiations with the Saudis—not the football authority, but the government. Saudi Arabia pushed for a match with England and eventually secured a Wembley fixture, for May 1998, just weeks before the World Cup finals in France—"a . . . fixture . . . not to fit in well with the England squad's preparations . . . Shortly afterwards, the Saudi government told the Minister for Sport that they would support England's bid" (31). Which of course they didn't, as informed analysts knew all along (Sugden and Tomlinson 1999a, 2002a). Around the same time as the unwelcome fixture was being confirmed by the British government, against the wishes of the English Football Association, two nurses convicted of murder in Saudi Arabia were returned to the United Kingdom. In Saudi Arabia, international football could be just another front for global political dealings. Saudi Arabia sent the son of the king to FIFA congresses, and Saudi membership of the IOC could tip the balance in votes on who would stage the Olympic Games. Close to the vote for the 2006 World Cup, won by Germany, Saudi Arabia would be receiving an unusual import of 1,200 bazookas from Germany, where trade constraints were lifted in special consideration of a nation whose vote was critical to Germany's successful candidature (Sugden and Tomlinson 2002a).

Back on the field of play, as Middle Eastern nations and their premier clubs sought rapid results at the highest levels, football mercenaries could earn large sums in short times. Brazilian Rivelino was reported, in the late 1980s, to have pocketed $2,000,000 for his coaching services. Another big Brazilian name, Santana, received $600,000 for an eight-month coaching stint at Jeddah's club Ali during the period of expansion. Arab playing star Majid Abdullah—in Colin Murphy's eloquent judgment "he could have fucking murdered the first division" in England[15]—was reportedly a billionaire at the end of the 1980s.

There were no limits to the resources poured into football development in the Gulf states, but the price might be high for perceived failure. Nowhere in the United Arab Emirates's own histories are the results of Italia 1990 mentioned—eleven goals against, two goals for, and three defeats in three matches. The UAE's capitulation by eight goals to nil to eventual finalist Germany at its opening game at Japan/Korea 2002 was a shaming moment that would brand all concerned, back in the kingdom, for life. And veteran Sudanese world sports leader Halim has commented that the price of some forms of extremism and cultural and political fundamentalism, which can lead to public humiliation, shame, and disgrace for players and officials returning to their home country, is unacceptable.[16] But these are the prices demanded in the corporatist societies for which football has been developed as a serious political commitment and cultural project. Away from the field of play, the not-so-enlightened despot or the far-from-benevolent dictator could shape or cull the football establishment at will—in the name of national pride, honor, and the priorities of the state.

MAKING CULTURE: JAPAN'S J-LEAGUE EXPERIMENT, SOUTH KOREA, AND SINGAPORE

"Olé, olé, olé, olé" was sung repetitively, droningly, and loudly behind a football goal by young fans of mixed gender bedecked in the expensive replica shirts of the successful football team. This was an unimaginable scene in Japan before the 1990s and the formation of the professional J-League. The growth of football in Japan and the professional experiment can be seen as interesting examples of the globalization of sport.[17] Top world stars from

East Europe and Brazil were imported to set the level; commercial sponsors and government backed the league, which was seen as crucial to the improvement and maintenance of the level of the national side; and the formation of the league was seen as an integral part of the bid by Japan's national football association to host the FIFA World Cup finals. All the paraphernalia of fan culture was put in place in an attempt to generate a professional football culture in a setting where its historical base was negligible.

This was an attempt to take football out of its amateurist, educational framework and professionalize it in modern form.[18] Football had featured in the school curriculum of the Shizuoka Prefecture from the beginning of the twentieth century and has been taught there ever since. The sport was introduced into the country as a consequence of opening up trade with the British in the late nineteenth century. An Englishman, Lieutenant Commander Douglas of the Royal Navy, is said to have introduced the game, and football came to feature in some schools, particularly in British-oriented educational institutions. Generally, though, baseball was the compulsory sport in Japanese schools. It was the international impact of the Olympic Games that gave football a higher profile in Japan, and the Japan Football Association was founded in 1921, a cup competition starting in the same year. The first winner was the Tokyo Club, and most winners throughout that inaugural and the following decades were university teams and clubs, from Tokyo or other major cities. Admission to FIFA came in 1929. But it was the international stage of the Olympics, and especially the country's staging of the 1964 Summer Games, that provided the platform for a fuller development of the game at a higher level of international performance. In 1960 the widely experienced FIFA coach Dettmar Cramer from Germany was hired to prepare the national team for the Olympics. A solid showing — victory over Argentina on the way toward the quarter finals, where Czechoslovakia won 4–0 — created a wave of enthusiasm for the game, and the following year the Japanese Football League was established. At the 1968 Olympics in Mexico, the national team went undefeated until its 5–0 semifinal defeat by Hungary and recovered well to take the bronze medal by defeating the Mexican hosts 2–0. This was the basis of football's development in Japan — an improving record of performance and achievement at high, but still amateur, level.[19] The heavy Olympic defeats in 1964 and 1968 were, of course, at the hands of East European, state-sponsored athletes — full-time professionals in all but formal status. The Football Association of Japan (JFA) was convinced that the next stage of development required a more sustained exposure to top international levels of performance. By the turn of the 1970s and the 1980s, the association was bringing the world's top national and club sides to Japan in the Kirin Cup (for invited national sides) and the Toyota Cup (for the club champions of Europe and South

America). Recognizing the widening interest in the game, the JFA saw the next logical stage as the creation of a professional league, linked to the plan to bid for the first World Cup ever to be staged in Asia.

JFA officials, sensitive to this evolutionary and incremental development of the game, understood that the game needed to be established in clubs and communities, not just imposed from above at an elite level. This was stated clearly in the declaration of "goals in establishing the J. League":

1. *To Promote Football as Culture*
    To spread the love of Japanese football more widely, thereby promoting the healthy and physical growth of the Japanese people and generating a rich sporting culture. To promote friendship and exchange with international society.
2. *To Strengthen and Foster Japanese Football*
    To invigorate Japanese football, improving the level to the point where Japan can qualify regularly for the Olympic Games and the World Cup, and to raise the status of football in Japan.
3. *To Raise the Status of Players and Coaches*
    To provide top-level players and coaches with worthwhile opportunities in the sport and to promote their standing in society.
4. *To Foster Stadium-development and other "Home-town" Ties and Facilities*
    To establish close ties between clubs and their communities through the provision of stadium and other facilities that enable local residents to experience first-class football at firsthand.[20]

This amounts to an ambitious project, at the levels of both community and nation. It is also a sophisticated conception, recognizing as it does that the task is one of cultural innovation and not just policy implementation, one in which inroads had to be made into established values. There are elements of social engineering within the vision, too—the cultivation of the healthy body, healthy mind, for instance—along with the sense that this can create conditions conducive to the production of national and international excellence. As J-League chairman and chief executive Saburo Kawabuchi put it, "We are also determined to build a new sport culture for Japan."[21] Such a culture would reposition Japan within the international sporting community, so contributing—as stated by Ryo Nishimura of the World Cup's Communications Department—to the post–World War II project of rehabilitation.[22]

Local government, industry, and companies proved to be responsive partners in the J-League initiative. The league itself set up a number of independent affiliated companies to handle visual rights (video and stills) and commercial rights, logo sales, and the like. Specialist outside companies, in 1996, dealt with data analysis of match records, result services, and schedule and match communications. All clubs in the 1996 lineup were sponsored (Table 3). The business and company names were consciously dropped from the team titles to emphasize community and locality roots and identities.[23] Such a lineup of influential and prominent industrial and commercial sponsors and substantial support from local and regional government enabled the J-League to develop from its solid start in 1993. It had been planned in the context of a booming "bubble economy" in the second half of the 1980s, benefiting from a climate of buoyant support from corporations. *Mécénat*, the sponsorship of sport and culture by corporations, provided the basis of its economic development.[24]

At the end of its third season, Kawabuchi commented that "we anticipated continued growth and excitement in 1995 and all of us are thrilled

TABLE 3. J. League club sponsors, 1996 season

Club	Sponsors/Founding funder
Kashima Antlers	Local government and companies; Sumitomo Metal Industries Ltd.
Jeff United Ichihara	Furukawa Electric Company Ltd.; East Japan Railway Company
Kashiwa Reysol	Hitachi Ltd.
Urawa Red Diamonds	Mitsubishi Motors Corporation
Verdy Kawasaki	Yomiuri Shimbun; Nippon Television Network Corp.; Yomiuri Land Company Ltd.
Yokohama Marinos	Nissan Motor Co. Ltd.
Yokohama Flügels	All Nippon Airways Co. Ltd.; Sato Kogyo Co. Ltd.
Bellmare Hiratsuka	Fujita Corp.
Shimizu S-Pulse	Local companies
Júbilo Iwata	Yamaha Corp.; Shizuoka Shimbun; Shizuoka Broadcasting System; and others
Nagoya Grampus Eight	Consortium of 20 major local companies
Kyoto Purple Saga	Consortium of local companies (core Kyocera); local government
Gamba Osaka	Matsushita Electric Industrial Co. Ltd.
Cerezo Osaka	Consortium of 17 Osaka companies, including Nippon Meat Packers Inc., Capcom Co. Ltd., and Yanmar Diesel Engine Co. Ltd.
Sanfreece Hiroshima	Consortium of 47 companies, including Hiroshima Prefecture, Hiroshima City, Mazda Motor Corporation, Chugoku Electric Power, and Hiroshima Bank
Avispa Fukuoka	Consortium of 44 local bodies and companies, including Fukuoka City, Kitakyushu Coca Cola Bottlers, and Sanyo Shimpan

Source: Details in this table are taken from *J-League Profile*, 1996 (English edition), 8–15.

that we achieved our goals."[25] This "thrill" sounded like a sigh of relief that the league was still prospering after a Japan-less World Cup in the United States the previous year. The Japan national side, having defeated its greatest rival South Korea, conceded a last-gasp equalizing goal to Iraq in Qatar, so allowing Korea to qualify for the U.S. finals: this traumatic moment became known in Japan as the Tragedy of Doha. Despite the 1995 growth, though, the 1996 season saw a decline in attendance and a lessening of television interest—interestingly, in the context of the league's first experience of a European-style single-stage schedule for the championship and FIFA's decision midway through the season that the 2002 World Cup be cohosted with Korea. The league reverted to the two-stage system with playoffs for the 1997 season, and sponsors remained committed. But a poor performance by the national side at the Eleventh Asian Cup (going out in a 0–2 defeat by Kuwait) had frayed the nerves of the Japanese football establishment. Nevertheless, the first four years of the J-League could be adjudged an overall success, particularly in the light of the longer-term project for cultural change. Whatever the poor showing of the national side in France for the 1998 World Cup finals, it had at least qualified—albeit through a suspicious-looking drawn match with archrival Korea, guaranteeing the qualification of both these nations—and so in its hosting role at the finals of 2002, Japan would not be making its first-ever appearance in the final stages.

Such success demonstrated the value of integrated planning and development based on commercial, political, and organizational alliances and partnerships. This was acknowledged by the AFC when its general secretary Velappan described Japan's "dedicated officials and players" as "definitely on the march with a promising new era ahead" and praised the JFA as "well structured and professionally managed, with good coach education, youth development, orderly crowds and, certainly Asia's, first professional women's football league" (Velappan 1996). World governing body FIFA and the AFC could claim a facilitating and monitoring role for the further international and continent-wide development of football at the national level. But it was private capital and state commitment, often working in tandem, which were required to put in place the J-League blueprint. Examples elsewhere in Asia show, albeit from discrete political contexts, the efficacy of such alliances.

The J-League, for instance, was adopted as a direct model for Singapore's S-League, incorporated as a company in June 1995, after a delegation visited Japan. The S-League's mission statement had more than a ring of the J-League's goals about it, stressing the promotion of excellence, opportunities for football professionals, community-based football environments, and the growth of youth development programs. FIFA's fair-play mission and AFC's drive toward professionalism were prominently cited in the S-League's mission.

In 1994 the Singapore national team, playing in the Malaysian League, won the League Championship and Cup double, and then resigned from the league. It had competed in the Malaysian Cup and League for many years, as did some teams from other countries (such as Brunei) on or contiguous to the Malaysian Peninsula. This internationalism of the Malaysian league reflected a colonial past in which Malaysia and Singapore had been part of a single imperial colony. More incongruously, while Singapore was completing its League and Cup double, the Singapore League itself included two Australian sides, Perth Kangaroos and Darwin Cubs, illustrating what Duke and Crolley (1996, 64) call "arguably the most bizarre concentration of cases involving economic pragmatism." The Perth Kangaroos hopped to the top of the league and won the Singapore Championship, but were not permitted to stay in the league. Its pleas were brushed aside, as confirmed in my interview of Football Association of Singapore secretary Tan Eng Yoon.[26]

In the interview with the Singapore secretary I also asked for details of the fallout with the Malaysian Football Association. Duke and Crolley (1996, 64) imply that the S-League was, in part, a pragmatic response to the Malaysian association's allegations that Singapore would not cooperate in punishing guilty parties in match-fixing scandals (Singapore had not been expected to complete a double). Tan Eng Yoon was reluctant to comment on the detail, but this all but confirms Duke and Crolley: "Some unhappiness set in and . . . I'm not sure I should mention, er, Singapore was not expected to win, so then they said that Singapore should not be invited, but the president of the Football Association of Malaysia is a sultan, and he wants Singapore to be in. They were going to put in a lot of restrictions about, er, er, vetting of players, and you know, so many regulations that came in just after we won, and to see whether they accept a player. There were so many restrictions. They didn't say why they go through a process of inspection by a group. And because there's so much unhappiness, Singapore—we felt that we want to remain good friends with Malaysia—let's try our own league." The implication of some commentators is that Singapore bribed its way to its historic double by match fixing and that while the Malaysian association acted by investigating more than one hundred officials and players, the Singapore association adopted a much more laissez-faire attitude and took no action.

In establishing the S-League, government support of S$19 million was provided (in March 1997, this translated to £8,265,00; US$13,186,000; and RM32,471,000). This was a large sum for a population a quarter or so of that of London. The minister of communications acted as adviser to the football association, and the Singapore government saw in football a means of bringing together ethnic groups—Chinese, Europeans, Malays, Singaporeans, Bangladeshi—in healthy competitive exchange, the minister, Mah

Bow Tan, referring to "this wonderful game which transcends status, age, religion and culture." The government also directed US$5 million per year to the league, from the national pools betting scheme.

Company sponsors of the S-League were Tiger Beer and Pioneer. Product sponsors were Pepsi, Visa, and life insurance company NTUC Income. Sponsorship of clubs and equipment came from sports goods manufacturers, audiovisual specialists, camera manufacturers, and travel companies. By the end of its inaugural season—and despite rumors that some later games in the season appeared to be played in suspiciously uncompetitive mode, not unconnected to betting syndicates—the basic elements were in place: an extended infrastructure, solid government support, and commercial sponsorship. More of the latter was needed, Tang Eng Yoon confirmed, each league club receiving S$400,000 from the S-League board, but needing S$1.2 million per year to run. Asia Pacific Breweries, manufacturers of Tiger Beer, was also funding the regional international event for the ASEAN national sides, popularly known as the Tiger Cup. The inaugural event was held in Singapore in September 1996, guaranteeing that teams such as Laos and Cambodia could be funded to gain international experience.

The case of South Korea also shows the power and effectiveness of such alliances of interest, though football was strongly established within Korean sport culture much earlier than in the Japanese case. British sailors are said to have introduced football into Korea in 1882, when the battleship *Flying Fish* arrived at Inchon. But they played only on the deck of the ship and were not allowed on land. Korean people nevertheless copied the game, the sailors having left their ball on departure. Firmer institutional roots for the game were established in educational establishments in the early years of the twentieth century, under the influence of European teachers and missionaries. In the 1920s, "All Korean" games and fixtures expanded, and their rapid growth has been "attributed to the Japanese colonial rule of Korea. Under the Japanese rule, sport quickly became a way of expressing national sentiment against the Japanese. People felt that although they were controlled politically, they could not be beaten in non-political areas such as sport" (Lee 1997). This national sentiment is so deeply rooted that "Koreans are eager to win in sporting competitions with Japan" (ibid.). The Korean League (dating from 1983) was Asia's first full-time professional football league. The Korean Football Association was clearly a far from autonomous or independent body. In 1997 its president was Chung Mon Joon, heir apparent to the Hyundai Corporation and already a regional and national politician. With highly developed ties between private capital, the state, and civil society in the form of the sport culture, South Korea demonstrated an extreme form of corporatist control and use of the football culture. The general secretary of the North and Central Americas confederation,

CONCACAF, Chuck Blazer, also noted this, in relation to the Korean bid for the 2002 World Cup: "The Korean bid was tremendously well coordinated. In all ways, things worked together, with the powers of the government, the private sector and sport combined."[27] Such a powerful congruence of interests fueled the ferocity of the bidding process for 2002.[28]

As hosts Japan and Korea both registered impressive performances at the World Cup 2002 to progress to the second stages of the finals, countless commentaries in the world media talked of turning points in the hierarchy of world football performances. Senegal had thrillingly beaten defending champion France in the opening game of the tournament, and the French exited the tournament without scoring a single goal. Senegal progressed from the group. The United States lost by just one goal to Germany, in its quarterfinal game. But a mere few months later, after a disappointing performance in an Asian tournament, Korea dismissed its coach, who had been deputy to Dutchman Gus Hiddink during the World Cup run. It would take more than the one successful run of performances on home territory—as disgruntled Spanish players would no doubt say after going out against Korea on penalties, after having two perfect goals disallowed—to confirm a lasting readjustment to the balance of power in the world game. But inroads were without doubt made into the respective national cultures, as the crowd responses for both Japanese and Korean matches and the abiding images of Japanese children on English fans' shoulders confirmed (Whang 2004). Whether those footballing nations continued to make a mark at the highest level would be dependent on more than just the fan base, though. It would need the continuing support of political and economic alliances at the highest levels.

Manufactured Sport

The English travel writer Jonathan Raban has documented the political similarities and the cultural, very often religious, differences between the new states and nations in what was once Arabia. Qatar, for instance, was lined up to be one of the members of the newly founded United Arab Emirates in 1971, but "Qataris belong to the Wahabi sect of Islam, while the other emirates are Sunni Muslims" (Raban 1980, 69). The tiny country—looking squashed out of the Gulf by its giant contiguous neighbor Saudi Arabia and the United Arab Emirates—decided to go it alone. In seeking access to these nations, Raban met with very different responses—helpful, hospitable responses from Qatar and from Bahrain (which did not even require a visa), and a cold unresponsive silence from Saudi Arabia. Generally, he observed, "In central and south Arabia nationhood is still a novel concept: the tribe and the family are much stronger and more real ideas, and the nation is thought of as a big family in which the visitor is either a guest or an intruder" (19).

T. E. Lawrence saw the tribesmen and townsmen of Arabic-speaking Arabia as "people of primary colours . . . who saw the world always in contour," characterized by "a universal clearness or hardness of belief": "They were a dogmatic people, despising doubt. . . . They knew only truth and untruth, belief and unbelief, without our hesitating retinue of finer shades" (1940, 36). In a society combining rapid transformation (through oil riches and post-colonial liberation) and sustained cultural, religious, and political conservatism, the football project would inevitably be a manufactured and controlled expression of the nation as family. In the context of rapidly transforming capitalist societies such as the tiger economies of the Far East, alliances between the state and industry could see in sport a project valuable to both national profiling and a regionally based community building. In such contexts, football has been manufactured, produced from above.

Sport has been used in a variety of ways to promote and sustain national identity, for example, by antidemocratic regimes in 1970s Argentina, by pan-Soviet administration across literally hundreds of suppressed, dominated cultures and nations, by governments for strategies of international rehabilitation as in the case of Japan. In all such cases, sport has to be understood as a tool of the state and an arm of the economy, whatever its populist and passionate base in the everyday life and popular culture of the people. Such alliances within corporatism, whereby the state has spoken for the people and in the most extreme cases infiltrated every layer of popular culture and whatever remains of civil society, have received extensive scholarly attention in the context of communist societies such as the Soviet Union (see Riordan 1996; and Edelman 1993), and Cuba (Sugden et al. 1990). The rise of the sporting profile, and in particular the football development of many Gulf states and Asian nations, is a further reminder of how important a sport culture is perceived to be in both the internal politics and culture of a society and the international dynamics of a postcolonial world.

PART III. LOCAL CULTURES

Local Cultures

The chapters in this section on the dimensions of sport and leisure cultures prioritize the local and the small scale. They are attempts to capture the sense of place and time that must to some extent shape people's experiences of sport and leisure. All the studies in this book have a historical dimension. It is difficult to conceive of an adequate analysis of global trends without tackling the question of historical legacies and influences. Whether the initial emphasis is on the global or the national, some sense of the meanings shaping the here and now must be sought. This analytical and interpretive imperative has underpinned all the work in this book. But this third part reverses some of the emphases, taking in one case a place, in the other cases particular practices in localities, and explores questions of locality, community, and tradition on the basis of leisure and sport lifestyles. Chapter 7 is a blend of contemporary history and sociological analysis of leisure lifestyles, rooted in the Southeast of England and, in particular, Brighton. Chapters 8 and 9 are social historical accounts of particular traditional sports of the industrial culture of Northeast Lancashire focusing on the small town of Colne, close to Nelson and Burnley on the edge of central England's Pennine Hills. I have lived in Brighton for almost a third of a century, and I was born and raised in Burnley. The chapters in this part are therefore local studies of localities that are hardly unfamiliar to me. It is worth considering whether this is of either interest or importance.

Eric Hobsbawm (1997, 230) recalls the response when he told his American students that he could remember walking home from school with his sister on January 30, 1933, the day on which Hitler became chancellor of Germany. His students looked at him "as though I had told them that I was present at Ford's Theatre when President Lincoln was assassinated in 1865. Both events are equally prehistoric for them." When I lecture to my British students on local cultures of the mid-twentieth century, for them I might as well be talking about ancient Rome. The vast majority of my students were not yet born when the videocassette recorder was invented. For them, Blockbuster Video rather than the post office is the community shop of the time. Like Hobsbawm's Americans, the young consumers in the University of Brighton's classrooms look at me as if I am a relic from a vanished world. It is inconceivable to them that a household could have a television without twenty-four-hour transmission. Yet I recall the morning in the early 1980s when breakfast television was first transmitted and attracted all the guests, in the guesthouse where I was staying, to an early breakfast in line with the television. Hobsbawm notes that any historian of the twentieth century simply knows, without any particular effort,

> *how much things have changed.* The past thirty or forty years have
> been the most revolutionary era in recorded history. Never before
> has the world, that is to say the lives of the men and women who
> live on earth, been so profoundly, dramatically and extraordinarily
> transformed within such a brief period. This is difficult for
> generations to grasp intuitively, who have not seen what it was
> like before. (1997, 232)

I have seen what it was like before in both Brighton and other parts of the Southeast of England and in Colne and its neighboring towns of Burnley and Nelson. But this does not lead me into nostalgia or sentimentalism for some kind of ravaged authentic past culture. Rather, it allows me to pose simple research questions with a lived, historically and biographically rooted interpretive empathy. This can only be helpful in approaching the analysis of cultural transformations on the sort of scale described by Hobsbawm. The three chapters in this part seek to capture the scale of cultural changes and transformations of the bases of everyday life, and the continuities—both constraining and positively enabling—that can be identified and accounted for within such a climate of change. At the workshop at which an early version of chapter 9 was first presented, social historian Alan Metcalfe reminded the participants that just because some people were dealing with the past, talking about the past, this did not necessarily make their work "historical." I took it that this was a reference, perhaps among others, to my own contribution. Just to talk about the past, he went on, is not enough to comply with the canons of historical scholarship. I sometimes describe my work as social historical, and if I were German I might call myself a cultural scientist of past and present sport and leisure cultures, but that would sound terribly pompous. I am, though, perfectly aware of the dangers involved in using oral historical sources, and in some cases I have gone to other sources (personal records, local statistics, newspaper accounts) to check on the recollection that I have recorded. Hobsbawm, recalling his earliest historical fieldwork—with accuracy, one hopes!—offers three warnings about interviews as a source of historical data. First, do your background research so that as far as possible when you speak with your respondents you know "more about the subject of the interview than they could remember." In my local studies, I have routinely immersed myself in the documents of the period and the place before interviewing people who were there. Second, "on any independently verifiable fact," the respondent's "memory was likely to be wrong." And finally, do not think that you can change people's ideas, "formed and set a very long time ago" (1997, 232). It is the context of genesis and framing of those ideas and associated practices that is the focus of the social historian of sport and leisure cultures. In reconstructing leisure biographies or sporting cultures of the past, such warnings need to be at the forefront of your methodological and epistemological concerns. The second warning warrants a few further reflections.

If I felt it necessary to do a check on the oral source or the interview data in every case, it could denigrate the oral historical and qualitative source as a method in itself. The popular memory often gets dates wrong in the retrospective haze, but why should the popularly memorized account not be quite as much an authentic piece of raw historical data as is, say, the contemporaneous newspaper account? If the popular memory of the past distorts a little, who is to say that it distorts any more than do the mass media or powerful and all-reaching institutions of social control? As Moore has noted, people might "describe events as if they were themselves participants in or eye-witnesses to the history . . . it should not be assumed that there is any absolute truth. . . . It is the interpretations of the events that are data" (1974, 234–35). Authoritative overviews of the whys and wherefores of oral history method are available in P. Thompson (1988) and Lummis (1987). As P. Thompson concludes his study: "Oral history gives history back to the people in their own words" (1988, 226). We do not simply reproduce those words. They are discourses, they become evidence, sources of interpretation, to lie alongside what you already know—Thompson again: "It is . . . generally true that the more one knows, the more likely one is to elicit significant historical interpretation from an interview" (166). Oral historical sources must be respected but not reified:

> By preserving memories oral history redresses the balance of experience against artifacts, and although it records the experience of all, it is especially valuable in preserving the history of those whose material possessions have been meagre, contemporary and transitory. (Lummis 1987, 154)

In looking to remedy such an imbalance, in my accounts of people's leisure and sporting cultures I have deliberately let many of the voices come through unchecked. But they are always edited, interpreted, analyzed.

People's history and the oral historical method have underpinned my approach to these analyses of local cultures, then, and to the Northeast Lancashire studies in particular. Another influence, sadly neglected by many aspirationally ethnographic sociological researchers, has been an everyday version of the French model of total history. This is the study of *mentalités*. Peter Burke, who did much to disseminate into English-language scholarship the work of the Annales School of synthesizing social historians, from Febvre to Braudel (Burke 1972, 1973), called *mentalité* the system of beliefs or the shared values of a time and place (Burke 1978). The concept could help us understand the web of interlocking beliefs of a culture and a period, Burke noted. And the concept offers a way of liberation from psychological anachronism and prevents us calling or labeling others stupid. As Burke adds, the latent rationality of any beliefs are brought out by the approach. Some of the lessons of the Annales School on how to evolve a synthesizing history of the long duration, focusing on everyday life and cultural beliefs, can be usefully applied to the study of change, continuity, and power in sport and leisure cultures. The everyday-ness of material life became a major focus for the Annales. As Braudel put it, the study of material civilization necessitates a focus on "the repeated movements, the silent and half-forgotten story of men and enduring realities, which were immensely important but made so little noise" (1974, 15). My generation of oral historical accounts of sport and leisure cultures, and qualitative data on leisure lifestyles and practices, is an attempt to make more noise on behalf of significant but ignored and sometimes marginalized cultures of consumption and leisure.

If I am drawn to any big theoretical or interpretive point from these local cultures, it is toward a critique of careless applications of categories such as the postmodern. Modernity itself has been complex enough, and I would hardly be quoting Hobsbawm if I believed that cultural changes have not been genuinely dramatic. And thinking through some implications of the term "postmodern" can be a useful exercise. Postmodernism has provided Rojek, for instance, with a set of points around which to retheorize leisure. First, it corrects a false emphasis on leisure as in some way "segmented from the rest of life as a charmed realm" (1995, 171). Second, it challenges modernist thought's privileging of the authentic above the inauthentic. Third, it "outflanks the notion of the integrated self which underpins modernist thought," presenting an alternative model of "the self as fissile entity" (172). Fourth, processes of circulation, production, and consumption expand the realm of identity politics and critical pluralism. Fifth, "postmodernism destabilizes the elitist authority structure of modernity" (172). This is an insightful list of the challenges of postmodern theorizing to "modernist pretenses and objectives" (171) in the leisure studies field. Despite allegedly throwing my hand in with analyses of "capitalist manipulation" (24) in my work on consumption (Tomlinson 1990a), and so being branded as one of those hegemony theorists whom Rojek's postmodern-informed agenda appears designed to decenter and supersede, I share an interest with Rojek's list of characteristics. But reconceptualizing leisure may not have needed the sort or scale of epistemological or paradigmatic break claimed by Rojek. Modernity itself, as historical work and contemporary sociological research have widely established, was never so certain or sure of itself. Unemployment and the problem of leisure were direct and threatening and real experiences for many of my respondents in the local studies. Going beyond the retheorizing of leisure, thinking through more fully the nature of the leisure-culture relation, Rojek grants a much lower profile to such postmodern breakthroughs. In his later theorizations of "leisure and culture" (Rojek 2000), in acknowledging that "the regime of leisure is still a mysterious thing," he makes a plea for "comparative and historical research" as "the best method for examining how the regime operates" (Rojek 1997, 396).

The stress on the local in the following three chapters is the basis of my own version of such a method for studying the nature—if not the operations—of sport and leisure cultures. Chapter 7 offers an analysis of leisure cultures and practices in modern Brighton, adopting an open-minded eclectic approach to understanding a local culture, stressing too—against some postmodernist accounts—classic sociological concerns such as class and inequality. Chapter 8 considers the importance of sport—in particular, Lancashire League cricket in the small town of Colne—in a local industrial culture of the 1930s, as a form of cultural cement through which communities might be bound together in identity-affirming and perhaps essentially conservative ways. Chapter 9 provides a case study of the traditional sport of knur and spell as a way of showing the specificities of the currency of a sporting form and local cultural practice and so confirming the influences that underlie the social formation, development, and dissolution of particular forms and practices.

7. Patterns of Consumption in Sport and Leisure Cultures

Urban Space and Suburban Fears

Researchers on leisure and mainstream themes such as leisure participation have been reminded in recent debates that cultural geography, in its insistence on the recognition of the social constructedness of space, has much to offer their field of study (Scraton and Watson 1998, 135). Feminist researchers in particular have made important contributions to such debates. Aitchison and Jordan point to "four related themes that examine the nature of gendered spaces within leisure and tourism" (1998, v): first, how the spaces of public and private leisure are influenced by gender, in their forms of construction and organization; second, how practices and modes of consumption in leisure are characterized by aspects of power and control that are "gendered"; third, how places, practices, and spaces of leisure can be used "to reinforce gendered identities or create new identities"; and fourth, how leisure relates to urban space and sexual identity, in cases such as lesbian, gay, or queer space. Aitchison and Jordan do not claim this as an exhaustive agenda; rather, these are the themes addressed by contributors in their volume. It is, nevertheless, a wide-ranging, challenging, and ambitious agenda. Sociologists of sport have also been urged to revitalize their sensitivity to the theme of space, drawing on the work of the French theorist Henri Lefebvre (van Ingen 2003). John Bale's work on sport and space has consistently reminded sport and leisure researchers of the value of such frameworks (Bale 1994), and without doubt the feminist research agenda brings contemporary theoretical issues to the fore of the field of study. But there is sometimes the danger that in identifying new theoretical directions, existing, and sometimes more orthodox, sources are overlooked. This chapter is about space, attitudes toward and uses of space, but contends that such concerns are far from altogether new and that many forms of data can inform such analytical and conceptual preoccupations. To demonstrate this, the chapter draws on a catholic range of sources in considering one particular urban space: the city of Brighton and Hove, in East Sussex, England, and some areas around the city. In the chapter I critically review sources (such as the General Household Survey and the data sets of the Henley Centre) that have provided data on national, general trends and patterns in leisure and sports participation in the United Kingdom. The argument for the pertinence of regional and local studies is then made on the basis of the methodological limitations of some of the general trend data and the theoretical imbalances or lacunae characteristic of some theorizing of contemporary forms of consumption.

In this chapter I employ the following letters to indicate specific Market Research Society Occupational Status Groupings:

A   Professional people: senior managers in business and commerce or top-level civil servants (including retired)

B   Middle management executives in large organizations; principal officers in local government; top managers or owners of small businesses, education, and services

C1   Junior management; owners of small establishments; all others in nonmanual positions

C2   All skilled manual workers and manual workers with responsibility for other workers

D   Semiskilled and unskilled manual workers, including apprentices or trainees to skilled workers

E   People dependent on state support

Empirical studies undertaken for a regional agency (Television South) and for Brighton Borough Council are then drawn on to indicate patterns of activity in sport and leisure; modes of involvement, participation, and activity; and class-based, age-based, and gender-based forms of involvement in particular activities.

Cultural consumption in any town or city will of course be multi-faceted. Anthony Seldon (2002) identifies no less than nine different cities in the one place of Brighton: a city of danger, vacations, the homestead, politics, loucheness, gays, high culture, popular culture, and the excluded. A zonal analysis clearly needs to be adopted if sense is to be made of the range of leisure activities that are engaged in across a town like Brighton (since 2000, the combined city of Brighton and Hove) with its various functions, including tourist destination, commuter belt, student city, regional shopping center, entertainment center, business and conference center, and its varied identities — one of the Southeast's traditional haunts for sexual pleasures, England's gay capital, hedonistic coastal resort, gentrified residence for professionals. "Brighton" has become a shorthand for a form of escape. Novelist Linda Grant has her heroine Evelyn recall, on several occasions, the smut and the fun of the end-of-the-pier shows in the 1930s (2000, 9, 54, 73). The city has provided the perfect setting for the dramas of the not-quite-belonging, captured here in Helen Zahavi's black-comic novel of the avenging heroine Bella:

> Sometimes she used to sit on the bench in Brunswick Square. It lost most of its trees in the great gale of '87, but it's still an elegant square. Apart from the flies, and apart from the dogs. The houses are Regency, with soaring columns and wide balconies. You can look from the sea to the houses and back again, and it's so calming that sometimes you feel like you almost belong. (1992, 15)

Nigel Richardson made himself belong, to this very area, in his summer ethnographic and novelistic raid on the city. His stories are of the dispossessed and the restored, the glamorous and the faded and jaded, the dreaming and the drunk. For one, the move back to Brighton from deprivation and despair in London, through the rolling green hills of the South Downs that provide the natural border north of the city, was restorative:

> When I've been away and I come back over those Downs and see the streets spread out over the hillsides, when I see the piers and smell the sea, when I get blown by the wind in those streets down to the sea, I think I've come home to the lost fucking tribe. (Richardson 1999, 137)

There is another Brighton, in the council estates hidden under the canvas of the downs, in Whitehawk and East Moulsecoomb, or in outlying suburbs such as Woodingdean, the latter focused on by Nick Danziger. Here the small parks are no-go areas for older people as young people congregate for talk, sex, drugs, or whatever they can lay their hands on—"no warnings to keep off the grass, and no parents to supervise them" (Danziger 1997, 257). Long-term residents recall the deep-rootedness of the problem: "There's never been anything for the young people to do here. Most of the building and the development took place here when I moved in the late fifties, there's been no new infrastructure since that time. It used to be cheaper to get to Brighton beachfront, money went further around, we're worse off now" (261).

These are environmental concerns common to any urban area, recurrent across generations, and include a middle-class preoccupation with the open green spaces of the city as an extension of their personal residential space (Ravenscroft and Speller 2002). Yet the most recurrent image of Brighton to the outside eye has been of its seductive yet threatening playfulness, of its exciting seediness. Graham Greene captured this in his novel of the Brighton underworld subculture, *Brighton Rock;* as did the lesser celebrated Patrick Hamilton in *The West Pier* and *Hangover Square*. In Keith Waterhouse's words, the town has the air of having been invited to help the police with their enquiries" (2003, 21), as Waterhouse has playfully and solipsistically reaffirmed in the dipsomaniacal meditations of his protagonist Chris Duffy, in *Palace Pier*. The late John Osborne, living in its theatrical subculture of the late 1940s, associated Brighton with decadent, sensual pleasures:

> As the word Brompton was to pain, Brighton was to pleasure. If I were to choose a way to die it would be after a drunken, fish-eating day ending up at the end of the Palace Pier. Brighton is like nowhere else. No other resort has its simple raffishness.... Brighton had randiness hanging in the air throughout the year. There was no close season on sex; sex was all year round. There was no drowsiness in the air as in Bournemouth, only randiness. Ozone in Eastbourne was spermatozoa in Brighton, burning brightly like little tadpoles of evening light across the front. Whenever I have lunch in Brighton, I always want to take someone to bed in the afternoon. To shudder one's last, thrusting replete gasp between the sheets at 4 and 6 o'clock in Brighton, would be the most perfect last earthly delight. (1982, 208)

For a long time elements of the town have been associated with sexual daring. In any seaside town the opportunity for personal display afforded by public spaces such as the seafront and the pier have long provided the frisson of sexual opportunity, a recognized and relatively safe space for the rituals of courtship. Patrick Hamilton identified the seafront and the pier of the early interwar years as a space in which a person's very presence was a statement of availability:

> The Pier was intimately and intricately connected with the entire ritual of "getting off." Indeed, without the Pier, "getting off" would have been to some minds inconceivable, or at any rate a totally different thing. The Pier was at once the object and arena of "getting off," . . . An invitation to go on the Pier was like an invitation to dance; it almost conferred upon "getting off" an air of respectability. (1953, 45)

In this sense Brighton is a space of carnival or transgression (to paraphrase Bakhtin), as G. Thompson (1983) has pointed out with reference to the northern English seaside town of Blackpool. Shields notes the place myth of Brighton as a "liminal destination, a social as well as geographical margin, a 'place apart'" (1992, 112). Moving from the northern English industrial city of Bradford to Brighton, in 1989, Jenny Bourne Taylor saw Brighton as "sunny, vibrant, youthful, camp. Well established as England's gay capital, it also provided a home for new yuppies and old hippies" (1992, 86). Though beggars sleep in shop doorways and there are tragic cases of gay bashing and gay murders, drug deaths, and sexual murders in the crematorium, Brighton has sustained this glossy image, nicknamed London by the Sea. Taylor captured this in contrasting the town with the somber industrial modernity of Bradford: "Brighton seems all surface—a town whose base is leisure: the celebration of the superstructural and the superficial . . . the epitome of postmodernity before the term was even thought of" (1992, 94). Well, as any flaneur familiar with Brighton's public spaces will testify, this is certainly what parts of Brighton seem. But it depends where you look and to whom you listen.

Urban leisure and consumption has to be negotiated on the basis of attributed meanings of distinct spaces and places. This has been at the heart of recurrent disputes over the status and desirability of different forms of leisure, historically manifest in terms of the disputes between the rough and the respectable (Bailey 1978, 1983) and recurring (in however veiled forms) in urban life throughout the modern period. Middle-class suburbs of the late nineteenth and early twentieth centuries provided golf clubs and tennis clubs as foci for a public culture of the new suburban classes, and it is the balance between safe space and social or sexual opportunity that proved ideal for women of the middle classes for whom the sporting activity might have otherwise been unavailable (Holt 1989, 1993). Forms of leisure consumption in cities and towns have been revealing public manifestations of cultural conflict and status, and the balance between the public and the more individualized private dimensions of leisure has shaped the landscapes and contours of everyday urban life. Some analyses claim that all space is collapsing into similarity, the local high street "invaded by cultures and capitals from the world over" (Massey 1994, 162). But as Massey rightly observes, arguments claiming that we are placeless and disoriented are far from proven: "There are debates to be had about how, anyway, we think about space and place" (163). Such debates can be enhanced by some close scrutiny of particular places and spaces.

There is little new in a call for such a focus. Classical Chicago School urban sociology (Wirth 1938) generated an accumulated ethnography of subcultural places, a sociology of zonal meanings, as confirmed in English variants such as John Rex and Robert Moore's analysis of the "urban game of leap frog" (1969). This sort of spatially aware urban sociology also addressed major questions concerning the capacity of human beings to challenge the dominant meanings of space within the power dynamics of local social structures. For some of a more humanistic literary leaning such as Raban (1975), the city is in a sense no more than the accumulated practices of the people who populate it. For Raban the city was in this sense "soft," malleable, open to various forms of remaking. Particular social groups reshape the city to their own ends. Interviewing ten people for her study of the North Laine area of Brighton, Emma Sola highlights the migratory pull of Brighton's place myth and image. None of her interviewees had grown up in Brighton. Six were contacts or friends made during her time at the University of Sussex. Jack, a twenty-three-year-old graduate originally from Oxfordshire, worked in music promotion and as a disk jockey and captures the identity-making draw of Brighton:

> Brighton is not about authenticity, it never was. It was built by the Prince Regent for him and his rich friends to come and live out their fantasies in an hallucinogenic heaven. . . . All of these shops and all of these chances to buy into an identity are part of that, there are still people coming down from London to buy into a culture that they see an affinity with, and something approaching authenticity can grow out of that. (Sola 1997a)

Here Brighton is the catalyst for the potential remaking of self. Julie "came to Brighton from London twenty years ago, had a wild and wicked weekend and never left," opening up a punk shop in the North Laine area alongside the traditional butchers and greengrocers still thriving at the time in Sydney Street, and has owned and run clothes shops in the area since. The North Laine, with its independent businesses, pavement culture, and bohemian feel, was perceived by twenty-five-year-old media studies academic Sarah as "a bit more authentic than going to Top Shop," as an alternative albeit middle-class dominated alternative to the working-class shopping areas of the Lewes Road or the London Road. "I mean," Sarah continued, "people that you see in Primark (a discount general goods shop on Western Road), you wouldn't see them here." Thirty-year-old Luke, masters graduate in English from Sussex University, working on thriller novels and now back in London, expressed his "hatred of chain stores." Sola's respondents were remarkably candid about the class dimensions of these consuming spaces. Sid, in his late twenties a veteran of Brighton's music scene, reiterated the zonal specificities of Brighton's consuming spaces:

> London Road is however you want to pigeonhole it, working-class families, and Lewes Road is the same, which is cool 'cos they'd feel totally lost and intimidated here, and trendy people say, "ooh that horrible grimy place over there." It should be that everyone's integrated, but we're not fluffy hippies.

And twenty-four-year-old Sussex graduate Gail, not working because she had independent means, originally from Surrey, when asked what kind of people go to the North Laine, disputed that it was "all sorts": "Well, no. Do you really get your scoomers or your hawkers (people from Moulsecoomb and Whitehawk estates) down there?" Gail would have treated a visit to these estates as an adventure on a par with touring the *favelas* of Rio de Janeiro. "If you look above the shops," she added, "all the buildings are really grotty, really dirty." Emma Sola expands on the place in the cityscape of the likes of Gail:

> She exemplified the snootiness of many university students who had come to Brighton from the more privileged locales (usually in the south). They liked Brighton's shabby glamour and the thrill of its potential danger at first but after a couple of years the dirt and the problems became a guilty reminder. Cafés, upmarket bars, fancy restaurants, rolling countryside, the plush interiors of private houses became their Brighton landscape, anything else caused a shudder and a dismissive giggle. Equality with these other, poor people was most certainly not on the agenda, and as soon as the degree was over it was to the leafier parts of London without delay. (personal communication)

This was Oxford-as-well-as-London-by-the Sea, a *Brideshead Revisited* for a fin de siècle constituency. Sola's perceptive study is a reminder of the value of highly focused qualitative work on space and consumption and on the strategic and semiotic possibilities of resistance in contemporary consumer culture (Sola 1997b). Brighton has been a gift to the sociologist of deviance or subculture thick-skinned or adventurous enough to march into a chosen cultural milieu. Muggleton (2000) based his subcultural study of style in Brighton, feeding so easily as it does his preoccupation with subcultures as forms of self-expression, individual autonomy, and cultural diversity, in many cases having an "elective affinity" with bohemian values. In thirty-eight separate interviews he spoke to forty-three men and fourteen women between late 1993 and early 1995, all between the ages of sixteen and thirty-four (average age, twenty-four). "Four non-subcultural people" were found as control group (one wonders where these were nabbed!). Subjects weren't hard to come by in Brighton:

> Subcultural informants were selected for this study on the basis of what I regarded as their unconventional appearance . . . regardless of the style and social background of the informants, were references to *freedom* — freedom from rules, structures, controls and from the predictability of conventional lifestyles. (Muggleton 2000, 171, 167)

One can ponder a little on Muggleton's impressionability, pouncing on his subjects in the clubs and pubs of the city. But this is a problem for all subcultural or ethnographic researchers, and his account rings very true to me, a long-term resident and even more anecdotal observer of Brighton's cultural and subcultural life than Muggleton. His study is a valuable addition not just to subcultural studies, but also to a contemporary urban sociology of cultural consumption.

Empirically, the rest of this chapter focuses on Brighton as a place, in order to raise some fundamental questions about people's relation to space in their own localities. But it is not so much the bohemian, erotic, or sensual Brighton that forms the focus of this analytical task—not the subculture, for instance, of its clubs, though these have been important public elements of the leisure-provision profile of the town, particularly for youth cultures (Redhead 1993), and young people and youth culture have been a vital focus for cultural policy and the consumer industries, as in other cities, as Chatterton and Hollands (2001, 2003) have vividly shown in their study of young people and consumption in Newcastle, in the Northeast of England, and Featherstone and Wynne (1990) in their focus on Manchester in the Northwest. Nor the July weekend when Fat Boy Slim (local disk jockey Norman Cooke made very big indeed) fills the town and the beach, "letting people do strange and different things" in the spirit of the place, as Fat Boy put it to the typically invisible Channel 4 conversationalist (Channel 4 2002)—what's great about Brighton, the voice of the documentary tells us, is that celebrities don't come to escape from it, they come home to it, to strut their wares. Nor the midsummer Gay Pride carnival in Preston Park, an event that with all the cheeky relish of the outed gay community shows how giant strides of understanding have been achieved since the 1970s, when gay couples were still seen as risqué should they dare to take a walk together, strutting their sitcom style, along the Brighton and Hove seafront. Rather, the concern of this chapter is with the mundanities of everyday living, the modes of everyday consumption that characterize the routine lives of the town's residents and their use of the town's facilities. How do people engage in the public culture of their area or locality? These are sometimes the least-understood aspects of contemporary leisure, lost in the grand sway of generalizing theories and fashionable constructions of the heterogeneous but category-defying contemporary consumer. This is no crude abstract empiricism; rather, it is the empirical imperative for any serious theoretical project for the study of everyday practices. Before reporting data from three pieces of empirical research that have illuminated these aspects, though, the limitations of some forms of trend data are commented on.

Broad Trends in Leisure in Contemporary British Society

Leisure has become recognized as both an increasingly important part of the everyday life of citizens and as a potential focus for the regeneration of local economy and infrastructure, with an ideological swing in the later 1980s and the 1990s toward the latter economic function. As Henry puts it, within this context the state has moved increasingly toward a marketization of leisure provision, with local authority policies embodying a new emphasis in the state's role vis-à-vis leisure: one of the "marketisation of service provision: leisure (and tourism) employed as a tool for economic rather than social regeneration; residual provision with leisure as a social policy tool in the inner city" (Henry 1993, 25).

Four features of leisure in the late 1980s caught the eye of one expert analyst: the growth of connoisseur leisure; some growth in outdoor leisure; home-centeredness, an intensification of home-based leisure; and an expressed concern about the collective use of space, manifest in the form of a perceived "threat of the mob" (Roberts 1989). Put another way (Tomlinson 1990a; Philips and Tomlinson 1992; Tomlinson 1992b), acceptable leisure has become increasingly a matter of privatized (often in-home domestic) and individualized consumption or packaged pleasures within orchestrated publics, such as theme parks, supermarkets, shopping malls, multiplex cinemas, and indoor all-seater stadia—particularly as some face-lifted traditional leisure practices (movies at the multiplex at Brighton Marina, snooker at the Brighton racecourse or in a vacated supermarket building) and some recently emergent leisure trends (health clubs and aerobic or activity centers in prime sites in town centers) are well provided for by the commercial sector.

Lest it seem that the outline above is painting too gloomy or partial a picture, it is worth reminding ourselves that some collective cultures of a committed, self-generated type do continue to flourish. The anthropologist Ruth Finnegan (1989) has documented the buoyant musical culture in the Milton Keynes district, and studies of the importance of the voluntary sector in leisure have emphasized the often underestimated significance of self-generated and self-organized, and often collectively produced and experienced, forms of leisure involvement (Bishop and Hoggett 1986; Tomlinson 1979, 1993; Crouch and Tomlinson 1994). Brighton offers the Dome as a venue for the high-profile concerts of Van Morrison in the summer of 1993; it is an equally important venue, in community terms, for the Crescent Operatic Society's performance of *Oklahoma* earlier in the year. Any understanding of everyday leisure in its publicly expressed forms must recognize the buoyancy of such elements and be sensitive to both the high-profile dimensions of the commercial entertainment markets (Brighton Races, the Tour de France in 1994) and the more modestly framed possibilities for participation in collective, localized, and sometimes community-led forms.

In its regular analyses, the Henley Centre has provided invaluable trend data, but with some important limitations. First, its regular surveys for *Leisure Futures* are market driven and client led. Profiles of the contemporary leisure consumer do not include the community activist, local sports club enthusiast, churchgoer, concertgoer, or library user because such activities are of little interest to mainstream consumer and leisure industries that comprise the center's core clients (and, no doubt, steady subscribers). Second, though the Henley Centre analyses offer some breakdown of trends by age, gender, and class, more typically they present a picture of the free-floating consumer, free to pick and choose according to market choice. Age is covered in fascinating detail when clearly identifiable as a burgeoning leisure market (Henley Centre 1994); inequality is identified in a commentary on the two-nations debate, in another issue, not as a social problem but as a warning to the leisure industries, a hint as to what and where to avoid, rather than an objective commentary on inequality in leisure and consumption activity and practices.

The Henley Centre identifies different intensities of participation, offering therefore more than one-shot Polaroid profiles. This provides valuable information, broken down by gender, on frequency of participation (Table 4). Clear gender patterns can be seen. Women, even when participating, participate in the activity on fewer occasions than do men. But for both men and women, it is the individual sport that tops the frequency table. What remains implicit rather than explicit in the Henley Centre data is the class dimension of such patterns, the material basis, too, on which such forms of participation must be premised—personal disposable income, assumed transport possibilities, cooperative domestic organization. For the Henley Centre, the ideal world is the world of the postmodern consumer, free to evaluate and act in response to the ever-expanding choices of a dynamic market: "In the postmodern age people are free to appropriate meanings into their lives from just about wherever they see it" (Tyrrell 1990, 9).

The data from the GHS (General Household Survey) have, in the years since a "leisure" question was first included in 1973, provided an invaluable database for the monitoring of national UK trends, broken down according to age, sex, and socioeconomic group. This has allowed researchers to report broad trends (Minten and Roberts 1989) and agencies to inform policy. But the GHS should be treated with caution as a longitudinal database, for in 1987 methodological changes (toward the use of prompt lists, shorter interviews, and less manual coding) meant that figures on participation suddenly looked very different:

> In 1987, 61% of all informants said they had done at least one
> of the sports activities shown on the prompt card at some time
> in the four weeks before interview. In 1986, with the old design of
> the section, 46% of informants had been identified as sports
> participants. It is likely that most of this apparent increase is
> because of methodological changes. (Matheson 1991)

Clearly, a reading of the raw data would be misleading here, indicating a rise in participation of more than a third in one year. Without such methodological caution, apologists for sport and leisure can verge not just on the messianic, but the bogus. For whatever the worthiness and benefits of physical recreation and informed exercise, regular engagement and participation remains a minority activity. Citing the GHS, the Sports Council massages general figures to claim "walking" as an activity contributing to sport as a majority activity (Sports Council 1992).

Coalter, Dowers, and Baxter have shown the statistical sophistication that can be brought to bear on GHS subsamples, demonstrating how social class categories must be seen in terms of other variables such as age and sex but warning that "the GHS remains an extremely limited source of information for detailed analysis of patterns of sport participation and the measurement of sectoral change" (1995, 72). Their "more general 'sociological' conclusion" was that "for most activities age is consistently the most powerful single discriminator between participants and non-participants" (72).

It is clear that sport and physical recreation are not among the most prominent of activities in any more general index of "activity participation" such as that of the Henley Centre. Billiards or snooker, aerobics, jogging, and darts (two of these being primarily based in pubs) are the only activities engaged in weekly; the long walk, swimming, going to a sports center, playing individual or team sports, and fishing are much more occasional forms of activity.

One in four or five people report going to the pub at lunchtime at least once a week. These will not easily be converted into active sport and

TABLE 4. Activity average frequency of participation per quarter (percent of those participating)

Activity	Total	Male	Female
Individual sports	18.7	19.3	17.3
Team sports	12.6	13.6	9.6
Visited sports center	12.1	13.2	10.8
Sports event spectator	5.0	5.3	4.5
Swimming	10.4	10.8	10.0

SOURCE: Henley Centre for Forecasting, *Leisure Futures*, 1993.

recreation enthusiasts in this lunchtime slot. The pub is often more fun, more sociable, and easier to get to.

These general and national indicators lead to two inescapable conclusions. Sport is a minority activity within our leisure culture, and that minority—despite some significant growth areas such as aerobics—appears to be relatively young, more male, and of "higher" occupational status. Also, the wider leisure culture in which sport and recreation must be contextualized is characterized by intensified forms of individualized consumption and in certain spheres by image and style.

Some of these points might be seen as indicating that the dominant contemporary pattern of leisure consumption is, paradoxically, its lack of pattern, its defiance of traditional categorization. But the general trend data are too selective (as in the case of the Henley Centre) or too blunt (as in the case of the GHS) for such interpretive leaps to be made with confidence. More needs to be known about these leisure consumers and their patterns of leisure and about the cultural context in which particular patterns of leisure participation prevail, as I have demonstrated in the profile of Brighton in the first part of this chapter. With this in mind, it is to the question of regional and local aspects of leisure that I now turn.

ASPECTS OF LEISURE ACTIVITY IN SOUTHEAST ENGLAND

A study of people in the Southeast (Parker and Tomlinson 1992), conducted at the turn of the decades of the 1980s and the 1990s, confirmed some of the national trends reported and discussed in the previous section (if not the local ambience of certain aspects of Brighton as captured by Hamilton and Osborne!). The survey was based on a representative quota sample of 1,010 respondents, interviewed in their homes or in the street in four locations: Tonbridge/Tunbridge Wells, Brighton/Hove, Bournemouth/Poole, and Basingstoke. The interviews were carried out by experienced interviewers coordinated in the field by Abacus Research of Uckfield, Sussex. The sample comprised 54 percent women and 46 percent men, spanning ages 18 to 69 and with an average age of 41 years.

Asked about sport and exercise, 61 percent of respondents reported "taking a walk for exercise" at least once a week, followed by 16 percent visiting a sports center, 15 percent an exercise facility, 13 percent swimming indoors, and 10 percent dancing. But it was interesting to see how many people "never did" those activities: 68 percent never visited an exercise or health facility, 54 percent never visited a sports center, 53 percent never did dancing of any kind, 50 percent never swam indoors, and 17 percent never went walking. It was also noticeable that people exercised or worked out either regularly or not at all.

Age differences were interesting in these activities, mostly in the categories of visiting sports centers and visiting exercise or health facilities. Weekly visitors to sport centers were young (22 percent of age group 18–34; 17 percent of age group 35–54; 5 percent of age group 55–69), as were weekly visitors to exercise or health facilities (19 percent of age group 18–34, 16 percent of age group 35–54, 5 percent of age group 55–69).

Across the sample, gender and occupational status differences (classified in terms of the Market Research Society's criteria) were evident. Many more women, for instance, were frequent swimmers indoors than were men (16 percent as opposed to 10 percent). Social grades D and E were much less physically active in their leisure than were social grades A and B: the figures for visiting sports centers weekly were, for those social grades respectively, 9 percent and 20 percent; for visiting exercise and health facilities, 5 percent and 20 percent; and for swimming indoors 9 percent and 17 percent.

Asked how satisfied they were with provision for leisure activities in their area, nearly three-quarters of the sample were very or fairly satisfied. A half of the Bournemouth sample was very satisfied with their leisure provision, compared with only around one in five in the other towns. Bournemouth and Brighton/Hove had the lowest proportions of people dissatisfied with leisure provision (7 percent and 18 percent respectively) and it would seem likely that this lower level of dissatisfaction is connected to being by the sea and to the availability of resources and facilities in a resort town. More of the As and Bs (37 percent) than the Ds and Es (20 percent) across the sample were "very satisfied" with their local leisure provision, though a third of the respondents considered leisure activities to be expensive. On the cost of leisure activities, more than half of all informants considered them to be "reasonably priced."

LEISURE, CONSUMPTION, AND LOCAL CULTURE IN BRIGHTON

Young people in the Brighton/Hove subsample of the *Life in the South* survey (Parker and Tomlinson 1992) were more active than other age categories: more than half of those who swam weekly were between the ages of 18 and 34, and two-thirds of those who swam once or twice a month were in that age category. For visiting a sports center, figures were similar: over half of those who visited weekly and over two-thirds of those who visited once or twice a month were in the 18–34 age category. Close to three-quarters of those visiting an exercise or health facility at least once a week were 18–34. Walking, too, showed a marked bias toward the younger adult years. Of those who walked for exercise at least weekly, 87.4 percent were 18–44, as were 73 percent of those who took a walk for exercise once or twice a month.

In the rest of this section, highlights from the Chelsea School Research Centre/Leisure Research Unit's three-phase Brighton Leisure Card Survey are presented. This project was implemented by the Leisure Research

Unit in the Chelsea School Research Centre (since superseded by the Sport and Leisure Cultures Research group). The work was conducted for a client, Brighton Borough Council (Marketing and Communications Department), as part of its evolving economic and community (rather than just leisure) strategy. The council was interested in patterns of leisure and consumption in the town as a basis for its decision-making vis-à-vis a possible leisure card (a discount ID for use in local municipal facilities) for people in the town and its potential partnership with, for instance, the French ferry town of Dieppe. The research instruments were therefore designed for policy and potentially commercial purposes, but their design was always a harmonious process of collaboration between the client (the council), the contractor (the Leisure Research Unit), and the subcontractor (market research company and consultant). The list of particular facilities about which respondents were asked was drawn up by the council itself, on the basis of commissioned research on commercial organizations conducted just prior to the Leisure Card Survey.

Drawing on this extensive database, perceptions of and issues around leisure and its provision are reported, general patterns of leisure activity according to frequency and form of activity are reviewed, the social profile of facility usage is commented on, and responses on sport and recreation from Brighton residents are broken down in detail to point to indicative if not "statistically significant" patterns of involvement. These data are then discussed in terms of the general question of the nature and significance of leisure and consumption in city life.

First, the highlights from the Brighton Leisure Card Survey.[1] The initial qualitative phase of the survey identified that attitudes toward Brighton's leisure facilities were mixed. Young people—who mainly used the cinemas, clubs, and public houses—were among the most contented of respondents. Those people particularly interested in cultural pursuits such as music and the theater also felt fairly contented. But sports enthusiasts were generally dissatisfied with what Brighton had to offer, particularly those who claimed some familiarity with leisure centers in the Midlands and the North of England. Older people born and bred in Brighton claimed that the range of activities for their age group had deteriorated over time. This is interesting, as in their lifetimes the range of facilities in both the private and the public sectors will certainly have increased. But of course there are critical questions to be raised here concerning the perception of the nature of space and the issue of access. Older women in a major northern English city, Leeds in Yorkshire, interviewed in the mid-1990s, did not consider the expanding cultural and consumer horizons of the changing city as an option for themselves: "Very few . . . put any emphasis on the city center as providing new opportunities for leisure. Far from new, 'postmodern cities' providing a democratized leisure setting for the consumption of culture, for many of

the women it remains a gendered and racialized space that offers few opportunities" (Scraton and Watson 1998, 134). Space is of course not equally
available to all, ready to be filled by the meanings of one's choice. New images
and structures in social space can be disorienting. Some respondents in the
Leeds study found a haven away from the threat of the new. For Cathy, the
market is her second home, and a shift from stalls to shops robs this space
of its familiarity; for Alice, only the market can counter the loss of the local
shop: "There were lovely shops on the Kirkstall Road . . . yes, you could buy
anything, but there isn't a butcher now, there isn't even a greengrocer . . .
there's nothing" (Scraton, Bramham, and Watson 1998, 117). The Leeds research confirms the continuing threat that city space can be perceived to
contain, particularly by the elderly women on whom the study focused.

In the Brighton study, further barriers to leisure were also identified
in the group discussions. These included lack of money, lack of time, and
for some an inadequate or (especially for the unemployed) an expensive
bus service. Disadvantaged respondents unsurprisingly identified a lack of
money as a constraint on their leisure. When the groups were probed for
spontaneous suggestions for "leisure card" benefits that would be appealing, sport and recreation and transport emphases were apparent: discounts
not just in chain stores and McDonald's but also in leisure centers and on
buses, and family discounts at swimming pools as well as cinemas. A particular benefit that would prove attractive to the more affluent and mobile
was the possibility of priority parking of some kind.

The groups stressed the sociability of sport—as one female discus-
sant put it: "I don't like doing sports on my own, but gardening—I like it on
my own then." Across the groups, sports provision in Brighton was criticized. Sports enthusiasts were among the least satisfied with Brighton. The
most critical respondents were those who had lived at some time in the
Midlands or in the North of England:

> Generally the North of England is miles better. Yorkshire is
> fantastic—Leeds and all round there. Nottingham is fantastic. I
> don't know what it is, but they've just put much, much more into
> the whole thing. (respondent from "disadvantaged women" group)

> There are some lovely leisure centres in the North of England. I
> came down here expecting to see them and they weren't here.
> (respondent from male group)

Brighton also fared badly in comparison with the capital, Londoners complaining that sports facilities were more expensive to use in Brighton:

> I think sports facilities in Brighton are bad. They're very expensive.
> Say if I wanted to go down and train for basketball, I couldn't do

it, whereas in London I could go and hire out a court for half an
hour. (respondent from "disadvantaged women" group)

Brighton's sports provision was also criticized for the location of the facilities, which were seen as "strung out" and "scattered" rather than located
together in any coherent and convenient fashion:

> They're there but they're all so scattered. If you want to go and
> run on the track, it's out at Withdean. There's a little bit of tennis
> and weight-lifting there, but if you want to go swimming you have
> to go somewhere else. (respondent from the male group)

One respondent argued that the sea was underexploited, there being a lack
of water-sports facilities in Brighton:

> Everywhere you go on the Continent, there are facilities galore for
> using the sea in the winter and the summer. Here we have nothing.
> If you want to water-ski, you have to know somebody who has
> their own boat. (respondent from the female group)

Clearly, from these responses, the scale and location of sports-based facilities was a cause of local concern. Old people too, echoing findings in the
Life in the South survey, were negative about Brighton's leisure facilities, noting that the range of activities was too narrow:

> There used to be a lot of tea-dances and things like that, which
> was very good, I used to love them. There's hardly anything for
> the older generation now, except Bingo. (respondent from the
> "disadvantaged man" group)

> There's very little in Brighton. It's disgusting, quite honestly,
> compared to what it used to be when I was young. (respondent
> from the female group)

The most contented respondents in these interviews were young people
(apart from those from the outskirts of the town), for whom Brighton's cinemas, clubs, and pubs provided a major source of satisfaction. Brighton's
club scene was seen to be second only to London's. And as generally stated
above, respondents interested in cultural pursuits also felt that Brighton
catered well for their leisure tastes, with a cosmopolitan repertoire in its
theaters. It was the sports enthusiasts who emerged as the least contented
in these interviews.

Harvey has noted that "the pluralistic stance of postmodernism"
recognizes as essential "the idea that all groups have a right to speak for
themselves, in their own voice, and have that voice accepted as authentic

and legitimate" (1989, 30). This phase of the project sought to mobilize some of those voices, to acknowledge their authenticity. But the range of voices suggested that they were emanating from social experiences that are cultural worlds away from the consumer and communications universe of postmodern discourses. This theoretical issue will be considered in more detail in the concluding section to this chapter.

In the narrative of the Brighton project, the group interviews were followed by a questionnaire survey comprising 478 face-to-face interviews in the two main shopping locations of the town. This second phase of the study (Lawrence and Tomlinson 1991) served as a pilot study for the third phase, the household survey of over 1,000 people. In general terms, the main findings of this third phase were as follows:

- The most leisure-active subgroups in the sample were the younger age groups, people in paid employment, those in A, B, and C1 occupational status groupings, and single people.
- The most popular activities were those requiring no entry fee, such as leisure shopping, walking by the sea or on the beach, eating out, and going to the pub.
- The least popular activities were sports activities (with the exception of swimming).
- Generally, participation in leisure activities is with other adults.
- The most popular facilities were high-profile and central sites, the Palace Pier (69 percent), the Royal Pavilion and Gardens (54 percent), and the Odeon Cinema (50 percent).
- Moulsecoomb Community Leisure Centre (6 percent)—a local facility—featured among the least popular facilities.
- 65 percent agreed that provision for the disabled left much to be desired.
- 69 percent agreed that more attention should be given to the development of leisure facilities in the peripheral areas of Brighton.
- 55 percent saw "fear of the dark" as a factor that more than any other hindered them from taking advantage of Brighton's leisure facilities as often as they would like.
- 52 percent found the cost of car parking a hindrance; 47 percent found the difficulty of car parking a hindrance.
- Daytime parking was such a hindrance for some that 11 percent resorted to going to another town.
- Over a third considered the cost of bus fares to be a hindrance.

Specific facilities did tend to attract particular subgroups of user, and it is illuminating to review sports facilities in terms of typical user profiles, followed by some consideration of theater and cinema use. A major subgroup using the Prince Regent Swimming Complex (overall usage 35 percent of the sample) was single or separated women aged 18–44, Brighton resident, and occupational status B and C1. Withdean Stadium (overall usage 18 percent of the sample) attracted in particular Brightonians aged 35–44, occupational status B. The 11 percent of the overall sample who had visited Stanley Deason Leisure Centre tended to be in the age groups 25–34 and 35–44, from Brighton. Users of the Hollingbury Golf Course (9 percent of the sample) were predominantly male. Those who used Moulsecoomb Community Leisure Centre (6 percent of the sample) tended to be Brighton residents aged 18–24 or 35–44, single, and occupational status C2. Middle-aged and older age groups were conspicuously underrepresented in the usage figures of sport and recreation facilities, apart from the golf course and Brighton Races. This could be related to the fact that people aged 65 or over, along with women across the age categories, were those subgroups of the sample for whom "fear of being in Brighton" after dark stood out as a major hindrance.

Cinemas were dominated by single young adults of "junior management" (in Market Research Society terms) occupational status; central theaters, by older adults of professional or middle management occupational status. The Palace Pier (despite having free admission) attracted very few people above the age of 55 or people dependent on state support. Differences in occupational status and gender were marked in the user profiles of the most central and, in a number of cases in terms of costs, accessible leisure sites and facilities.

I have commented that the broader the profile presented, in sources such as the Henley Centre's survey work, the blunter the analysis—the broader the profile of the consumer, the more likely it is that differences are ironed out. Looking at usage profiles and underrepresentation in use of facilities confirms the continuing—however informal—cultural zoning characteristic of contemporary leisure. In order to look at this in more detail, some data have been generated on the particular patterns of activity of subsamples of the Brighton residents in the survey. These data are drawn on in the rest of this section and followed by a concluding discussion on methodological and theoretical implications of the studies.

The data have been rerun on the basis of the postal districts of Brighton, which themselves served as the sampling frame for the questionnaire survey in the third and main phase of the Brighton Leisure Card Survey, and produced an occupational status profile as follows: occupational grouping A, 3 percent of the sample; B, 23 percent; C1, 29 percent; C2, 25 percent; D, 10 percent; E, 10 percent. The numbers that are the basis of this kind of locality or residential analysis must be treated with some caution: they are too small for the application of tests of statistical significance. So in terms of any quantitative canon, data reported on this are indicative rather than definitive.[2]

The Brighton residential communities, as manifest in the postal districts, are Central; Preston/Preston Park; Patcham; Coldean; Kemp Town/Elm Grove/Whitehawk; Queen's Park/Hanover; Moulsecoomb; the Outer Deans, that is, Ovingdean, Woodingdean, and Rottingdean. The Coldean sample included a higher level of age group 65 and older and fewer in the age group 25–34. In Queen's Park there was a higher percentage of age group 18–44 and fewer in the groups 60–64 and 65 and older. In Moulsecoomb there was also a higher percentage of those over 60 in the sample. There was a higher percentage of people not in paid employment in Patcham and Coldean and a higher percentage of full-time workers in Queen's Park and Hanover. The category of "chief wage earner" for a household was used in the survey; there was a higher percentage of chief wage earners in the respondents in Queen's Park/Hanover and a higher percentage of non–chief wage earners in Preston/Preston Park and the Outer Deans.

There were differences in the distribution of occupational status. As and Bs were prominent in Preston/Preston Park. Bs were prominent in Queen's Park/Hanover. C2s and Ds were prominent in Coldean. And Es (people dependent on state support) were prominent in Queen's Park/Hanover. The Queen's Park/Hanover subsample had a higher percentage of single respondents (as did Central) and a higher percentage of separated/divorced respondents. The subsamples in Patcham, Coldean, and the Outer Deans had a higher percentage of respondents who were married or cohabiting. A higher percentage of respondents in Preston/Preston Park was widowed. The Queen's Park/Hanover subsample had a higher percentage of respondents with no children at home, in contrast to the Outer Deans, whose subsample had a higher percentage of respondents with children still living at home. In Patcham home ownership was especially prominent in contrast to, especially, Moulsecoomb, where renting predominated.

Differences were found in response to the questions, "How would you rate Brighton's leisure facilities for you personally? Do you feel that Brighton offers you . . . a wide range of leisure facilities? A moderate range of leisure facilities? A fairly limited range of leisure facilities?" A higher percentage of respondents in Coldean answered "fairly limited," whereas in Queen's Park/Hanover respondents answered "a wide range." The profile of the residential community and its central or peripheral location are clearly important in how leisure experiences and possibilities are experienced and perceived.

Indicative expressions of opinion on the quality of Brighton's sports facilities were acquired in response to the statement "The sports facilities are poor compared to those in other parts of the country." In Central, 32 percent disagreed and 26 percent agreed with the statement. In Preston/Preston Park, 35 percent agreed and 26 percent disagreed. In Patcham 44 percent agreed (though none "strongly") and 26 percent disagreed (though hardly any disagreed "strongly"). Forty-eight percent agreed and 22 percent disagreed in Coldean. In Kemp Town/Elm Grove/Whitehawk, 37 percent agreed and 22 percent disagreed. In Queen's Park/Hanover, 34 percent agreed and 19 percent disagreed. In Moulsecoomb, 37 percent agreed and 33 percent disagreed. And in the Outer Deans, 25 percent agreed and 25 percent disagreed. The tendency here was for more people in less central communities to agree to the statement—or at least to choose not to disagree with or contradict the statement.

When faced with the statement "More attention should be given to developing the leisure facilities in the peripheral areas of Brighton," people clearly expressed their views on the basis of their residential experience. In Central, 34 percent agreed and 24 percent disagreed. In Preston/Preston Park, 74 percent agreed and a mere 12 percent disagreed. In Patcham, 65 percent agreed and 26 percent disagreed. In Coldean, 65 percent agreed and 17 percent disagreed. In Kemp Town/Elm Grove/Whitehawk, 73 percent agreed and 11 percent disagreed. In Queen's Park/Hanover, 64 percent agreed and 9 percent disagreed. In Moulsecoomb, 70 percent agreed and 13 percent disagreed. In the Outer Deans, 80 percent agreed and 15 percent disagreed. There is an element of self-interest in these responses, but without doubt a very strong feeling across the town that outlying areas are not well provided for in terms of leisure.

In looking at particular facilities and activities, the influence of the residential communities is again marked. There are clear differences in cinema, theater, pub, and club going—in close-to-the-center, fashionable Queen's Park and bohemian Hanover this is very predominant; in more outlying Patcham and Coldean less so. The pattern is the same for walking by the sea and eating out and going to concerts or live music. A higher percentage of people from Coldean never goes to a swimming pool (Moulsecoomb shares this characteristic) or a leisure center. Queen's Park/Hanover has a higher percentage of people going to the swimming pool (as does the Outer Deans) and to a leisure center. In terms of all these forms of activity, Coldean—and to a lesser extent Patcham—might as well not be in Brighton at all.

With regard to specific facilities, the Stanley Deason Leisure Centre was used more by people from Kemp Town/Elm Grove/Whitehawk and the Outer Deans (as was, more surprisingly, the Moulsecoomb Community Leisure Centre), almost never by people from Coldean. The Moulsecoomb Centre was virtually never used by people from Queen's Park/Hanover. Withdean Stadium was used by people from Preston/Preston Park and not used by people from Coldean. In a highly mobile society, locality of access continues to be an important consideration.

CONCLUDING COMMENTS

This chapter is a rather hybrid beast, made up on the one hand of reports from projects that were client-led and on the other of methodological and theoretical concerns that were not central in the planning and implementation of those projects, spiced too by a contextual cultural portrait of the city of Brighton. To switch metaphors, it might look like rather an odd sandwich, with the conceptual bread pressing far from neatly around the filling of the empirical projects. But the novelty of putting those together at all is indicative of the paucity or inadequacy of empirical referents in prominent discussions of the nature of contemporary leisure.

There is no shortage of sophisticated and eloquent theorizing about spaces such as the theme park as a "zoned space for pleasure, contingent on and convenient to the city, yet apart from it" (Philips 1998, 75), less vibrant and expressive and multivocal than relatively uncontrolled city spaces such as the fairground, the local carnival, or the market place (81). How female recreational sportswomen construct their own body fashions and negotiate their physical identities in sports space has also received close attention (Fasting 2000, 157). Such focused work continues to be invaluable and illuminating of contemporary trends, and alongside such work the aim of this chapter is comparatively modest. Some geographic approaches have also prioritized the study of leisure or tourism as the study of encounters (Crouch 1999), and perhaps such an approach might usefully reprise the brilliant work of Erving Goffman in this area. For Goffman, encounters or "focused gatherings" included the examples of "a *tête-à-tête*; a jury deliberation; a game of cards; a couple dancing; a task jointly pursued by persons physically close to one another; love-making; boxing" (1972, 18). In this sense, though, many leisure cultures and practices might constitute unfocused gatherings. We can sit in the cinema or the theater on our own, in close proximity to hundreds of (in many cases like-minded) human beings, and have no encounter whatsoever with any one of them. The combination of a cultural geography allied to the nuances of a Goffmanesque symbolic interactionism affords the leisure researcher some stimulating possibilities. Within the newer cultural geography mentioned in the first section of this chapter, too, there are novel and stimulating new challenges: the senses are given prominence in Urry's research agenda: "People's pleasures in leisure can be interrrogated and even enhanced," he writes (1999, 44), promoting an analysis of leisure according to categories such as sense and smell. Urry reports that "recent leisure-related trends include . . . some appreciation that the preservation of landscapes involves not just issues of visualisation, but also of threatened smellscapes" (43). This chapter has aspired to no such level of insight into the sphere of the sensory. It has, rather, sought to review the evidence in a local case for an understanding of the reasons why more than a few in a local population might have restricted prospects for meaningful "encounters" in relatively local "smellscapes," threatened or otherwise.

In John Urry's eloquent, insightful, and accessible study of tourism he recognizes that "by no means all" aspects of contemporary culture are characterized by postmodernist "processes of de-differentiation" and "that there are other important cultural elements that will be present in a given society (pre-modern, realist, modernist etc.)" (1990, 86). But the postmodern perspective dominates his analysis of contemporary culture, and as argued elsewhere, Urry's tourist emerges "as a passive recipient of a constructed experience, as a malleable and uncritical consumer of increasingly spectacle-ised places and spaces" (Crouch and Tomlinson 1994, 311). Yet the gaze is not all consuming, and sociability continues to be a central dimension of leisure activity and urban consumption, not just in the spectacular subcultures of bohemian or youth groups, or the collective self-generated consumption of the voluntary sphere, but also in the everyday practices of recreational walking, shopping, or eating and drinking out and everyday tourist behavior.

Summarizing a socioeconomic analysis that places a mediated condition of hyperreality at the center of its framework, Rojek makes four points: that new more flexible forms of capital and the fragmentation and insecurity that they generate are "reflected in leisure experience which becomes more restless and preoccupied with gaining permanent distraction from the worries of life" (1993, 286). Second, with the collapse of distinctions between elite culture and popular culture, "cultural affiliation and compliance in leisure practice" is (further) complicated. Third, new forms of leisure practice stimulated by the media emphasize "simultaneity and integration," weakening distinctions between the domestic and the global. Fourth, electronic forms of communication emphasize discontinuity, simulation negating the principle of authenticity: "The screen replaces the street as the axis of leisure identities, associations and practices" (287). There is no doubt that these points depict important dimensions of the condition of contemporary leisure culture. But late nineteenth-century social and cultural life in Britain could be characterized in a number of similar ways, with fragility of identity and the loss of traditional certainties at the core of the experience of British society: "It could be seen . . . in a certain latent instability throughout the industrial world, in an assumption that change was a norm of life in a way that had not been true in past ages . . . a society in which rootlessness was endemic and in which people felt themselves to be living in many different layers of historic time" (Harris 1993, 5). Before accepting wholesale the postmodern diagnosis, it is important to keep asking what people do, where they do it, and with whom they do it. It is still possible to be skeptical about the screen and friendly on the street—more difficult, perhaps, in some urban contexts and localities, but possible. As Sola says of Brighton's St. James's Street, close to the town center and the seafront and highly transformed and consumerized in the late 1990s:

> St James's Street is a real changing animal, every day a new premises changes from old fashioned to new and trendy. . . . the Safeway has rebranded itself as a "Metro" store [which] fits with the projected idea of the area as full of busy urban types, who don't have time to cook.
>
> The image St. James's Street wants is constantly under threat from the people that use it, gay businesses come under regular attack (the Candy Bar, a lesbian bar, had its windows broken many times before it ever opened), there have been a few gay murders this year, there are a lot of homeless drug users and alcoholics on the street, some really heartbreakingly covered in sores and clearly very distressed, mums ask kids to hold their hands tightly, but it is still a place where people stop to chat and smile hello.[3]

The surveys reported in this chapter were commissioned and generated not in response to diagnoses of the postmodern moment, but in the context of a concern with understanding some of the specificities of regions and urban localities. This sort of concern is conspicuously absent in many discussions of the momentum and pervasiveness of the postmodern in contemporary social and cultural life.

The picture of leisure consumption that emerged in these studies of the Brighton population is one of discrete activity markets for particular age and status groups, rather than any free-floating patternless consumerism. This is not to deny the force of social and cultural changes affecting domestic and public culture (Tomlinson 1990a, 1990b; Philips and Tomlinson 1992). Rather, it is to recognize that the model of the quintessential postmodern consumer is premised on an infrastructure of resources, access, and income, and that for many individuals and social groups such a dizzy world of consumption is something from which they remain culturally disenfranchised. Cities are reshaped by cultural and consumer identities and public leisure cultures. This can generate forms of material displacement, as a result of gentrification, and cultural colonization (Tomlinson 1983). When patterns of consumption in urban leisure culture are scrutinized in any detail, participation in the most everyday and mundane of leisure practices away from home can be seen to be bounded by classic sociological influences of class, gender, and age. Henry recognizes the contemporary mix of some elements of the postmodern and other aspects, commenting that "Cultural fragmentation is developing apace, with growing individualization and

privatization. The merging of authentic and fake in hyperreality is an identifiable and significant phenomenon. However, the focus on these contemporary cultural phenomena to the exclusion of other significant features of
social existence is mistaken" (1995, 56). The regional and local studies cited
in this chapter remind us of the persistence of social divisions based on
class, status, gender, and age and of how these overlap with spatial influences such as residential location. They constitute evidence of inequality as
well as lifestyle choice.

Too much postmodern theorizing remains ignorant of the nature of
social structure, social relationships, and cultural life. Norris has condemned
Baudrillard for peddling "a form of wholesale anti-realist doctrine" and
offers his rejoinder in the observation that "there are real and present facts
of experience—inequality, deprivation, urban squalor, unemployment, massive and increasing differentials of wealth and power—which make non-
sense of Baudrillard's sophisticated case that nothing exists outside the
endless circulation of ungrounded arbitrary signs" (1990, 188). Such facts of
experience continue to construct and constrain the possibilities for leisure
experience and consumption, and such facts—despite Roberts's wise reminder that sometimes, in the case of social class measures, the selected
mode of analysis may well "yield the expected results" (1995, 3)—can best be
explored in terms of the specificities of regional and local cultures and the
patterns that characterize those cultures over and above the unique experiences of the single individual.

The residential subsamples in the Brighton study confirm the distinctiveness of localized leisure cultures and consumption possibilities and
preferences within any urban context. A particular kind of population in
central areas feels on the whole well catered for; as one moves toward the
periphery of the town, public leisure cultures seem increasingly insignifi-
cant. The city center is a mecca for the young, a no-go zone for many of the
elderly. As any open-eyed contemporary observer or sociologist must recognize, this is in part a consequence of lifestyle choice and the centrality of
home-centeredness in current patterns of leisure consumption (the video
not the movies, the four-pack not the pub), but it is also in part a consequence of barriers to and inhibitions on leisure. The cost of transport, the
time to do things, the concern over personal safety—all of these affect the
leisure choices that individuals make and can be seen to be bound up with
persisting social influences, so reminding us that classic sociological categories and divisions such as class, gender, and age are still major determinants of the cultural landscapes and human networks of urban life.

8. The Politics of Men's Leisure

Northern English Working-Class Culture in the 1930s

How are the cultural practices of traditional working-class culture related to new developments in the consumer market? This has been a central question in oral history, social history, and related fields concerned with the study of the place of sport, leisure, and popular culture in the everyday life of the working classes. To answer such a question, it is important to look not just at working-class institutions one by one (the family, the club, work, and so on), but to look at the nature of working-class culture as a *whole;* to see precisely how it is made, remade, consolidated, or undermined. It is also important, in doing this, to look at elements in working-class culture that are not explicitly progressive (or emergently challenging)—which is what Richard Hoggart did in part one of his study of working-class life (1958)— but also at those which might constitute a conservative (I say conservative, and not reactionary or residual) core at the center of working-class culture. I will say more about this conservative core in the final section of this chapter, when I discuss the way in which aspects of working-class leisure show how social actors can recognize injustices and reject dominant values but simultaneously choose to retreat into their own familiar social world.

A working-class culture characterized by a mixture of privatized social life, industrial or political struggle, and a stress on locality-cum-community and hedonism is a much more complicated phenomenon than a master-servant view of history would imply. To understand the complexity of working-class culture, therefore, we need to consider how individuals and groups are positioned in relation to the labor process and the labor market—on which theoretical ethnographics of past and present working and everyday life are very much needed. And to come anywhere close to grasping what working-class culture is and has been, we need to take the task of historical reconstruction very seriously indeed. In other words, past and present ethnographies are required—ethnographies on how the general social processes that we know to be at work in modern industrial capitalism are actually *lived through* and experienced by the working class in specific places and at particular times. This sounds straightforward enough, but the need for such work warrants a theoretical and methodological rationale alongside the reporting of the case itself. In this chapter, therefore, I report and speculate on a small-scale focused study of working-class sports and leisure in Colne, a small industrial community in northeast Lancashire, concentrating on the interwar years of the twentieth century. In doing this, I want to feature very prominently the voices of the working-class respondents to whom I talked when conducting the study in the mid-1980s. The question, "How was Colne, as an entity, possible in a period of massive social divisiveness?" will be at the heart of the discussion.

THE CONTINUING NEED FOR SOCIAL HISTORIES OF SPORT

My own work on the 1930s developed out of a dissatisfaction with what was available in the field of sports history. We have no shortage of histories of sports (results, personalities, and so on) but when undertaking this study, I was conscious that there were few *social* histories of sports. This has been to some extent remedied since with the appearance of single studies and also valuable collections (Mason 1989). These have tended to tell the story of the erosion of traditional forms of working-class culture and document the triumph of the forces of commercialism. They challenge the historian to reassess the kind and level of significance that more traditional sports had in working-class culture. My study of Colne was led by such concerns. When I encountered some references to a sport called knur and spell in some Northern towns in England, I wanted (a) to reconstruct this sport's history in truly social, rather than "quaintly archaic" historical ways (see Tomlinson 1992a; and chapter 9 of this book) and (b) to consider in some detail the nature of and influences on working-class sport and leisure in one small town in the interwar years. As has been commented about this period: "We probably know more about Victorian pubs, coffee rooms and clubs than we do about those of the 1920s and 1930s" (Howkins and Lowerson 1979, 57). So a general aim in my two tasks was simply to reconstruct the sports and leisure activities within the cultural life of a working-class community, using interviews with local people, reporting their experiences in their own voices and names.

The 1930s is a fascinating period, too, for comparison with the 1970s and 1980s. As Howkins and Lowerson noted, "Interwar Britain presents a mixed picture . . . in the first place we see an enormous growth of leisure both in terms of time and expenditure. . . . The second area of importance is . . . enforced leisure created by unemployment" (55). And perhaps one of the most important questions about both periods is this—how are massively significant creases in the social fabric smoothed out? How is it that working-class males continue to gather together in tens of thousands to watch a game of football, rather than to demand bread or social justice? I am not alone in commenting on the lack of work on this. Listen to what Stuart Hall has to say (his "us" refers to a gathering he was addressing at a *History Workshop* conference):

> It isn't by chance that very few of us are working in popular culture
> in the 1930s. I suspect there is something peculiarly awkward,
> especially for socialists, in the non-appearance of a militant, radical,
> mature culture of the working-class in the 1930s when to tell you
> the truth—most of us would have expected it to appear. From the
> viewpoint of a purely "heroic" or "autonomous" popular culture,
> the 1930s is a pretty barren period. This "barrenness"—like the
> earlier unexpected richness and diversity—cannot be explained
> from *within* popular culture alone. (1981, 230)

So we must look at the underlying social relations embodied in the popular cultural forms of Hall's "barren" period. What Hall implies here is that popular culture must be autonomous, set apart from the dominant culture and pitted against it. What kind of social relations, though, are bound up with nonheroic, nonautonomous popular cultural forms such as sport? They cannot simply be taken for granted, the question put to one side. It is this question that drives the analysis in this chapter.

Working-Class (Popular) Culture in Colne

Colne is a small, northeast Lancashire cotton town at the end of a line of four townships that runs through a valley typical of the kind of townships that grew up early in the industrial revolution. Beyond this line lies the pretty wild area of the Yorkshire moors, famous for fueling the extraordinary imaginations of the Brontë family. The town rises up the foothills of the Pennine hills and is surrounded on all sides by hills and moorlands that are immediately accessible. Closed in by hills it has *the feel* of a self-contained, if not isolated, community (this local topography is further expanded in chapter 9). Only a few miles away lies one of northern England's biggest wool towns, Bradford. But that is in a different county—Yorkshire—and Colne retains a strong sense of its Lancashire affiliation. Although Colne surrendered its independence as a separate borough in 1974—to be absorbed into the new Borough of Pendle (total population 85,600), which incorporates half a dozen other towns and village—it has retained, among its smallish population, a fiercely partisan sense of its own local identity.[1] The population of the town in the mid-1980s was under 20,000, and within a couple of miles of it lie several industrial villages that were seen, in the interwar years, as separate and distinct "communities" and whose culture was based very much on the chapel. A tradition of political support for the Labour Party was rudely interrupted in the 1970s, when a swing to Conservatism reflected the crisis of British labor politics. That is the context, then. I now describe the range of activities that characterized working-class culture, say something about the range of lived cultures *within* the working class generally, and consider some of the influences on and meanings of particular cultural practices.

There was a range of male-dominated cultural forms still thriving in the 1930s (many of which still thrived half a century later). The working-men's club, the brass band, the pigeon-fanciers' club—these are just some of the voluntaristic or self-provided and self-organized types of activities. There was also a strong commercial base to leisure experience: the cinema, boxing and wrestling three nights a week, dancing, and the pub. Local amateur football and cricket were extensively played. So too were games of various kinds (ranging from stick games to whippets or pigeons) clustered around betting or gambling. One of the main characteristics of such activities is the dominance of the male. Outlets for leisure activities for women were severely restricted. For most married, working-class women away from the church, the chapel, the women's institute, or the cinema, patterns of leisure were a matter of creating forms of sociability within the workplace of the home or the communal washhouse (see, for an example of this in the culture of the South Wales working class, Crook 1982; on Salford (north of Manchester), England, Davies 1992; and on East Sussex, England, though for a later period, Tomlinson 1978). Sociability was created in much the same way as in male shop floor culture, which could attempt to usurp industrial labor time for nonwork purposes (see Hollands 1988). It is really the rise of the commercial sector on a new large scale in, for instance, the cinema and dance hall, which created spaces where women could go and be accepted. Mrs. Baxter recalls her "courting" days in the early years after World War I:

> We used to go to t' pictures and I was only allowed out on
> Wednesday night and Saturday and Sunday and I used to 'ave to
> be in at nine o'clock at 21 years of age. . . . Ooh, pub, no, never
> 'eard of.

This is quite a change from her own mother's social life, which had revolved exclusively around the chapel and which had been an early influence in Mrs. Baxter's own life:

> I used to be in concerts . . . oh, yes, and especially when the talking
> pictures came, yes, we used to go to t' pictures Christmas Eve—
> operatics, we've seen quite a lot and I still go to operatics now.

Mrs. Baxter's patterns of leisure changed after marriage, coming closer to how she recalls her own mother's routinized week—"Oh, routine, Mother used to wash Monday . . . and ironin' on Tuesday. . . . Bakin' days, oh they *were* bakin' days." And so "after marriage" Mrs. Baxter no longer went "dancin'"; instead she "went to plays—that were my pleasure." Dancing, then, was a space for the unattached or courting woman, not for the married one. After marriage, the domestic site and its responsibilities put constraints on the social life of the woman. And we should not imagine that popping in and out of houses was a firmly entrenched activity within the working class. Mr. Billy Baxter is emphatic in recalling that, though support was always available in a crisis, neighbors were not there to be imposed on: "As soon as yer start tea-partyin' yer start fallin' out." And so, within the commercial sector, the cinema offered a potentially liberating space for women's leisure, a space in which the surroundings of everyday life could be temporarily escaped. In the words of Andrew Faulds:

> It could open up a new world . . . standard of living . . . if your own rotten, miserable life were spent in a stinkin', dirty cotton mill [or the home] you wanted to get away from that and be transferred . . . call it what you like . . . and then you could see there were somethin' else in life beside work.

It is not coincidental that one of the biggest stars in British cinema in the 1930s was Gracie Fields, the "lass from Rochdale" who so easily found a responsive audience among the working-class cinema audiences of the times (Aldgate 1981). It is in what one writer has called the "growth of the industries of entertainment" (Wild 1979, 59) that working-class women found the possibility of experiencing newer forms of leisure away from the spheres of male-dominated leisure that were so central to Colne's working-class culture. Bingo, for instance, was an important example of this in the second half of the century (Dixey 1983). We have, then, to see gender—male dominance within the sites of leisure, if not in the home—as an absolutely central dimension of working-class culture. Although women might not be actually debarred from certain kinds of activities, and could, as they did in the bigger working-class town of Bolton, attend wrestling matches, this was not approved of by other elements within the culture. Evidence on audiences at wrestling matches in Bolton indicates that the women who attended did so in order to see specimens of male virility ("real men") the like of which were not available, claimed some respondents, at home (Mass Observation 1939). But such activities met with double disapproval: they were seen as nonfemale activities, and they were seen as lacking in any moral dimension. Women were doubly damned for invading male territory and lacking morals. The first general point, therefore, that I want to make about working-class culture in Colne at this time is that it is gender distinctive.

My second point refers to the elements within the working class itself. For in Colne at this time there was no single, easily identifiable, homogeneous working-class culture. There was a range of lived cultures within the working class itself. Hugh Cunningham has illustrated this beautifully with reference to the nineteenth century (1980); Engels lionized the autodidactic English working-class figure for whom economic, scientific, and aesthetic lectures provided the ideal leisure pursuit (1958, 272). There were without doubt such groupings in Colne too. But Anthony Delves has emphasized how popular culture can be influenced by the outcome of intra- and interclass relations (1981). And it is always worth remembering that when Karl Marx got round, in the *18th Brumaire* (Marx 1979), to talking about *class* in given moments, at particular points, he proposed long lists of factions across and within class lines. So we must beware of any simple notion of a pure working class. All elements within working-class culture might share a common situation in terms of, say, their relation to capital (though things are complicated here by the persistence in the interwar years of transient, casual labor as a means of supporting oneself), but there are other mediating influences that partially structure the experience of particular groups — such as the church, the kind of worker-employer relation characteristic of the workplace, and a sense of neighborhood or extreme locality.

There was, then, no single working class within Colne. It is worth breaking down some of the separate elements: first, according to location or place; second, according to what I will call the local social structure.

At the bottom of the town's steep high street was the station area, described to me by one respondent (Norman Atkinson) as a separate, self-contained area with its own shops, its own services, and even its own hawking system; in the middle of the town, into the 1930s, there was the notorious Windy Bank, a kind of center for the "rough" working class, where "Irishmen" might also come in as casual immigrant labor for the haymaking season; there was "Waterside," a self-contained, respectable working-class area around the town's river valley; and there were the surrounding villages, which often clustered around the chapel as a major influence. There is no single, united view of the world to which these different cultural worlds subscribed. They need to be explored separately and yet in the context of the processes prevailing in the time of which they are all a part.

These areas had distinctive class cultures. In Windy Bank, before it was redeveloped out of existence in the mid-1930s, a "rough" working-class culture prevailed. It was a culture that in the interwar years was subjected to a systematic attack by decision-making bodies in the local community.

Perceiving Windy Bank as a threat to "respectable" elements in the town, the town's council drew up, in 1931, a ten-year plan that included the demolition and redevelopment of the Windy Bank area and of two other areas, Waterside and Nineveh. Windy Bank's seven streets had 315 residents (when not swollen, presumably, by Irish labor)—a mere 1.3 percent of the town's population of 23,791 in 1931. But it was in a central position in the town, running down one side of the high street, a sore sight for respectable eyes. In this sense, it never stood a chance when the image of the town began to be worked on systematically. Waterside was the next "clearance area" in 1934, when 516 people in twelve streets with three pubs were redeveloped out of their own culture. (My figures on these processes are culled from the work of a local historian, Crombie 1978). What, then, in this interwar period was so distinctive about the culture that it was undermined so effectively by "respectable" citizens of the town?

One local historian has said that "off the main streets of Colne were many courts and alleys where closely knit communities had to make do with the most meagre living standards. . . . The warren of buildings behind the Robin Hood in Waterside survived until the early 1930s" (Spencer 1971, 27). But, with the welcome exception of Davies's (1992) work on Salford, there has been little investigation of what the life of such "closely knit" communities was like. A pictorial representation of Colne refers to a number of the characters of Windy Bank, but says little about the area itself (Crombie 1978, 12–13). I have spoken in depth to one of the cited characters, Jim Hird, and to Jimmy Hines, the brother of another. There seems little doubt that life could be rough in the area. This is what Jimmy Hines told me:

> JIMMY H.: Fighting was popular among the locals themselves . . . street fighting . . . it was a rough area you know was Windy Bank . . . the Heaps and the Leonards, they was the main culprits, it was like a vendetta with 'em, it were a rough quarter you know, but they'd be the best of pals next day. People never held grudges against one another . . . they were good people . . . them days down Windy Bank policemen didn't go down there singlehanded, there were two or three at a time . . . I've no idea what it [the fight] was about, but they were always at it.

> A.T.: What happened with all the other people in the neighborhood? Did they gather round?

> JIMMY H.: Oh aye they all watched . . . they all loved a good fight . . . it'd take sometimes half an 'our.

> A.T.: What was it . . . just fists?

JIMMY H.: Oh it were the lot, the boot and the lot went in, then it
nearly always was a free-for-all, and the police 'ud come down an'
break it up . . . it were, like, telegraph.

A.T.: Were women ever involved in this?

JIMMY H.: Oh, they were at it anole . . . What do they call 'er? Big
Maggie, Maggie Mackenzie . . . un Big Willie 'ud fight over nothing.

Unsurprisingly, Windy Bank bred fighters. Jimmy Hines himself was an
experienced local boxer and his brother Laddie, who died at twenty-one,
had already won 81 of his 90 fights. The Hines were involved with a few
gyms in the area, and boxing booths came to town with the local fair, and
then were set up on a more regular basis in the town. Windy Bank was a
"rough" area where toughness was respected. Toughness as a trait of working-
class culture has lacked serious investigation, apart from one detailed exploration of a London boxer at the turn of the century (Shipley 1983). Life
in Windy Bank may also have been less routinized or structured than in
other parts of town, for work discipline may not have been so rigorously
formalized. Joseph Hird, for instance, was born in 1908 to a gypsy family in
Windy Bank and was raised in the area. Joseph's motto was "Ad 'awk owt for
a bob," which means, to the nonlocal, "I'd sell anything for a few pennies or
a shilling (or a few dimes)." Joseph Hird lived in Colne all his life, though he
farmed for thirty-three years on the edge of town:

JOSEPH H.: I never worked for nobody in mi life. I've bin on
mi own since I left school . . . used to 'awk when I were
young, used to 'awk fruit you know . . . earn a bob where we
could . . . an' when we earned a bob in them days it were yer
own, an' we used to mek thi own sports.

Married at twenty-one, Joseph Hird lived in Puddling Pond in one of a row
of six houses. His rent was six shillings and four pence per week and included two bags of coal. He lived there throughout the 1930s, in a small
"two-up-two-down terraced house," before taking up his farming: "There
were no baths them days . . . there were nowt like that . . . outside toilets."
Joseph's brother also lived in Windy Bank; he ran a rough-and-ready
utility store there for most of his working life. Windy Bank had more than
just a "rough" everyday culture to worry the local authorities. It also had a
local informal or "black" economy. These combined to create a specific culture of the casual laboring class. In such parts of the town as the Station
area and Waterside, more "respectable" working-class cultures made their
contribution to the entity known as Colne. Further divisions could operate within these categories, and it is important to recognize religion and

politics as sources of such divisions. Two major cultural categories within the working class, then, could be seen as the nonconformist religious work-ing class and the secular culture of the working class. It is with elements that contribute to the latter that I have been most concerned so far. In the 1920s, the local authorities had banned the sport of bowling stones, and in a legendary 1920s police raid on the moors around the town the gambling networks had been broken.

So what I have been looking at in talking about Windy Bank and in instancing forms of street culture is a predominantly hedonistic element in secular working-class culture, which was under attack from the "respectable" local society. It is worth noting that most of my respondents, with whom I made contact on the basis of networks of sport and leisure, had little and often absolutely nothing to do with political associations.

In other sections of the working class, popular culture revolved around the chapel, which could be an all-embracing influence on social life, particu-larly in the small industrial villages around the immediate countryside. Vic-tor Bertwhistle talked to me about life in tiny Trawden, a mere mile or two outside Colne. As a boy, he would play any of a wide range of games available, all of them based on the street and items of everyday life. Nicknacking involved a thread and a drawing pin. Tin in t' Ring, Billet and Stick, Wooden and Iron, Hoops, Whip and Top, Devil Up Pipe, and Statues were all street games, several of which were of an obviously irritating type to the adults in the community. Yet, from his boyhood, it was the chapel that constituted the major influence on his nonwork life. Leisure time, for both men and women within such networks, became increasingly defined and structured by the chapel. Victor Bertwhistle recalls the early 1920s:

> In the evenings at winter time, well, the churches would have
> events . . . socials, concerts, at-homes, pantomimes, and what
> have you . . . there was the Church of England, the Primitive
> Methodist, the Trawden Wesleyan, the Zion Independent, and
> then the Inghamites . . . there were five churches . . . and organized
> by the Sunday School scholars you'd 'ave the annual outing and
> you'd go to Ilkley or something like that which was a great event. . . .
> In 1920–21 we went to Ilkley from our Sunday School on what was
> a converted coal wagon and thought it was absolutely marvellous
> to go to Ilkley . . . that was like going abroad.

Ilkley is only a few miles from Trawden. It is difficult to overemphasize the significance of locality in working-class culture of the time. To reiterate, Colne and the area around it was defined by the hills and the landscape as well as by place-names and boundaries. The area, and areas within it, are physically enclosed communities. This had the effect, in the pre-motor age, of solidifying the local culture. Around the church or the chapel, in places like Trawden (where the places of worship outnumbered by more than two to one the places of drinking) and certainly in areas within Colne itself, Victor Bertwhistle and people like him could structure their social and family lives almost completely around the church or the chapel; many of the activities in this setting were self-generated and self-organized and contributed to an energetic and dynamic participatory culture.

I have spent most time in this chapter describing the "rough" variant within secular working-class culture and the respectable religious working-class culture. There were, within working-class culture, all sorts of shaded areas between these somewhat polarized extremes. Mrs. Baxter, quoted earlier, went to dancing as well as to chapel. But proponents of the latter generally retained a strong sense of disapproval of the former, and so the tension between the religious and the secular in working-class culture produced many different types of cultural experience at and between the two extremes. My point is a simple one in the end. It is that we must be aware of the diversity *within* the working class if we are to develop an adequate sense of the vibrant cultures of the local social structure of the time. Besides these various working-class cultures, the other elements in the local social structure were the middle classes (traders, professionals, teachers, and "public administrators"), and the local squirearchy, made up of "significant" families that had, through ownership of land or factories or through trade, assumed the position of the local "leaders."

The single most significant fact about this local social structure in the interwar period is that it survived intact, discrete from, apart from, the rough working-class culture, which was "redeveloped" away. This survival took place during two decades of almost uninterrupted crisis in the local cotton industry, intensified by the stock market crash and the depression years in the 1930s. The crash did not plummet a secure world into an unanticipated crisis. As one specialist has put it, "In the 1920s and the 1930s the threat of unemployment hung over most workers in Britain irrespective of where they lived" (Constantine 1980, 17). Cotton, coal, shipbuilding, and the iron and steel industries (the great boom industries of early industrialization) were in permanent decline at the beginning of the interwar period. Constantine refers to the gross "inefficiency" of an industry that "had been slow to convert to ring-pinning, automatic looms and electric power before the war," and therefore became increasingly uncompetitive in the world market between the wars (12). The slump intensified a crisis already well-entrenched, particularly in towns dependent on single industries. In a bigger cotton town—Blackburn, some twenty miles away—the figures illustrate this well. In Blackburn, where 60 percent of the workforce was employed in the cotton industry, the 1931 slump "left 46.8 per cent of workers unemployed"

(19). Here, "the dawn of affluence" and the expansion in the "range of entertainment" (Stevenson and Cook 1979) were clearly far from the general experience.

The central question is how, in times (long-term times, not simply occasional moments) like these, times of obvious tension in the social fabric, the diverse elements in the social structure of Colne could continue to constitute Colne as an entity. In answer to that question it is important to point to the experiences of the people in the community that show how Colne could be experienced as a common point of reference, despite the potential tensions built into the social relations of the time. The example that I take to illustrate this is the game of cricket.

In the 1920s and the 1930s, Lancashire League cricket drew big crowds to watch teams representative of small towns or areas within larger towns play each other. To play for the team, residence or employment within the town or area was a qualification, though each club was allowed one full-time professional. The Lancashire League still operates at the beginning of the twenty-first century, along much the same principles but with nowhere near the same crowds. In cricket, the social relations of the time (or at least a central aspect of them) became manifested in a prominent local cultural form. This can be usefully explored by considering how individuals of diverse types came to construct a common subjectivity around the popular cultural form of cricket. This is most dramatically exemplified in the reception given to Indian and West Indian cricketers who came to the towns of northeast Lancashire as club professionals in the Lancashire League. The game of cricket introduced black people into the local culture long before the waves of post–World War II immigration from the Commonwealth territories. From 1935 to 1938, for instance, Lalah Amar Singh played as a professional for Colne and entered the local mythology through his sporting feats. An Indian, he scored 2,700 runs as a batsman and took 336 wickets as a bowler in his three seasons with Colne, and once, it was recorded, he hit a score of 110 not out in only twenty minutes. Singh died, tragically, on the way home to India in 1939, aged only twenty-nine.

Perhaps the most famous black person to play Lancashire League cricket was Learie Constantine, who played for neighboring Nelson. It is recorded that the largest-ever crowd for a Colne versus Nelson match gathered in 1929, when Constantine was playing (Crombie 1978). And a 1935 match, with Singh the professional for Colne, drew a gate (a total income from admission fees) of 367 pounds, 13 shillings, and 7 pence, at sixpence each for admission. This represents between 14,000 and 15,000 spectators in a town with a population of just under 24,000. I asked Ellis Dickinson, a former Colne player, how the black players were perceived by the local people:

Well, there weren't a lot of black uns about in them days yer see . . .
a black chap it didn't matter . . . 'e were an attraction as a cricketer
if 'e were a good un.

There was, in fact, more to Constantine than that he was a "good un at
cricket." The West Indian writer C. L. R. James has related to an English
writer a tale that shows that Constantine was more than a mere sportsman:
it was he who urged James to "'come over here' to Nelson, if you want to get
published" (Ward 1983, 475). James took Constantine's advice and got his
manuscript published by a small publisher in Nelson, Colne's neighboring
town, which was known as one of Lancashire's "Little Moscows." Yet it was
exclusively for his cricket that Constantine was recognized as "a good un"
and welcomed by the local populations. In this sense, the sporting experience has the capacity to supersede differences. And if you were "a good un"
a lot of privileges might come your way. This was as true of working-class
sportsmen as of the black club professionals from the other side of the
world. By concentrating in detail on the career of Ellis Dickinson, it can
be seen how the bonding of community can be experienced, lived out, and
partially achieved in the sphere of sports.

Ellis Dickinson was born in 1906 in the nearby village of Earby. At the
age of fifteen, he started working in the mill—"you've got to go into t' mill,
that's all there were knockin' about 'ere in those days . . . I worked in a small
mill and I were determined to get out as quickly as ever I could." Cricket
became Ellis's escape route from unrelenting work in the cotton mill. At one
point, he was asked to practice with the Yorkshire County Cricket Club,
which paid traveling expenses and ten shillings a day and thirteen shillings
for an appearance in a second team match. Another county in the West
Midlands also approached Ellis, asking him to join them as a wicketkeeper.

Ellis resisted the approach from Worcestershire in the Midlands
and, in the end, the approach from the Yorkshire club. Pulled in one direction by the club—to play for its second team—and in another by his uncle—
to join the local police force—he chose the latter. At the age of nineteen,
Ellis saw this as offering a secure future, and he recalls that "I never valued
sport as a career for the simple reason you're only as good as what you
are." But Ellis was not happy in the police force, and only lasted fourteen
months—"I didn't like it a bit an' I soon chucked out of that." Having left
the police force he went back to the mill as a weaver, and it was now that
his sporting prowess began to affect the direction his life was taking. Colne
Cricket Club wanted him to play for them but, living and working in Earby,
he did not fulfill the residential or the employment qualifications. Nelson
Cricket Club moved for him, and this prompted the Colne Club to act with
more urgency. Ellis was offered work in Colne itself:

Things were pretty bad in t' local village in Earby you see an' they
offered mi work in t' town. Well chairman of Colne Cricket Club,
thi called 'im Scase . . . he belonged to cricket club as a lot of
influential men in t' town were in them days.

And they sort of offered you talent money and all sorts of
things to mak' sure you 'ad a good income like . . . back 'ander shall
we say and all sorts of things and then Harry Scase he offered me a
job there an' I worked there and played wi' Colne.

So Ellis moved to Colne:

> ELLIS D.: They found me a house in Colne, so I worked there and
> then 'ad a working qualification and living qualification . . .
>
> A.T.: Did you pay rent?
>
> ELLIS D.: No I didn't really. They paid it like . . . a man on t'
> Committee let mi 'ave it for next to nothing.

Ellis worked for more than twenty years at the engineering firm that had
offered him the job. I asked him what his view of influential local men such
as his first club chairman was:

> Yes, very interested, different to what they are today. . . . If you did
> well, shall we say . . . supposin'. . . I used to get talent money, I
> used to get seven and six for everyone I caught and stumped . . .
> well that were a guinea . . . and then there were fellers that ran
> mills or . . . same as I'd tell yer my boss . . . he'd er . . . and various
> people that had money them days who were interested in t' club
> who'd think nothin' about comin' and stickin' a ten bob note in yer
> 'and and say "Here you are . . . you've 'ad a good day today" and
> sometimes you might pick a couple of quid up . . . as much as yer
> wage were for workin' for a week in them days—well you never
> turned yer nose up at things like that and if yer were lucky to get a
> 50 or anythin' like that . . . well you'd get a collection of 20 . . . well
> that were big money in them days.

Benefiting from the patronage of local businessmen, Ellis nevertheless still
retained a strong sense of his class position. "What about the team? You
were a working man. Were the rest of the team working men?" I asked him.
Ellis held a team photograph from the mid-1930s in his hand and went
through the lineup:

> ELLIS D.: Well this were team about when I cum . . . This feller
> were what thi call a warp dresser . . . that were Freddie Hanison.
> That's Norman Spence, he were a weaver—this feller were a warp

dresser connected wi' t' mill . . . this feller worked in t' mill. This
feller worked in t' mill . . . it were Stan Wright . . . this chap here,
Jim Gough he were a florist, his father 'ad a florist shop. Now this
were Ernest Dyson, you've 'eard of Dyson 'appen and Bracewells . . .
'e's just retired now . . . 'e were apprentice tailor . . . that's Armagh
Singh . . . that's Jack Hardacre, 'e were t' manager of Stanroyd
Mill, down Cottontree . . . it were Courtauld . . . 'e were a good
cricketer Jack Hardacre, one of t' best all-round cricketers in
league, were Jack . . . 'e could bat, 'e could bowl, 'e could field.
Now that's misself of course.

   This lad, they called 'im Jim Pollard . . . 'is father 'ad what
they called an oatcake business . . . They were working men . . .
when I came to Colne at first thi' were a little bit o' school tie
attached to it but it faded away when I cum to Colne and round
about then for the simple reason that . . . were sort o' wouldn't
wear it . . . you know what I mean . . . I were one o' them I din't
care . . . an' I always thought like it din't mak no difference to me
whether they were solicitors or schoolteachers or whatever they
were . . . if they were good cricketers they were all right . . . it din't
matter to me whether they were well off or they weren't . . . if they
could play cricket it were just OK wi' me.

A.T.: What about the committee . . . Did you get on well with the
committee?

ELLIS D.: Well aye . . . we 'ad difference of opinion . . . differences
of opinion of course but generally speaking we voiced us opinion . . .
but yes . . . I think we did.

This, then, is how cricket (as one popular cultural form) can constitute community. Ellis is fully aware of his class position, but all differences are irrelevant when the team cooperates to represent the locality. Colne transcends
class as the structuring influence. Despite the differences between the committee (of local dignitaries) and the team (predominantly made up of working men in the area), the ultimate affiliation is to Colne, to the locality. Local
identity and community as experienced through sport contribute to the perpetuation of a local set of social relations in which bourgeois hegemony—
the position of the local plutocracy and squirearchy as the apparently "natural" leaders of the community—is successfully reproduced, despite the
tensions of the time. Look at some of Ellis's phrases—"if they were good
cricketers they were all right . . . if they could play cricket it were just OK
wi' me." Ellis also experienced the material advantages of the patronage
system (not unlike some of the "pedestrians" or runners in the early days of
working-class athleticism)[2]—and even though he also played cricket on
Tuesday afternoons, this was no economic deprivation either. As Ellis recalls:

> I used to get mi wages just same 'cos chairman of club were boss
> of this firm and 'e let me off and I got "loss of work" off cricket
> club, well that were a good do.

There are forms, therefore, in which class conciliation is achieved. Lancashire League cricket was neither primarily a middle-class cultural form nor a working-class cultural form; it was a form in which the vertical relations of class and status were central, but in which such relations were often superseded by the sense of shared community. To be a Colner, as player or spectator, could be more important than to be a member of this or that class. If you were "a good un" or, in terms of spectatorship a "keen un" or a "knowledgeable un," then whether you were black, bourgeois, or proletarian was in a sense immaterial. You were part of a united community; you were a Colner.

John Clarke has argued that "locality" as an element of working-class culture "continues to act as a focus in a number of forms . . . to act as a focus for some working-class cultural identifications, often among those who are in some senses marginal to production and to the collective solidarities generated there" (1979, 251). Locality, for Clarke, becomes a base for a "magical" or "imaginary" reconstitution of community (as in, say, youth cultures such as skinheads) and operates as a form of limited oppositional consciousness that, ultimately, has little effect on things. Clarke is talking about the meaning that locality can have in a period of what Ian Taylor emphasizes as one of dislocation rather than one of ideological reproduction.[3] Locality, though, can be the source of major reaffirmative and conservative aspects of working-class culture. And "community" in interclass relations can be more than merely imaginary. It might serve one group's interests rather than another's, but that does not make the shared experience any less real. Within processes of ideological reproduction, community is lived through and experienced consciously as a major influence. In a very real everyday sense it is the actual experience of community that makes the reproduction of the status quo possible. In Colne, in the 1930s, it was a very real way of making sense of your place in the world.

There could, though, be tensions *within* the community that could be literally "played" out. I will go back to the cricket field to illustrate this in one way at least. Listen to Hyndeman Snell, a loom maker born in 1906, who was a fast bowler for the Colne cricket team—also recruited by "the boss where I worked, he was on the committee at Colne." Hyndeman started playing for the Colne First Eleven regularly in 1943 but had played occasionally for them, and quite regularly for the second team, in the 1930s. He had, he recollects, not got right into the first team in the late 1920s and 1930s because his father was a "Labour man." So community was not always achieved smoothly.

Hyndeman displays a strong sense of class differentiation in his recollection that when he took the wicket of some opponent, he would be especially pleased if his victim was a local toff. He also took much pride from being a "better" or more effective player than other "posher" or more middle-class members of his own team. Community prevailed, though, and Hyndeman, after playing at a lower level in his fifties, returned to the Colne club to run a fourth team for two years before becoming a member of the committee himself. He was excluded from the club as a young man—because of, he claimed, his family Labour connection—then asked in a few years later, when the power of "the old school tie" seemed to fade, and eventually finished up as a club committee member himself. Hyndeman's life history in cricket captures the underlying social relations in which a community identity prevails over a class identity. Throughout all this, community is rooted (as in the case of "enlightened" factory owners such as the Quaker chocolate manufacturers) in unequal social relations: the local middle class, the dignitaries, ran the club and so controlled an activity watched and played, on the whole, by "working men." Within this process, new recruits like Hyndeman Snell himself might be incorporated into the established power structure. But community was still experienced—it was not imaginary. To be from Colne and not from some other Lancashire township was what gave people a large part of their collective social identity. To be a "Colner" was a way of making sense of an otherwise "difficult to situate" wider world.

Community was also "achieved" in other, more coercive ways, as I have already indicated with reference to urban redevelopment and police action against street sports and gambling. The latter two phenomena are worth looking at in more detail. Gaming and gambling were "policed" out of existence when, in the early 1920s, a raid was made on gambling in the local hills. As Andrew Faulds has told me (drawing on the gossip of the time rather than direct experience), in 1923 uniformed police in a furniture van raided the main organized gambling area around a pub on the moors outside Colne, where three to four hundred gamblers gathered regularly. Faulds sees this event as

> the result of so many complaints going into the police station about men working in the mill, drawing their wages and going straight up to Coldwell and the wives never saw the wages . . . the wives made the complaint.

Wives, the churches, the police, the local judiciary; this was a powerful cross-sectional alliance indeed, formed to attack a major cultural form of the "rough," or at least not-so-respectable, working class. Andrew Faulds recalls that gambling carried on around street corners, but this was no more than "little lads' stuff" and was policed more mildly.

In the 1920s, the local sport of bowling stones, still played in defiance of local laws, was more vigilantly policed and so forced out of existence in the town. In 1928, for instance, police started motorcar patrols to stop the sport. This game involved throwing a fist-sized round stone from point A to point B—both "points" usually being drinking places. The thrower to reach point B in the least number of throws was the winner. The sport had been illegalized and opposed for generations. "Bowling stones on the highway," went one report in the *Colne Times* (May 16, 1885): a local weaver from Colne, Robert Taylor, was summoned by the aptly named Police Constable Hardman for the offense of "bowling stones between Monkroyd and Reedshaw Moss." Three more Colne men (a fork maker and two weavers) and a weaver from Winewall "were charged with aiding and abetting":

> The officer said he was on duty in plain clothes at 12 o'clock on the 3rd inst., along with PS Parkinson, and he saw the defendant Taylor. . . . The other four defendants were marking and carrying defendant's clothes. He got within six yards of them, and they had been watching them for forty-five minutes. On seeing the officers the defendants ran away, but he told them they had no need to run, as he knew them all.

Taylor had been answering a similar charge just the month before, and one of the others "had been up six times previously; once for bowling." Bowling on the highway had been banned by various acts of Parliament for over a century. But as late as the 1960s the *Colne Times* could report that a few local men could remember watching the game, and some even played it occasionally:

> Law or no law, the game went on. Every fine Sunday morning about 100 years ago men would leave the district to play bowls on quiet country lanes well out of reach of the arm of the law.
>
> There was gambling on a large scale. Enthusiasm ran high. Often wagers ran as high as £50 a side . . . bowling stones . . . was regarded as one of the most popular sporting pastimes of the age . . .
>
> Country lanes were rarely absolutely straight. And this was where the top-ranking bowler came into his own. Selecting a bowl with the correct amount of bias demanded no small degree of skill and patience. They were usually hewn roughly from local quarrys and then chipped and rounded to exactly the right size and weight.[4]

As streets were built, as transport emerged on these streets, bowling stones began to be seen as an undesirable and "rough" activity, incompatible with a developing sense of petty bourgeois civic pride. So it had to go. The conditions for "community" were certainly not purely organic; they were in the making, the social construction of particular class groups with power and influence but also of the social relationships that were forged across and within classes in everyday life.

And sometimes, if community was threatened—or seen, even remotely, to be threatened—then more coercive steps would be taken to reinstate the sense of common community. My last example of this comes from a Colne man recollecting an incident in the early 1930s in the next town down the valley, Nelson—the Little Moscow mentioned earlier. I asked Andrew Faulds whether forms of policing were directed against forms of working-class political life in the interwar period. He recalled direct policing of, for instance, the National Unemployed Union's collective action. A police charge of "absolute brutality" was mounted against a demonstration, in the early 1930s, in Nelson:

> *Battleship Potemkin* showed at the Regent in Nelson and the damn silly idiotic authorities . . . the police surrounded the cinema . . . because they thought people were goin' to get ideas into their 'ead about revolution . . . the silly idiots . . . Oh, they surrounded the cinema, dear me, it were idiotic.

Such measures, particularly in Colne, were not always necessary. The powerful pull of locality—with cricket matches played between teams of striking workers and teams of employers/manufacturers—was often sufficient to serve as a foundation for the reconstitution of community.

Class, Community, and Conservatism in Sport Culture

How can case studies of working-class culture in the past be most adequately theorized? And the question posed earlier in the chapter, about the interwar period, how are creases in the social fabric ironed out in the sphere of sport and popular culture? There is a threefold answer to this second question. First, new class conciliations are constantly in the making. There is no single, unitary working class ready to condemn the inadequacies and injustices of the capitalist system. Second, as a consequence of some new class alliances, "undesirable" elements of the working class are redeveloped or policed out of existence in ways meant to suggest that things were "improving," environmentally and morally, despite the social problems. And third, social relations are often lived out around the principle of community, through experiences like sport, in spite of the objective membership of different individuals and groups to particular social classes.

It is easier to live with the world as it is than to change it. Working-class culture has, in many of its elements, a strong traditional and conservative core that has as a major characteristic an inveterate hedonism. It is not adequate to talk just about whether or not hegemony is achieved. Bourgeois hegemony certainly was achieved—or, more accurately, sustained—in Colne in the interwar years, but some sort of hegemony is often achieved wherever the social fabric remains intact. In Colne, it was achieved or reproduced through the real, lived experience of locality and community. But it is not an explanation of a social process to point to the existence or nonexistence of hegemony. The processes through which hegemony is negotiated are what must always be given detailed consideration. To say that hegemony is achieved is a starting point in a more revealing general inquiry into how and why it is achieved at all. So my first major concluding point arising from the case study is that the notion of hegemony must be seen as a starting point rather than a conclusion in the exploration of working-class cultural forms.

Second, we should be careful not to read into cultural practices meanings that were not there. If we have a chance to hear the voices of the social agents whose practices we are examining, the chance should be taken. It would be easy to take a cultural practice like sport and to read off a meaning from it that might fit a particular view of the world. But this can lead to extremist readings of, say, sport as repression or as an opiate (Hoch 1972; Brohm 1978) or of sport or play as some kind of utopian category in which images of a new future society can be glimpsed (Hearns 1978). To plunder and pillage the past for meat to put on the bones of a skeletal model of history is to ignore the complex mediations through which experiences are actually lived. Forms of sport and leisure arise in specific sets of social conditions. Forms of domination may well be potentially resisted by play forms, but there is no inherent characteristic within sport that makes of it a utopian or a subversive category with regard to structures of domination. Close study of the nature of the play form in the particular social setting has to take place. There can be no substitute for this sort of detailed, and sometimes ethnographic, work.

My third point is that forms of sport and leisure are often essentially conservative simply because of the good sense they make to human agents in terms of how the social world can be comprehended and accommodated. By this, I mean that the hedonistic element in working-class culture often operates to produce collective modes of social closure (Parkin 1974, 1979).[5] This is a complicated process, but it has developed alongside new forms of inter- and intraclass relations in ways that often contribute to the reproduction of the status quo—of existing relations of domination. In sport and leisure, too, strategies of social closure have often exhibited the same male-dominated traits that are characteristic of forms of social closure in the workplace and in politics. The point to emphasize here is that forms of social closure can often seem to be initially disruptive of the established order but are usually incorporated into that order or at least ultimately unthreatening to it.

Fourth and finally, it is critical to develop, in the study of working-class culture, an adequate notion of what social bonds are both within working-class life and between the working class and other classes. Social actors do not simply mouth words written by some omnipotent scriptwriter. They often write, with great self-consciousness, their own scripts. But such scripts are often permeated by a realistic view of the world that recognizes the odds against changing things as they are. Social actors recognize the nature of their bonds in everyday life. Too much work on the working class has underemphasized this. Sports can, in some circumstances, be experienced as a realm of apparent freedom or collective bliss (in, say, open competition or through team effort), but the sport and leisure forms within working-class culture are bound up with what Dahrendorf has called ligatures (or bonds, constraints) rather than options (1979). Ellis Dickinson, in Colne, could get a job, a house, and local fame as a cricketer. But his really big options were a gamble, or illusory, and he knew it. The advantages that did become available to him had as a premise his experience of community as a ligature, as an ultimately constraining "allegiance, bond or linkage" (Dahrendorf 1979) that limits the ways in which Ellis could move out of or beyond his position in the local social structure. Fully aware of the nature of these bonds — of the balance between ligature and option — Ellis Dickinson, Hyndeman Snell, and others could nevertheless manage to have some good times in the bad times of the 1930s.

The points raised in this final section suggest that the study of working-class culture in the interwar years has yet to be developed in ways that might point toward some form of adequate account, rather than mere description. We might live under capitalism, but we are also members of communities. We might be British, but we are also "Colners," people of particular places. There is a rich vein of work on working-class culture in the period of its emergence, in its making and remaking (to quote the classical terms derived from E. P. Thompson 1963, and Stedman Jones 1974). We have gone beyond the bird's-eye overview of a certain descriptive approach (as in, say, Mowat 1968). There is also much work on the experience within working-class culture of the period after World War II, when various influences have been said to have altered fundamentally the social and economic basis of everyday working-class life. Generally, it has been acknowledged that "historians would now place greater emphasis on the geographical determinations of culture: cities, towns and villages might all have distinctive cultures of their own" (T. Harris 1995, 12).

But what was the nature of the culture that was made, once it was actually made, in the phase of its consolidation? This is what work on the interwar period can help us understand. In this chapter I have stressed the diversity of working-class culture — pointing to the different elements within the working class itself—and considered two major ways in which cross-class relations were achieved (the one coercive, the other more subtly based on the experience of community) in the 1920s and the 1930s in a particular working-class cultural context in northern England. Some might mourn the lack of a "mature culture of the working-class," to use Hall's term again. But by "mature culture" Hall means political practice—he is using the word in a highly specific developmental sense, rather than in the sense of a general process. There were plenty of "matured" popular cultural forms in working-class life in the interwar period. They reminded women of their allocated position in working-class culture. And some of them, in the spheres of sport and leisure, showed that elements within the working class were perfectly aware of their objective position as exploited worker, but nevertheless chose not to sacrifice the good times of the here-and-now on the altar of a vision of the good (or at least a better) society. It was more than a matter of contesting the dominant and looking to develop emergent forms of culture (Williams 1977a, 1977b) or of the making of an alternative culture (E. P. Thompson 1963). Everyday culture was more pragmatically and realistically negotiated than that.

Many chose to reconstitute themselves as Colners rather than to mount an offensive against the social order, and to carry on "having a good time" rather than to seek to transform the structures that gave them a sense of their own subordinate place in the world but a more "equal" place in Colne. We must never "diminish the rationality and stature of the actors and underestimate the self-awareness of illiterate people. They may not have read *Mythologiques,* but they had their own notions as to what they were turning out about" (E. P. Thompson 1993, 510). Thompson was talking of the makers of "rough music," that "rude cacophony, with or without more elaborate ritual, which usually directed mockery or hostility against individuals who offended against certain community norms" (467). We must listen to our respondents, respect their own hermeneutic integrity, and seek to reconstruct the *mentalité* of a particular time and place. The analysis in this chapter has given voice to some prominent actors in the cultural scene of Colne's working-class communities in the 1930s. Asking how hegemony might be secured, we must allow some of the voices and perspectives that contributed to its accomplishment to be heard in their own terms. The politics of working-class leisure and sport in the period and context considered in this chapter were essentially conservative—through good times, they contributed to the reproduction of bad times.

9. Continuities and Change in Male Working-Class Leisure
The Case of Knur and Spell

This chapter presents a single case study in the context of an exploration of social and cultural change and the major influences affecting patterns of working-class culture in interwar and postwar twentieth-century Britain. The case study is of knur and spell, a form of working-class sport (also known as tipping or poor man's golf) in the northwest region of England. The study draws on newspaper, other documentary, and oral sources. It is presented as evidence of the unevenness of cultural change, and so in one sense as a challenge to overgeneralized conceptions and theories of social and cultural change. The case study is also a reminder that mainstream and dominant understandings of sport may in themselves be merely partial contributions toward any truly comprehensive history and sociology of ludic culture or the history of popular pleasures and practices.

In his book *Sport and the British,* the historian Richard Holt establishes as the main theme "the tension between the forces of continuity and the 'otherness' of what we call 'modern' sport" (1989, 67). From the perspective of the social historian, Holt is keen to detect and record the occurrence and recurrence of links between "old and new ways of playing" (67). It is not just what people did that is of interest to Holt or in what physical environment or facilities they did it; rather, it is the values and meanings that underlay what they did. As examples he cites cricket and horse racing; some aspects of their appeal lay in "the sense of the pastoral they evoked" (67). Sports therefore can represent complex cultures and values intertwined in far from simple ways with contemporary social processes and historical legacies.

Holt looks at two examples of "explicit survival" of forms of sporting practice; knur and spell in the north of England and the Celtic sport of hurling (also known as shinty) in the Scottish Highlands and the west of

Ireland. Quoting an encyclopedic source, Holt discusses the regional following of knur and spell: "Champions like Billy Baxter, who became 'world
champion' at Colne in 1937, was a kind of folk-hero in many a northern
household" (1989, 68). Holt has also recognized that "a careful ethnography
of England would no doubt throw up many more such figures" (1996b, 143),
such as Billy Baxter, the knur and spell world champion whom I feature
centrally in this chapter. Across the North and South regions of England,
there may be more such as "Cumbrian or Devonian wrestlers like Abraham
Cann, for instance, who was honoured by Palmerston among others" (1996b,
143). The fact of survival of sports forms such as knur and spell calls for a
historicized sociological investigation of the social and cultural basis of their
persistence and an evaluation of the social change processes that have determined the forms of their survival.

The sport has been threatened by newer, modern forces and alternative leisure forms and practices throughout two centuries. Enclosure led
to a widespread "loss of playgrounds," in the words of Hammond and Hammond (1947, chapter 6). Fairweather Green was an open space of twenty to
thirty acres, near Bradford. Joseph Ellison, a witness to the Health of Towns
Committee, confirmed the importance of the green as a major recreational
resource for the community within a radius of five or six miles. A local pro-
prietor was threatening this resource by sponsoring a private bill through
Parliament to enclose this green and other wasteland, totaling 170 acres.
The act preserved a mere three acres for "Exercise and recreation for the
neighbouring population," protested Ellison:

> On Fairweather Green, he pointed out, it was the custom to play
> at cricket, and "a game we call spell and nur; they will drive a ball,
> 10, 11, 12, 13 and 14 score; they cannot play at those games in three
> acres." (Hammond and Hammond 1947, 86)

But men of these industrial villages, like some of their mining brethren
with "one foot in the mines, the other in the land" (Mingay 1979, 134)
could find ways of preserving their popular recreations, and it is the forms
and resilience of such survivals that sociological models of change often
underestimate.

In this chapter I describe and account for the contemporary history
of knur and spell and add to the social and cultural context of what Holt
calls "one of the most remarkable examples of survival" (1989, 68). The case
study also demonstrates the value of historical scholarship and particularly,
where possible and appropriate, oral history, for a sociology of contemporary culture.[1] Before presenting the case study though, the rationale for
such detailed case studies in the sociology of sport needs to be justified.

The Case for Case Studies

Much of our grasp of general patterns of sport and leisure is based on official sources that provide, particularly in the case of formal sports, statistical data on participation rates. Large-scale surveys can tell us who does what, and sometimes how often, in a way that provides a sociography of leisure and sport participation. Why people engage in the particular activity and how they do it are questions to which such large-scale quantitative sources are rarely designed to respond. Small-scale and qualitative studies are essential if the meaning of leisure is to be adequately understood.

Survey data also lack historical perspective. For a full understanding of the culture and politics of leisure it is not enough just to document the meanings of contemporary activities; it is essential to account for how certain meanings prevail in particular times and places. Why do the zoological gardens give way to the theme park, or the zoo to the "world of adventures," the municipal swimming pool to a range of "splashworlds," the community spectator sport to the membership-based media entertainment?

Key questions arise here concerning the role of popular pleasures and the shifting significance of types of leisure within everyday cultural life. In 1988 in the United Kingdom, the traditional pleasures of older and lower-class people were subjected to a sustained attack by programmers in commercial television. Greg Dyke, chairman of the Independent Television sports subcommittee (a little over a decade later, the director general of the BBC), expressed the committee's interest in changing the audience profile of sports viewers away from people ages fifty-five and over, particularly those in social groups D and E (Perera 1988, 3). Dyke also saw traditional light entertainment programming as anachronistic.[2] With wrestling, darts, snooker, and bowls about to be removed from or reduced in the schedule, Dyke and others were complying with the demands of advertisers for higher income, bigger spending, and younger audiences. The potentially equal but simultaneously tenuous and tense relationship between sports and the broadcast media has become a major influence on the world of sport itself and marks a fundamental shift in the social development of many leisure sports.

A critically informed sport and leisure study must focus on such transformations if it is to go beyond the limited scope of the sociographic approach. A concern with the historical and the qualitative will enable the production of what Stuart Hall calls a historical periodization capable of apprehending shifts in cultural relations characteristic of the development of popular culture:

> There is no simple historical evolution of popular culture from
> one period to another. The study of popular culture has been

somewhat bedevilled by this descriptive approach, tracing the internal evolution of popular pastimes, from hunting wild boar to collecting garden gnomes, strung together by an evolutionary chain of "things" slowly "becoming" other things. Against this approach I want to insist that historically, we must attend to breaks and discontinuities: the points where a whole set of patterns and relations is drastically reshaped or transformed. We must try to identify the periods of relative "settlement" . . . when not only the inventories of popular culture, but the relations between popular and dominant cultures, remain relatively settled. Then we need to identify the turning points, when relations are qualitatively restructured and transformed . . . the moments of transition. (Hall 1986, 23)

Even sophisticated and sociologically apposite models of the development of modern sport have presented too simplistically this apparently smooth process of becoming, which Hall is disputing. Guttmann's model (1978) of the characteristics of sports in various ages lists seven features: secularism, equality, specialization, rationalization, bureaucracy, quantification, and records. Dunning and Sheard (1979), in their seminal study of the development of rugby football, listed fifteen structural properties separating modern sports from folk games. Both models have identified major characteristics of sport and leisure in the modern period, but both remain somewhat reflectionist (sport is said to be a mirror image of the society: part of the Protestant ethic for Guttmann, part of the civilizing process for Dunning) and also, as linear models, overly simplistic (implying that sports have inexorably become modern).

Such all-embracing interpretations run the risk of understating the range of variations within the development of sport in terms of characteristic features, time scale, and the cultural relations of which they are a part. In this sense such typologies, as Gruneau (1988) has argued, are too formalistic, sidelining the part that negotiation, contestation, and struggle have played in the framing of modern sports and marginalizing the question of any substantively periodized analysis.

To further test or refine such models, there is a need for detailed case studies of sport and leisure practices and of the conditions of their existence and their relationship to hegemonic sport and leisure cultures. What are the influences behind the persistence, reproduction, or dissolution of distinct sets of practices? Many sports did not simply die or fade away. They were rendered marginal and/or redefined in light of new influences. Like the monasteries of England in the reign of Henry VIII, they were often forcibly dissolved.

It is not adequate, then, to talk about the "natural" demise of particular activities in the organic language of birth, development, and death. If leisure forms flourish, they do so in a particular set of social and cultural relations. If they become more marginal it is because they begin to be seen in new ways, or are perceived as undesirable, or are superseded by aggressive and expansionist new forces. It is the periods of transformation and the influences on such processes that must be the focus of any adequate analysis.

The work needed to rectify these inadequacies is not mere antiquarianism. It can have much contemporary resonance in a time when traditional leisure cultures, such as the allotment (Crouch 1989), are under siege from developers.[3] Detailed case studies can remind us that there are more leisure cultures and lifestyles in our cultural legacy than official sports bodies or tourist development think tanks might claim. I am not arguing for a project to unearth a heroic culture, as Hall (1981) tends to do; nor am I pleading for recognition of the character and remains of an unneutered virile indigenous culture such as that of Cunningham's (1980) mid-nineteenth-century working class. But there does remain a suppressed history of sports and leisure, an account of once prominent and sometimes dominant forms, to which people's history and, where possible, oral history grant access.

It is worth reminding ourselves of Raymond Williams's methodological comments on the analysis of culture:

> We need to distinguish three levels of culture, even in its most
> general definition. There is the lived culture of a particular time
> and place, only fully accessible to those living in that time and
> place. There is the recorded culture, of every kind, from art to the
> most everyday facts: the culture of a period. There is also, as the
> factor connecting lived culture and period culture, the culture of
> the selective tradition. (1965, 66)

Inevitably, then, interpretation and cultural analysis becomes a matter of selectivity, guided by what Williams calls the composed tradition of new periods. Some periods elevate one interpretation above another, marginalizing once prominent practices. Cultural analysis therefore becomes, in no small part, a matter of exploration, discovery, and retrieval. A leisure culture that was once persistent and pervasive might be seen in contemporary terms as quaint, as little more than a curious revival. But it is the way in which cultural credibility is granted to particular activities that is of interest, and an analysis of the context of and influences on such developments will offer a route toward a periodized understanding.

In this chapter, then, I draw upon primarily oral historical and newspaper sources to outline the history of knur and spell in one northeast Lancashire community (Colne) in the first half of the twentieth century and in nearby northern towns in the adjacent county. The sport was popular in other parts of the north of England too, surviving "at least through the period of modernisation" (Lowerson 1989, 3) in parts of Yorkshire and the Sheffield region. Analysis of advertisements in Yorkshire newspapers (Collins 2000) has shown the rising profile of the sport in the period immediately following the Great War, in the early 1920s. The major features of the activity are outlined, and the voices of three former world champions are woven into an interpretation of the social context and cultural significance of the sport. Such work could form the basis of a social history of sport and leisure that might be seen as a history of secular nonconformism. By this, I mean that in everyday life, beliefs and values could be hewn out of the common and traditional practices of a locality and sustained, often against mounting odds and in defiance of the encroaching prevalence of a dominant new cultural force.

KNUR AND SPELL IN COLNE

Knur and spell thrived throughout the nineteenth century in cotton-mill and mining communities in Yorkshire and northeast Lancashire. One source, a pamphlet entitled *Out-Door Games* published in the northern English city of Newcastle, undated but probably from the late eighteenth century, provides a descriptive account of the game:

> Northern-Spell
> Northern-spell is played with a trap, and the ball is stricken with a
> bat, or stout stick, at the pleasure of the players, but the latter is
> most commonly used. The performance of this pastime does not
> require the attendance of either of the parties in the field to catch
> or stop the ball, for the contest between them is, simply, who shall
> strike it to the greatest distance in a given number of strokes; the
> length of each stroke is measured, before the ball is returned, by
> means of a cord made fast at one end, near the trap, the other end
> being stretched into the field by a person stationed there for that
> purpose, who adjusts it to the ball, whatever it may be; the cord is
> divided into yards, which are properly numbered in succession, so
> that the person at the bottom of the ground can easily ascertain
> the distance of each stroke by the number of the yards, which he
> calls to the players, who place it to their account, and the ball is
> thrown back. This pastime possesses but little variety, and is by no
> means so amusing to the bystanders as Trap-Ball.[4]

The center of the Lancashire game was Colne, a small cotton-mill town close to the moorlands of the Brontë country and the Yorkshire dales. "Bonny Colne upon the hill," it is a town proudly defensive of its traditions. Allison has shown how such traditions become a core of self-endowed celebrity, so that Colne is "famous, if for anything, for Luddite riots and Hovis advertisements and for producing Wallace Hartley, the brave bandmaster of the Titanic" (1984, 139). The long-term residents claim a tightly knit sense of their community and continuity (P. Smith 1989). The bonds of community and locality among the older generation have persisted in such a way that though many of the old industrial workers may die, memories of the old days wither, and it becomes too easy to romanticize the past, the old memories do nevertheless "seem to challenge our lives today" (ibid.). Much of the talk of the old days concerns the ways in which hardships were surmounted, and it is couched in a language of fatalistic acceptance of things as they were. It was enough to have survived and to remember the characters who survived with you. As one of Smith's anonymous male respondents said, "If tha doesn't expect owt tha'll not often be disappointed" (ibid.). A female respondent recalls train trips to the working-class seaside mecca of Blackpool for the annual holiday and holidays in the resort when everybody knew each other, and the apartments they occupied for the holiday were known to everybody: "You might 'a just as well 'a stopped in Colne, because everybody knew everybody" (ibid.) was her observation about going for a walk on Blackpool promenade.

Colne is a web of steeply falling and climbing streets, straddling "a savage-shaped ridge, 800 feet high and in a bowl of higher hills" (Allison 1984, 139). Nowhere in Colne do you feel that the town has colonized the country. The higher hills, stretching to the wild moors of the Pennines, always dwarf the town itself. No amount of gentrification, urban redevelopment, or roadway construction has dislodged this balance. In Colne the legacy of the industrial past lives on:

> The textile communities stretching up the valley from Burnley to Colne all came to boast the same kind of pioneering roughness of far-flung frontier towns. This abrasive newness, coupled with the scarcity of large-scale mill-owners, became grafted on to existing democratic traditions that flourished locally. (Liddington 1984, 34)

But any such pioneering roughness must be understood in the context of the natural environment of the town, which always appears to be at the mercy of a countryside that continues to dominate the landscape. As Allison puts it in typically provocative style, "north of Alkincoats Park in Colne there is open country right through to the North Pole" (1984, 139). Colne is a town with an assertive self-identity, hewn out of a lived sense of community and fiercely defended, and a town with a distinctive socioecological profile.

Knur and spell was played mainly in the open countryside, field, or moorland. The equipment was basic: a primitive form of golf driver (a pummell or stick) with a squared wooden head, a small round wooden or pot ball (the knur), and some system whereby the ball could be suspended in order to be struck (a "pin" or a "spell"). In Colne a string was used to dangle the pot knur from the gallows-like spell, ready to be struck. Two forms of contest have predominated. The first is the total distance of all strikes, the winner being the player with the highest aggregate, the one who has hit the knur farthest from the declared number of "rises" or "strikes," or "knocks." This way of playing is usually known as a match of scores. The other form of playing is the "long knock" the winner being the player who drives the ball farthest with any single knock. This mode of contest developed as a popular and prominent one at the turn of the nineteenth and the twentieth centuries. In either mode, distances struck are measured in twenty-yard units known as scores.

Contests usually took place on the grounds or in the vicinity of a drinking place (pub or inn). Betting was a central element for the spectators: it offered a form of incentive to top players, excitement for onlookers, and business potential for local gambling entrepreneurs. Betting and gate money produced the revenue that guaranteed the stakes and covered expenses. Knur and spell has not made it into the Olympic program; it has never sent delegates to the Central Council for Physical Recreation in Britain or applied for Sports Council subsidies. But for several centuries it featured significantly in the local cultural life of some industrial communities. In Colne this took the form of a series of revivals of varying impact:

> "Knur and Spell"—At the Craven Heifer Grounds, Cullingworth, a large crowd of Lancashire and Yorkshire sportsmen assembled on Monday on occasion of the meeting of Joe Machin, of Greenside, and W. Driver ("Strong") of Colne to decide the longest knock in 25 rises each at knur and spell, with wood heads and knurs, for 90 pounds. Betting was brisk, opening at 5 to 4 on Machin, and closing at 11-10 on Driver. Driver won with his eighteenth rise, which measured 13 score seven yards 9 inches. Machin's tenth rise was his best, and measured 12 score 17 yards 1 foot. (*Colne and Nelson Times*, March 25, 1898, 5)

> "Knur and Spell Match"—About 500 people witnessed a game of knur and spell at the Alma Grounds, near Colne, on Saturday. The contestants were Harry Benson, of Cottontree, and Robert Spencer, of Colne, who competed for the longest knock, 25 rises each, 1/2 oz pot knurs, for 40 pounds. After having 20 strikes each Spencer was leading by about a score yards and, the wind having dropped, the match looked as good as over. The unexpected, however, happened for at Benson's 23rd rise he sent the winning stroke, which measured 8 score 17 yards to Spencer's 8 score 14

yards, thus winning by three yards. (*Colne and Nelson Times*, March 27, 1908, 5)

The final of a knur and spell handicap held by the landlord of the Old Duke Inn took place on Saturday at the Shale Hill Ground . . . a large crowd witnessed it. (*Colne and Nelson Times*, October 22, 1937, 7)

"Youngest entrant wins knur and spell final"—The revival of the ancient game of knur and spell continues . . . despite having to use mothballs for practicing purposes because of a shortage of knurs. On a bitterly cold Sunday morning, standing on the old St. Andrew's golf-course at Laneshawbridge watching the final of a handicap, rounds of which have been played throughout the winter months, was no joke. It was freezing. Yet over 100 enthusiasts turned up to watch the six competitors battle for supremacy. (*Colne Times*, March 14, 1958, 12)

The emphases in the reports change. The technical detail in the earlier reports is replaced by the novelty value of the revivalist reports. But for some twenty years after the last cited report there was a renaissance of the sport. Its cultural resonance was such that enough cognoscenti, enthusiasts, and raw recruits would be found to revive the game. The 1958 report goes on to describe how the youngest entrant, twenty-three-year-old Stuart Greenfield, won the contest. Greenfield was to become world champion in 1973, by which time sponsors had donated £200 for the winner. A number of sponsors were by this time showing real interest in the sport, attracted by the sport's local rootedness and regional specificity. Gannex, a raincoat manufacturer—famous as the brand of everyman's coat worn by the Labour prime minister Harold Wilson—showed some interest, as did some local breweries. The game's revival featured in broadcast and print media too, though usually in the patronizing tones of the amused and often metropolitan outsider.

The sport's cultural significance, though, is best understood by listening more fully to the voices and recollections of its major figures rather than relying on the whimsical reporting of the media commentator. One figure straddling the years of buoyancy and revival was Billy Baxter, world champion in 1937 and one of Greenfield's advisers and supporters thirty years later.

Billy Baxter and Other World Champions
I talked to Billy Baxter and Stuart Greenfield about their sporting lives in February 1981 and to three-times world champion Len Kershaw almost

twenty years later. I use the real names of the players, and I personally interviewed them in Colne. They were all warmly welcoming and generously responsive to my inquiries, though initially cautious given some of their experiences with the popular media, which they perceived as superficial, haughty, and untrustworthy in their dealings with the local culture.

Billy Baxter was born in 1909 in Foulridge, a village near Colne, but he lived in Colne since the age of five. Upon leaving school, Baxter worked on a farm for ten shillings a week before going into the mill, attracted by a weekly wage of fifteen shillings a week. "That's worst thing ah ever did," commented Billy, a countryman in origin and heart all his life. But if he had continued to work on the land, his work and leisure life may have taken a different course. Working on the land, enmeshed in the temporal cycles of the more natural rhythms of primary production, Billy would have had no real space for leisure activity or spare-time pursuits.

Moving to millwork—he worked at one mill for twenty years, another for thirty-five years—he became a loomer and a twister. Industrial work immediately gave him a five-and-a-half or six-day working week, with very clearly defined nonwork hours. He played a lot of casual football and cricket in his leisure time and was introduced to knur and spell around the mid-1920s. He was taken to his first match in neighboring Trawden by a man whose hens he used to look after. This was Billy's first sight of the sport and of those who played it, known in Colne as "tippers" and sometimes as "laikers." Billy's sixpence entry fee was paid by his patron and employer:

> An then when I saw these tippers, yer know, 'e says, "I 'ave some
> tackle at home, tippin' tackle," he says. "We'll 'ave a bit of a do
> some time." So I went from there, yer see, an' I seemed to like do
> very well, yer see, an' I got interested in it an' they couldn't keep
> me away from it, yer know, after that. . . . Aye, I started joinin
> 'andicaps, yer see.

Billy never lost his job in the mill, but during the 1920s and 1930s he was often on reduced working hours:

> Yer see, a lot of it was yer might 'ave 'appen only half a week in,
> yer see, an you'd only 'alf a week's wage, yer know, there was no
> Conservative's "You've never ad it so good" goin' on then.

As Billy became keener, his playing would take up "nine weeks out of ten," some of the weekend (often Sunday morning), and he would also compete in or watch a handicap on a Saturday afternoon. Billy's other enthusiasm was pigeons, and he was a member of the Colne Homing Society. His leisure culture was very much an outdoor one and also included a lot of exercise:

"You walked it both ways up to the Alma practisin' or up to Noyna; yer know, there were no buses, even if there were buses you wouldn't 'ave 'ad the money, you couldn't afford to go."

Billy recalls knur and spell as an exclusively male, working-class activity. It was working men who played; owners or the middle class might sometimes have shown interest but they did not play. The golf clubs were providing the sites of pleasure for other classes. To Billy, the golf club was just another "closed shop." Crowds were often large. Billy recalls a gate of £75 from a sixpence admission fee (approximately three thousand paid admissions), a significant crowd for a town whose population in 1931 was 23,791. There might also be a good number who would gain entry without paying: "There'd be a lot get in climbin' over t' walls. They'd 'ave nothing, yer see."

Equipment was made locally and sometimes by the players themselves: "We got us own equipment for makin' it. We started makin' it usselves." This gave outstanding players reputations as canny craftsmen and not just prima donna performers. The stick head in particular was seen as a local work of art:

> There was a man in Yorkshire, thi called 'im Archie Robinson an 'e was a good tipper but 'e was the best maker of 'eads that I've ever come across. They were beautiful, they were works of art were 'is eads. They were like what yer might say Chippendale furniture among somethin' that's no good, beautiful, a work of art.

Different, often neighborhood-based groups rivaled each other. The Alma Lot, Waterside, Savage Club, and the Red Lion Lot. These sorts of groupings would stage, host, or initiate handicaps. "They were different places, they congregated at each," recalled Billy Baxter. Challenges were based around individual prowess:

> There was allus a bit rivalry among 'em, thi'd 'ave a man that 'ud say like, well, we fancy like so-an'-so. . . and 'ave you anybody like 'ud do 'em, yer know, an' then that's 'ow matches would come about, yer see.

The language of male rivalry—to be able to "do" the other, that is, beat him—would guarantee a regular round of challenges. So matches would be made and staged, often at the grounds of local pubs or in cooperative farmers' fields. With practice, handicaps, heats, and all the surrounding cultural life of the activity—the gossip, the challenges, the disputes, the followup—knur and spell was a full and time-consuming commitment:

> Well, yer see, if you were really interested in knur-and-spell you 'adn't a lot of time for anythin' else, yer see, 'cos yer kept goin'

practisin' . . . only yer couldn't be goin' doin' somethin' else, in yer
spare time yer went practisin', yer couldn't do anythin' else.

Billy's estimate of the number of regular players was four or five hundred:

They were up at t' Alma every night . . . they was at Foulridge,
Noyna, night after night. Oh, there was ever so many fields where
they went.

The pub was usually the first port of call, and Billy remembered the rhythms
of his day:

Ah've come over from the Alma at night in summertime at about
11 o'clock when we've been commin' 'ome and there's been the
owls 'ootin, it's been beautiful, lovely night, yer know, an' then
when ah've got 'ome ah've 'ad a bit of a swill an' to bed an' then
ready for work an ah were thinkin' about goin' again the night
after, aye.

Billy never made very much money, a few shillings perhaps in his time as
champion. In the various revivals in the 1950s and 1970s more significant
cash sums became available through sponsors. But by this time whatever
momentum the particular revival had built up, it undoubtedly fit less inte-
grally with the cultural climate of the times, with the contemporary leisure
culture. "Burly" Bill Baxter and his peers would be respected locally and celebrated within the local culture. But knur and spell would be seen by outsiders as an oddity, a cultural relic, a premodern activity hauled out of the
attic of history from time to time to titillate the curiosity of the more
urbane cosmopolitan or to highlight regional stereotypes—like television
advertisements or situation comedy.

In one group photograph from the mid-1930s (Tomlinson 1992a,
201, photo 2), Billy Baxter stands proudly, second from the left, wearing a
raincoat, clogs on his feet and hands in his pockets. This photograph shows
young and old knur and spell players in a gathering of like-minded enthusiasts, all male. Forty years later, spectators at a big event included women,
children, and media personnel covering the Knur-and-Spell World Championships in its revived form. In a 1979 newspaper report of this event, Billy
Baxter bemoaned the lack of real competition among youngsters interested
in the game. The real competition lay elsewhere now, in the possibilities
within the consumer culture that would have looked like fantasy to the
young Billy and his playing peers.

Stuart Greenfield, champion in 1973 and third in the 1979 contest,
was introduced to the game by his father, who was friendly with some old
players and became involved in one of the revival phases:

Me dad must 'a' said, like, well our Stuart'll 'ave a go. But 'e 'adn't
any tackle so 'e provided me with a stick and a head an' I went in
that particular dinner time—I didn't know anythin' about this
until I arrived at this pub for a drink, yer see, at dinner time—an'
mi dad walked in with this stick an' 'ead an' 'e said, "I've entered
yer for this 'andicap an' there's yer tackle." So that were first thing
I knew about it.

In the interview with Stuart Greenfield it was clear that the social and cultural base of the sport had changed. He spoke realistically but with some
sadness of the culturally peripheral nature of the sport in contemporary life
and with suspicion of outsiders who came along to express an interest in
the sport. Too many expressions of interest by such outsiders had led to a
caricature of this important aspect of the sporting culture of Colne, and he
now seemed protective of the dignity of his local culture. I spoke to Len
Kershaw, fellow expert player with Greenfield, in December 2000. This
confirmed that the tipping tale is not yet dead. In the later 1980s and the
1990s contests were arranged and the odd world championship event staged.
BBC local radio would usually cover this, occasionally the national press
would show some interest, and a curiosity feature was also made for television by Transworld Sport. In a predictable fashion, a local sponsor would
emerge to offer one-off support. Len Kershaw was used to this. He had
been runner-up in an autumn tournament at the Hare and Hounds, Black
Lane Ends, in 1981, with a longest knock of 175 yards, five yards behind Stuart Greenfield. A spokesman for the organizers told the local newspaper
that "Following the success of the competition, and the interest it aroused
and the following it is attracting once again, it is hoped to hold another
tournament up at the Hare and Hounds in Spring."[5]

Kershaw won the world title in 1974. His second came in 1991. In
April, at the Otley Cricket Club, Yorkshire, he won a massive gold trophy,
a cash prize of £100, and, defeating 160 rivals, the championship, with a
knock of nine score and two yards.[6] Greenfield finished second. 1991 was a
heyday of the sport's revivalist profile. Kershaw won his third title at the
Bradshaw Tavern, Halifax, Yorkshire, in May, with Greenfield and Griffiths
taking second and third places. Channel 4 broadcast the Transworld Sport
feature of his achievement on July 20.

Kershaw was still the world champion in 1995 when along with
"Colne Giant" Ted Griffiths he was involved in organizing a showcase handicap match, with £200 prize money put up by local Lancashire brewery
Thwaites (Eveleigh 1995). But as with Gannex thirty years earlier and Web-
ster's brewery earlier in the 1990s, sponsors did not stick around for long.
The sport's world champion contenders were by now all in their fifties or
sixties, no new generation saw the sport as anything but a curious relic of a

simpler age and time, and "Len Kershaw" would become the answer to a local pub quiz question, "Who is the reigning world champion of knur and spell?" well into the new century. No one had emerged to challenge Kershaw, and in December 2000 I talked to him in his second home, the Royal British Legion club in Colne. It was 10 p.m. on a Sunday evening, the Legion was full, its two full-size snooker tables occupied, its clientele chatty, cozy, familiar, and old. I had interviewed prominent tippers in here more than a decade and a half before, but the club had had a makeover and was clearly thriving and a haven to an aging population in a tight-knit community. There were couples, singles, women as well as men, and I heard no accent that could be other than East Lancastrian. Len Kershaw took me into a quiet back room where we could talk, interrupted only by the odd offer of a drink from one of his friends. Len sipped the local East Lancashire favorite, Benedictine with water, brought back to Britain by surviving World War I veterans from the French front. We discussed the highs and lows of the sport throughout the previous few decades. He was a reluctant interviewee, saying outright that he didn't like doing interviews. I was reminded of my earlier phase of research in the town and the complexities that arise when you make the journalistic or researcher's raid and are assaulted by that guilt generated by a voyeuristic position in which different accounts have to be balanced against each other, some maybe privileged over others (Tomlinson 1997a). I began to feel intrusive, this professor from the South barging in on a weekend ritual. "Are you from round 'ere?" Kershaw asked me. "Yes," I replied, "from Burnley" (which is a mere four or five miles down the valley). "Oh, not Colne though," Kershaw corrected me. Some ice was broken when my tape's microphone refused to cooperate. "Well yer certainly not professor o' tape-recordin'," Len wryly observed. This was a privileged place to be, as a guest in a local culture and network of a special kind. Midway through his description of his own unique playing style, Len was offered a drink. He broke off from his technical description to a stranger, speaking to himself as much as to me—"That's Frank, 'e's a joiner, a good man and friend, he buried mi wife two years since." This was an enclosed world, a world of community as lived, and relationships as long-standing and reciprocated. It was a world that might last little longer than the story of knur and spell itself.

Len resumed his account of his playing style. He'd recently had a replacement hip and confided that if anyone challenged for his championship now, at the age of sixty-four, he would have to turn down the challenge and give up his title. He began to mime his unique style. "I 'ad a unique style. I developed mi own style. . . . I'd address it like this, swingin' the stick up right round me 'ead." He looked as much like a shot-putter as a golfer, and you could see in this moment how some commentators have been tempted to link knur and spell with the pastimes of the Vikings.

Len was coached in the sport by his father Harry, a local bookmaker who ran the book for sports such as tipping. He was initially "secretly" coached by his father, who also refused to accept any bets on his son, and emerged from nowhere as one of the top players of the new younger generation during the mid-twentieth-century revival of interest in the game. How did he get the equipment? "Yer made it yerself, I got some timber stockpiles off the railway, and Leonard Crabtree shaped mi two sticks." The head of the stick could be any size or shape you liked—"yer could 'ave it like a fryin' pan if yer wanted"—but a kind of intuitive design engineering all but standardized it. Len reflected that making the equipment now might cost a fortune, but he was supported by enthusiasts. "It were a labour o' love for t' old chaps that knew 'ow to do it. Jimmy Annis, 'e made lots of 'eads, 'e gave mi two 'eads." One turned out to be flawed and split, but the other lasted Len throughout his playing lifetime. He never made his own heads, but recalled that Stuart Greenfield "started makin' some reasonable 'eads." Len had worked in the mill, as a tackler and at other tasks, for thirty years before becoming a traffic warden. Tall, wiry, and lean, with striking white hair, you could picture him policing the double yellow lines of Colne High Street with a decisiveness and military bearing acquired in the National Service of his youth and never lost. As a young man he'd practiced knur and spell on Sunday mornings and every night of the week before events, handicaps, or championships. Len didn't let this interfere with his personal life. He took his personal life out into the fields. "She'd come out wi' mi, while I were practisin', and she'd go lookin' for t' knurs."

Knur and spell was not Len's only sporting passion or leisure activity. He played other team sports like football and cricket and was known as a competitive snooker player in the local leagues. He also starred in amateur operatics in a local Glee Union. Combining his work, leisure, and sporting profiles, Len had from time to time made himself available as a local speaker in an act that he called "Park, Hit, Sing." He'd tell tales about his job as a traffic warden, and then about his tipping hits or strikes, and finish with a song (he'd often taken the lead in the Glee Union productions, and "I'll sing 'owt'"). A year from retirement when I interviewed him, Len was considering expanding this public presentational profile and working up a fuller presentation on his time as a prominent knur and spell player, including exhibitions. If he gave such exhibitions, he said with a self-knowing smile, he would put clogs on and a handkerchief around his neck, though he never played in such attire. Len knew the game and knew how some saw his game and his culture. "We sold some stuff once to a feller in America, some knur and spell tackle . . . hi said 'e were goin' to do a lot wi' it, but we never 'eard nowt back from 'im." Len had heard a lot from the sponsors, the pundits, the cultural entrepreneurs over the years. He knew that interest could be insensitive, patronizing, superficial, and most of all transient and fleeting. And he knew that the game was never going to revive. When those who taught him the game boosted its main revival in the 1930s, "there were nowt else to do, now they've got so much, computers and whatnot." Len talked of the grip of the game: "It gets under yer skin, it's a good game, there's a lot to knur and spell, the right 'ead on the day, the trajectory for the lay of the land." He recalled one victory when he'd outwitted and outthought the field, striking the knur on a lower trajectory to take the ball under a wind, while all others were hitting the knur high and getting shorter distances as the wind held the knur back.

I asked Len to recall some special moments during his playing career. He recalled his longest knock of all, when he struck the knur fourteen and a half score (that's what my notebook says, though it sounds too long to be true, but by now it was almost midnight at the end of a weekend), coming only second to the legendary Selwyn Schofield. This was at Spring Rock, in farmer and fellow player Dan Binns's field. Spectators put "their coppers in t' milk pails next to t' stile." This was in the early 1960s, Len confirmed. A world of glee unions, self-organized leisure, and local sports contests might seem quaint and marginal in a networked world of mediated and individualized consumption. But it still has its legacy, and the world that produced and sustained Colne and its generations of knur and spell enthusiasts is a reminder that sport and leisure lifestyles need not be solely about the search for the new or the assertion of the regularly and frenetically reconstituted identity.

Cultural Transitions

Billy Baxter and the knur and spell players of 1930s Colne were of course rooted and raised in different patterns of work and leisure from the generations raised in postwar Britain. More work, more overtime, expanding choices of what to do in one's spare time, increased mobility via the automobile, new and more individualized and home-based forms of consuming—all these factors characterized this key transitional period in the social history of leisure and everyday life. Billy's own symbol of this postwar shift is the transistor radio: "Well, I think, yer see, that these young uns, they'd got other occupations. They 'ad these 'ere boxes they carried about with 'em blarin' out, what do they call 'em, disco-jockeys or somethin'." Billy may have placed transistors and portable sound systems a decade or two before their time but the observation is an evocative one. The simpler values of knur and spell were scarcely compatible with the embryonic consumer culture.

Consumer culture is, in John Hargreaves's view, "a specifically modern, pagan version of the good life" (1986, 133). It is hedonistic, based on individual choice and a sense of freedom and self-fulfillment anchored in the deeply personal. In consumer culture, Hargreaves notes, collective concerns are absent, displaced to a level of personal reality in which the individual has sole responsibility for his or her condition (1986, 150–51). Such a description could hardly be less appropriate for the older generation of Colners, to whom contemporary forms of living offer little compared with the happiness and contentment of a simpler and at times harsher way of life: "Perhaps we were more satisfied because we simply didn't know there was anything else" (P. Smith 1989). It is around the features of a consumer culture, though, that the "new bourgeoisie" has initiated an "ethical retooling" in which new needs are produced; the logic of the economy favors "a hedonistic morality of consumption, based on credit, spending and enjoyment" (Bourdieu 1986, 310). Model lifestyles emerge, to which we are directed by forms of "sly, imperative advice"; overall, "the new tastemakers propose a morality which boils down to an art of consuming, spending and enjoying" (311).

Bourdieu argues that exclusion from this new art constitutes "a new form of the sense of moral unworthiness" (311). The model lifestyles at the heart of this art are premised on a conspicuous form of spending. Forms of consumption other than those blending these elements of expenditure and pleasure into a formula for distinction remain outside the new ethic, ill-fitted for the new morality and thus by definition lacking in moral worthiness. It is in this way that Billy Baxter's culture begins to look out of place, to the bearers of the lived culture of the new generations as well as to the new tastemakers. And it is in this way that the apparent "naturalness" of the modern marginalizes alternatives and distorts the cultural legacies of some times and some places. Knur and spell has been a significant cultural activity for several centuries. Essentially a component of male working-class popular culture, it continued across numerous generations and historical periods to represent a set of values that do not fit easily with widely held conceptions of modern sport. Its major characteristics have been as follows:

- working class
- male dominated
- self-engendered
- nonbureaucratized
- inexpensive
- self-administered
- spatially unconfined
- passed on by example and oral tradition
- regionally varied
- equipment self-made
- entwined in local economy of beer and betting

The game provided those elements described by Williamson as central to the leisure of his grandfather, a miner in a Northumberland (Northeast England) village—autonomy, self-respect, some independence, security—important sources of self-esteem that work could never provide (Williamson 1982, 116). No consultants were needed to lay out the tippers' playing area; no further specialization complicated the sport. One stroke or knock could win the day. Knur and spell is no more a cultural freak than is the hammer throw, the shot put, the javelin, or the discus. But its closeness to the mainstream form of modern golf has served to render it as marginal.

Much of Britain's national sporting culture has been based on the formalization and standardization of particular sporting practices and the "canonization" of particular conceptions of physicality, skill, and leisure. One major element in this development has been to specify the boundaries of an activity in terms of time and space, to contain it in a predictable format. Contemporary versions of this issue are now being addressed. With regard to televising darts, bowls, and snooker, Greg Dyke observed, "they overrun . . . they are not guaranteed slots like football, rugby and boxing, which go for a certain time and where a company can say 'We'll take the half-time slot'" (Perera 1988, 3).

When Billy Baxter and his rivals overran, no one—except perhaps long-suffering spouses or partners—breathed down their necks complaining about interrupted schedules. Modern sports have and continue to become increasingly dependent on sponsorship and media patronage, packaged and commodified for standardized production and global consumption. But it is worth reminding ourselves that breaks and shifts have been less all-embracing and smooth than such processes often imply. Modern might in fact be seen as a euphemism for dominant.

Yeo and Yeo have pleaded for a popular cultural analysis that focuses on "arousing sleeping forms" (1981, 142). While cultural analysis can hardly play the role of suitor to the Sleeping Beauties of a past culture, such arousing could perform a valuable interpretive task, for it would reveal to us the narrowness of a conception of sporting practice based only on the most powerful, established, and dominant of sporting interests or the recorded evidence and claims of such dominant interests. Any such narrow conception will misrepresent the range and variety of elements in a culture, for dominant definitions and high-profile chronicles do not capture the fullness of an extant culture. In its different phases of popularity and prominence, knur and spell has always represented a comparatively simple form of pleasure and enjoyment, not too demanding in terms of cost, easily and spontaneously accessible, and closely linking the acts of production and consumption. Knur and spell was a very different act of consuming compared to that which the new tastemakers have for some time been proposing.

Jackson (1968) has argued that the world of middle-class lifestyles and packaged values could learn a lot from working-class life. Particularly concerned with forms of working-class community in the late 1950s and early 1960s, Jackson highlighted three qualities of working-class life that any civilized society should try to absorb: a deeply ingrained habit of cooperation, a habit of valuing people rather than concepts, and a directness of emotional response (1968, 159). Tipping in Colne, as a self-made activity, exhibited this degree of cooperation, spiced by the recurrent rivalries of different groups. In celebrating yet never idealizing players, it valued people and judged personalities, not just concepts. And in the rivalries between groups—Billy Baxter's friend, Herbert Bateson, recalls disputes over interpretation of rules: "They were all rebels, they'd never meet to sort things out. They were deadly enemies"—competitive rhetoric provided a means for uninhibited and direct emotional response and rivalry. Knur and spell players often had expressed and committed loyalties, playing out of sub-localities within the town, and these intense rivalries were fueled by the absence of any formal series of matches. But in sport's special fashion, local affiliations could be temporarily suspended and transcended when rivalries were regionally inflected, expressed, in Colne's terms, against the neighboring county of Yorkshire in big cross-county matches and challenges and in the world championship.

The values of the enduring qualities of knur and spell stand in contrast to the pervasiveness of media and consumer culture. The new tastemakers operating in the worlds of sports sponsorship, corporate hospitality, and the production of media spectacles must be reminded continually that there is more to the world of sport than meets the televisual eye. If they are not reminded of this, then their tastemaking will go uncontested as the contours of our popular cultural life are "drastically reshaped, qualitatively restructured and transformed" (Hall 1986, 23). The cultural dynamics at the heart of any such transformation are a focus of illuminating study. Theoretically, the rise of the modern should be seen as a far from naturally inevitable process (Gruneau 1988). Interpretations are needed that illustrate the relation of everyday practices to power relations and key shifts of social influence (Kew 1989; Whitson 1983). Such interpretations of the role of sports in leisure culture will highlight the part that sport has played as a form of secular nonconformism, expressing important values not necessarily at one with those placed at the center of the dominant sport culture. In focusing, too, on heretofore neglected sports and their champions, such work can also complement our understanding of the contribution of sport to national identity (Englishness, for instance [Holt 1996a]). Holt has valuably outlined four "stages in the history of the sporting hero" (1999, 13). This covers the early champions of the eighteenth century, the time of the gentleman amateur in the nineteenth century, the ascendant "quiet suburban" modern professional player, and modern "performer and celebrity, an ostensibly classless product of market values and the media." Local celebrities in traditional sports would be increasingly marginalized as these later stages became dominant.

But the knur and spell players of Colne represented, certainly for much of the first half of the twentieth century, alternative values that were to be perceived as increasingly anachronistic as the modern consumer era encroached on more traditional cultures of sport and leisure. When "in an increasingly international consumer culture" sport's commodification continues "apace," "the sphere of 'the popular'—which centrally includes sport and the body—will be more important than ever before in the formation of social and political identities" (Gruneau 1993, 99). In this context of sweeping consumerism, through the clarity of comparison and juxtaposition, the cultural institution of knur and spell is a source of more than mere cultural curiosity or retrospective amusement. At a time when so much of our leisure activity is either private and individualized or public and orchestrated (Philips and Tomlinson 1992), the echoes of resilient traditional forms and practices are worth listening for.

Gruneau has argued that sport retains a capacity for autonomy in several ways. First it is set apart, as a dramatic form, from other spheres of social life. Second, its spontaneity offers a sense of "voluntary action and agency" in social living; its profane nature "can never be completely incorporated into modes of domination" (Gruneau 1983, 150). And third, it can conjure up a sense of ultimate possibilities, for it is, or at least can be made, by and for its participants. The latter two elements might operate at the level of metaphor in Gruneau's view, that is, sport stands for these values, but in all these ways the sphere of sport offers to participants a range of human possibilities. That range, as the cultural life of knur and spell laikers/ players in the north of England has shown throughout the modern period, is far from exhausted by classificatory schema that run the risk of constituting the modern as the one and only, as the natural.

If historical ethnography is at all possible—the reconstruction of the lived culture of a time and a place and the recognition of the range of expressions of that culture—then a sociology of sport adequately informed by such approaches will avoid the kind of error and risk that can produce a form of scholarship that is little more than the celebration of the currently dominant. Such work can also be a sobering reminder that glossy cosmopolitanism and individualized consumption are not the only sources of sporting pleasure and leisure experience. Any study of the ascendancy of the global is dislocated and unrooted speculation, merely posing as sociological theory, unless it simultaneously recognizes the persistence of local cultures and is sensitive to the conditions and nuances of cultural change that enable different generations and populations to negotiate their personal and collective leisure identities. To ignore such local cultures is to under-estimate the scale of what Willis (1990) has called a "grounded aesthetic," to ignore the role of collective and self-organized leisure and cultures of commitment (Tomlinson 1979; Bishop and Hoggett 1986; Crouch and Tom-linson 1994; Tomlinson 1993), and to stay far more faithful to the mantra of globalization than any adequately ethnographic and sociological imagination should allow.

.

Conclusion

Observations and Research Directions

I concluded the introduction to this volume with a quote from Walter Benjamin, linking conclusions with courage (or lack of it). Initially I planned no concluding section to this collection of studies. The selection and organization of the sections and the chapters are of course an act of interpretation, a statement of position. So, somewhat obliquely, a mite quixotically—some might say evasively or elusively—I planned for the studies to stand alone, connected in their obvious ways (to me at least) by the rationale for and structure of the overall text. Not in splendid isolation, I must reaffirm, but in embryonic, incipiently coherent, integration. Two influences have changed my view on this. First, my editors (Ann Hall and Toby Miller) stimulated me to rethink the shape of the book, edging me toward a cohering revision of parts of the manuscript, including the introductions to each part. Not toward any false synthesis or bogus mono-theory, but toward a reminder to the reader and the field that these are not merely separate studies, they are, as claimed in the introduction, studies of interrelated cultural phenomena and social processes. Therefore the chapters speak across the separate sectional locations, to connecting themes central to the significance, study, and understanding of sport and leisure cultures. The second influence is one that I thought I would never write about, as what is there left to say on the question of the impact of the September 11, 2001, attacks on the Pentagon and on the World Trade Center in New York? Some of the world's top creative writers and political commentators have sought to make sense of that day and its aftermath. Why should a sport and leisure cultures researcher even consider commenting on such an issue? There is one obvious, general reason: after September 11, it is more important than it has ever been to grope toward integrated forms of intercultural understanding in a crisis-ridden but intensifyingly globalized world. Sport is the quintessential expression of an increasing internationalization of global culture, in

mediated mega-events and elite contests sponsored by nation-states, multi-
and transnational corporate organizations, and recently enriched governing bodies of sports themselves — in the 2002 tennis world, number one for
the second year running was Australian Lleyton Hewitt, defeating Swiss and
Spaniard en route to his final championship victory of the year in Shanghai,
during the week in which a new generation of China's political ruling body
was introduced to the world. Sport also provides ready-made ceremonies
where values and ideologies and particular cultural messages can be show-
cased: the U.S. Olympic Committee gained permission to overrule Olympic
protocol in the Winter Olympic Games at Salt Lake City in February 2002
and raise the tattered, battered national flag retrieved from the rubble of
the collapsed twin towers in the opening ceremony of those Games. Leisure
and consumption are crucial drivers of the world economy, too, in cultural
industries from fashion to rock music as well as sport, from tourist packages to alcohol sponsorship of sports institutions. Reactions to the September 11 tragedy — and to outrages such as the bombing of a nightclub in
Bali in 2002 — include a reevaluation of the scale and nature of consumerism
and consumption in contemporary life. If this sounds like scaremongering,
ask the unemployed workers of bankrupt airline companies, the idling taxi
drivers of Bali, the busy beneficiaries of self-catering property bookings in
the UK holiday market. Sport and leisure cultures, as analyses in this book
have confirmed, are not immune from wider social and cultural influences
and forces or from the fallout from the September 11 tragedy and its cultural and political consequences. We are read differently for the moment,
since that date, as we travel the world. Just take the time to look at how you
are now looked at in the immigration queue, smiled through in the domestic nationals' gate; scowled through more slowly when formally framed as
an outsider or a cultural other.

So, taking Benjamin's advice, from unfamiliar desks overlooking first
the rough winter seascapes of Brighton and Hove and finally from a Trini-
dadian terrace facing the plush green hills of the island's tropically drenched
interior, I have summoned the necessary courage to draw some conclusions
from this volume. And as Benjamin also noted, it is a far from pleasurable
act. Conclusions, in works of cultural analysis based on interpretive strategies and presented in appropriately discursive style, remain difficult, persistingly, perplexingly contingent. It is easy to take an orthodox line, simply
restating what the chapters of the book have said and done. But you have
already — or may soon have — read them for yourself. Why go over them again
here? And as many of my (successful) graduate students would confirm —
and they do agree that the restating strategy is often a fatigued way of coping
with waning energy — there is usually more to it than that. For in the kind
of work undertaken in this book, the "more to it" requires a particular type

of leap, from confident focused analyses of selected societies, cultures, practices, or forms to general processes or themes. What themes, then, bind together the diverse and discrete but interconnected studies contained in this book?

First, sport and leisure cultures have been transformed, particularly in the last quarter of the twentieth century, in ways that have increased their profile in everyday life and their importance as social, cultural, political, and economic presences, sometimes even forces. How these different presences interrelate and intersect is the central and recurrent question and focus for a critical social scientific and social historical analysis of sport and leisure. It would be a mistake to see these presences, influences, and forces as separate. In the high-profile sports event, for instance, political, economic, and cultural dimensions coalesce. An Olympic Games or a Grand Slam tennis tournament articulates the history and the culture of a time and place as well as the new formative alliances of a globalizing culture and economy. To study and understand such phenomena requires a recognition of political economy (of the power of economic relations and the specific political interests that such relations might serve) and a simultaneous sensitivity to cultural analysis (to the meanings and values and ideologies built into the event or the activity, the sports form or the leisure practice). Take that pivotal Summer Olympic Games in Los Angeles as a case in point, as referenced in chapter 1. To analyze at all accurately the nature and impact of that event demands an awareness of the following: the Cold War context of the genesis of the event, the internal domestic Reaganite context of the moment, the contemporaneous crisis of the Olympic movement, the nature of volunteering in U.S. civic culture, the emergence and profile of corporate sponsors in the mounting of such events, and the West Coast–based Hollywood culture of entertainment and display. This is not an optional list. It is an essential one if the social history and sociocultural analysis of sport and leisure is to be anything more than a descriptive Book of Genesis account (as warned against in Tomlinson 1999a, chapter 2) of what people do. Here, the cultural is the political, and the political is the cultural.

Second, most prominent in that coalescence of forces that has reshaped sport is the economic corporate presence. Not that this is absolutely new, as attested by Coca-Cola's long-standing investment in the Olympic Games and the football World Cup, and by Adidas's and Horst Dassler's role in the reshaping of sport finances in exclusive sponsorship deals with influential organizations such as the world governing body of football, FIFA, and the International Olympic Committee. The scale of impact of these forces can hardly be underemphasized in any analysis of sport's contemporary political economy. Analyses in part I of the book color this context. But some of this is also true of general leisure consumption, in everyday practices and local cultures. As shown in chapter 9, a vibrant local culture can be corroded at the very moment of its apparent revival. Local sponsorship in partnership with local and regional media can offer false hope to a culture, highlighting its novelty value alone, branding a culture with a history as little more than antiquarian, rustic, or just plain eccentric. This is how the heritage industry works, consumerizing histories and cultures, obsessed with potential markets rather than actual meanings. On a different scale but expressive of a parallel logic is the dilemma of Australian Rules football. In September 2000 I was invited into the radio commentary box at the Melbourne Cricket Ground for the semifinal game between two top Melbourne-based sides. It was a memorable annual event, with about ninety thousand people in the stadium, and two games all but sold out for the single weekend. I was asked what the game should do to solve its current crisis. "What crisis?" I thought, with this unique game, guaranteed crowd, locally bred heroes. The question was really about globalization and corporate markets. How can the game increase its national and international profile, attract more multinational sponsors, generate more money for its superstars? It all seemed very simple to me. If you did all that you'd change the format of the game so much that it wouldn't be Australian Rules any more. Keep the unique cultural product, I urged—whatever you do, don't listen to Rupert Murdoch's seductive whisperings.

Third, as the range of studies in the book shows, the collective dimensions of sport and leisure remain extraordinary. They can reinvigorate human aspirations and reinforce oppressive political ideologies, as national studies in part II clearly demonstrated. They provide a context and opportunity for the potential articulation of dimensions of human expression greatly at odds with some of the prevailing, privatized tendencies of contemporary consumption. Many sports, for instance, create that momentary public space in which you can feel bound to strangers, as cases in the chapters in part I showed in the context of the sport mega-event. After September 11, New Yorkers followed the valiant progress of the New York Yankees that season with a reciprocal empathy. Resuming sport fixtures was heralded as "a potent symbol of recovery from the attacks" (Reuters 2001, 194). Major league baseball started up again at the Coors Field in Denver on September 17, where players from the Colorado Rockies and the Arizona Diamondbacks held a giant American flag across the diamond. Other teams across the United States paid similar tributes, from Los Angeles to Philadelphia. The New York Mets team resumed its competitive calendar in Pittsburgh: "The Mets players wear baseball caps wearing the logos of the NYPD and the New York Fire Department to honour the victims" (Reuters 2001, 198). The first game to be played in New York after the tragedy was at Shea Stadium on September 21, against the Atlanta Braves. American flags were waved throughout the crowd, and singer Liza Minnelli performed *New York, New York* accompanied by city firefighters and police officers, clapping and shuffle-stepping with her during the seventh inning stretch of the game. A giant Stars and Stripes was unfurled in the center of the field at Yankee Stadium on September 25, when the Yankees played their first home game since the attacks. Yankee Stadium had been the venue for the "A Prayer for America" service just two days before. At a time of such tragedy, shock, and grief, the sport setting and encounter provided a key symbolic collective context for the expression of national feeling. In immeasurably less dramatic circumstances, in the context of the mundane rhythms of everyday life and the sporting calendar, Lincoln Allison has noted the symbiosis of the performer and the crowd. He instances the case of celebrity football striker Ian Wright scoring an apparently meaningless goal for Burnley Football Club, playing at only the third division level of the national football leagues:

> An ordinary goal with relatively little meaning. What made the moment extraordinary was his reaction to scoring and the crowd's reaction to him. . . . The atmosphere was like a revivalist meeting . . . a demonstration of the pure joy of scoring goals . . . which is the more realistic idea of the core of amateurism. (Allison 2001, 137–78)

Garry Whannel concludes his study of media sport stars with what I see to be a comparable recognition of the pull of the emotions, drawing on the Barthesian notion of bliss, conveyed in the French word that is a literal translation of "orgasm." Sport is, Whannel agrees, more and more the "playground of corporate capitalism":

> Yet the very uncertainties of sport . . . and the ability of sport to produce fleeting moments of *jouissance* can always, albeit briefly, escape the calculations of the corporate marketeers and entrepreneurs. . . . For those brief moments, sport provides glimpses of the marvellous, which enliven the spirit . . . inspirational glimpses of the ability of humans to transcend the calculable. (Whannel 2002, 216)

This might not last long, but like orgasm, it can happen again. There is a collective bliss in sport that has yet to be fully understood, a persisting expression of supraindividual identity. It applies equally to other leisure activities where the potential for the expression of the collective remains strong. And such forms of collective expression might well fuel a further revitalization of local cultural forms in the wake of widening disillusionment with the project of globalization.

Finally, the studies in this book embody a particular approach to social and cultural analysis, in which the ethnographic and the qualitative are crucial, the investigative a major challenge (Sugden and Tomlinson 1999c, 2002c). This is not a call for a reductionist approach to some concentration on mere individuals. In one of the most sophisticated theorizations of sport's big international events, Maurice Roche has reaffirmed the importance of central sociological questions such as the individual-society relationship and the relationship between individuals as "conscious and choosing agents" and the determining influence of social systems (Roche 2000, 229–31). Qualitative, investigative work is vital if we are to understand sport and leisure cultures at all adequately as both the expression of the agency of actors and simultaneously the articulation of the interests and influences of structural forces. To come at all close to accomplishing this, the interdisciplinary imperative of my first concluding point must be matched by a methodological openness to the relevance and generation of data and sources. As I draft this concluding paragraph, I await phone calls from individuals who control the revenues and committees of the CONCACAF football confederation (representing thirty-five national associations across North and Central America and the Caribbean). They might never ring, but they've got my message and my number. And I have their documents and their claims, and the false tickets for my payment at three international games during the last week. The home crowd was highly displeased at the last of these, Trinidad and Tobago's home loss to tiny St. Lucia. Of course they focused on the players and the manager as the ecstatic St. Lucia players slid in celebration across the waterlogged pitch of the Dr. João Havelange Centre of Excellence, Tunapuna, across and down the road from the disappeared site of the Tunapuna Cricket Club ground, where C. L. R. James first cultivated his own love of team sports almost a century earlier. The fans, as fans routinely do, aimed their disappointment at the players. But maybe one day those fans will be interested in hearing why no tickets were issued for the game, old tickets from past tournaments were used, and how the CONCACAF president Jack A. Warner lands so many profitable football-related deals for his own companies. I have written to Warner seeking an interview, though he's not ringing back. But I understand the joy of the St. Lucia giantkillers, the shame of the Trinidad and Tobago squad (even though they scraped through the qualifying group of the confederation's Gold Cup), and what motivates Mr. Warner. I couldn't have done all that with telephone interviews and SPSS (Statistical Package for the Social Sciences). Studying real-world sport and leisure cultures demands that you sample the cultures, hear the voices, interrogate the producers. The phone might ring at any moment, there is work yet to do, and there is no predictable end to the investigative trail. It has been said by some that what I do is not really sociology. But it usually illuminates, always engages with, and sometimes acts back on sport and leisure. That sounds sociological enough to me. It's also far from idiosyncratic. If sociology doesn't engage at all directly with living issues, why do it? You might as well stick with social theory and sloppy philosophy. Alan Touraine's contribution to the International Sociological Association's Brisbane conference on global order or divided world in July 1992 recognized as much. Thinking his way, after a lifetime of engagement with the biggest sociological questions of his time, toward a definition of the object of sociology, at a time in which sociological inquiry might establish a zone of "peace and creation between aggressive forms of communitarianism and a market economy which destroys all forms of social, political, cultural and autonomous life," he concluded that the "object of sociology is to seek the path to liberty through the chaos of a landscape disrupted by war, growth and crisis" (Touraine 2003, 131). These are brave things to say, and with this spice of utopianism not at all easy to say. They are propositions that tear at the mind, as I could see as I sat next to him on the plane from Singapore to Brisbane, a big man furiously annotating his manuscript, crumpled in economy class and not letting go for a minute of his commitment to the sociological project. You could sense the urgency in his intense preoccupation. For there remains much to be done if the sociological project is to have any real bearing on social development. And to return to my own modest, but at least focused, preoccupations, there is also much yet to do if the research emphases and directions at the heart of this book are to be sustained and the continuing importance and impact of sport and leisure cultures properly understood.

Notes

2. Sport, Politics, and Identities
This chapter draws on presentations made at "Culture and Identity: City, Nation, World," the second Theory, Culture, and Society conference, August 10–14, 1995, Berlin; and "Popular Culture and Collective Identity," a workshop held at the Fondation Nationale des Sciences Politiques, University of Paris, July 4, 1996. I am grateful to John Sugden with whom I worked on aspects of these conference presentations; to participants in those events for critical and supportive responses; to Professor Alan Bairner for discussions on the cultural context of football in Northern Ireland; and to Maurice Roche, organizer of the Paris event and editor of a consequent volume on sport, popular culture, and identity, for a stimulating, rigorous, and scholarly response to the initial oral presentation and written submission.

1. Quotes are taken from match reports in the *Mirror* ("Double Spice Karlheinz Stuns Euro Kings Juve," 33); the *Independent* (D. Milne, "Juventus Wrecked by German Bite," 32); and the *Guardian* (R. Williams, "Riedle Double Sinks Juve," 26)—all on Thursday, May 29, 1997.

2. No doubt I run the risk of being perceived as crudely empiricist in this intent; I am certainly making claims that any understanding of sport and popular culture should involve observation of concrete sociocultural realities with complex historical legacies. In this I am guided by C. Wright Mills and his warnings against grand theory. For Mills, grand theory is "the associating and dissociating of concepts"; grand theory's basic cause is "the initial choice of a level of thinking so general that its practitioners cannot logically get down to observation. They never, as grand theorists, get down from the higher generalities to problems in their historical and structural contexts" (Mills 1970, 34 and 42). For Mills, grand theorists are also guilty of fetishizing the Concept.

3. I would argue that both concepts illuminate the central dilemma for modern societies—how to generate coherence out of diversity, to promote forms of collectivity in an age of individualism? For Marx, the answer was economic and political transformation. For Durkheim, the modern work organization—the corporation—provided the potential to fill the moral vacuum of which anomie was the

symptom. Although it may seem to be an unfashionable, unorthodox, and perhaps even controversial view, I see both alienation and anomie as indices of the disintegration of a more collective human experience. Widespread concern with questions of identity is an echo of this classical sociological issue.

4. Durkheim himself was not entirely consistent in his discussion of the different forms that mechanical and organic solidarity take, implying in one case that there might be weaker social ties in the former than in the latter. For the purposes of the analysis in this chapter, I am most concerned with the importance of grasping the persisting relevance of the conceptual category of social solidarity for any adequately sociological understanding of cultural identity. I am indebted to Maurice Roche for pointing out the ambiguity in Durkheim's analysis.

5. In discussing the ways in which one can move across and between forms of the collective, it is interesting to consider Victor Turner's notions of *liminality* and *communitas* (Turner 1967, 1969, 1974, 1982). Liminality refers to a phase—often transitional—"betwixt and between" positions or states: "the liminal community or comity of comrades and not a structure of hierarchically arranged positions" (1967, 100). Communitas is "a perception of shared emotional states" (1982, 21), linked to a deemphasis on the "logical, linear, and classifying functions associated with social structuring" (21). Communitas—along with *sacra* (sacred things) and *ludic recombination* (the element of play)—is one of the major components of the liminal process: "a direct, spontaneous and egalitarian mode of social relationship" (202). For Turner, liminal states of communitas are potentially transformative, processual, and constitute a kind of cultural time-out potentially threatening to social structure itself. A full sociological and cultural application of Turner's ideas to sport spectacle and sport cultures would be an intriguing contribution to understanding the sources of identity and symbolic meaning in popular culture. MacAloon, for instance, has drawn on the notions of liminality and marginality in his brilliant study (1981) on de Coubertin and the birth of modern Olympism.

6. Interviewed in FNB Stadium (Soccer City), Johannesburg, January 1996.

7. Interviewed in Durban, South Africa, January 1996.

8. Although the reported views are those of white journalists, black activist sports writers also recognize the problem of deep-rooted corruption in African football administration, as well as its progressive potential. See Sugden and Tomlinson 1998, chapter 6; Quansha 1996; and Maradas 1996.

9. This summary of the documentary is taken from Tomlinson 1996a.

10. See Tomlinson 1986; and Bellos 2000. Havelange was deeply distrusted for the reforms of the Brazilian league that he undertook in the 1960s and 1970s. His influence was long-standing, too. When the Brazilian league championship, renamed the João Havelange trophy, was decided on the last Saturday of December 2000, second division Sao Caetano contested the title (losing to Vasco da Gama) without ever having played in the top division. This was due to an idiosyncratic knockout and play-off system designed to revive a moribund league left in neglected shape two and a half decades earlier, when Havelange's legacy to his national sport at home was to leave the sport shorn of any infrastructural stability. The final to this championship cum cup "caps six farcical months" of the new season's "byzantine structure," as one commentator (Bellos 2000, 2) put it.

11. To fail to recognize this is to commit the fallacy of the fetishization of

the concept, to analytically privilege a notion of identity within modernity that is too often read from reaffirming textual sources rather than observed in the complex and confusing contexts of cultural and social settings.

12. Interview in *L'Équipe*, Tuesday, May 27, 1997, no. 15879, 8 (my translation).

3. FIFA and the Men's World Cup

1. The following discussion of Rimet draws on two main sources—Guillain 1998 and Sir Stanley Rous's memoir (Rous 1978). It uses material, too, that is also reported in Sugden and Tomlinson 1999c, chapter 2; and Tomlinson 1999d.

2. Winterbottom was talking in a BBC radio tribute to Rous, and in a personal interview with me, November 24, 1996. This synopsis of Rous's background is based on Tomlinson 1999c.

3. S. Rous, "Post-war development—a memorandum prepared by the War Emergency Committee for the Consideration of the Council," May 1943; and "Post-war development—an Interim Report," October 1944. Both these papers are in the minute books of the Football Association's Council.

4. This annotated document is in the Sir Stanley Rous papers kept by Rose Marie Breitenstein, a copy of which is in the Rous papers in the Sports Cultures Archive for Investigative Research (SCAIR), Sport and Leisure Cultures, Chelsea School Research Centre, University of Brighton.

5. This discussion of Havelange's background and style draws on Sugden and Tomlinson 1998c, 1999a; Yallop 1999; Farah 1996; and an interview with the author in Cairo, September 1997.

6. And this was reiterated in FIFA 1994: "Havelange transformed an administration-oriented institution into a dynamic enterprise brimming with new ideas and the will to see them through" (6). A decade more of new ideas, still the same wording and tribute.

7. This discussion of Blatter is based on my personal observation of proceedings during the FIFA Congress in Paris, on June 8, 1998, and of Blatter at various hotels, stadia, and functions throughout that tournament as well as continued monitoring of his style and impact during his first four-year tenure and the first six months of his second cycle in the presidential office. On how Blatter so successfully sustained voting loyalties for his election victory in 2002, I have drawn on Tomlinson 2002.

8. On England's bidding, see Sugden and Tomlinson, 1999b, 2002a. On England's struggle to get back into the corridors of power, see Sugden and Tomlinson 1999d. On the public relations elements of the offer to Wales, see Tomlinson 1999e.

4. Sport, Cultural Diversity, and National Identity

1. Simmel (1991) made interesting observations, first published in 1885, on Alpinism as an example of the democratization of access to the natural world, which he saw as an important dimension of modernity.

2. My thanks to Martin Putter for corroboration of this point.

3. Etzioni's writings on the notion of communitarianism have influenced revisionist left-wing politicians such as the UK prime minister Tony Blair. In his reflections on the nature and spirit of community he argues for "'a new moral, social, public order—without puritanism or oppression' . . . based upon shared values, the

renewal of social bonds and the reform of public life" (Tomlinson 1999g, 23). Speaking of how such an order could be achieved, Etzioni instanced school games and team sports (Etzioni 1994).

4. This multilevel of provision explains some at-first-glance surprising statistics. For instance, the average amount of broadcast hours of the UEFA Champions' League 1995/96 was 48 hours per European country. But Belgium broadcast 75 hours 40 minutes, and Switzerland 109 hours 33 minutes, for the games had to be simultaneously covered on several different language channels in those two countries (see TEAM 1997).

5. See Codding (1961, 161–62) for a summary, up to 1961, of Swiss involvement with international organizations. These ranged from the International Red Cross Committee (1864) to technology, communications, and financial organizations. Specialized agencies of the United Nations — such as the World Health Organization and the World Meteorological Organization — were also based in Geneva.

6. Martin Putter was presenting at the Sport in Divided Societies symposium, University of Brighton, Sport and Leisure Cultures, at the Sussex Arts Club, Brighton, on May 23, 1997.

7. A summary and a record of Swiss football performance on the international stage can be found in Oliver (1995, 534–46).

8. On the IOC, see Simson and Jennings 1992 and Jennings 1996; on FIFA, the governing body of world football, see Sugden and Tomlinson 1998c.

9. Research and policy debate is featured in its review, *Macolin*. Stamm and Lamprecht, for instance, debate how to translate the knowledge that all occasional sports participants have of the health benefits of regular sport and exercise into patterns of more regular forms of commitment and involvement. They suggest targeting groups such as women, particular age groups, and men with children with strategies of encouragement. See Stamm and Lamprecht 1996a.

10. Office fédéral de la statistique 1990. The data reported in this section are all taken from this source.

11. See Mathys 1977; Burgener 1974, 1981; and Huguenin et al. 1981.

6. EASTERN PROMISE?

1. "S-League Ball: Gala Dinner and Awards Presentation '96," dated November 15, 1996. This was kindly provided by the Football Association of Singapore.

2. This is the first paragraph of the conclusion to Dato' Peter Velappan, *Asian Football in the New Millennium*, presented at the media seminar held in conjunction with the Eleventh Asian Cup, Abu Dhabi, United Arab Emirates, on Saturday, December 14, 1996. I am indebted to the general secretary of AFC, Dato' Peter, for support in acquiring media accreditation for the event and responding to further approaches. Much of this chapter, when dealing with AFC perspectives on the development of the game, draws on Dato' Peter's expertise as expressed at the seminar, in interviews, and in AFC publications.

3. Ibid.

4. My thanks to AFC Marketing Ltd., Hong Kong, publisher (on behalf of the AFC) of *Asian Football Confederation News*. Thanks too to Michael Church, editor of the latter, for informing discussions during matches at the Eleventh Asian Cup, in Abu Dhabi in December 1996, and for his department's generous response in

providing documents during a visit to AFC in Kuala Lumpur, March 1997. His rationale for a neutral, football-only approach to Asian football writing also confirmed for me the intense partisanship at the heart of the extended Asian football family: so intense between the national associations, that it seemed that an official publication of the AFC could not contemplate commenting on much more than purely playing matters.

I retain some skepticism concerning the definitiveness of FIFA's rankings, for they are based on all games played, in or out of tournaments, and do not capture the vicissitudes of performance—planned, for instance, in terms of seasonality or peak performance—that are critical to top-level tournament play. But the compilers of the rankings—Hans Peter Stamm and Markus Lamprecht of SLS, Zurich—argued convincingly, during a hospitable and civilized lunch in Zurich in May 1996, that their tables have a predictive value, indicating genuine form teams, the up-and-coming winners (for example, South Africa at the African Cup of Nations, on its home territory in January/February 1996). The Asia table, compiled before the Asian Cup of December 1996 held in the United Arab Emirates, confirms their claims. Japan and Korea appeared, at that tournament, to be in decline, the United Arab Emirates and Kuwait performed in improving fashion, and Saudi Arabia stood firm. China flattered to deceive, but only Iran's stirring renaissance performances confounded the rankings' predictive value.

5. See, too, Stamm and Lamprecht 1996c.

6. Interview with author, Abu Dhabi, December 1996. See also Sugden and Tomlinson 1997b.

7. "What Is a Case?" Jennifer Platt (1992) has asked. In her critical review of the use of "cases" in sociological work, she shows that much case study theorizing has been conceptually confused. My own use of the case studies is an intramethodological, inductive aspect of a wider study of the context of which the cases are apart.

8. The main source of data cited on the United Arab Emirates is *UAE Yearbook 1996*. On the growth of soccer in the United Arab Emirates, I have drawn on pages 18–25 of the Official Souvenir Program of the Eleventh Asian Cup.

9. For further contextual comment on this elision of the Asian Cup event with the UAE president's jubilee celebrations, see my two pieces in *Gulf News* (Tomlinson 1996b and 1997b).

10. Home page of Asia Cup 1996, December 3–21, http://www.asiacup96.org.ac/.

11. Ibid.

12. This vignette of the structure of top-level football is based on an interview with Abbas Mohammad Hassan at the headquarters of the UAE Football Association, Zayed Sports City, Abu Dhabi, December 17, 1996. Hassan, an expert on football matters in the United Arab Emirates, was also a FIFA referee of twenty-two years' standing and acted as a commissioner and instructor with the AFC.

13. "Locals" and "nationals" in the United Arab Emirates refers to, respectively, people of Emirate origin and people who have been granted UAE nationality. Large numbers of people—migrant workers and expatriates—being neither of these, are perceived as outsiders.

14. I follow Winkler's definition of corporatism, which is characterized by unity, order, nationalism, and success. See Winkler 1977.

15. Author's archives.

16. Interviewed in London, June 12, 1997.

17. See Horne and Jary 1994.

18. The following account of the growth of Japanese football and the formation of the J-League is based on documentation provided by the J-League, the Football Association of Japan, and the 2002 World Cup Preparatory Committee Secretariat in March 1997. This material includes *Japan Football Scene* monthly newsletters; the 1996 annual report of the Football Association of Japan; *Sharing Our Goal with the World*, a dossier of the World Cup Japan Bidding Committee (January 1996); and the *J-League Profile* 1996 (English edition). Interviews with Tadao Murata and Ryo Nishimura at the offices of 2002 World Cup were also most valuable (Friday, March 21, 1997, Tokyo). My thanks go also to Derek Bleakley for interpreting during parts of the interviews and for providing—with the historical pedigree of a Preston North End fan!—insights on the specificities of Japan's football history and development. His splendidly detailed knowledge has been incorporated into the collection on the 2002 World Cup edited by Horne and Manzenreiter (2002). See, too, Watts 1998 and Horne and Manzenreiter 2002. Watt's observations echo my own: "supports" chanting is orchestrated by an appointed leader (1998, 198).

19. This legacy was evident in Japan's victory in the final of the World Student Games football competition in Fukuoka, Japan, in 1995.

20. *J-League Profile*, 1.

21. Ibid.

22. Interview by author, March 21, 1997.

23. This was confirmed in discussion with Chris McDonald, JFA adviser, at the Yokohama Marinos stadium on March 29, 1997.

24. Sayama (1997) writes: "The word *Mécénat* is originated from the name of the Roman empire politician Maecenes. Historically, the word indicates the sponsorship of culture by the Medicis. Today *Mécénat* is the term for sponsorship of sports and culture by corporations called the out-manager system." Interestingly, the Japanese inflection on *Mécénat* equates the notion of public contribution with the private sponsoring corporation: amounting to what is really a combination of outreach, philanthropy, and public relations.

25. "J. League Enjoys Best Season Ever," update, *Japan Football Scene*, January 1996.

26. Tan Eng Yoon, interview by author, Jalan Besar Stadium, Singapore, March 14, 1997.

27. Chuck Blazer, interview by author, New York City, February 20, 1997.

28. See Sugden and Tomlinson 1998c, 111–21; and Sugden and Tomlinson 1999a, chapter 13.

7. Patterns of Consumption in Sport and Leisure Cultures

1. The survey comprised a series of five group discussions carried out in November 1990; a questionnaire survey, involving interviews of seven to ten minutes, administered to 478 members of the public in Brighton in February and March 1991; and a household interview survey of on average just over half an hour with 1,026 respondents, administered in October and November 1991 (60 percent of these respondents were Brighton residents, 40 percent were from Hove, the Portslade

postal districts, Lewes, Peacehaven, Haywards Heath, and Burgess Hill). Reports of these phases of the study (Magness 1990; Lawrence and Tomlinson 1991, 1992) are the source of these highlights.

2. It may repay to reconfigure the residential analysis by combining some postal districts and constructing a zonal typology—town center, off-center districts, outer districts, for instance. This would produce more numerically valid results on, say, the gender breakdown of the use of particular facilities and the type of transport used for getting to individual facilities.

3. Personal communication, August 2001.

8. The Politics of Men's Leisure

1. For a collection of studies on the pull and nature of identity in local sport cultures, see Hill and Williams 1996.

2. There is a biography/obituary, for instance, of a seventy-three-year-old athlete in the 1929 *Craven Herald* (August 16). This man, from Cowling, a few miles outside Colne, was a professional athlete from the age of nineteen to his fortieth year. He lived on this skill and had sports trophies worth £250. His first handicap was set up by a sporting entrepreneur (Alec Whipp, from a town twenty to twenty-five miles away): there were seven heats, four in each heat, over 120 yards. At the age of twenty-five (1881) he jumped across the canal. At one Lake Sports he won all the field events, getting an extra ten shillings and a week's "royal hospitality" from a local gentleman. Patrons supported him. When he was not supported, in between his athletic activities he took on factory work making pillboxes, drumming in a theater band, and jumping over galloping horses in a circus. Hustling was also his forte. He would wear an old cap, a worn-out coat, thin trousers, and laced-up clogs and then challenge some local jumping champion for £25 a match and usually win easily.

3. This point was made by the late Ian Taylor at the workshop at which this analysis was first presented, at Queen's University, Kingston, Ontario, Canada.

4. "What Are They?" *Colne Times*, October 16, 1962.

5. Although some of the cultural forms discussed in this chapter can be understood as forms of closure, the point also relates widely to gender-based associations or clubs within working-class culture, which I mentioned early on in the third section of this chapter but to which I have not given any detailed consideration.

9. Continuities and Change in Male Working-Class Leisure

1. I have argued this case on methodological and conceptual grounds in more detail elsewhere, in terms of the project of cultural studies (Tomlinson 1981, 1989b).

2. *News of the World*, August 7, 1988, 1.

3. Allotments are municipally owned plots of land rented out to local citizens and usually used for a mixture of gardening, horticulture, and getting away from it all.

4. Pages 44–45. The booklet quotes Dr. Johnson, but the spelling is very modern, and the males leapfrogging on the front cover picture look most likely to be from the late eighteenth century (though there is no definitive confirmation that the cover image is contemporaneous with the writing and publication date). The

booklet is from Sport box 15, in the John Johnson Collection of Ephemera, at the Bodleian Library, University of Oxford. "Bowman, Publisher, 20, Newgate Street, Newcastle; London Agent: G. Golding, 18, Houghton Street, Newcastle Street, Stroud. Price One Penny."

5. "Champ Stuart—Pubs and Clubs," *Colne Times,* December 4, 1981.

6. "Champion of the World," *Colne Times,* April 12, 1991.

Bibliography

Adair, G. 1986. "The Light Ages." In *Myths and Memories*. London: Flamingo.

AFC (Asian Football Confederation). 1994. *Asian Football Confederation, 1954–1994*. Kuala Lumpur: Asian Football Confederation.

Aitchison, C. 2000. "Poststructural Feminist Theories of Representing Others: A Response to the 'Crisis' in Leisure Studies Discourse." *Leisure Studies* 19, no. 3: 127–44.

Aitchison, C., and F. Jordan. 1998. "Gender, Space, and Identity: Introduction." In *Gender, Space, and Identity: Leisure, Culture, and Commerce*, ed. C. Aitchison and F. Jordan. Eastbourne, UK: Leisure Studies Association.

Alabarces, P., A. Tomlinson, and C. Young. 2001. "Argentina versus England at France '98: Narratives of Nation and the Mythologizing of the Popular." *Media, Culture, and Society* 23, no. 5: 565–84.

Aldgate, T. 1981. "British Cinema in the 1930s." Unit 7, block 2, "The Historical Development of Popular Culture in Britain," 2, course U203 Popular Culture. Milton Keynes, UK: Open University.

Alegi, P. 2000. "Contracts of Joy in South African Football, c. 1940–76." *International Journal of the History of Sport* 17, no. 4: 1–20.

Allison, L. 1984. "Walking Home." *New Society*, August 16, 138–39.

———. 2000. "Sport and Nationalism." In *Handbook of Sports Studies*, ed. J. Coakley and E. Dunning. London: Sage Publications.

———. 2001. *Amateurism in Sport: An Analysis and a Defence*. London: Frank Cass.

Andrews, D. L., R. Pitter, D. Zwick, and D. Ambrose. 1997. "Soccer's Racial Frontier: Sport and the Suburbanization of Contemporary America." In *Entering the Field: New Perspectives on World Football*, ed. G. Armstrong and R. Giulianotti. Oxford: Berg.

Appadurai, A. 1999a. "Ethnic Violence in the Era of Globalization." In *Globalization and Identity: Dialectics of Flow and Closure*, ed. B. Meyer and P. Geschiere. Oxford: Basil Blackwell.

———. 1999b. "Globalization and the Research Imagination." *International Social Science Journal* 160: 229–38.

Arbena, J. L. 1993. "International Aspects of Sport in Latin America: Perceptions,

Prospects, and Proposals." In *The Sports Process: A Comparative and Developmental Approach*, ed. E. G. Dunning, J. A. Maguire, and R. E. Pearton. Champaign, IL: Human Kinetics.

Bailey, P. 1978. *Leisure and Class in Victorian England: Rational Recreation and the Contest for Control, 1830–1885.* London: Routledge and Kegan Paul.

———. 1983. "Ally Sloper's Half-Holiday: Comic Art in the 1880s." *History Workshop Journal* 16: 4–31.

Bairner, A. 1999. "Masculinity, Violence, and the Irish Peace Process." *Capital and Class* 69: 126–44.

———. 2000a. "After the War? Soccer, Masculinity, and Violence in Northern Ireland." In *Masculinities, Gender Relations, and Sport*, ed. J. McKay, M. A. Messner, and D. Sabo. London: Sage.

———. 2000b. "Sport and Peace: An Uneasy Dialogue." In *Memories of the Present: A Sociological Chronicle of Ireland, 1997–1998*, ed. E. Slater and M. Peillon. Dublin: Institute of Public Administration.

———. 2001a. *Sport, Nationalism, and Globalization: European and North American Perspectives*, Albany: State University of New York Press.

———. 2001b. "Sports Studies and Politics: Reflections on the Irish Experience." Presentation at "History and Politics in Sports Studies," workshop of the British Sociological Association Sociology of Sport Study Group, University of Ulster, and the Sports Council for Northern Ireland, February 9–10.

———. 2003. "On Thin Ice? The Odyssey, the Giants, and the Sporting Transformation of Belfast." *American Behavioral Scientist* 46, no. 11: 1519–32.

Bairner, A., and P. Darby. 2001. "The Swedish Model and International Sport: Lennart Johansson and the Governance of World Football." *International Review for the Sociology of Sport* 36, no. 2: 337–59.

Bairner, A., and P. Shirlow. 1998. "Loyalism, Linfield, and the Territorial Politics of Soccer Fandom in Northern Ireland." *Space and Polity* 2, no. 2: 163–77.

Bale, J. 1994. *Landscapes of Modern Sports.* Leicester, UK: Leicester University Press.

Banks-Smith, N. 1984. "Where Eagles Dare." *Guardian*, July 30, 9.

BBC (British Broadcasting Corporation) World Service. 2002. "World Football." November 9.

———. 1999. News item, December 8.

Beck, P. 1999. "British Football and FIFA, 1928–46: Going to War or Peaceful Coexistence?" Paper presented at British Society of Sports History annual conference, University of Brighton, March 31–April 1.

Bellos, A. 2000. "Juninho Back at the Top." *Guardian*, December 30, sport section, 2.

Benjamin, W. 1970. *Illuminations*, ed. H. Arendt, trans. H. Zohn. London: Collins/Fontana Books.

———. 1978. *Reflections: Essays, Aphorisms, Autobiographical Writings*, ed. P. Demetz, trans. E. Jephcott. New York: Harcourt Brace Jovanovich.

Berlin, P. 1994. "Where Dribbling Is Child's Play." *Financial Times*, July 7, 4.

Bernstein, K. 1995. "Born in China, Made in Brazil." *Independent on Sunday Magazine*, July 9, 8–11.

Bhaba, H. K. 1994. *The Location of Culture*. London: Routledge.

Bishop, J., and P. Hoggett. 1986. *Organizing around Enthusiasms: Patterns of Mutual Aid in Leisure.* London: Comedia.

Black, D. R., and J. Nauright. 1998. *Rugby and the South African Nation: Sport, Cultures, Politics, and Power in the Old and New South Africas*. Manchester: Manchester University Press.

Block, R. 1996. "Team That Truly Represents a Nation." *Independent*, February 5, sport section, S12.

Bondi, L. 1998. "Gender, Class, and Urban Space: Public and Private Space in Contemporary Urban Landscape." In *Gender, Space, and Identity: Leisure, Culture, and Commerce*, ed. C. Aitchison and F. Jordan. Eastbourne, UK: Leisure Studies Association.

Bonjour, F. 1920. *Real Democracy in Operation: The Example of Switzerland*, trans. C. Leonard Leese. London: George Allen and Unwin.

Booth, D. 1998. *The Race Game: Sport and Politics in South Africa*. London: Frank Cass.

Bose, S., S. Sarkar, and A. K. Chatterjee. 1994. "Gymnastic and Sport in Switzerland." *Research Bi-annual for Movement* (Maharashtra State, India) 10, no. 2: 53–57.

Bourdieu, P. 1986. *Distinction: A Social Critique of the Judgement of Taste*. London: Routledge and Kegan Paul.

———. 1999. "The State, Economics, and Sport." In *France and the 1998 World Cup: The National Impact of a World Sporting Event*, ed. H. Dauncey and G. Hare. London: Frank Cass.

Braudel, F. 1974. *Capitalism and Material Life, 1400–1800*. London: Fontana/Collins.

British Olympic Association. 1996. "*Modern Olympic Movement.*" In British Olympic Association Olympic Pack. London: British Olympic Association.

Brohm, J.-M. 1978. *Sport: A Prison of Measured Time*. London: Ink Links.

Bromberger, C. 1994. "Football Passion and the World Cup." In *Hosts and Champions: Soccer Cultures, National Identities, and the USA World Cup*, ed. J. Sugden and A. Tomlinson. Aldershot, UK: Ashgate.

Bulletin of Sports Information. 1991. "Suisse: Evolution de l'infrastructure sportive de 1963 à 1986." *Bulletin d'Information Sportive* 24: 1815–16.

Burgener, L. 1974. *Education physique en Suisse: Histoire et situation actuelle*. Derendingen-Soleure, Switzerland: Editions Habegger.

———. 1981. "Games and Physical Exercises in Switzerland in the 15th and 16th Centuries." *Olympic Review*, no. 162: 237–40.

Burke, P., ed. 1972. *Economy and Society in Early Modern Europe: Essays from Annales*. London: Routledge and Kegan Paul.

———, ed. 1973. *A New Kind of History, from the Writings of Febvre*. London: Routledge and Kegan Paul.

———. 1978. "Annales School and *Mentalités*." Paper presented at sociology research seminar, University of Sussex, February 2.

Calgari, G. 1963. *The Four Literatures of Switzerland*. London: Adam Books.

Carpozi, G., Jr. 1999. *Nazi Gold: The Real Story of How the World Plundered Jewish Treasures*. Far Hills, NJ: New Horizon Press.

Cart, J. 1994. "$7 Million for World Cup Boss." *Los Angeles Times*, October 19, C1, C7.

Chaney, D. 1994. *The Cultural Turn: Scene-Setting Essays on Contemporary Cultural History*. London: Routledge.

Channel 4 (UK). 2002. *Big Beach Boutique*, March 2.

Chatterton, P., and R. Hollands. 2001. *Changing Our 'Toon': Youth, Nightlife, and Urban Change in Newcastle*. Newcastle: University of Newcastle upon Tyne.

————. 2003. *Urban Nightscapes: Youth Cultures, Pleasure Spaces, and Corporate Power.* London: Routledge.

Childs, P., and R. J. P. Williams. 1997. *An Introduction to Post-colonial Theory.* London: Prentice Hall.

Clarke, J. 1979. "Capital and Culture: The Post-War Working-Class Revisited." In *Working Class Culture: Studies in History and Theory*, ed. J. Clarke, C. Critcher, and R. Johnson. London: Hutchinson.

Coalter, F., S. Dowers, and M. Baxter. 1995. "The Impact of Social Class and Education on Sports Participation: Some Evidence from the General Household Survey." In *Leisure and Social Stratification*, ed. K. Roberts. Leisure Studies Association Publications no. 53. Eastbourne, UK: Leisure Studies Association.

Codding, G. A., Jr. 1961. *The Federal Government of Switzerland.* London: George Allen and Unwin.

Collins, T. 2000. "Sport and Gambling: An Historical Overview." Presentation at British Society for Sports History annual conference, University of Liverpool.

Connell, R. 1999. Foreword to *Class, Sports, and Social Development,* by R. Gruneau. Champaign, IL: Human Kinetics.

Constantine, S. 1980. *Unemployment in Britain between the Wars.* London: Longman.

Cooley, C. H. 1969. "Looking-Glass Self." In *Symbolic Interaction: A Reader in Social Psychology*, ed. J. G. Manis and B. N. Meltzer. Boston: Allyn and Bacon.

Coser, L. A. 1971. *Masters of Sociological Thought: Ideas in Historical and Social Context.* New York: Harcourt Brace Jovanovich.

————. 1984. Introduction to *The Division of Labour in Society,* by E. Durkheim, trans. W. D. Halls. London: Macmillan.

Crombie, G. R. 1978. *1926–1951: A Colne Festival.* Lancashire, UK: MM Publishing.

Crook, R. 1982. "'Tidy Women': Women in the Rhondda between the Wars." *Oral History* 10, no. 2: 40–46.

Crouch, D. 1989. "Patterns of Co-operation in the Cultures of Outdoor Leisure: The Case of the Allotment." *Leisure Studies* 8, no. 2: 189–99.

————. 1999. "Introduction: Encounters in Leisure Tourism." In *Leisure/Tourism Geographies: Practices and Geographical Knowledge*, ed. D. Crouch. London: Routledge.

Crouch, D., and A. Tomlinson. 1994. "Collective Self-generated Consumption: Leisure, Space, and Cultural Identity in Late Modernity." In *Leisure: Modernity, Postmodernity, and Lifestyles*, ed. I. Henry. Eastbourne: Leisure Studies Association.

Cunningham, H. 1980. *Leisure in the Industrial Revolution, c. 1780–c. 1880.* London: Croom Helm.

Dahrendorf, R. 1979. *Life Chances: Approaches to Social and Political Theory.* Chicago: University of Chicago Press.

Danziger, N. 1997. *Danziger's Britain: A Journey to the Edge.* London: Flamingo.

Dauncey, H., and G. Hare, eds. 1999. *France and the 1998 World Cup: The National Impact of a World Sporting Event.* London: Frank Cass.

————. 2000. "World Cup France '98: Metaphors, Meanings, and Values." *International Review for the Sociology of Sport* 35, no. 3: 331–47.

Davies, A. 1992. *Leisure, Gender, and Poverty: Working-class Culture in Salford and Manchester, 1900–1939.* Buckingham, UK: Open University Press.

DCMS (Department of Culture, Media and Sport). 2000. "Staging of International Sporting Events: The 2006 World Cup Campaign." December 8. Memorandum submitted by the Football Association to the House of Commons Culture, Media, and Sport Committee (document reference SF20). London: House of Commons.

De Coubertin, P. 1986. "Switzerland, Queen of Sports." *Olympic Review*, no. 228: 599–603.

———. 2000. *Pierre de Coubertin, 1863–1937: Olympism; Selected Writings*, ed. Norbert Müller. Lausanne: International Olympic Committee.

Delves, A. 1981. "Popular Recreation and Social Control in Derby, 1880–1850." In *Popular Culture and Class Conflict, 1590–1914: Explorations in the History of Labour and Leisure*, ed. E. Yeo and S. Yeo. Brighton, UK: Harvester Press.

DSR (Department of Sport and Recreation). 1995. *Sport and Recreation in South Africa*. DSR: file://A:\sportrec.htm, accessed October 28, 1999.

Dixey, R. 1983. "The Playing of Bingo: Industry, Market, and Working-Class Culture." In *Leisure and Popular Cultural Forms*, ed. A. Tomlinson. Eastbourne, UK: Leisure Studies Association.

Douglas, J. D. 1976. *Investigative Social Research: Individual and Team Research*. London: Sage Publications.

Duke, V., and E. Crolley. 1996. *Football, Nationality, and the State*. London: Longman.

Dunning, E. 1999. *Sport Matters: Sociological Studies of Sport, Violence, and Civilization*, London: Routledge.

Dunning, E., and K. Sheard. 1979. *Barbarians, Gentlemen, and Players: A Sociological Study of the Development of Rugby Football*. New York: New York University Press.

Durkheim, E. 1984. *The Division of Labour in Society*, trans. W. D. Halls. London: Macmillan.

Edelman, R. 1993. *Serious Fun: A History of Spectator Sports in the USSR*. Oxford: Oxford University Press.

Egger, E., and E. Blanc. 1974. *Education in Switzerland*. Geneva: Swiss Educational Documentation Centre (Palais Wilson, Ch 1211, Geneva 14). July.

Engels, F. 1958. *The Condition of the Working-Class in England*. Trans. and ed. W. O. Henderson and W. H. Chaloner. Oxford, UK: Basil Blackwell.

Etzioni, A. 1994. *The Spirit of Community: The Reinvention of American Society*. New York: Simon and Schuster/Touchstone.

Eveleigh, R. 1995. "Spellbinding." Pictures by Kevin Rogers. *Lancashire Life*, May, 34–37.

Farah, E. J., ed. 1996. *Young Havelange: FIFA in the Third Millennium*. São Paulo: J. S. Propaganda.

Fasting, K. 2000. "Seeing and Being Seen: Body Fashion in Female Recreational Sport." In *Sport, Leisure Identities, and Gender Spaces*, ed. S. Scraton and B. Watson. Eastbourne, UK: Leisure Studies Association.

Featherstone, M. 1996. "Localism, Globalism, and Cultural Identity." In *Global/Local: Cultural Production and the Transnational Imaginary*, ed. R. Wilson and W. Dissanayake. London: Duke University Press.

Featherstone, M., and D. Wynne. 1990. *Lifestyle and Cultural Consumption in the City*. Economic and Social Research Council application, UK. April.

FIFA. 1984. *History of FIFA*. Zurich: FIFA.

———. 1994. *90 Years of FIFA: Souvenir Edition 1994*. Zurich: FIFA.

Finnegan, R. 1989. *The Hidden Musicians: Music-Making in an English Town*. Cambridge, UK: Cambridge University Press.

Foulds, S., and P. Harris. 1979. *America's Soccer Heritage: A History of the Game*. Manhattan Beach, CA: Soccer for Americans.

Fynn, A., and L. Guest. 1994. *Out of Time: Why Football Isn't Working*. London: Simon and Schuster.

Gardner, P. 1994. "Lightweight Bill in Vegas." *World Soccer* 34, no. 4: 4.

———. 1995. "Pipe Dream: Paul Gardner Is Not Convinced by Major League Soccer's Plans to Lay a Pipeline to the Stars." *World Soccer* 35, no. 8: 46–47.

George, N. 1992. *Elevating the Game: Black Men and Basketball*. New York: Harper Collins.

Giddens, A. 1991. *Modernity and Self-identity: Self and Society in the Late Modern Age*. Cambridge, UK: Polity Press.

Giulianotti, R. 1999. *Football: A Sociology of the World Game*. Cambridge, UK: Polity Press.

Glanville, B. 1995. "No Time for This Rubbish." *World Soccer* 35, no. 8: 72.

Goffman, E. 1959. *The Presentation of Self in Everyday Life*. New York: Doubleday Anchor.

———. 1968. *Asylums*. Harmondsworth, UK: Pelican.

———. 1972. "Fun in Games." In *Encounters: Two Studies in the Sociology of Interaction*. Harmondsworth, UK: Penguin University Books.

Gow, D. 1997. "Wiesel to Head Swiss War Fund." *Guardian*, May 2, 23.

Grant, L. 2000. *When I Lived in Modern Times*. London: Granta Books.

Gruneau, R. 1983. *Class, Sports, and Social Development*. Amherst: University of Massachusetts Press.

———. 1988. "Modernization and Hegemony: Two Views on Sport and Social Development." In *Not Just a Game: Essays in Canadian Sport Sociology*, ed. J. Harvey and H. Cantelon. Ottawa: University of Ottawa Press.

———. 1993. "The Critique of Sport in Modernity: Theorising Power, Culture, and the Politics of the Body." In *The Sports Process: A Comparative and Developmental Approach*, ed. E. G. Dunning, J. A. Maguire, and R. E. Pearton. Champaign, IL: Human Kinetics.

———. 1999. *Class, Sports, and Social Development*. Champaign, IL: Human Kinetics.

Guelke, A., and J. Sugden. 1998. "Sport and the 'Normalising' of the New South Africa." In *Sport in Divided Societies*, ed. A. Bairner and J. Sugden. Aachen, Germany: Meyer and Meyer.

Guillain, J.-Y. 1998. *La coupe du monde de football: L'oevre de Jules Rimet*. Paris: Éditions Amphora.

Guldemont, H., and B. Deps. 1995. *100 ans de football en Belgique*. Brussels: Union Royale Belge des Sociétés de Football Association.

Guttmann, A. 1978. *From Ritual to Record: The Nature of Modern Sports*. New York: Columbia University Press.

———. 1993. "The Diffusion of Sports and the Problem of Cultural Imperialism." In *The Sports Process: A Comparative and Developmental Approach*, ed. E. G. Dunning, J. A. Maguire, and R. E. Pearton. Champaign, IL: Human Kinetics.

Hall, S. 1981. "Notes on Deconstructing 'the Popular.'" In *People's History and Socialist Theory*, ed. R. Samuel. London: Routledge and Kegan Paul.

———. 1986. "Popular Culture and the State." In *Popular Culture and Social Relations*, ed. T. Bennett, C. Mercer, and J. Woollacott. Milton Keynes, UK: Open University Press.

———. 1990. "Cultural Identity and Diaspora." In *Identity: Community, Culture, Difference*, ed. J. Rutherford. London: Lawrence and Wishart.

———. 1991. "Old and New Identities, Old and New Ethnicities." In *Culture, Globalization, and the World-System: Contemporary Conditions for the Representation of Identity*, ed. A. D. King. London: Macmillan.

Hamilton, P. 1953. *The West Pier.* London: Constable.

Hammersley, M., and P. Atkinson. 1983. *Ethnography: Principles in Practice.* London: Routledge.

Hammond, J. L., and B. Hammond. 1947. *The Bleak Age.* Rev. edition (first published 1934). West Drayton, Middlesex, UK: Penguin Books.

Hannerz, U. 1999. "Epilogue: Some Reports from a Free Space." In *Globalization and Identity: Dialectics of Flow and Closure*, ed. B. Meyer and P. Geschiere. Oxford: Basil Blackwell.

Hargreaves, Jennifer. 2000. *Heroines of Sport: The Politics of Difference and Identity.* London: Routledge.

Hargreaves, John. 1983. "Sport and Hegemony: Some Theoretical Problems." In *Sport, Culture, and the Modern State*, ed. H. Cantelon and R. Gruneau. Toronto: University of Toronto Press.

———. 1986. *Sport, Power, and Culture: A Social and Historical Analysis of Popular Sports in Britain.* Cambridge, UK: Polity Press.

———. 1996. "Catalan Nationalism, Spanish Identity, and the Barcelona Olympics." Paper presented at the British Sociological Association annual conference, Reading, UK, April.

———. 2000. *Freedom for Catalonia? Catalan Nationalism, Spanish Identity, and the Barcelona Olympic Games.* Cambridge, UK: Cambridge University Press.

Hargreaves, John, and A. Tomlinson. 1992. "Being There: Cultural Theory and the Sociological Study of Sport." *Sociology of Sport Journal* 9, no. 2: 207–19.

Harris, J. 1993. *Private Lives, Public Spirit: A Social History of Britain, 1870–1914.* Oxford: Oxford University Press.

Harris, T., ed., 1995. *Popular Culture in England, c. 1500–1850.* London: Macmillan.

Harvey, D. 1989. *The Condition of Postmodernity: An Enquiry into the Origins of Cultural Change.* Oxford, UK: Basil Blackwell.

Harvey, J., and F. Houle. 1994. "Sport, World Economy, Global Culture, and New Social Movements." *Sociology of Sport Journal* 11, no. 3: 337–55.

Harvey, J., G. Rail, and L. Thibault. 1996. "Globalization and Sport: Sketching a Theoretical Framework for Empirical Analysis." *Journal of Sport and Social Issues* 20, no. 3: 258–77.

Hearns, F. 1978. *Domination, Legitimation, and Resistance: The Incorporation of the Nineteenth-Century English Working Class.* Westport, CT: Greenwood Press.

Henley Centre for Forecasting. 1993. *Leisure Futures.* Vols. 1–4. London: Henley Centre.

———. 1994. *Leisure Futures.* Vol. 1. London: Henley Centre.

Henry, I. 1993. *The Politics of Leisure Policy.* London: Macmillan.

———. 1995. "Leisure and Social Stratification: The Response of the State to Social Restructuring in Britain." In *Leisure and Social Stratification*, ed. K. Roberts. Eastbourne, UK: Leisure Studies Association.

Hill, J. 1999. "Cocks, Cats, Caps, and Cups: A Semiotic Approach to Sport and National Identity." *Culture, Sport, Society* 2, no. 2: 1–21.

Hill, J., and J. Williams, eds. 1996. *Sport and Identity in the North of England.* Keele, UK: Keele University Press.

Hobsbawm, E. 1995. *Age of Extremes: The Short Twentieth Century, 1914–1991.* London: Abacus.

———. 1997. *On History.* New York: New Press.

———. 1999. *The New Century (in Conversation with Antonio Polito)*, trans. Allan Cameron. London: Abacus.

Hoch, P. 1972. *Rip Off the Big Game: The Exploitation of Sports by the Power Elite.* New York: Doubleday Anchor.

Hoggart, R. 1958. *The Uses of Literacy.* Harmondsworth, UK: Penguin.

Hollands, R. 1988. "Leisure, Work, and Working-Class Cultures: The Case of Leisure on the Shop Floor." In *Leisure, Sport, and Working-Class Cultures: Theory and History*, ed. H. Cantelon and R. Hollands. Toronto: Garamond.

Holt, R. 1989. *Sport and the British: A Modern History.* Oxford: Oxford University Press.

———. 1992. "An Englishman in the Alps: Arnold Lunn, Amateurism, and the Invention of Alpine Ski Racing." *International Journal of the History of Sport* 9, no. 3: 421–32.

———. 1993. *Stanmore Golf Club, 1893–1993.* Stanmore, Middlesex, UK: Stanmore Golf Club.

———. 1996a. "Cricket and Englishness: The Batsman as Hero." In *European Heroes: Myth, Identity, Sport*, ed. R. Holt, J. A. Mangan, and P. Lanfranchi. London: Frank Cass.

———. 1996b. "Heroes of the North: Sport and the Shaping of Regional Identity." In *Sport and Identity in the North of England*, ed. J. Hill and J. Williams. Keele, UK: Keele University Press.

———. 1999. "Champions, Heroes, and Celebrities: Sporting Greatness and the British Public." In *The Book of British Sporting Heroes*, comp. J. Huntington-Whiteley. London: National Portrait Gallery Publications.

Honigsbaum, M. 1997. "The Heist Meister." *Observer Review*, December 14, 3–4.

Horne, J., and D. Jary. 1994. "Japan and the World Cup: Asia's First World Cup Final Hosts?" In *Hosts and Champions: Soccer Cultures, National Identities, and the USA World Cup*, ed. J. Sugden and A. Tomlinson. Aldershot, UK: Arena/Ashgate.

Horne, J., and W. Manzenreiter, eds. 2002. *Japan, Korea, and the 2002 World Cup.* London: Routledge.

Houlihan, B. 1994a. "Homogenization, Americanization, and Creolization of Sport: Varieties of Globalization." *Sociology of Sport Journal* 11, no. 3: 356–75.

———. 1994b. *Sport and International Politics.* London: Harvester Wheatsheaf.

Howkins, A., and J. Lowerson. 1979. *Trends in Leisure, 1919–1939.* London: Sports Council/Social Science Research Council.

Hudson, D., and R. J. Boewadt. 1995. "Youth and Collegiate Soccer Participation in America: A Foundation for Major League Success?" In *Policy and Politics in*

Physical Education, Sport, and Leisure, ed. S. Fleming, M. Talbot, and A. Tomlinson. Eastbourne, UK: Leisure Studies Association.

Huguenin, A., B. Unger, and F. L. Bare. 1981. "100 Years of the International Gymnastics Federation, 1881–1981: Essay on the Development and the Evolution of Gymnastics within an International Federation." Lyss, Switzerland: International Gymnastics Federation.

Inglis, S. 1988. *League Football and the Men Who Made It*. London: Willow Books/Collins.

IOC (International Olympic Committee). 1992. *1992 Olympic Broadcast Analysis Report: The World Is Watching*. Lausanne: International Olympic Committee.

———. 1995. *The Olympic Charter*. Lausanne: International Olympic Committee. June 15.

Ireland, P. R. 1994. *The Policy Challenge of Ethnic Diversity: Immigrant Politics in France and Switzerland*. Cambridge, MA: Harvard University Press.

Jackson, B. 1968. *Working-Class Community: Some General Notions Raised by a Series of Studies in Northern England*. London: Routledge and Kegan Paul.

Jacques, M. 1989. "Britain and Europe." In *New Times: The Changing Face of Politics in the 1990s*, ed. S. Hall and M. Jacques. London: Lawrence and Wishart.

Jarvie, G. 1985. *Class, Race, and Sport in South Africa's Political Economy*. London: Routledge and Kegan Paul.

Jarvie, G., and J. Maguire. 1994. *Sport and Leisure in Social Thought*. London: Routledge.

Jenkins, J. R. G. 1986. *Jura Separatism in Switzerland*. Oxford, UK: Clarendon Press.

Jennings, A. 1996. *The New Lords of the Rings: How Olympic Gold Medals Are Bought and Sold*. London: Simon and Schuster.

Jennings, A., and C. Sambrook. 2000. *The Great Olympic Swindle: When the World Wanted Its Games Back*. London: Simon and Schuster.

Johnston, P., and B. Scribner. 1993. *The Reformation in Germany and Switzerland*. Cambridge, UK: Cambridge University Press.

Jones, G. L. 1994. "How Wrong Can You Be?" *Soccer Illustrated 1994 World Cup Review*, 28–31.

Jury, L. 1997. "Swiss Stop Saying Sorry for Nazi Gold." *Independent*, December 1, 8.

Keech, M. 2000. "At the Centre of the Web: The Role of Sam Ramsamy in South Africa's Readmission to International Sport." *Culture, Sport, Society* 3, no. 3: 41–62.

Keech, M., and B. Houlihan. 1999. "Sport and the End of Apartheid." *Round Table: The Commonwealth Journal of International Affairs*, no. 349: 109–21.

Kew, F. 1989. "How Games Change: The Structuring and Restructuring of Games." In *Sport in Society: Policy, Politics, and Culture*, ed. A. Tomlinson. Eastbourne, UK: Leisure Studies Association.

Klein, N. 2000. *No Logo: No Space, No Choice, No Jobs*. London: Flamingo.

Kohn, H. 1978. *Nationalism and Liberty: The Swiss Example*. Westport, CT: Greenwood Press. First published 1956 by G. Allen and Unwin.

Kuhn, T. 1970. *The Structure of Scientific Revolutions*. 2nd ed. Chicago: University of Chicago Press.

Kuper, S. 1994. *Football against the Enemy*. London: Orion.

Lacey, D. 1993. "Draw Poker in the Land of Stars and Hypes." *Guardian*, December 18, 18.

Lamprecht, M., and H. Stamm. 1995. "Expansion and Integration versus Differentiation and Segregation: The Case of Recreational Sport in Switzerland." Paper presented at International Sociological Association Conference, Bielefeld, Germany.

———. 1996. "Age and Gender Patterns of Sport Involvement among the Swiss Labour Force." *Sociology of Sport Journal* 13, no. 3: 274–87.

Lanfranchi, P. 1998. "Le role de la Suisse dans le développement du football en Europe." Unpublished manuscript, University of Geneva/UEFA.

LAOOC (Los Angeles Olympic Organizing Committee). 1984. *Official Report of the Games of the XXIIIrd Olympiad, Los Angeles, 1984*. Los Angeles: LAOOC.

Larrain, J. 1994. *Ideology and Cultural Identity: Modernity and the Third World Presence*. Cambridge, UK: Polity Press.

Lawrence, L., and A. Tomlinson. 1991. *Brighton Leisure Card Survey Report (Phase Two)*. Brighton, UK: Leisure Research Unit/Chelsea School Research Centre, Brighton Polytechnic.

———. 1992. *Brighton Leisure Card Survey Report (Phase Three)*. Brighton, UK: Leisure Research Unit/Chelsea School Research Centre, Brighton Polytechnic.

Lawrence, T. E. 1940. *Seven Pillars of Wisdom: A Triumph*. London: Jonathan Cape.

Lawson, M. 1993. "Moving the Goalposts." *Independent Magazine*, May 29, 26–30.

Lee, J.-Y. 1997. "World Cup Co-hosting and the Korean Society." Japan Society of Sport Sociology, international conference. Ritsumeikan University, Kyoto, Japan, March 26–28.

Lenskyj, H. J. 2000. *Inside the Olympic Industry: Power, Politics, and Activism*. Albany: State University of New York Press.

Liddington, J. 1984. *The Life and Times of a Respectable Rebel: Selina Cooper, 1864–1946*. London: Virago.

Lovejoy, J. 1993a. "Pythonesque Circus in a Football Desert: FIFA Keen on World Club Competition." *Independent*, December 18, 24, 26.

———. 1993b. "World Cup 1994." *Independent (II)*, December 20, 32.

Lowerson, J. 1989. "Sheffield Triumphant? Some Views on Sport and the Regions." *British Society of Sports History Bulletin*, no. 9.

Lummis, T. 1987. *Listening to History: The Authenticity of Oral Evidence*. London: Hutchinson.

MacAloon, J. 1981. *This Great Symbol: Pierre de Coubertin and the Origins of the Modern Olympic Games*. Chicago: University of Chicago Press.

———. 1992. "The Ethnographic Imperative in Comparative Olympic Research." *Sociology of Sport Journal* 9, no. 2: 104–30.

Macrae, K. D. 1983. *Conflict and Compromise in Multilingual Societies: Switzerland*. Waterloo, Ontario: Wilfred Laurier University Press.

Magness, A. 1990. *Report on Research into the Concept of a Leisure Card (Phase 1): Group Discussions*. Brighton, UK: Brighton Borough Council/Leisure Research Unit, Brighton Polytechnic.

Maguire, J. 1994. "Sport, Identity Politics, and Globalization: Diminishing Contrasts and Increasing Varieties." *Sociology of Sport Journal* 11, no. 4: 398–427.

———. 1999. *Global Sport: Identities, Societies, Civilizations*. Cambridge, UK: Polity Press.

Mandel, E., and G. Novack. 1970. *The Marxist Theory of Alienation*. New York: Pathfinder Press.

Mangan, J. A. 1981. *Athleticism in the Victorian and Edwardian Public School: The Emergence and Consolidation of an Educational Ideology.* Cambridge, UK: Cambridge University Press.

———. 1985. *The Games Ethic and Imperialism: Aspects of the Diffusion of an Ideal.* London: Viking.

Maradas, E. 1996. "The Long Road to South Africa." *African Soccer Souvenir,* January, 16–17.

Markovits, A. S. 1988. "The Other 'American Exceptionalism': Why Is There No Soccer in the United States?" *Praxis International* 8, no. 2: 125–50.

———. 1990. "The Other 'American exceptionalism': Why Is There No Soccer in the United States?" *International Journal of the History of Sport* 7, no. 2: 230–64.

———. 1998. "Reflections on the World Cup '98." *French Politics and Society* 16, no. 3: 1–29.

Markovits, A. S., and S. Hellerman. 2001. *Offside: Soccer and American Exceptionalism.* Princeton, NJ: Princeton University Press.

———. 2003. "The 'Olympianization' of Soccer in the United States." *American Behavioral Scientist* 46, no. 11: 1533–49.

Marx, K. 1979. "The Eighteenth Brumaire of Louis Bonaparte." In *Collected Works,* vol. 2, *Marx and Engels, 1851–1853,* ed. K. Marx and F. Engels. London: Lawrence and Wishart.

Mason, T. 1980. *Association Football and English Society, 1863–1915.* Sussex, UK: Harvester Press.

———. 1986. "Some Englishmen and Scotsmen Abroad: The Spread of World Football." In *Off the Ball: The Football World Cup,* ed. A. Tomlinson and G. Whannel. London: Pluto Press.

———, ed. 1989. *Sport in Britain.* Cambridge: Cambridge University Press.

———. 1995. *Passion of the People? Football in South America.* London: Verso.

Mass Observation. 1939. "All-in, All-out." In *Britain by Mass-Observation.* Harmondsworth, UK: Penguin.

Massey, D. 1994. *Space, Place, and Gender.* Cambridge, UK: Polity Press.

Matheson, J. 1991. *Participation in Sport.* London: Office of Population, Censuses, and Surveys/Her Majesty's Stationery Office.

Mathys, F. K. 1977. "National Games in Switzerland and Their Relations to Other European Games." In *History of Physical Education and Sport: Research and Studies,* ed. Y. Imamura, M. Verhaegen, and J. Narita. Tokyo: Kodansha.

McFee, G., and A. Tomlinson. 1995. "Notes on Bodily Culture and Sports Ideology: The Case of Leni Riefenstahl." In *Entre tradition et modernité: Le sport: Regards historiques et sociologiques sur une siècle de culture corporelle: Trajectoires et enjeus,* ed. C. Pigeassou. Agde/Montpellier, France: Actes du colloques Sport, Culture, Tradition.

———. 1999. "Riefenstahl's *Olympia*: Ideology and Aesthetics in the Shaping of the Aryan Athletic Body." *International Journal of the History of Sport* 16, no. 2: 86–106.

McLennan, G. 1998. "Sociology and Cultural Studies: Rhetorics of Interdisciplinary Identity." *History of the Human Sciences* 11, no. 3: 1–17.

Media Sports Business. 1994. July 31, no. 171. Carmel, CA: Paul Kagan Associates.

Merkel, U. 1999. "Sport in Divided Societies: The Case of the Old, the New, and the

'Re-united' Germany." In *Sport in Divided Societies*, ed. A. Bairner and J. Sugden. Aachen, Germany: Meyer and Meyer.

Metcalf, R. 2000. "Home Comforts in Short Supply for Americans." *Independent*, February 15, 26.

Miller, T., G. Lawrence, J. McKay, and D. Rowe. 2001. *Globalisation and Sport: Playing the World*. London: Sage.

———. 1999. "Modifying the Sign: Sport and Globalization." *Social Text* 60: 15–33.

Mills, C. W. 1970. *The Sociological Imagination*. Harmondsworth, UK: Penguin.

Mingay, G. 1979. *Rural Life in Victorian England*. London: Futura Publications.

Minten, J., and K. Roberts. 1989. "Trends in Sport in Great Britain." In *Trends in Sports: A Multinational Perspective*, ed. T. J. Kamphorst and K. Roberts. Voorthuizen, Netherlands: Giordano Bruno Culemberg.

Moore, R. 1974. *Pit-Men, Preachers, and Politics: The Effects of Methodism in a Durham Mining Community*. Cambridge, UK: Cambridge University Press.

Moorhouse, H. F. 1995. "One State, Several Countries: Soccer and Nationality in a 'United Kingdom.'" *International Journal of the History of Sport* 12, no. 2: 55–74.

Moragas, M., N. K. Rivenbergh, and J. F. Larsan. 1995. *Television in the Olympics*. London: John Libbey.

Mouzelis, N. 1995. *Sociological Theory: What Went Wrong? Diagnosis and Remedies*. London: Routledge.

Mowat, C. L. 1968. *Britain between the Wars, 1918–1940*. London: Methuen.

Muggleton, D. 2000. *Inside Subculture: The Postmodern Meaning of Style*. Oxford, UK: Berg.

Muldoon, M. 2001. Address to British Sociological Association Sociology of Sport Study Group, Northern Ireland Sport Council, February.

Murray, B. 1994. *Football: A History of the World Game*. Aldershot, UK: Scolar Press.

———. 1995. "Cultural Revolution? Football in the Societies of Asia and the Pacific." In *Giving the Game Away: Football, Politics, and Culture on Five Continents*, ed. S. Wagg. London: Leicester University Press.

Nelson, G. 1995. *Left Foot Forward: A Year in the Life of a Journeyman Footballer*. London: Headline Book Publishing.

Norris, C. 1990. *What's Wrong with Postmodernism: Critical Theory and the Ends of Philosophy*. London: Harvester Wheatsheaf.

Novak, M. 1976. *The Joy of Sports: End Zones, Bases, Baskets, Balls, and the Consecration of the American Spirit*. New York: Basic Books.

Office fédéral de la statistique. 1990. *Loisirs et culture: Microrecensement 1988—Données de base*. Statistique officielle de la Suisse, no. 305. Bern, Switzerland: CP-Institut AG.

Oliver, G. 1995. *The Guinness Book of World Soccer*. 2nd ed. London: Guinness.

Osborne J. 1982. *A Better Class of Person: An Autobiography*. Harmondsworth, UK: Penguin Books.

Palmer, M. 1994. "A Whole New Ball Game." *Sunday Telegraph Review*, June 12, 1–2.

Parker, S., and A. Tomlinson. 1992. *Life in the South: The Paradox of Prosperity*. Chelsea School Topic Report 1. Eastbourne, UK: University of Brighton/Chelsea School Research Centre.

Parkin, F. 1974. "Strategies of Social Closure in Class Formation." In *The Social Analysis of Class Structure*, ed. F. Parkin. London: Tavistock.

———. 1979. *Marxism and Class Theory: A Bourgeois Critique*. London: Tavistock.

Perelman, R. B., ed. 1985. *Olympic Retrospective: The Games of Los Angeles*. Los Angeles: Los Angeles Olympic Organizing Committee.

Perera, S. 1988. "'Downmarket' Sports Fear Loss of Cash Lifeline as ITV Axes Minority Coverage." *Guardian*, June 2, 3.

Phaidon. 1985. *Switzerland: A Phaidon Cultural Guide*. Oxford, UK: Phaidon.

Philips, D. 1998. "Carnival and Control: The Commodification of the Carnivalesque at Disneyland." In *Tourism and Visitor Attractions: Leisure, Culture, and Commerce*, ed. N. Ravenscroft, D. Philips, and M. Bennett. Eastbourne, UK: Leisure Studies Association.

Philips, D., and A. Tomlinson. 1992. "Homeward Bound: Leisure, Popular Culture, and Consumer Capitalism." In *Come On Down: Popular Media Culture in Postwar Britain*, ed. D. Strinati and S. Wagg. London: Routledge.

Pieterse, J. N. 1995. "Globalization as Hybridization." In *Global Modernities*. ed. M. Featherstone, S. Lash, and R. Robertson. London: Sage.

Platt, J. 1992. "Cases of Cases . . . of Cases." In *What Is a Case? Exploring the Foundations of Social Enquiry*, ed. C. C. Ragin and H. S. Becker. Cambridge, UK: Cambridge University Press.

Quansha, E. 1996. "The Cup to Surpass All Cups." *Africa Today* 2, no. 1: 27.

Raban, J. 1975. *Soft City*. London: Fontana.

———. 1980. *Arabia through the Looking-Glass*. London: Fontana.

Rappard, W. E. 1936. *The Government of Switzerland*. New York: D. Van Nostrand Company.

Ravenscroft, N., and G. Speller. 2002. "Green Spaces in Brighton and Hove: Preliminary Reports from Focus Group Interviews." Presentation at Hove Town Hall, October 10.

Raynor, R. 1992. *Los Angeles without a Map*. London: Flamingo.

Redhead, S., ed. 1993. *Rave off: Politics and Deviance in Contemporary Youth Culture*. Aldershot, UK: Avebury/Ashgate Publishing.

Reich Collection. 1985. Transcripts of interviews with Los Angeles Olympic Committee personnel. Los Angeles: Amateur Athletic Foundation of Los Angeles.

Reuters. 2001. *September 11: A Testimony*. London: Pearson Education.

Rex, J., and R. Moore. 1969. *Race, Community, and Conflict: A Study of Sparkbrook*. London: Routledge and Kegan Paul.

Richardson, N. 1999. *Breakfast in Brighton: Adventures on the Edge of Britain*. London: Indigo.

Riordan, J. 1996. "Sport and Nationalism in the CCCP, Socialist Internationalism versus a Strong Russian State." Paper presented at the British Sociological Association annual conference, University of Reading, April 1–4.

Roberts, K. 1989. "Great Britain: Socio-economic Polarization and the Implications for Leisure." In *Leisure and Lifestyle: A Comparative Analysis of Free Time*, ed. A. Olszewska and K. Roberts. London: Sage. Reprinted in *Sociology of Leisure: A Reader*, ed. C. Critcher, P. Bramham, and A. Tomlinson. London: E and FN Spon, 1994.

———. 1995. *Leisure and Social Stratification*. Eastbourne, UK: Leisure Studies Association.

Robertson, I. 1987. *Blue Guide: Switzerland*. 4th ed. London: A and C Black.

Robertson, R. 1990. "Mapping the Global Condition: Globalization As the Central Concept." *Theory, Culture, and Society: Explorations in Critical Social Science* 7, nos. 2–3: 15–30.

Roche, M. 2000. *Mega-events and Modernity: Olympics and Expos in the Growth of Global Culture*. London: Routledge.

Rogenhagen, A. 1995. *The Final Kick*. Directed by Andreas Rogenhagen and directors from forty countries. Litchblick Production in coproduction with Last Border, in cooperation with arte. Broadcast in BBC 2 TX series (November 25). Series editor John Wyver.

Rojek, C. 1993. "After Popular Culture: Hyperreality and Leisure." *Leisure Studies* 12, no. 4: 277–89.

———. 1995. *Decentring Leisure: Rethinking Leisure Theory*. London: Sage.

———. 1997. "Leisure Theory: Retrospect and Prospect." *Society and Leisure* 20, no. 2: 383–400.

———. 2000. *Leisure and Culture*. London: Macmillan.

Rous, S. 1978. *Football Worlds: A Lifetime in Sport*. London: Faber and Faber.

Rowe, D. 2003. "Sport and the Repudiation of the Global." *International Review for the Sociology of Sport* 38, no. 3: 281–94.

Samuel, R., ed. 1981. *People's History and Socialist Theory*. London: Routledge and Kegan Paul.

Sayama, I. 1997. "Soccer: The Limit of the Japanese Society and the Bitter Reflection of Its Possibility." Paper presented to the Japan Society for Sport Sociology annual conference, "How Sport Can Change the World," March 27–28, Ritsumeikan University, Kyoto. Conference proceedings, 62–71.

Sayer, I., and D. Botting. 1998. *Nazi Gold: The Story of the World's Greatest Robbery and Its Aftermath*. Edinburgh: Mainstream Publishing.

Schlagenhauf, K., and J. Schiffer. 1976. "German and the Swiss Club." *International Review of Sport Sociology* 14, no. 3/4: 87–96.

Schlossberg, H. 1996. *Sports Marketing*. Oxford, UK: Basil Blackwell.

Scraton, S., and B. Watson. 1998. "Gendered Cities: Women and Public Leisure Spaces in the 'Postmodern City.'" *Leisure Studies* 17, no. 2: 123–37.

Scraton, S., P. Bramham, and B. Watson. 1998. "'Staying In' and 'Going Out': Elderly Women, Leisure, and the Postmodern City." In *Leisure, Time, and Space: Meanings and Values in People's Lives*, ed. S. Scraton. Eastbourne, UK: Leisure Studies Association.

Sebald, W. G. 1999. *The Rings of Saturn*, trans. Michael Hulse. London: Harvill Press.

Segalman, R. 1986. *The Swiss Way of Welfare: Lessons for the Western World*. New York: Praeger.

Seldon, A. 2002. *Brave New City: Brighton and Hove; Past, Present, Future*. Lewes, UK: Pomegranate Press.

Shields, R. 1992. *Places on the Margin: Alternative Geographies of Modernity*. London: Routledge.

Shipley, S. 1983. "Tom Causer of Bermondsey: A Boxer Hero of the 1980s." *History Workshop: A Journal of Socialist and Feminist Historians*, no. 15: 28–59.

Simmel, G. 1991. "The Alpine Journey." *Theory, Culture, and Society: Explorations in Critical Social Science* 8, no. 1: 95–98.

Simson, V., and A. Jennings. 1992. *The Lords of the Rings: Power, Money, and Drugs in the Modern Olympics.* London: Simon and Schuster.

Sinha, D. 1994. "World Cup USA: A Different Perspective." *Economic and Political Weekly* 29, no. 31: 1996–97.

Sklair, L. 1991. *Sociology of the Global System.* London: Harvester Wheatsheaf.

———. 2000. *The Transnational Capitalist Class.* Cambridge, UK: Polity Press.

Smith, H. W. 1975. *Strategies of Social Research: The Methodological Imagination.* London: Prentice/Hall International.

Smith, P., host. 1989. *Northern Lights.* BBC Radio 4, March 3, 10, 17, 24, 31, and April 7.

Sola, E. 1997a. "'Be What You Want To Be': Consuming Spaces and the Construction of Identity." Unpublished course assignment, University of Sussex.

———. 1997b. "Quit Your Job for 'Bob': Possibilities for Resistance in Contemporary Society." Master's thesis, University of Sussex.

Sontag, S. 1983. "Fascinating Fascism." In *Under the Sign of Saturn.* London: Writers and Readers.

Spencer, W. 1971. *Colne As It Was: Photographs Selected and Introduced by Wilfred Spencer.* N.p.: Hendon Publishing.

Spivak, G. C. 1987. *In Other Words: Essays in Cultural Politics.* New York: Methuen.

Sports Council. 1992. *Sport in the Nineties: New Horizons—A Draft for Consultation.* London: Sports Council.

Sports Industry News. 1995. February 3, 48. Reported in *North American Society for the Sociology of Sport Newsletter,* winter, 13.

Stamm, H., and M. Lamprecht. 1995. "Social Stratification, Lifestyle, and Leisure Choice: The Case of Switzerland." In *Leisure Cultures: Values, Genders, Lifestyles,* ed. G. McFee, W. Murphy, and G. Whannel. Eastbourne, UK: Leisure Studies Association.

———. 1996a. "Qui sonts les sportifs occasionnels?" *Macolin: Revue Mensuelle de l'EFSM et de Jeunesse et Sport* 4: 7–9.

———. 1996b. "Sport Organizations in Switzerland." Working paper for the research group Sport Organizations in Europe.

———. 1996c. "Factors Governing Success in International Football." *FIFA Magazine,* August, 7–11.

Stedman Jones, G. 1974. "Working-Class Culture and Working-Class Politics in London, 1870–1900: Notes on the Remaking of a Working-Class." *Journal of Social History* 7: 460–508.

Stevenson, J., and Cook, C. 1979. *The Slump.* London: Quartet Books.

Stevenson, T. B., and Alaug, A.-K. 1997. "Football in Yemen: Rituals of Resistance, Integration, and Identity." *International Review for the Sociology of Sport* 32, no. 3: 251–65.

———. 1999. "Football in the Yemens: Integration, Identity, and Nationalism in a Divided Country." In *Sport in Divided Societies,* ed. A. Bairner and J. Sugden. Aachen, Germany: Meyer and Meyer.

Sugden, J. 1994. "USA and the World Cup: American Nativism and the Rejection of the People's Game." In *Hosts and Champions: Soccer Cultures, National Identities, and the USA World Cup,* ed. J. Sugden and A. Tomlinson. Aldershot, UK: Arena/Ashgate Publishing.

————. 1997. "Fieldworkers Rush In (Where Theorists Fear to Tread): The Perils of Ethnography." In *Ethics, Sport, and Leisure: Crises and Critiques,* ed. A. Tomlinson and S. Fleming. Aachen, Germany: Meyer and Meyer.

Sugden, J., and A. Bairner. 1992. "'Ma, There's a Helicopter on the Pitch!' Sport, Leisure, and the State in Northern Ireland." *Sociology of Sport Journal* 9, no. 2: 154–66.

Sugden, J., and A. Tomlinson, eds. 1994a. *Hosts and Champions: Soccer Cultures, National Identities, and the USA World Cup.* Aldershot, UK: Arena/Ashgate Publishing.

————. 1994b. "Soccer Culture, National Identity, and the World Cup." In *Hosts and Champions: Soccer Cultures, National Identities, and the USA World Cup,* ed. J. Sugden and A. Tomlinson. Aldershot, UK: Arena/Ashgate.

————. 1994c. "One Night in New York." *Leisure Studies Association Newsletter* (Eastbourne, UK), no. 39: 25–27.

————. 1995a. "One Day in LA." *Leisure Studies Association Newsletter* (Eastbourne, UK), no. 40: 25–32.

————. 1995b. "Hustling in Havana: Ethnographic Notes on Everyday Life and Mutual Exploitation between Locals and Tourists in a Socialist Economy under Siege." In *Leisure Cultures: Values, Genders, Lifestyles,* ed. G. McFee, W. Murphy, and G. Whannel. Eastbourne, UK: Leisure Studies Association.

————. 1996a. "What's Left When the Circus Leaves Town? An Evaluation of World Cup USA 1994." *Sociology of Sport Journal* 13, no. 3: 236–54.

————. 1996b. "The Price of Fame." *When Saturday Comes,* no. 109: 39.

————. 1997a. "Global Power Struggles in World Football: FIFA and UEFA, 1954–1974, and Their Legacy." *International Journal of the History of Sport* 14, no. 2: 1–25.

————. 1997b. "A Gulf in Class." *When Saturday Comes,* no. 120: 36–37.

————. 1998a. "Sport, Politics, and Identities: Football Cultures in Comparative Perspective." In *Sport, Popular Culture, and Identity,* ed. M. Roche. Aachen, Germany: Meyer and Meyer.

————. 1998b. "FIFA's World Cup Wars." *New Statesman,* May 1, 38–39.

————. 1998c. *FIFA and the Contest for World Football: Who Rules the Peoples' Game?* Cambridge, UK: Polity Press.

————. 1999a. *Great Balls of Fire: How Big Money Is Hijacking World Football.* Edinburgh: Mainstream Publishing.

————. 1999b. "War of the Worlds." *When Saturday Comes,* no. 143: 28–29.

————. 1999c. "Digging the Dirt and Staying Clean: Retrieving the Investigative Tradition for a Critical Sociology of Sport." *International Review for the Sociology of Sport* 34, no. 4: 385–97.

————. 1999d. "Out of Their League." *When Saturday Comes,* no. 144: 22–23.

————. 2002a. "International Power Struggles in the Governance of World Football: The 2002 and 2006 World Cup Bidding Wars." In *Japan, Korea, and the 2002 World Cup,* ed. J. Horne and W. Manzenreiter. London: Routledge.

————, eds. 2002b. *Power Games: A Critical Sociology of Sport.* London: Routledge.

————. 2002c. "Theory and Method for a Critical Sociology of Sport." In *Power Games: A Critical Sociology of Sport,* ed. J. Sugden and A. Tomlinson. London: Routledge.

————. 2003. *Badfellas: FIFA Family at War.* Edinburgh: Mainstream Publishing.

Sugden, J., A. Tomlinson, and P. Darby. 1998. "FIFA versus UEFA in the Struggle for the Control of World Football." In *Fanatics! Power, Identity, and Fandom in Football*, ed. A. Brown. London: Routledge.

Sugden, J., A. Tomlinson, and E. McCartan. 1990. "The Making and Remaking of White Lightning in Cuba: Politics, Sport, and Physical Education 30 Years after the Revolution." *Arena Review* 14, no. 1: 101–9.

Szymanski, S. 2002. "A Licence to Print Money." *Soccer Analyst* 3, no. 2: 11–12.

Taylor, J. B. 1992. "Re: Locations: From Bradford to Brighton." *New Formations*, no. 17: 86–94.

Team Marketing Report. 1994. *Sport Sponsor Factbook (Spring)*, 660 Grand Avenue, Chicago, IL 60610.

TEAM. 1997. *UEFA Champions League Review 1995/96.* Lucerne, Switzerland: TEAM (Television Event and Media Marketing AG) and UEFA.

Thompson, E. P. 1963. *The Making of the English Working Class.* London: Gollancz.

————. 1993. "Rough Music." In *Customs in Common.* Harmondsworth, UK: Penguin.

Thompson, G. 1983. "The Presentation and Consumption of Leisure: Blackpool As a 'Site' of Pleasure." In *Leisure and Popular Cultural Forms*, ed. A. Tomlinson. Eastbourne, UK: Leisure Studies Association.

————. 1999. "Introduction: Situating Globalization." *International Social Science Journal*, no. 160: 139–52.

Thompson, J. B. 1990. *Ideology and Modern Culture: Critical Social Theory in the Age of Mass Communication.* Cambridge, UK: Polity Press.

————. 1995. *The Media and Modernity: A Social Theory of the Media.* Cambridge, UK: Polity Press.

Thompson, P. 1988. *The Voice of the Past: Oral History.* 2nd ed. Oxford: Oxford University Press.

Thürer, G. 1970. *Free and Swiss: The Story of Switzerland.* London: Oswald Wolff.

Tomlinson, A. 1978. "Leisure, the Family, and the Woman's Role." In *Leisure and Family Diversity*, ed. Z. Strelitz. Eastbourne, UK: Leisure Studies Association.

————. 1979. *Leisure and the Role of Clubs and Voluntary Groups.* London: Sports Council and Social Science Research Council.

————, ed. 1981. *Leisure and Social Control.* Eastbourne, UK: Leisure Studies Association.

————. 1983. "The Illusion of Community: Cultural Values and the Meaning of Leisure in a Gentrifying Neighbourhood." In *Leisure and Popular Cultural Forms*, ed. A. Tomlinson. Eastbourne, UK: Leisure Studies Association.

————. 1984a. "The Sociological Imagination, the New Journalism, and Sports." In *Sport and the Sociological Imagination*, ed. P. Donnelly and N. Theberge. Fort Worth: Texas Christian University Press.

————. 1984b. "De Coubertin and the Modern Olympic Games." In *Five-Ring Circus: Money, Power, and Politics at the Olympic Games*, ed. A. Tomlinson and G. Whannel. London: Pluto Press.

————. 1986. "Going Global: The FIFA Story." In *Off the Ball: The Football World Cup*, ed. A. Tomlinson and G. Whannel. London: Pluto Press.

————. 1988a. "Good Times, Bad Times, and the Politics of Leisure: Working-Class

Culture in the 1930s in a Small Northern English Working-Class Community." In *Leisure, Sport, and Working-Class Cultures: Theory and History*, ed. H. Cantelon and R. Hollands. Toronto: Garamond Press.

———. 1988b. "Images of Sport: Situating *Chariots of Fire*." *British Society of Sports History Bulletin*, no. 8: 27–41.

———. 1989a. "Representation, Ideology, and Sport: The Opening and Closing Ceremonies of the Los Angeles Olympic Games." In *The Olympic Movement and the Mass Media: Past, Present, and Future Issues*, ed. R. Jackson and T. McPhail. Calgary: Hurford Enterprises.

———. 1989b. "Whose Side Are They On? Leisure Studies and Cultural Studies in Britain." *Leisure Studies* 8, no. 2: 97–106.

———. 1990a. "Consumer Culture and the Aura of the Commodity." In *Consumption, Identity, and Style: Marketing, Meanings, and the Packaging of Pleasure*. London: Routledge.

———. 1990b. "Home Fixtures: Doing It Yourself in a Privatized World." In *Consumption, Identity, and Style: Marketing, Meanings, and the Packaging of Pleasure*, ed. A. Tomlinson. London: Routledge.

———. 1991. "North and South: The Rivalry of the Football League and the Football Association." In *British Football and Social Change: Getting into Europe*, ed. J. Williams and S. Wagg. Leicester, UK: Leicester University Press.

———. 1992a. "Shifting Patterns of Working-Class Culture: The Case of Knur-and-Spell." *Sociology of Sport Journal* 9, no. 2: 192–206.

———. 1992b. "Whose Game Is It Anyway? The Cultural Analysis of Sport and Media Consumption." *Innovation in Social Science Research* 5, no. 4: 27–42.

———. 1993. "Culture of Commitment in Leisure: Notes Towards the Understanding of a Serious Legacy." *World Leisure and Recreation Association Journal* 35, no. 1: 6–9.

———. 1994. "FIFA and the World Cup: The Expanding FIFA Family." In *Hosts and Champions: Soccer Cultures, National Identities, and the USA World Cup*, ed. J. Sugden and A. Tomlinson. Aldershot, UK: Arena/Ashgate Publishing.

———. 1995. "Patterns of Consumption in Urban Leisure Culture: A Case-Study of Brighton." Paper presented at British Sociological Association annual conference, University of Leicester, April.

———. 1996a. "Olympic Spectacle: Opening Ceremonies and Some Paradoxes of Globalization." *Media, Culture, and Society* 18, no. 4: 583–602.

———. 1996b. Feature in *Gulf News* 1.

———. 1997a. "Flattery and Betrayal: Observations on Oral and Qualitative Accounts." In *Ethics, Sport, and Leisure: Crises and Critiques*, ed. A. Tomlinson and S. Fleming. Aachen, Germany: Meyer and Meyer.

———. 1997b. Feature in *Gulf News* 2.

———. 1998a. "Domination, Negotiation, and Resistance in Sports Cultures." *Journal of Sport and Social Issues* 22, no. 3: 235–40.

———. 1998b. "Sport, Cultural Diversity, and National Identity: The Swiss Case." In *Sport in Divided Societies*, ed. A. Bairner and J. Sugden. Aachen, Germany: Meyer and Meyer.

———. 1999a. *The Game's Up: Essays in the Cultural Analysis of Sport, Leisure, and Popular Culture*. Aldershot, UK: Ashgate Publishing.

———. 1999b. "Whose Feet in Which Time? Sport and Leisure in Contemporary Culture." In *The Game's Up: Essays in the Cultural Analysis of Sport, Leisure, and Popular Culture,* ed. A. Tomlinson. Aldershot, UK: Ashgate.

———. 1999c. "Going Global: The FIFA Story." In *The Game's Up: Essays in the Cultural Analysis of Sport, Leisure, and Popular Culture.* Aldershot, UK: Ashgate.

———. 1999d. "FIFA and the Men Who Made It." *Soccer and Society* 1, no. 1: 53–71.

———. 1999e. "Executive Distress." *When Saturday Comes,* no. 18–19.

———. 1999f. "Interpreting the Growth of Sports: Debates in History and Theory." In *Understanding Sport: An Introduction to the Sociological and Cultural Analysis of Sport,* J. Horne, A. Tomlinson, and G. Whannel. London: E and FN Spon.

———. 1999g. "Industrial Society, Social Change, and Sports Culture." In *Understanding Sport: An Introduction to the Sociological and Cultural Analysis of Sport,* J. Horne, A. Tomlinson, and G. Whannel. London: E and FN Spon.

———. 1999h. "Staging the Spectacle: Reflections on Olympic and World Cup Ceremonies." *Soundings: A Journal of Politics and Culture,* no. 13: 161–71.

———. 2000a. "A Bid Too Far." *When Saturday Comes,* no. 162: 22.

———. 2000b. "Carrying the Torch for Whom? Symbolic Power and Olympic Ceremony." In *The Olympics at the Millennium: Power, Politics, and the Games,* ed. K. Schaffer and S. Smith. New Brunswick, NJ: Rutgers University Press.

———. 2000c. "From the Field: Sydney 2000 and an Olympics Research Agenda." In *Issues and Values in Sport and Leisure Cultures,* ed. M. Keech and G. McFee. Aachen, Germany: Meyer and Meyer.

———. 2002. "FIFA Family Fortunes." *Soccer Analyst* 3, no. 2: 7–9.

———. 2004. "The Making of the Global Sports Economy: ISL, Adidas, and the Rise of the Corporate Player in World Sport." In *Sport and Corporate Nationalisms,* ed. M. Silk, D. Andrews, and C. L. Cole. Oxford, UK: Berg.

———. 2005. "Los Angeles' Olympics: 1932 and 1984." In *National Identity and Global Sports Events: Culture, Politics, and Spectacle in the Olympics and the Football World Cup,* ed. A. Tomlinson and C. Young. Albany: State University of New York Press.

Touraine, A. 2003. "Sociology without Societies." *Current Sociology* 51, no. 2: 123–31.

Tuastud, D. 1997. "The Political Role of Football for Palestinians in Jordan." In *Entering the Field: New Perspectives on World Football,* ed. G. Armstrong and R. Giulianotti. Oxford, UK: Berg.

Turner, V. 1967. *The Forest of Symbols: Aspects of Ndembu Ritual.* Ithaca, NY: Cornell University Press.

———. 1969. *The Ritual Process.* Chicago: Aldine.

———. 1974. *Dramas, Fields, and Metaphors: Symbolic Action in Human Society.* Ithaca, NY: Cornell University Press.

———, ed. 1982. *Celebration: Studies in Festivity and Ritual.* Washington, DC: Smithsonian Institution Press.

Tyrrell, B. 1990. "Postmodernism and Leisure Markets." In *Leisure Futures,* 5–10. London: Henley Centre for Forecasting. August.

UAE Yearbook. 1996. London: Trident Press.

Urry, J. 1990. *The Tourist Gaze: Leisure and Travel in Contemporary Societies.* London: Sage.

———. 1999. "Sensing Leisure Spaces." In *Leisure/Tourism Geographies: Practices and Geographical Knowledge,* ed. D. Crouch. London: Routledge.

U.S. Internal Revenue Service. 1991/92. Form 990, 1991: Return of Organization Exempt from Income Tax, "For the Calendar Year 1991," relating to "World Cup USA 1994, Inc., 2049 Century Park East, Suite 4400, Los Angeles, California 90067."

———. 1992/93. Form 990, 1992: Return of Organization Exempt from Income Tax, "For the Calendar Year 1992," relating to "World Cup USA 1994, Inc., 2049 Century Park East, Suite 4400, Los Angeles, CA 90067."

Usborne, D. 1994. "OJ and the Knicks Put the World's Game in a Twist." *Independent*, June 20, 39.

Vahed, G. 2001. "'What Do They Know of Cricket Who Only Cricket Know?' Transformation in South African Cricket, 1990–2000." *International Review for the Sociology of Sport* 36, no. 3: 319–36.

Van Ingen, C. 2003. "Geographies of Gender, Sexuality, and Race: Reframing the Focus on Space in Sport Sociology." *International Review for the Sociology of Sport* 38, no. 2: 201–16.

Van Niekerk, P. 1996. "Mandela Is the Cheerleader as Sport Unites All South Africans." *Observer*, February 4, 19.

Velappan, P. 1996. *Asian Football in the New Millennium*. Presentation at Media Seminar, Asian Football Confederation, held in conjunction with the Eleventh Asian Cup, Abu Dhabi, United Arab Emirates, December 14.

Waddington, I., and M. Roderick. 1996. "American Exceptionalism: Soccer and American Football." *Sports Historian*, no. 16: 42–63.

Wagg, S. 1995. "Mr Drains, Go Home: Football in the Societies of the Middle East." In *Giving the Game Away: Football, Politics, and Culture on Five Continents*, ed. S. Wagg. London: Leicester University Press.

———. 1995. "The Business of America: Reflections on World Cup '94." In *Giving the Game Away: Football, Politics, and Culture on Five Continents*, ed. S. Wagg. London: Leicester University Press.

Wahl, A. 1986. "Le footballer français: De l'amateurisme au salariat (1890–1926)." *Le Mouvement Social*, no. 135 (April–June): 7–30.

Wallechinsky, D. 1993. *The Complete Book of the Winter Olympics*. 1994 ed. London: Aurum Press.

———. 1996. *The Complete Book of the Olympics*. 1996 ed. London: Aurum Press.

Walzer, M. 1983. *Spheres of Justice*. New York: Basic Books.

Ward, C. 1983. "We Are All Historians Now." *New Society* 64, no. 1075: 475–76.

Waterhouse, K. 2003. *Palace Pier*. London: Sceptre.

Watson, D. 1994. *Dancing in the Streets: Tales from World Cup City*. London: Victor Gollancz.

Watson-Smyth, K. 1998. "Swiss Face Fresh Scandal after Claims of Labour Camps for Jews." *Independent*, January 6, 3.

Watts, J. 1998. "Soccer Shiunatsubai: What Are Japanese Consumers Making of the J. League?" In *The World of Japanese Popular Culture: Gender, Shifting Boundaries, and Global Cultures*, ed. D. P. Martinzed. Cambridge: Cambridge University Press.

Weber, M. 1978a. "Classes, Status Groups, and Parties." In *Max Weber: Selections in Translation*, ed. W. G. Runciman, trans. E. Matthews. Cambridge: Cambridge University Press.

———. 1978b. "Postscript: The Concepts of Status Groups and Classes." In *Max Weber: Selections in Translation,* ed. W. G. Runciman, trans. E. Matthews. Cambridge: Cambridge University Press.

Weir, T. 1993. *USA Today*, December 17, 3C.

Whang, S.-H. 2005. "Supporters and Consumers at Japan/Korea 2002." In *National Identity and Global Sports Events: Culture, Politics, and Spectacle in the Olympics and the Football World Cup,* ed. A. Tomlinson and C. Young. Albany: State University of New York Press.

Whannel, G. 2002. *Media Sport Stars: Masculinities and Moralities.* London: Routledge.

Whitson, D. 1983. "Pressures on Regional Games in a Dominant Metropolitan Culture: The Case of Shinty." *Leisure Studies* 2, no. 2: 139–54.

Wild, P. 1979. "Recreation in Rochdale, 1900–40." In *Working Class Culture: Studies in History and Theory,* ed. J. Clarke, C. Critcher, and R. Johnson. London: Hutchinson.

Williams, J., and R. Giulianotti. 1994. "Introduction: Stillborn in the USA?" In *Game without Frontiers: Football, Identity, and Modernity,* ed. R. Giulianotti and J. Williams. Aldershot, UK: Arena/Ashgate Publishing.

Williams, R. 1965. *The Long Revolution.* Harmondsworth, UK: Penguin Books.

———. 1977a. "Dominant, Residual, Emergent." In *Marxism and Literature.* Oxford: Oxford University Press.

———. 1977b. "Literature in Society." In *Contemporary Approaches to English Studies,* ed. H. Schiff. London: Heinemann.

———. 1983. *Keywords: A Vocabulary of Culture and Society.* London: Flamingo/Fontana.

Williamson, B. 1982. *Class, Culture, and Community: A Biographical Study of Social Change in Mining.* London: Routledge and Kegan Paul.

Willis, P. 1990. *Common Culture: Symbolic Work at Play in the Everyday Cultures of the Young.* With S. Jones, J. Canaan, and G. Hurd. Milton Keynes, UK: Open University Press.

Wilson, J. 1994. "The Big Kickoff (the Sporting Scene)." *New Yorker,* August 1, 52–58.

Wilson, P. 1991. "America Slow on Draw for Big Shoot-Out." *Observer (Sport 2),* December 8, 39.

Winkler, J. T. 1977. "The Corporate Economy: Theory and Administration." In *Industrial Society: Class, Cleavage, and Control,* ed. R. Scase. London: George Allen and Unwin.

Wirth, L. 1938. "Urbanism as a Way of Life." *American Journal of Sociology* 44, no. 1: 1–24.

Yallop, D. 1999. *How They Stole the Game.* London: Poetic Publishing.

Yeo, E., and S. Yeo, eds. 1981. *Popular Culture and Class Conflict, 1590–1914: Explorations in the History of Labour and Leisure.* Sussex, UK: Harvester Press.

Zahavi, H. 1992. *Dirty Weekend.* London: Flamingo.

Žižek, S. 1997. "Multiculturalism, or The Cultural Logic of Multinational Capitalism." *New Left Review,* no. 225: 28–51.

Index

Alan Tomlinson is professor of leisure studies, Chelsea School Research Centre, University of Brighton, United Kingdom.